MAN, GOD AND MAGIC

BOOKS BY IVAR LISSNER

MAN, GOD AND MAGIC

THE CAESARS: *Might and Madness*

THE LIVING PAST

IVAR LISSNER

MAN, GOD
AND MAGIC

Translated from the German
By J. MAXWELL BROWNJOHN, M.A. (Oxon.)

G. P. PUTNAM'S SONS NEW YORK

901.91
L77m

A WORD OF THANKS

I SHOULD LIKE TO EXPRESS MY GRATITUDE TO THE DIS-
*tinguished authorities who have assisted me by offering
advice and valuable suggestions or by checking individual chapters of this book.*

HEINZ BÄCHLER, *student of prehistory and master at the
Kantonschule, Saint Gallen*

HERMANN BAUMANN, *Ph.D., Professor of Ethnology
and Director of the Institute of Ethnology, Munich
University*

HANS DIETRICH DISSELHOFF, *Ph.D., student of early
American cultures, Director of the Museum of Ethnology, Berlin*

W. EHGARTNER, *Ph.D., Lecturer in Anthropology at
Vienna University and President of the Anthropological Society, Vienna*

HERBERT FRANKE, *Professor of Oriental Culture and
Philology at Munich University*

MARTIN GUSINDE, *Professor, Nanzan University, Na-
goya, Japan, formerly Professor of General Anthropology at Chile University*

JOSEF HAEKEL, *Ph.D., Professor of Ethnology and
Director of the Institute of Ethnology, Vienna University*

W. JAHN, *Ph.D., Munich Observatory*

A WORD OF THANKS

WILHELM KOPPERS, *Ph.D., Professor of Ethnology, Vienna University*

SIEGFRIED LAUFFER, *Ph.D., Professor of Ancient History, Munich University*

OSWALD MENGHIN, *Ph.D., Professor of Prehistory at Buenos Aires University, Director of the Centro Argentino de Estudios Prehistoricos, Editor of Acta Praehistorica, Buenos Aires*

KARL J. NARR, *Ph.D., Lecturer in Prehistory at Göttingen University*

CONTENTS

MAN, GOD AND MAGIC

CHAPTER 1

SPIRITUALITY IS LIFE

We trusted that science could and would tell us everything worth knowing and everything we need for guidance in our life, but science has delivered us to destruction by reducing man to an "electron-proton complex," to a "combination of physico-chemical elements," to "an animal closely related to the ape or monkey," to a "reflex mechanism" or "a variety of stimulus-response relationship," to a "special adjustment mechanism," to "psychoanalytical libido." Some indeed go so far as to deprive man even of mind, or thought, or consciousness...reducing him to a purely behavioristic mechanism of unconditioned and conditioned reflexes.

P. A. SOROKIN, *The Crisis of Our Age*, New York, 1941, p. 121

REALLY great truths are invisible, and the realms of knowledge are a few scattered islands in a boundless and uncharted sea of ignorance. Man is the one recalcitrant creature which strives to push forward from the tangible into the remote and inaccessible regions of spirituality.

Man is constantly engaged in this struggle and always has been. Never satisfied merely with the palpable, the visible and material, he possesses a superabundance of spiritual momentum which propels him forward, far beyond the purely positive. Thus, in contrast with animals, he has driven an immense cleft between himself and nature, and created an abyss which cannot be bridged. He has thrown off the primeval bonds which link nature and the animal world. He is alone, and the more lonely he becomes the more he vainly seeks to rediscover his lost paradise. And because he is, in a sense, sundered from his environment, biology cannot encompass the reality of human life—nor, indeed, of the human being himself.

One can only marvel at the perseverance with which man has striven, throughout his history, to reach outside himself. His energies were never directed solely toward the necessities of life. He was forever questing, groping his way further, aspiring to the unattainable. This strange and inherent urge in the human being is his spirituality. It is constantly leading him on toward a goal which is just beyond his reach. And that goal is God.

An animal's faculties are focused on the palpable, on the immediately apparent, on the positive. Animals are, in a sense, the only true positivists. But man is neither an animal nor a plant nor a purely materialistic creature. His appetites cannot be satisfied merely with food or material possessions, and that is why benevolent politicians and philanthropists who promise an earthly paradise where all will be clothed, shod and fed are no more than would-be administrators of a vast zoological garden. It is not consistent with his nature that man should be content with material blessings alone.

This superabundance in man, this striving to reach outside himself and grasp the spiritual and transcendental—religion and God—has been the motive power behind the truly great achievements in history. Man's attempts to approach the imperishable and eternal have provided the foundation of all art and culture. It was in the service of God and immortality that the pyramids came into being, that the Chinese built their pagodas and the Mayas reared their amazing temples to the skies. It was faith which gave birth to the temples of Greece, turned the pictures and altars of the Middle Ages into mute prayers filled with simple humility, caused the great works of the Renaissance painters to burst their two-dimensional bonds, became embodied in the windows of Romanesque and Gothic churches.

Man traded the visible for the invisible countless millennia ago. Whole peoples served the images of their dreams, figures which alone spurred them on to spiritual and artistic endeavor. It was not hunger which piled huge blocks of stone upon the pyramids or dragged them into the Peruvian wilderness to build massive cities and temples, but the extraordinary determination which man has always shown when building in the service of his faith. Innumerable myths, countless thousands of legends and vast numbers of religious cults all testify to the enormous energy which, since time immemorial, man has devoted to the spiritual side of life. It is just this which represents the fundamental difference between man and beast. Man is not content merely to sleep, eat and warm himself, but is molded and permeated by the spirit. All the civilizations of mankind that have ever existed were rooted in religion and a quest for God. Without faith, religion and God, civilization is inconceivable.

Man has not always been free, of course, and the small flames of freedom which he secretly tries to kindle in times of oppression are constantly being extinguished, only to flare up once more. There have been autocrats who denied and scorned God, but none who did not fear Him as something which raises men up, will not long tolerate naked and soulless force, and always humbles it in the end. Freedom has been extinguished in parts of our world in our own day, but man will not be forced to serve the state, the machine and the productivity curve for ever. What are forty or fifty years in comparison with six hundred thousand—the estimated duration of man's existence? To attain salvation or earthly bliss merely through the manufacture and enjoyment of dead things is no sort of objective for creatures driven by this inexplicable craving for the spiritual. Civilization could never have originated solely in the struggle to sustain life and win a ration of daily bread. Civilization is much too comprehensive, delicate and multiform a phenomenon to have had such primitive parents. It was born of the impetus which man received from God and the depths of his own soul.

Civilization is not constituted solely of a roof overhead, food, clothing, warmth and industrial production, but of the human spirit.

Wherever men's attentions are directed only toward material ends there come into being the great vacua, the areas without spiritual freedom, without a quest for truth, without uninhibited philosophy, without art. What has become of the authors, dramatists, painters, sculptors and architects in states whose inhabitants are compelled to live exclusively in the service of increased production? But we should not spend our whole time reproaching the rulers of these vacua. They ought to be a constant reminder of our own wealth of ideas, of the thing which spurs us on and the goal toward which we strive.

The belief in God is age-old, and it cannot be an accident that we meet this belief in primitive peoples as far removed from each other as the Andamans in the Gulf of Bengal, the Bambuti Pygmies of the Ituri River in Central Africa, the Negritos of the Philippines and the peoples of the Far North. Since the oldest races in the world brought their belief in God with them from primeval times, it is probable not that God was born in the depths of the human soul like some natural phenomenon but that the religious awareness of so many quite distinct races depends on a genuine experience of some sort. This experience is probably as old as mankind itself. It may be blurred and obscured, but much has been unearthed in the past hundred years and many questions solved by questioning primitive peoples whose powers of recollection are all the stronger because they have no written language. No one who has carried out research among the oldest primitive peoples can fail to understand that they all conceive of God, that they possess a lively awareness of a supreme being and are deeply convinced of his omnipotence and goodness. This store of ideas is unimaginably ancient. It did not "develop." It was there when bipeds first began to think like men.

Man is in large part inaccessible to pure science, for the one truly human factor, spirituality, is not susceptible of any scientific elucidation. Who knows whether science is reality, whether man-made criteria can be "objective," whether the artificial worlds to which man has given the designation "sciences" are any truer than dreams, visions or inspirations? It is well known that the world of ideas did not begin with science but with an ability to fashion myths. Unlike the animal, man is free, released from nature and therefore from coercion. And he has always stood in a free relationship to the Supreme Being whose existence has been affirmed in the myths of the oldest peoples on earth for several hundred thousand years. Freedom possesses the greatest prospect of immortality, for it dwells in man and can only be conquered when the human spirit itself is conquered.

No ideology or "ism," tyranny or dictatorship, cure-all philosophy or graven image lasts for ever. This is a lesson taught not only by history but also by prehistory, whose depths are only now beginning to be explored. It is a symptom of crass historical ignorance to regard as eternal and immutable any political system which fails to preserve the freedom of free men, and it is a symptom of deficient education to wish to help men in a purely material way when their greatest craving and fiercest energies are directed toward intellectual and spiritual ends.

All thought is subjective. There is really no such thing as objective knowledge or objective truth or absolute proof. Einstein said: "No amount of experimentation can ever prove me right. A single experiment may at any time prove me wrong." Sir Arthur Stanley Addington, famous English astronomer and physicist, wrote: "We cannot pretend to offer proofs. Proof is an idol before whom the pure mathematician tortures himself. In physics we are generally content to sacrify before the lesser shrine of plausibility."

I believe that the mechanical plays a far smaller role in the life of nations than the spiritual, for the essence of man is his intellect and his soul. I believe that all men are very similar since they are all provided with souls. I believe that there is a supreme being and that this supreme being was once associated with man in the act of creation, as Saint Paul implies in his Epistle to the Romans (I, xix). I believe that God is the apex of spirituality, because, if we are to give the human element preference over the mechanical and put the principle of spirituality before that of industrial production, we must conceive of such a supreme spirituality and supreme ideal.

I do not believe that machines, ships, airplanes, rockets, associations, political parties or trade balances are realities. They are perishable and evanescent things which must ultimately wither, decay and come to nothing. If one could ask the dead of this earth, who stand in a billionfold majority to the living, to review all the things which they once possessed and are now scattered to the winds, they would confirm this.

I believe that the only truths are imagination, the soul and inspiration. We know that Homer's songs, once passed on by word of mouth alone, have survived longer than the civilization which produced them. Christ's Sermon on the Mount will still exist when man's last machines and missiles have been consumed by fire, when his skyscrapers and fortresses have been ground to dust and the lonely wind moans across an earth destroyed by his own hand.

The wealth of things still undiscovered is infinitely greater than that of the already discovered and the frontiers of ignorance have scarcely receded at all. There is an infinite number of truths and forces of which we as yet know nothing. It may not be long before we set foot on the moon, but we have not yet managed to plumb the depths of our own souls. Love itself remains beyond our power.

CHAPTER 2

THE PROBLEM OF OUR TIME

Endless invention, endless experiment,
Brings knowledge of motion, but not of stillness;
Knowledge of speech, but not of silence;
Knowledge of words and ignorance of the world:
All our knowledge brings us nearer to our ignorance,
All our knowledge brings us nearer to death,
But nearer to death no nearer to God.
Where is the life we have lost in living?
Where is the wisdom we have lost in knowledge?
Where is the knowledge we have lost in information?

CHRISTOPHER DAWSON, *Religion in*
the Age of Revolution, Part III,
The London Tablet, 1936, p. 179

WE come and go. Doors open, only to close once more. Entire nations have lived here on earth whose traces have been scattered to the winds or buried beneath sand and stone.

Where are the people of Palmyra, the once thriving capital of Queen Zenobia? Shall we ever learn the dying hour of the Sardi, the highly civilized race who lived on the island of Sardinia in prehistoric times? What fate befell the pre-Indo-Germanic inhabitants of Hellas, the Leleges and Pelasgi? What became of the Alpine Rhaetians, and why has their language perished? Who were the mysterious founders of Tarentum, the so-called Parthenians, and how did they meet their end? How were the Sicanians of Sicily exterminated? Why did the magnificent Minoan culture of Crete take to the grave the secret of its destruction in 1400 B.C.? What religiously inspired race trundled huge blocks of stone to Tiahuanaco, 12,000 feet up in the Andes, and to what wars or natural catastrophes did these dwellers by Lake Titicaca fall victim? Why, having reached its prime in the latter half of the third millennium B.C., did the Indus civilization perish forever at the close of the same millennium? What sort of life did Pithecanthropus pekinensis lead 300,000 years ago, and why did his kind die out? Why did the last of the Neanderthal men, who once hunted over three continents, die out completely in about 30,000 B.C., after a life span of 40,000 years and probably much longer?

One civilization after another has passed away, and all that has survived for us to discover amounts to nothing when we consider what has vanished into dust or lies hidden beneath land and sea. Where did we come from and where are we going? Every generation has attempted to solve this mystery. The Old Testament tells us of the beginnings of mankind, and Christ describes the Resurrection. It is from the Bible that the Western world has culled its ethical, artistic and literary ideas, and from the Bible that there has flowed an unquenchable stream of comfort, inspiration and sanctity.

And what of God? Did God arise from the store of ideas, the yearning and imagination of mankind described in these ancient stories? We call the Bible an old book, but the earliest written accounts of Old Testament traditions go back no farther than 1,300 years before Christ, the period when Moses, one of the greatest statesmen and lawgivers in history, renewed the faith of his people. Abraham lived, roughly, between 1900 and 1700 B.C., David sang his songs about 1000, and Solomon sat in the judgment seat some 950 years before Christ's birth. But these were but the last few yards of the infinitely long and thorny path down which man had been wandering for hundreds of thousands of years before the stories in the Old Testament were compiled.

God is much, much older, as modern science can prove. Hundreds of thousands of years before the Book of Books was written, man was on earth, clearly distinguishable from animals not only by his relationship to fire and manufacture of tools but, above all, by his belief in God. God has always been here, man's constant companion ever since He created him perhaps a million years ago.

How do we know all this, and can we prove it?

We live in a world where everything has to be scientifically established. People insist on wringing out of lifeless stones what was once reliably and credibly handed down from generation to generation by word of mouth. We have lost the inclination to believe in words and prefer to put our trust in stone and iron, whirring wheels, physics and chemistry. We have become skeptics, yet we preserve a blind confidence in the exact sciences and a deep faith in machines. In a world where matter threatens to overwhelm mind, where many people are incapable of believing anything save what they actually *know*, and where God is regarded as little more than a pious fairy tale, there can be no more crucial question than this: Was God really here? Has the biped Homo known God since the Creation? Was he half-conscious of his becoming man? Or is God merely a man-made invention? If a genuine encounter with God led to the biped's becoming a human being, any drawing away from God must lead to dehumanization, to bestialization and the extinction of the human race. That is why it is so important to study this problem in the concrete terms of ethnology and prehistory.

There are only two fundamental urges in life, one toward spirituality and the other toward material advancement. Just as intellectual interests and increased spirituality are the only source of happiness on earth and material possessions alone never bring true contentment, so the only ladder that leads to a higher form of existence is the link which binds man with God. William F. Albright, famous American Orientalist, at present professor of Semitic languages at Johns Hopkins, wrote in 1946 in his book *From the Stone Age to Christianity:* "Nothing could be farther from the truth than the facile belief that God only manifests Himself in progress, in the improvement of standards of living, in the spread of medicine and the reform of abuses, in the diffusion of organized Christianity."

Our hopes of continued existence and survival depend on the extent to which the world is guarded and controlled by men of spirituality. If it passes into the hands of purely materialistic interests, into the hands of pure technicians, chemists and atomic physicists, if the Arts wither and die, if people cease to reflect on existence, God and goodness, if they become apathetic and lose their will for freedom, if there is a blunting of the desire to preserve the heritage of spirituality that has been handed down to us over hundreds of thousands of years—if this happens, mankind is finished. The fate of humanity should not be allowed to depend on rivalry in the exact sciences. It must be guided by great, universal minds which are close to the secrets of the transcendental and throw more into the scales than mere weight of technological progress.

If there is one ominous indication of the much-sung decline of the West (in which I do not personally believe), it is the fact that more and more young people and their parents are giving preference to an education in the sciences as opposed to the humanities and spiritual education in general. According to Helmut Kuhn, professor of philosophy and since 1943 editor of *The Journal of Philosophy*, "Spengler felt no scruples in applying his results to problems of the day and he advised his readers to stop writing poetry and to take to engineering because the new Iron Age made inwardness an art absolute." I do not share Spengler's views. The new Iron Age does not make art superfluous nor will it stifle men's inward yearnings. On the contrary, it cries out for a spiritual counterpoise. I believe that we should devote more time and attention to Western culture and ideological truths in general. Our material life has far too greatly outdistanced our spiritual development. Every civilization has a supreme value, and the apex of our spiritual civilization is God. If we hold that material objects, the work of human hands and visible natural phenomena represent the sum total of existence, we shall either deny God or silently dismiss Him as having never been. Sometime, somewhere, the idea of God must have arisen. "No one saw Him," a Yuki Indian told me, "but I think that someone must have seen Him, or we should never have known of Him."

Even in recent years, people of the West believed that mankind had moved upward in its religious beliefs, on an evolutionary spiral which began in earliest times with superstition, mingled with sorcery and magic, to the triumphant evolution of monotheism. This theory held that as man became more civilized he came to see more and more clearly that magic was false and at last reached the highest level of monotheism or belief in one God. Yet, as we will see, a belief in a single supreme deity and creator is found among all the ancient peoples whom we in our arrogance call primitive.

Ethnology has established an extremely interesting fact which is all too little appreciated. All the primitive peoples in the world possess a tradition of a supreme god, and all primitive peoples are aware of a divine manifestation. Wherever we trace the origins of the oldest religions we are forced to recognize that men did not create their religion by themselves. The oldest races believe that the supreme being once, in primeval times, dwelt on earth with men, and it can scarcely be an accident that the divine has appeared in some form or other to every race of men.

A recollection of primeval times has best been preserved and retained among the still-surviving tribes of hunters who live in the Northern Hemisphere. No one who visits these circumpolar peoples and lives among them can fail to recognize that there once existed a universal, primordial religion, and that this primordial religion, far from gaining in strength, has become more and more atrophied. All the circumpolar peoples trace their religion back to a supreme being. But nowhere on earth has this primordial religion experienced growth or refinement, only decay as polytheism, magic, sorcery, animism, shamanism and idolatry grew up gradually in the course of centuries.

It is strange that people of today are generally interested only in the last seven thousand years of their history, even though their forefathers have been living on earth as human beings for some six hundred thousand years. Seven thousand years are no more than a few minutes in the existence of mankind, and the only means of probing more deeply into the past is to study ethnology and prehistory, lines of approach which can yield us information about things which occurred before these last few "minutes" in the whole of human history.

Ethnology is the science of races, and descriptive ethnology is known as ethnography. There are thousands of erroneous conceptions latent in all our sciences. History begins, we are told in school, wherever written evidence first comes to hand; i.e. history begins with writing. Races who have left no documentary evidence of their existence are sometimes termed "anhistorical" races, although it is obvious that the stuff of history is the mere existence of a race. People who have no system of writing are termed "primitive," whereas Chinese, Indians, Near Easterners, Egyptians and Europeans are said to possess "high cultures." Yet there has never been a race which did not have a history and there has never yet been a race entirely without culture.

The so-called primitive peoples are closer in their culture to the beginnings of the human race. They are aware of the origins of their existence and still mindful of the ladder that leads to God. Because we cannot build without a knowledge of foundations; because we shall not long survive without a comprehension of the whole of human history and, with it, our responsibility in respect of origination and eternity; because, finally, we shall meet increasing hazards on the highway of human history, we must attempt to trace our way back into the gray dawn of the primeval past. And, in doing so, we must learn to do something which Europeans find immensely difficult: to unlearn the habit of constantly applying our own standards to the cultures of primitive peoples.

Culture consists of a countless multitude of human thoughts, human inventions, human achievements and accomplishments. Customs contribute to it, as does daily behavior. It is the sum total of the harmony of man's coexistence with nature, his environment and fellow men. The American anthropologist, ethnologist, and professor of prehistory Cornelius Osgood defined it as follows: "Culture consists of all ideas of the manufacturers, behavior, and ideas of the aggregate of human beings which have been directly observed or communicated to one's mind and of which one is conscious." If, despite immense difficulties, we wean ourselves of this habit of regarding material achievements as culture, we shall have come a step nearer the most important truth of all: that the most advanced culture is not necessarily that with the fastest machines or the largest cities, and that there is no fundamental difference between the primitive and the civilized.

CHAPTER 3

MAN 600,000 YEARS AGO

We in South Africa have collections which rival those of Chou-kou-tien. We have about 200 teeth of our Australo-pithecines, and they are quite as important as those from Peking. We have 5 good skulls, and 8 imperfect ones, and we have more important remains of the skeleton than have so far been found in China. It will take years before all the material we now have can be adequately described; and all the time we are adding more and more to our knowledge of the South African fossil forms. Our caves have so far only been scratched. Thousands of caves and cave deposits have never been examined.

ROBERT BROOM and J. T. ROBINSON, *Further Evidence of the Structure of the Sterkfontein Ape-Man Plesianthropus*, Transvaal Museum Memoir, No. 4, p. 13, Johannesburg, 1950

THE earth is about three and a half billion years old. This has been elicited from the frequency distribution of radioactive elements. Since we can now establish how much time has elapsed since the formation of the oldest radioactive minerals, only still-older minerals need be dated in approximate terms, and we can at least deduce the earth's minimum age. The formation of substances such as uranium, actinium and thorium must have begun about two to three billion years ago, for if they were older they would already have disintegrated. The earth's age cannot be much less than three and a half billion years, however, because the minimum age of certain minerals has been fixed at 2,200 million years. The English geophysicist Arthur Holmes, who has devoted his whole life to this problem, puts the earth's age at 3,250 million years.

The earth circles the sun in company with the other eight major planets, but the sun is also circled by several thousand small planets or asteroids and by a comparable number of comets which describe elliptical courses.

Our sun belongs, together with some hundred million other suns, to the cosmic unit known as the Milky Way. This "galactic" system takes the shape of a round but distinctly oblate ellipsoid. The Milky Way, with an equatorial diameter of about 100,000 light-years and a polar diameter of 15,000, rotates slowly about its polar axis. The sun, which is 30,000 light-years distant from the central point of this galactic system, completes one revolution every 250 million years, traveling at a speed of about 190 miles per second, or ten times faster than the earth rotates about the sun itself.

Our galactic system is only one unit among the millions of others which can be identified by means of modern telescopes. Astrophotographers, who now have enormous reflectors at their disposal, have demonstrated that many galactic systems similar to our own exist in the universe, and that these are also constructed in the shape of ellipsoids and sometimes rotate on their polar axes. These galaxies are entirely divorced from our own Milky Way and can only be measured in millions of light-years. Nebulae M31 of the constellation of Andromeda, for instance, is "only" a million and a half light-years away, while Nebulae M51 of the constellation of Canes Venatici is separated from us by six million light-years. The more distant galaxies are so far away that no single star can be distinguished even by the most powerful reflectors. The astronomer Baade used the hundred-inch reflector at Mount Wilson to photograph groups of galaxies in the Coma Berenices constellation, which, lying at a distance of some 500 million light-years, represents the limit of this reflector's photographic efficiency. We shall doubtless see the day when astronomers penetrate the universe to a depth of one billion light-years.

However, none of this means that we possess an "insight" into the cosmos. Despite all these dizzy numbers, we know only a small part of it, and our observations are extremely inexact. We cannot even explain why the planets, which all come from the sun, are so far away from it, why the majority of matter has been retained by the sun, and why the whole of the rotary momentum has been imparted to the planets. Although we think we know a great deal, actually we know very little, since our knowledge embraces such a minute portion of the universe, considering its infinite magnitude, and because our information is so very fragmentary.

For about three and a half billion years, or almost the whole duration of its existence, the earth circled the sun unencumbered by human beings. Man is so relatively new a phenomenon to the planet which we rather presumptuously call "our" earth that his brief span of existence is like a mere puff of wind in the everlasting cosmic storm. The bipeds whom we classify under the genus *Hominidae* and the species *Homo* have been walking this tiny rotating speck in the universe for only about 600,000 years.

Man has survived some violent climatic changes in his time. Four Ice Ages moved across northern Europe, North America and northern Asia during the Quaternary period; i.e. during the last 600,000 years. The mean temperature dropped. Glaciers moved down from the Poles and mountains, pushing masses of stone and sand before them to form what are known as moraines. The four glacial periods were interspersed by three temperate periods. Using spectral analysis, the Jugoslav astronomer Milutin Milanković defined these glacial and interglacial periods in absolute terms, and the extremely interesting results of his research were further amplified by the Russian archaeologist Vladimir Köppen in 1924. Each Ice Age lasted roughly 50,000 to 100,000 years. Man probably arrived in time to experience the first glacial period (600,000–540,000). The fourth Ice Age lasted from 118,000 to about 10,000 B.C. We are living in a post-glacial period which has so far lasted about 12,000 years, and it may be surmised that a new Ice Age will begin some 50,000 or 60,000 years hence. Several of the large Alpine glaciers and part of the glacial mass in the Arctic Circle are relics of the last great freeze-up.

Man thus arrived on earth at a relatively late date. Furthermore he appeared suddenly, and despite diligent research and archaeological endeavor science has never yet discovered any evidence to prove incontrovertibly that Homo evolved from an animal or is descended from one. The sudden appearance of man only half a million years ago is all the more surprising because as long ago as 250 million years the humid, marshy forests were inhabited by air-breathing arthropods and flying creatures with huge, unretractable wings. About 160 million years ago, in the Mesozoic period, the earliest mammals evolved from reptilian progenitors. The earliest finds of true mammals of the Jurassic period hail from Germany, England and South Africa. About 80 million years ago, in the Senonian period, saurians became extinct. At the beginning of the Tertiary period, or about 58 million years ago, mammals finally gained predominance over reptiles and became dispersed throughout the earth. Most of today's mammalian species first appeared about seven or eight million years ago.

And man?

The earliest traces of genuinely human existence found so far are at most 600,000 years old.

In 1900 Dr. Haberer, assembling a fossil collection for a Munich professor, bought a few fossilized bones from a Chinese apothecary. These fossils had been intended, according to ancient northeast Asian practice, to be ground into powder and used for medicinal purposes. In 1903 the paleontologist Max Schlosser discovered in the Haberer collection a strange tooth which, it occurred to him, might have belonged to an as yet unclassified species of ape or a very early type of man. While conducting excavations outside the city of Peking in 1926, the Austrian anthropologist Otto Zdansky unearthed two teeth, also belonging to an early man. One year later a third tooth was discovered by a young Swedish geologist, Dr. B. Bohlin, and discussed by Dr. Davidson Black, professor of anatomy at the Rockefeller Institute in Peking, in an article entitled "Tertiary Man in Asia" which appeared in the *Bulletin* of the Geological Society of China in 1927. The name given to this Tertiary man was Sinanthropus pekinensis. The hill of Chou-k'ou-tien, with its early Paleozoic limestone caves, stood only twenty-five miles southwest of the former imperial city. Here, in 1928, the Chinese archaeologist Pei Wen-chung discovered a parietal bone, a fragmentary frontal bone and numerous teeth. On December 2, 1929, he dug up a skull. This was the signal for larger quantities of stone to be removed and examined, and a second and fairly well preserved skull came to light. By the year 1940 the fossilized remains (almost exclusively skull fragments) of forty-five human or semihuman beings had been discovered. It was the French scholar M. Boule who suggested that Peking man should be classified as Pithecanthropus (ape-man) pekinensis.

Although Darwin's successors continued to believe that they had unearthed the bones of an ape-man dating from the middle of the glacial period, that our ancestor was either semianimal or semihuman, and that he was capable neither of thought nor reason, modern science has reached quite different conclusions about Pithecanthropus pekinensis. All the indications are that the fossils of Chou-k'ou-tien are the remains of truly human beings. For one thing, their teeth offer strong evidence of this. Indeed, the incisor-like shape of one of the lower canines is, in the opinion of the Swiss anthropologist Joseph Kälin, more "human" than the incisor of a modern man. The average cranial capacity of a modern European lies between 1,350 and 1,500 cubic centimeters. Pithecanthropus pekinensis had a cranial capacity of 915 to 1,225 cubic centimeters. Even though bulk is not in itself a decisive indication of the brain's efficiency, the similarity of volume is striking. The Italian palethnologist Alberto Carlo Blanc has gone so far as to deduce, from the development of part of the left upper frontal region, that Sinanthropus was able to speak articulately.

The Pithecanthropus type from Chou-k'ou-tien already possessed a culture of his own. He manufactured tools, scrapers, blades, points and burins—all out of quartzite, a poor material. In one area, measuring only 33 feet by 14, no less than 2,000 hand-worked fragments of stone were unearthed. Peking man used these rudimentary tools to shape animal bones, for large numbers of bones betrayed signs of his handiwork. Apart from bones, cut sections of deer's and gazelle's horn were also worked on, presumably for subsequent use as tools. During the visit to the caves of Chou-k'ou-tien in 1932, Abbé Henri Édouard Breuil, the eminent French ethnologist who discovered many prehistoric caves and has published a great number of learned treatises, personally established that the large antlers were first exposed to fire and the singed portions then carved with the aid of quartz tools. "I satisfied myself," wrote this distinguished student of prehistory, "that it was not the work, say, of hyenas."

The remains of a hundred different types of vertebrates, among them more than eighty mammals, has provided scholars of every nationality with material for the most diverse conclusions. For instance, is it entirely inconceivable that the skulls which Pithecanthropus pekinensis assembled at Chou-k'ou-tien are evidence of some sacrificial cult, as the Swiss professor of prehistory Otto Tschumi has suggested? Bearing in mind all we know of the earliest Stone-Age cultures and comparisons with primitive peoples, it is even possible that Peking man already believed in a single god and made sacrifice to him. Polytheism, as the German ethnologist P. Wilhelm Schmidt demonstrated some years ago in his monumental multivolume work on the origins of the idea of God, was not present at the beginning of human history.

Heaps of ash indicated that Peking man was familiar with the use of fire. Breuil identified burnt and scorched animal bones, stones with nestlike hollows stained with soot and even a fragment of charred wood. The burnt residua stood—interspersed with layers of limestone, rubble and red clay—twenty-three feet high, and must have formed a veritable mountain in the days of Peking man. In Breuil's view, this suggests that fire was kept burning here for a remarkably long time and that living flame played an extremely important part in the existence of the Chou-k'ou-tien people.

Another very noteworthy fact was discovered: all the skulls that were found had been broken at the base. The German anthropologists Hans Weinert, Franz Weidenreich and G. H. R. von Koenigswald have deduced that Peking man may have been a cannibal, and that this may even have been an instance of ritual cannibalism. Modern ethnology has taught us, however, that cannibalism is never to be found among primitive hunters and food collectors. Except where men have turned to cannibalism in dire emergency—and this has so far been found only among a few Eskimos who were entirely cut off from supplies of food—the eating of human flesh has always and everywhere been a sacramental act. It is, curious as it may sound, a sign of advanced culture. Cannibalism has been identified among tribes who were already plant growers and thus culturally much more developed than the simple hunters and food collectors of the Pithecanthropus pekinensis type.

It is also possible that Chou-k'ou-tien was once a burial ground and used as such over a long period. Yet another possibility is that a much more advanced man, a higher form of hominid, used to hunt Pithecanthropus and animals and leave the remains of his prey in this particular spot. What makes this theory unlikely is that the remains of another form of man should also have been found, whereas the actual Chou-k'ou-tien layers contained only the bones of Peking man. (The site known as the Upper Cave, though included in the famous Locality 1 and containing the fossil remains of a far later man who belonged to the Homo sapiens group, is not contemporaneous.) A further suggestion is that Peking man may have carried the skulls of his relatives or tribe about with him as a token of respect for the dead and finally left them lying at Chou-k'ou-tien. All living members of the tribe must then, for unknown reasons, have abandoned the place. Death cults of this kind are known among peoples as ancient, ethnologically speaking, as the Andamans, Negritos and Tasmanians.

The fact that Peking man exhibited technical competence and had mastered fire compels us to regard him as the heir of still older progenitors. But where are their remains, and why was Pithecanthropus pekinensis found so far away from all the other early men discovered so far?

Intellectual achievements such as hunting and the use of fire, tools and weapons are incompatible with the predicates "ape-man" or "pre-man." The earliest tokens of cultural activity should not, fundamentally speaking, be assessed any differently than the ability of the pioneers who built the first steam engine and are now harnessing atomic energy. Every cultural achievement involves the same human factor.

Even though the average cranial capacity of Pithecanthropus (1,075 cubic centimeters) was less than that of modern man (1,350 to 1,500 cubic centimeters), even though his forehead was flat and the bones of his skull noticeably thicker, he was a human being who

The major sites of discovery on the island of Java.

enjoyed a measure of mental and cultural development. Estimates of the age of Peking man differ widely. Alberto Carlo Blanc puts it at between 520,000 and 500,000 years. Lately, however, Pithecanthropus pekinensis has been placed in the Pleistocene, which lasted from about 435,000 to 187,000 B.C. This is a very broad estimate, but if one settles for the middle of this vast period it means that Peking man lived on earth about 300,000 years ago. Frederick E. Zeuner, professor of anthropology at the University of London, in his book *Dating the Past* takes the view that the absolute age of Pithecanthropus pekinensis and his tools is in the region of 500,000 years.

Peking man was not alone in the world. Other members of his species lived at widely scattered points. Between 1891 and 1892, near Trinil on the River Solo in Java, a Dutch medical officer named Dubois found the vault of a skull (*calotte*), a femur and a tooth, and announced that these finds belonged to a man whom he christened Pithecanthropus erectus. Java man possessed a cranial capacity of about 1,000 cubic centimeters, that is to say, considerably less than the average modern man. Since 1936 the celebrated German geologist and anthropologist G. H. R. von Koenigswald has discovered still further traces of Pithecanthropus in Java, at Sangiran and Modjokerto. In 1939, on the eastern bank of Lake Eyasi or Nyarasa, forty-seven miles south of Oldoway in Northern Tanganyika, Dr. Kohl-Larssen unearthed some splintered skull fragments which likewise belonged to a Pithecanthropus of 500,000 years ago. Weinert named this creature Africanthropus.

Finally, mention must be made of the find unearthed in 1907 by a schoolmaster named Schoetensack in a sand pit at Grafenrain bei Mauer, near Heidelberg in Germany. This consisted of an extremely clumsy and receding lower jaw which displayed a set of teeth approximating those of modern man. Homo heidelbergensis was at first regarded as a species intermediate between man and ape, but modern research classifies him in the Pithecanthropus group. "Everything suggests that we are dealing with a europid representative of the Pithecanthropus group," writes Joseph Kälin. Nevertheless, Heidelberg man is probably older than Peking man and Java's Pithecanthropus erectus.

This brings us to the astonishing conclusion that the same man, a creature who was probably already capable of some degree of abstract thought, exhibited completely human characteristics, possessed an intellect and manufactured tools, was living in Java, East Africa and Europe half a million years ago. We are today confronted by the fact that the first human being known to have used fire was a creature who had to some extent mastered his environment and exercised free will in fashioning his existence, a creature with no perceivable direct relationship to the pongids, i.e. chimpanzees, gorillas and orangutans. All evidence indicates that pongids and hominids sprang from a common stock but diverged at an early date. That such a common stock once existed is now accepted by science, just as it is accepted that the earth detached itself from the sun, but the reasons for the parallel development of man and ape remain shrouded in mystery. The most that can be said is that the question of man's physical evolution is, "despite all the various theories and disregarding the countless valuable finds which archaeological research has brought to light in the past few decades, very far from solved." In saying this, the Viennese anthropologist Wilhelm Ehgartner once more underlines the fact that an intermediate stage between man and beast, a genuine "missing link," has never yet been found.

The same applies to what is probably the most interesting discovery of this century, Australopithecus africanus (literal translation: "African south-ape"). It is not yet clear whether Australopithecus represents a very highly developed form of ape or one of the most primitive forms of man.

In 1924, at Taungs in Bechuanaland, the facial bones, lower jaw and a perfect cast of the skull of a manlike creature were discovered. These fossil remains obviously belonged to an immature individual who displayed both anthropoid, or apelike, and hominid, or manlike, characteristics. Dr. Raymond A. Dart, Professor of Anatomy at Witwatersrand University, worked on these finds and later published the results of his research. He named the newly discovered creature Australopithecus africanus, *australis* being the Latin for "southern."

It is extremely difficult to classify fossils phylogenically when they belong to an immature individual and thus have not yet reached their final stage of development. In 1936, however, the doctor and paleontologist Robert Broom discovered the fossil skull of an adult (Plesianthropus) in a limestone cave near Sterkfontein in the Transvaal, forty miles from Johannesburg. In June 1938, guided to the spot by a schoolboy, Broom discovered fossil remains of a second skull (Paranthropus robustus), this time in an abandoned limestone quarry at Kromdraai, about two miles from Sterkfontein. And in 1939 the South African experts Gregory and Hellmann grouped all three finds under the name Australopithecidae.

In 1947 came the discovery of a complete occiput belonging to an Australopithecine of this type near Makapansgat, ten miles northwest of Potgietersrust in Central Transvaal. This find was given the name Australopithecus prometheus because chemical analysis of the surrounding breccia disclosed apparent signs of carbonization. While they are probably attributable to the effects of fire, this does not in itself prove that Australopithecus prometheus was familiar with its use.

Another extremely interesting conjecture has been made. It is possible that Australopithecus prometheus used the longer bones of hoofed animals as a form of club. Kälin bases this suggestion on the peculiar chipping marks visible on the joints of some of these bones. Numerous baboon skulls belonging to the accompanying fauna of the Australopithecidae display indentations and apertures whose

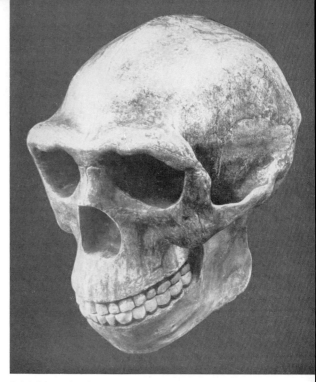

[1] The skull of Peking man or Pithecanthropus pekinensis, whose remains were unearthed at Chou-k'ou-tien, twenty-five miles southwest of Peking. This individual lived about 300,000 years ago, manufactured stone tools and used fire. (Photograph of a cast made by the anthropological laboratory attached to Musée de l'Homme, Paris.)

[2] Tools used by Peking man about 300,000 years ago included scrapers, blades and points made of soft quartzite.

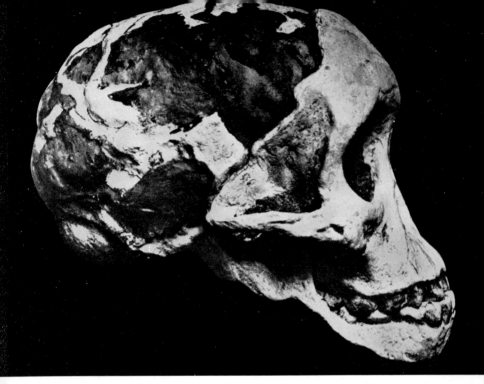

[3] Australopithecus africanus means literally "African south-ape," but this skull belonged to a human being who lived about 600,000 years ago. The Australopithecines are the earliest men so far discovered.

[4] Homo heidelbergensis is the name given to the man whose lower jaw was discovered eighty feet below ground near the village of Mauer, six miles southeast of Heidelberg, on October 21, 1907. Modern scientists classify this man in the pithecanthropus group. Homo heidelbergensis may have been a contemporary of Peking man, who probably resembled him closely, but many authorities believe that the Mauer mandible is older and put its age at between 300,000 and 500,000 years.

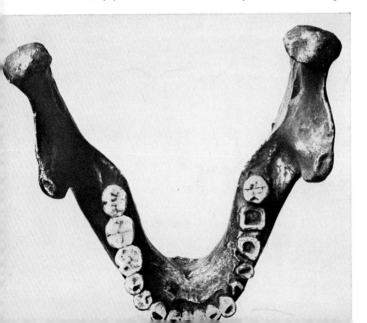

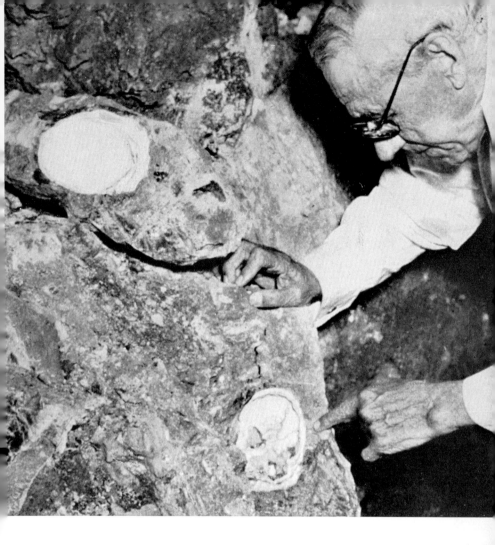

[5] The fossil skull of an adult (plesianthropus) discovered in 1936 by the doctor and paleontologist R. Broom near
Sterkfontein in the Transvaal, forty miles
from Johannesburg. This man is also a
member of the Australopithecines, who
lived about 600,000 years ago.

[6] Coups de poing from the Acheulian, so named after the site of its discovery at Saint-Acheul in the valley of the Somme. This period reached its zenith between 150,000 and 300,000 years ago.

[7] Man's earliest tool. Side and front view of a hand-fashioned coup de poing from the Abbevillean found on the Somme in France. This implement belongs to the Lower Paleolithic period and may be between 300,000 and 400,000 years old. Another French term for the coup de poing is "biface."

[8] Used for polishing bone tools, interesting grooved stones such as this have been found in large numbers.

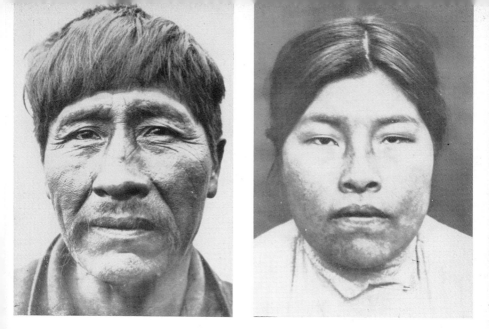

[9] and [10] The Yaghan call themselves Yamana, or "people." These people live on the south coast of Tierra del Fuego and are nearly extinct today. The Yaghan spend most of their time in canoes and are called Canoe Indians. (*Left*) A fifty-five-year-old Yaghan called Hálupens. (*Right*) A twenty-two-year-old Yaghan girl called Lauixweliskipa.

[11] and [12] The Selknam (Ona) came to Tierra del Fuego after the Yaghan and the Alacaluf. They lived on Isla Grande, did not travel by canoe and were therefore called Foot Indians. They were nomads who hunted the Guanaco and Cururo with bow and spear. (*Left*) A Selknam man called Wáteni. (*Right*) A twenty-six-year-old Selknam woman called Korsieyan. The red paint applied on her face from her nostrils to her ear lobes is a beautification often resorted to when visiting or receiving friends.

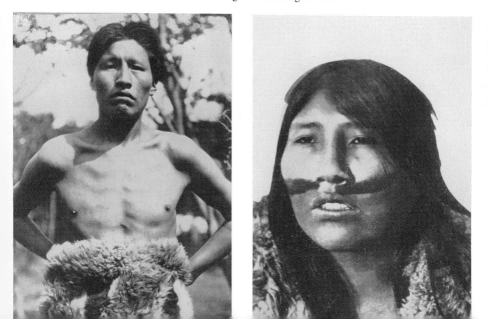

[13] and [14] The Alacaluf are probably the oldest American Indians. From 50 to 100 live today in the western islands of Tierra del Fuego. Martin Gusinde and Junius Bird have studied this interesting people. (*Left*) A thirty-year-old Alacaluf. (*Right*) A twenty-two-year-old girl called Julia by Gusinde.

[15] This old Copper Eskimo from Coronation Gulf belongs to the Kilusiktok Group and is called Apattoaq.

[16] Vast and almost uninhabited, the taiga is threaded by huge gold-bearing rivers.

[17] (*Following page*) Unbroken forest stretching from horizon to horizon. The area bounded by the Amur Bend, the Volga and the Urals contains the largest forests in the world.

shape furthers the assumption that the bones of various animals were used in this way. Dart tried in 1949 to prove that 80 per cent of the baboon skulls found showed signs of deliberate blows, but even this does not clarify the question of whether the Australopithecid was really a man. As Kälin says: "The instrumental use of objects for the attainment of an objective under a given set of circumstances is not beyond the mental capabilities of animals or even invertebrates." All the remains of the so-called Australopithecus africanus had been deposited alluvially in the caves and crevices of a dolomitic limestone system. They were not, however, the only things to be washed into these caves, for they were accompanied by vast quantities of bones belonging to mammalian animals of the same period which had gradually turned into a solid mass of bone breccia. Dart believes that the huge number of mammals found in the Australopithecines' company indicates that the primeval inhabitants of South Africa were big-game hunters.

Excavation began on a large scale. Six hundred tons of rock were sifted *in situ* and ten tons brought to Johannesburg for closer scrutiny. More and more fossil relics of this mysterious creature came to light. In 1949 and 1950 Broom and the South African anthropologist J. T. Robinson unearthed skull fragments, a hipbone and a mandible, until eventually more than a hundred fossils had been assembled. At the fourth summer seminar of physical anthropology in New York, these were ascribed to the early Pleistocene Age. To be more precise, the Australopithecines' span of existence probably lasted from the late Pliocene to about the middle of the Pleistocene, so they lived at a period which lies between 550,000 and 600,000 years in the past.

Were the Australopithecines' mastery of fire proved beyond all doubt it could scarcely be disputed that they were men, but the traces of fire are open to more than one interpretation. On the other hand, it is believed that the Australopithecines could stand and walk in an approximately human manner and that they were of a fundamentally human build which nevertheless revealed, in certain important respects, distinct signs of pithecoid ancestors. Egon von Eickstedt, Wilfred Le Gros Clark, professor of human anatomy at Oxford, and other authorities group the Australopithecines among

The major sites of discovery of Australopithecus africanus. Here in South Africa were unearthed the earliest known human fossils, about 600,000 years ago.

the hominids. J. T. Robinson's research indicated that they were of small stature (about 4 feet tall), in which case their small cranial capacity would not necessarily be a sign that they belonged to the anthropoids. Wilhelm Ehgartner declares that all the Australopithecine bones so far found bear a much closer relationship—despite many deviations—to the human type than the anthropoid or ape type.

It might perhaps be conjectured that hominids or human beings have evolved direct from the "African south-ape" and that the Australopithecines are thus the direct ancestors of human beings. This is the view taken by Broom and Robinson, in "Further Evidence of the Sterkfontein Ape-Man Plesianthropus," published as a Transvaal Museum Memoir in 1950:

The child skull of Australopithecus, the adult skull of Paranthropus and the jaw of the young child, and the many skulls and parts of skeletons of Plesianthropus reveal to us a group of Primates that are nearly human, but not quite, and a group that approaches man so closely as to leave little doubt in our opinion that it was from a member of this family, the Australopithecidae, or a closely allied form, that man arose.

This is highly improbable, for a very "human" mandible was discovered in Swartkrans together with fragments of Australopithecines, from which it may be deduced that the Australopithecines and hominids existed contemporaneously. Australopithecus probably belonged to one of humanity's blind alleys. He may have been a creature which possessed all the physical prerequisites for becoming human but died out or was exterminated by a more highly developed man before he had a chance to exploit them.

Fossils discovered in a brown coal layer at Monte Bamboli in the Italian province of Grosseto have given rise to the most audacious theories. Here, between 1868 and 1958, increasing numbers of fossil remains were unearthed, all belonging to a strange creature, first investigated by the French paleontologist Paul Gervais in the year 1872, which bears the scientific name Oreopithecus bambolii Gervais. Although Rütimeyer dismissed Oreopithecus as a form of gibbon as early as 1876, Professor Johannes Hürzeler of Basel recently (in 1958) put forward the theory that Oreopithecus was an early man or hominoid. To quote his exact words (*Oreopithecus bambolii Gervais*, p. 5): "I gained the conviction that Oreopithecus is a typical hominoid." According to Hürzeler, therefore, this so-called hominoid is a proto-man dating from a period between six and twelve million years in the past. No such early man existed, however. In 1959 the Kiel zoologist Professor Remane positively identified Oreopithecus as an ape. Remane's examination of the fossil remains of Oreopithecus at Basel effectively quashed a scientific sensation which had sprung from the hypothesis that, far from being at most 600,000 years old, as hitherto assumed, man was between ten and twenty times older.

The Quaternary, which covered a span of one million years, is the only period of man's earthly existence. The preceding Tertiary period lasted for 60 million years. No fossil of any kind has yet been discovered in the Tertiary which could plausibly be attributed to an ancestor of man. The German anthropologist Paul Overhage says:

> No genuine 'missing link' exists. All this underlines the difficult, one might almost say comfortless, position in which research into man's "family tree" still finds itself at the present time. We cannot traverse the glacial period. We possess no remains, Le Gros Clark asserts, which antedate the Australopithecines and Pithecanthropus.[1]

France's greatest paleontologist, Henri Victor Vallois, who was director of the Musée de l'Homme in Paris, professor at the National Museum of Natural History and member of the Academy of Medicine, devoted exhaustive study to the question of whether mankind evolved from various roots or only one. The nineteenth-century German naturalist Karl Vogt still believed that humanity consisted of three groups which were descended from the "recent" anthropoids, i.e. gorillas, chimpanzees and orangutans. The French anthropologists Abel Hovelacque and Georges Hervé (1887) as well as Paul Broca and other scholars shared this view, modifying it to a greater or lesser degree to fit their own particular conception. But Vallois declared in 1929 that none of the many human racial types in existence displayed any characteristics which indicated a direct connection with the anthropoids. The typical features of the anthropoids are absent in all human racial groups, and the distinguishing features of the various human races are lacking in all anthropoids.

[1] *Das Stammesgeschichtliche Werden der Organismen und des Menschen,* Freiburg 1959, p. 238.

Despite racial differences, all living men are extraordinarily similar; far more similar, at any rate, than any race of men is to any form of anthropoid. It is impossible to reproduce here the whole of Vallois' scientific argument. Suffice it to say that he reaches the conclusion which comparative anatomy wholeheartedly endorses in every respect: that men and anthropoids are fundamentally different. They are two quite distinct groups which may possibly have evolved from a single stock but have never been capable, since they diverged, of merging again. Anatomy tells us that any logical view of the human species *must* concede its monophyletic origin—in other words, its origination from a single stock—and that it presumably shares this original stock with the anthropoids.

The difference between anthropoid and hominid does not lie in the physical sphere alone. The abyss between ape and man owes its existence to the human intellect. Only man grew out of an existence ruled by instinct and blind urge and into a life of free will. Only man started to comprehend the reality that lay outside his own person, to "reach outside himself" spiritually, to aspire to God. And this groping for the spiritual could not have arisen from man's physical and natural disposition alone. It must once, in the beginning, have been awakened or called into being. There must be an outside power, a power we cannot perceive, an unknown creative force which summoned man, and no other living creature, to burst the bonds of instinct. For, were such a development naturally conditioned, some other form of life might eventually have reached the same stage.

Not even that exhausts the definition of man, for he does not consist only of body and intellect. There is a third constituent, the soul. The body of man and, to a certain extent, his intellect may both have developed in an evolutionary manner—i.e. have developed from animal origins. That is why they were and are variable from one period to another. The soul was born of creative power, summoned into being spontaneously and at a single point in time by outside intervention. That was the true beginning of the human race, the moment when man became Man. Man is a trinity made up of body, intellect and soul, and nothing can subtract from this, mask or obscure it: neither the fact that man is a vertebrate and a mammal and must obey the laws of nature just as other vertebrates do; nor that he has overtaken all other living creatures intellectually and has at some stage crossed a frontier in his development which we cannot conceive of his having crossed under his own power; nor that his share of the divine reposes in a soul which is immutable and therefore immortal. Science will one day be compelled to give full recognition to this third element, the existence of the soul, and acknowledge it as a constituent part of man, something inexplicable, perhaps, but nonetheless something which irrefutably exists.

CHAPTER 4

NO MORE PRIMITIVE THAN OURSELVES

But, if the essence of humanity be laid bare, we are confronted by a primordial human occurrence whose enormous significance rests on the fact that two things came into being contemporaneously: man and man's handiwork; that man is at once creature and creator, sculptor and stone, tool, material and workshop. How much more momentous must have been the period in which the wonder of the human body came into being than all the later periods, which merely use that body and adorn it!

GEORGE KRAFT, *Der Urmensch als Schöpfer,* Tübingen, 1948, p. 231

BY about 600,000 years ago, when the era of the four Ice Ages began, man already had made a timely discovery: the use of fire. They were no "warmth-accustomed ape-men," these creatures who came upon the idea of fire, nor—as Hans Weinert surmises—did "beings whom we should still describe as ape-men sit round a deliberately laid fire and snugly enjoy its warmth and the protection it afforded against dreaded predators," nor—yet another supposition of Weinert's—did these ape-men "roast their prey in the fire and enjoy the unaccustomed flavor."

No, fire surrendered its secrets to quite another sort of creature. No animal or semianimal would have been capable either of grasping the complicated procedure involved in the artificial use of fire or of exploiting his discovery. Only man, not being tied to impulse and instinct, could have succeeded in absorbing such an idea. Only man, being endowed with free powers of reasoning and the ability to act independently of a given set of material circumstances—only Homo could have bridged the vast mental gulf between a desire for warmth and artificial lighting and the kindling, obtaining and use of fire. The culture of primitive fire users has always been linked with a primeval sense of magical associations which modern man has lost, but there is no doubt that Pithecanthropus of 500,000 years ago still felt something of this magic. In order fully to comprehend the com-

plex train of thought which must precede the kindling and maintenance of a fire, modern man must go off into the forest without a
box of matches and try to emulate the achievement of Pithecanthropus.

The greatest riddle of human existence is that our forefathers were
somehow miraculously spared the closely circumscribed physical
specialization which subordinates everything to determinate physical
requirements, and that, instead, their limbs were left free to perform
an infinite number of diverse and delicate physical functions in
obedience to the brain's most complex commands. Thus, the human
hand is neither clawlike, hooked, prehensile nor scansorial like that
of an ape or monkey, but can be used to grasp physical objects of
almost any shape. It is perfectly adapted to carry out the many and
various commands of a highly developed brain. Similarly, the human
face is not distinguished by a prominent mouth or masticatory apparatus, but keeps these features tucked in beneath the cranium
which dominates the human head. Among apes, cerebral growth
halts shortly after birth, while muzzle and masticatory equipment
develop swiftly and to a marked extent. In human beings the brain
continues to develop until the seventh year, whereas facial development lags considerably. Because his masticatory equipment has receded, man, in contrast to all types of ape, possesses a triangular
chin. Likewise, the proportions of his arms and legs (unsuitable for
climbing), the construction of his feet, his upright stance, the horse-
shoe- and not U-shaped dental arches of his upper and lower jaw,
even the shape of his pelvis—all these conform to the needs of a
thinking creature and one which mentally dominates its environment.

Only this can explain why the climatic vicissitudes of some 600,000
years of glacial and interglacial weather failed to extinguish human
life. Being incapable of adapting himself physically to nature and
lacking the toughness and resilience of many other mammals, man
was thrown back on his intellect. Needless to say, there were wide
areas available to him which were spared the rigors of an Ice-Age
climate, so he could always move southward, but if he had been
unable to think constructively, even in those days, he would undoubtedly have become extinct. Our whole existence, our life and,

above all, our future survival are founded on powers of intellect which we possessed in a remarkably high degree at least half a million years ago. However long ago they lived, all the human beings whose fossils have been unearthed were "intellectual," for intellect is a definitive attribute of the species Homo, not merely of a few of the most creative members of that species.

As the various Ice Ages progressed, so a number of animals each time adapted themselves with notable success to the abnormally harsh climatic conditions. Only adaptation or adjustment and not an intellectual discovery like that of fire could have saved these animals from extinction. We have only to think of the peculiarly hirsute exterior of the *Elephas primigenius* or mammoth, which did not die out until the most recent Ice Age, or about 15,000 years ago, and of which remains have been found in the North Siberian ice surrounding the Arctic Sea, throughout Europe, and in North America as far south as the Gulf of Mexico. All unadaptable species became extinct during the glacial periods. For instance, the second Ice Age proved too much for the saber-toothed tiger, the *Elephas australis*, the broad-browed elk and the Etruscan rhinoceros, while the last Ice Age snuffed out the cave lion, cave panther, cave hyena, cave bear and woolly rhinoceros. By the end of the last glacial period only a remnant of the original wealth of animal life still survived; only those animals, in fact, which had learned how to live with nature or avoid it. Avoidance was still possible because southern Europe and the whole of Africa remained unaffected by glaciation. Ice, therefore, was not the only natural hazard to life. The extinction of certain forms of animal is one of the great enigmas in the history of organisms, for some animal species die out in temperate periods, too, and none of the many explanations which have been put forward— some of them on a philosophical plane—are fully satisfactory.

But man remained, having survived four glacial periods each lasting between fifty and a hundred thousand years, hunting, collecting food and successfully defying the limitless wastes of inland ice. In northern Sweden the ice lay between eight and ten thousand feet deep. In Germany the climate resembled that of modern Russia's Arctic coasts. Man endured temperatures as low as −58° Fahrenheit, but he kept away from the largest ice masses and most menacing glaciers, avoiding their grim frozen expanses. The outlying regions of frosty tundra, bare or almost bare of vegetation, were also devoid of inhabitants or at most scantily populated. The biped Homo probably lived in a herb and grass tundra, but principally in the chilly steppes of the southeast and in the southwestern scrub tundra. These lay north of the Pyrenees, at the foot of the Alps, in the Carpathian Mountains in southern Russia and in the central regions of Asia. Of course, man also lived farther south where the climate was rainy but mild. Being an outdoor dweller who fed on fruit and game, he naturally gravitated toward the more temperate regions. The Lehringen finds near Verden on the Aller (Hanover, Germany) provide positive proof that men of the last interglacial period about 130,000 years ago hunted wild animals individually, as do the far older finds at Chou-k'ou-tien, where large quantities of game were eaten. Seventy per cent of the animal bones left behind by Peking man belonged to deer, but other wild animals including the gazelle and horse were also hunted. We even know that men used to feed on small cherrylike fruit. What we do not know is how they hunted. They may have dug pits or driven their quarry together by kindling forest fires, but it is improbable that early hominids used traps, snares or other technical apparatus. It is also uncertain whether Peking man was a cannibal, for no such far-reaching conclusion can be drawn from broken human fossils.

Older than all the human skeletons discovered are the tools which human beings left behind them. It used to be fashionable to trace the origins of man back to increasingly early times, for he could, on the face of things, have coexisted with the pre-Quaternary mammals who lived about twenty or thirty million years ago. Attempts were made, therefore, to deduce the existence of human beings from certain stones which had apparently been shaped by hand. In fact, large quantities of stones were discovered which *could* have been tools, so-called eoliths or "stones of the dawn" (a compound of the Greek words *eos* and *lithos*, "dawn" and "stone").

If human handiwork existed in the Tertiary, if there really was such a thing as an eolithic culture, if, in fact, these stones were actually fashioned by human hands, they ought logically to present an extremely primitive and rudimentary appearance. But this is not the case. Some of these stones seem to display better workmanship than the far later tools of Peking man. The formation of all eoliths can be attributed to natural causes. Pressure, displacement and subsidence of geological strata, fire, glacial motion, splitting—all these natural phenomena contributed to their formation. Tempting though it may be to dream of inheriting a legacy in stone from someone who lived ten or even twenty million years ago, all such conjectures must be consigned to the realm of fantasy.

The English have always been famous for great practical discoveries because they possess a sportsman's passion for investigating, with great verve and enthusiasm, the only-just-possible. Being brilliant and taciturn individualists who love to see fantasy verified, they are not easily deterred from bold ventures into practical research. The successful researcher must, to a degree, be a crank, for society tends to be inhibited by doubt and hesitation and enjoys throwing cold water on audacious theories, mainly from an instinctive and understandable reluctance to allow anyone to burst the barriers of its own mediocrity.

Evidences of human activity were discovered very early in England. We owe our knowledge of the (allegedly) oldest proofs of human existence to J. Reid Moir, an indefatigable archaeologist who has persistently sought to demonstrate that certain tool-like flints bear traces of human handiwork. Moir's finds were made at Ipswich, Cromer, Shelly and Foxhall. If his view that flints dating from the beginning of the Quaternary were artificially shaped is scientifically tenable, it means that human toolmakers existed before the first Ice Age, 600,000 to 800,000 years ago. However, these English finds have now been discounted, and, in any case, they would not be older than the earliest stone tools since discovered in South Africa.

But are we on the right track? May not the whole study of prehistory be so clouded by theory and countertheory that we now fail to recognize possibilities which might otherwise present themselves? May there not have been cultures which produced no flaked or hand-fashioned stone? Does the use of stone tools really represent the earliest form of human culture? May there not have been an even earlier wood culture of which nothing or next to nothing has survived?

The French archaeologist and prehistorian R. Forrer excavated a campsite belonging to a diluvial community of huntsmen who possessed wooden implements and probably nothing else. These wooden relics, which hailed from the Mindelriss near Spichern in Alsace, were made of spruce, fir and pine and included a form of windbreaker, the earliest token of man's quest for artificial protection from the elements. They were accompanied by fossils belonging to only one animal, the *Rhinoceros merckii*, and it must be assumed that the hunters devoured their quarry on the spot. The earliest layer of the flake-tool culture in the so-called Clactonian (named after Clacton-on-Sea in Essex) yielded what some have identified as a quite skillfully made spear point of wood, fifteen inches long and nearly one and a half inches thick, though the thickness of the wood has understandably caused the German scholar Karl J. Narr to doubt whether it really is a spear.

Greater importance should, it seems, be attached to a noteworthy discovery made at Lake Dalai Nor in Outer Mongolia, near the northwest Manchurian frontier, where the remains of bones and man-made wooden tools were found lying forty-five feet below ground level. Also unearthed there was a fragment of wickerwork which may once have belonged to a basket. No stone tools lay in the vicinity of these objects, and it has been asserted that the remarkable traces of the people of Dalai Nor date from the oldest part of the Quaternary—in other words, that they go back 800,000 years. However, the age of these relics is a very delicate question, and we must remember that the glacio-chronological terminology often employed in the case of eastern Europe and Asia makes such things appear much older, in comparison with European discoveries, than they really are. Moreover, wooden utensils of great age are never datable with certainty, however strong our inclination to believe that wood was used before stone.

The wooden implements from Spichern, the spear point from Clacton and the Dalai Nor finds may not in themselves be sufficient to prove the existence of a pre-Stone-Age wood culture, but it is hard to dismiss the possibility. Some very early diluvial layers contain no forms of tool at all, yet they also contain traces of fire which seem to indicate that man was there. Even this primitive man must have possessed tools, and if none were found it is difficult to escape the conclusion that they were made of wood and have therefore disintegrated in the course of hundreds of millennia.

It is always possible that traces of ash or carbonization are attributable to natural causes, but on the Giebelstein near Krölpa in Thuringia, charcoal and ash were found in company with animal bones, an indication of human activity. Once again, the complete absence of stone tools may mean that men were working with wooden implements. Apart from this, wood offers the easiest method of obtaining fire. The fact that man knew of fire and exploited it very early, the fact that we have found traces of fire three, four or five hundred thousand years old at Chou-k'ou-tien near Peking and that remains of fires have been discovered even in places where the presence of implements or tools can no longer be detected—all this indicates that a knowledge of artificially induced fire is older than all the tools so far unearthed.

How did man obtain fire 600,000 years ago? It has been suggested that at the very beginning he merely tended and maintained fire which had originated naturally. However, every wood fire goes out from time to time for some natural reason, whether because of heavy rain, neglect or mere mischance. It is simply one of the hazards of an outdoor life. Anyone who has lived in the open without a tent for any length of time will know that no system of watches and reliefs, however well planned, will keep a fire going indefinitely. And, when a fire goes out, man is once more faced by the problem of how to relight it.

It is probable, therefore, that the use of fire was linked from the very start with the great secret of how to kindle it. There are various methods of obtaining fire. Some authorities assert that percussive kindlers consisting of a flint and one or two pieces of iron pyrites represent the earliest implements ever used to produce fire. However, while it is easy enough to strike sparks from a flint, it is exceedingly difficult to trap such sparks in tinder. That explains why the practice of obtaining fire from flint is not more widespread. There is, however, a simpler method and one which is much more common among the still-surviving primitive peoples of the world.

A piece of wood is placed on the ground. In this piece of wood is a recess, and into the recess is inserted a tightly fitting vertical wooden stick. If the horizontal piece of wood is held firmly in place with the feet and the vertical stick is twisted backward and forward like a drill, this produces a frictional heat in the horizontal stick which prolonged drilling increases until the wood smolders and eventually catches fire. This method of obtaining fire is termed "drilling." Another way, "plowing," is to scrape a small, hard stick briskly backward and forward along the grain of a piece of softer wood. Some primitive peoples obtain fire by pulling a length of liana to and fro against a piece of rough wood. This is termed "sawing."

The most convenient method, that of drilling, encourages us to assume that a man who possessed fire also possessed a wood culture. And, because traces of fire are among the very earliest evidences of human existence, it is likely that the use of wood as a tool or weapon was contemporary with the use of stone. I am informed by the renowned Austrian archaeologist Oswald Menghin, now professor of prehistory at the University of Buenos Aires, that in his opinion wood, bone and stone were all in use from the very first, but that wood, for obvious reasons, was employed in larger quantities. As a matter of interest, all races on earth today know how to kindle and use fire. The only possible exceptions are the Bambuti Pygmies of the Ituri River in Central Africa and the Andamans, an Asiatic people who live in the Andaman Islands in the Gulf of Bengal. Until recently, they only tended fire and were unacquainted with methods of obtaining it.

When we come to 300,000 years ago, some of the mystery surrounding man's existence on earth has already been dispelled. The first two glacial periods are now in the past, and we learn to our astonishment that the whole of the Old World—Asia, Africa and Europe—was inhabited. "Inhabited" does not, of course, mean that the people of the time tilled the soil or carried out any form of cultivation. They were hunters and food collectors who lived in the open air, but they were far from being tree dwellers.

Two different methods of working with stone were evolved at a very early stage, the core-tool technique and the flake-tool technique. The first, which confined itself almost entirely to the making of *coups de poing* or hand axes, involved the progressive removal of flakes from a stone until the finished tool was fashioned from and included the core. Users of the second technique detached flakes and then fashioned tools from them in which the actual flake surface formed part of the finished article. Tools of this type included scrapers, points, disks and choppers.

Are we dealing with two different types of men who manufactured tools independently of each other and under different circumstances? This is unlikely. The core-tool and flake-tool cultures were probably not divorced. The flake-tool culture is known only in the immediate vicinity of the core-tool or pebble industry, and is usually of more recent date.

The early craftsmen manufactured their coups de poing by chipping the edges of a stone until they had a pear- or almond-shaped tool which could be easily grasped. The coups de poing still lying buried beneath the sands of the Sahara would no doubt fill a large number of freight trains on their own. But, while Africa was probably the hub of this culture, it also spread, during the interglacial periods, to the Near East, Italy, Spain, France and even to northern Germany.

The earliest known stage of cultural development in Africa is the so-called pebble culture, which goes back 600,000 years or more to the early Pleistocene. Pebbles have been found on the Kageran River near Nsongesi which reveal signs of fierce natural friction and possibly, too, of human handiwork. These are the utensils of the Kafuan culture, so named after the Kafu River in Uganda. It is impossible, however, to state categorically that the Kafuan stones are the earliest tools so far identified because there is no absolute proof that they are products of human activity.

Scientists have recently come to the conclusion that the earliest tools so far unearthed are those from Oldoway in Tanganyika, a discovery site which has yielded a large number of tools confidently identifiable as human handiwork. This East African culture was christened the Oldowan by its discoverer, the English anthropologist L. S. B. Leakey who, in 1931, found quantities of pebble tools, i.e. natural stones which had been transformed into tools by being chipped in a few places. Typical of the Oldowan culture are the so-called chopping tools which Ice Age man manufactured by striking chips from both sides in order to obtain a serrated cutting edge. Since this serrated edge is lacking in the chopping tools of the oldest Kafuan pebble industries, it is thus possible that they came into being naturally and were not artifacts. In that case, the Oldowan implements would be the earliest stone tools so far discovered anywhere in the world. In a lecture delivered on October 7, 1959, Dr. Leakey declared: "This culture has now been recognized from Portugal to South Africa and right across the continent of Africa as the oldest well-defined Stone-Age culture known to us, since most of what used to be called Kafuan has had to be abandoned as uncertain, and the balance clearly belongs to Oldowan."

In 1958, Dr. and Mrs. Leakey once more undertook excavations in what is known as Bed I and succeeded in bringing to light an almost complete skull. Since the oldest stone tools so far discovered occupied the same layer this find was extraordinarily interesting, for it became clear that the earliest toolmakers hitherto known had once lived here. Moreover, because the fossils of large animals such as the giant ostrich, giant antlered giraffe, giant pig, giant wild sheep, giant wild cattle and giant hippopotamus were also discovered in the neighborhood of the skull, and because most of these animal bones were broken, Leakey surmised that the man in question was the owner of the camp, not the victim of animals or another form of human being. Leakey named his extremely important discovery Zinjanthropus boisei. The skull resembles Australopithecus in many respects, but also shares certain features with later forms of Homo. He says:

The great importance of the discovery is that it gives us a skull which from the geological age and from the morphological point of view can lead direct to Homo. Finally I have some special news. I was sure that the living floor, if further explored, would yield us the rest of the skeleton. Among the bones found during the last few days of the excavation before funds ran out was a tibia, which I have every reason to believe belongs to Zinjanthropus.

The quantity of chopping tools belonging to the Oldowan seems to suggest that a certain density of population may have existed even in very early times—about 500,000 years ago, in the opinion of Dr. Kenneth Oakley of the British Museum of Natural History. Exactly what man did with his coups de poing and how he used them has not, despite numerous conjectures, been positively established. They could have been used for splitting, piercing or perhaps even for drilling, an operation for which the examples with sharpened points would have been particularly well suited. Coups de poing may also have been used for digging purposes.

The French scholar G. de Mortillet named this culture the Chellean, after the finds made at the gravel pit at Chelles near Paris. Because the core-tool culture of Chelles is more recent, however, students of prehistory have christened the earliest stage of core-tool development Abbevillean, after the town of Abbeville. Just outside the town lay the gravel pits of Porte du Bois, where stone tools and the fossils of extinct mammals were found in the year 1847.

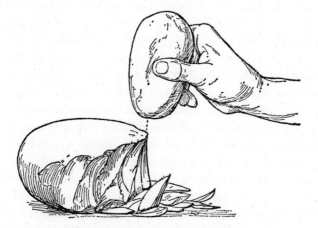

Percussion-flaking a flint in Paleolithic times.

The man responsible for this great discovery was Jacques Boucher de Perthes, famous French archaeologist, who had steadfastly endured years of hostility and derision on account of his unpopular theories. Just over thirty miles upstream from Abbeville on the outskirts of Saint-Acheul-sur-Somme the Abbeville finds were confirmed and amplified by further discoveries of coups de poing. It was established that what were initially rough-and-ready tools later became neater and more delicate. Indeed, hand-fashioned stones of pronounced geometrical regularity indicated that a strong aesthetic sense had been at work.

Coups de poing were often found in the company of tools which had been manufactured by flaking pieces of stone. These sharp-edged flint flakes or chips constituted the blades of the Stone-Age craftsman. The splitting technique may possibly have been employed by men who for that and perhaps other reasons, too, belonged to quite another cultural milieu.

Both cultures, core-tool and flake-tool, flourished contemporaneously in Europe for a long time. In the coastal regions of north Africa, in Spain, Italy, France and northwest Germany and along the coasts of Syria and Turkey, the two techniques partially overlapped. It is probable that they always existed together, for flake tools have been discovered in large numbers even in the earliest genuine pebble industries. Modern French West Africa and central Africa have mainly yielded coups de poing. No deserts existed in west Africa in those days, although central Africa has boasted huge tropical forests from time immemorial. The core-tool people probably hunted in what is now Abyssinia as well as in Somaliland on the Indian Ocean and in the rain forests of India. Menghin believes that the stone implements characteristic of core-tool cultures were suited to life in the primeval forests, and he therefore assumes that the core-tool culture's point of departure was a region of tropical forests, perhaps southern Asia or the sweltering heart of Africa.

Because it was impossible to exist in the primeval forest with only one form of tool, the coup de poing, and because man stood in need of cutting implements, flake tools were also manufactured and employed. Apart from that, wood was so readily available in the forest that it must surely have found a use. Naturally, wooden implements would not have survived the passage of hundreds of thousands of years, but there is no reason to suppose that Stone-Age man was unaware of the potentialities of that material. Bamboo, for instance, is ideal for making cutting tools. It is probable, too, that coups de poing were sometimes mounted on a wooden shaft and used as axes, though it is not clear how such axes were used to fell trees or how flints were used for hunting purposes. Anyone who holds a coup de poing in his hand will find it hard to imagine how it could have been used to tackle a tree, still less an animal. At all events, most coups de poing have been found in the tropics, so it may be reasonable to assume that the tropical rain forest was the original home of these strange and clumsy implements.

The blade culture probably evolved primitive forms of stone dagger and spear, weapons which were well adapted to steppe life. It may thus be supposed that the blade culture came into being in central Asia—perhaps, as some scholars believe, in the Ordos desert region in north China, for the flake-tool culture extended a long way eastward to the Caspian Sea and across the Urals into southern Russia and Mongolia. Elsewhere, the existence of flake-tool areas in northern France and southern England (Clacton) leads one to assume that they formed an independent cultural group.

Little by little, the two cultures merged. Perhaps the coup de poing people and the blade people got to know each other better. Certainly, the two forms of industry exercised an increasing influence upon one another until they eventually became amalgamated. However, the two major cultures of the Lower Paleolithic coexisted more or less unalloyed in the same areas of the Northern Hemisphere for hundreds of thousands of years before, in about 130,000 B.C., the forms and characteristics of the two industries started to mingle.

After 130,000 B.C., Menghin believes that there was a third culture in existence, namely a bone culture. This probably debouched into central Europe from the northeast and gained a foothold in the Alps. The idea of using bone for tools and hunting equipment would have come naturally to people who had to endure a violent contrast between summer and winter temperatures. Being compelled to cover vast distances, they could not carry heavy weights, i.e. stones, with them. Their whole way of life was founded on mobility and speed.

However, it is exceedingly difficult to identify cultures which lie hundreds of thousands of years back in the darkness of prehistory, and the question of whether an independent bone culture existed remains entirely unsolved. It is at least probable that the people who used bones as tools were bear hunters and that their home lay in northern Siberia, in the area east of the Urals and north of the trans-Asiatic mountain chain. Perhaps the men who were familiar with this technique eventually brought their knowledge with them to Switzerland and employed it on the cave bears there.

We have now entered a new culture, the Mousterian, so named after the site of its discovery, Le Moustier. Though it lingered on until about 50,000 B.C., this culture flourished between 130,000 and 80,000, the period when a strange creature known to science as Homo neanderthalensis walked the earth.

The core-tool and flake-tool cultures lasted from about 540,000 until 130,000 B.C., and throughout the whole of that period—some 410,000 years—men had been manufacturing and using the same primitive stone implements. We are thus confronted by yet another unsolved mystery; namely, the reason for this alarmingly—or comfortingly—sluggish development in technique. How is it possible or even conceivable that throughout this disconcertingly long period man persisted in the same technical methods, developed his implements in this slow and imperceptible manner and continued to use the same form of tool, even though he had taken the coup de poing with him on his world-wide wanderings from Gibraltar to the Ordos desert and from Germany to South Africa? Coups de poing and pebble tools have even been found at Gongenyama, not far from Tokyo.

Karl J. Narr, professor of prehistory at the University of Göttingen, has pointed out that the numbers, density of population and life span of the people of the Lower Paleolithic were all very much less than those of modern man. This diminished their chances of garnering and passing on the fruits of experience. If the average man lived to an age of only twenty-five or thirty-five his adult existence could have lasted only five to fifteen years. This is rather different from the forty years of adulthood which the average modern man enjoys, a span of time during which his store of experience is continually increasing. Considerably more can be built on this than on judgments and faculties which can only be exercised for a mere five or fifteen years, and skills once acquired are much easier to pass on.

Technical development accelerates like the traditional snowball rolling down a hill. Its speed is contantly increasing. It becomes—as we moderns with our love of comparisons would say—"better." Yet its course, to pursue the snowball analogy, is necessarily downhill, and that may be symbolic of its true worth. Intellect and moral consciousness, on the other hand, are not subject to this "law of gravity," but have been sustained by creative power for 600,000 years and probably longer. We may well find, if we have not already done so, that technical progress is a nettle which mankind has been overeager to grasp.

I believe that the answer to the question of man's initially slow technical development can also be sought in the human conception of time, in the human attitude toward past, present and future. It is well known that primitive peoples have a very different relationship to time than the peoples of the river-valley cultures. Granted that man originally possessed no experience of time, that he had no sense of time or tradition of chronology, it must have been hundreds of thousands of years before he forfeited that state of blissful unawareness.

Knowledge, perception and presentiment undoubtedly go hand in hand with a mature relationship to time. They form a trinity which presupposes an understanding of time, a trinity made up of knowledge of the past, perception of the present and presentiment of the future. But this is still far removed from a real preoccupation with time and a direct struggle against its remorseless advance. Primitive races teach us that the passage of time is less painful to them, that time does not press and that it need not always be filled with activities. They teach us, in fact, that the present can be taken as it comes.

To the extent that man has reached outside himself, so he has been forced to make decisions about the present. To the extent that he has queried the source and origin of things, so he has shouldered the weight of the past, present and future. Knowledge of the past and anticipation of the future lead him to exploit the present, to fill it as his peculiar conception of progress encourages him to think desirable, to create, to work, to invent, to devise and to philosophize.

The people of the early Paleolithic were probably nearer to God. They were probably more receptive, less possessed by the present than possessors of it, not so conscious of things outside and beyond themselves as to be tormented by the past or harassed by thoughts of the future. But if they were less aware of time they were no more primitive than ourselves, for culture can be measured only in terms of morality, not of machines. Persevering, using the things they knew, unhurriedly evolving new techniques, not hastening to destruction but happily ignoring the passage of time, they patiently survived the natural hazards of an existence which spanned hundreds of thousands of years.

CHAPTER 5

EARLY MAN IN AMERICA

I wrote a letter on April 27, 1931, to the Honorable C. M. Babcock, state commissioner of highways, suggesting that his department cooperate with the University of Minnesota in reporting any subsurface discovery of human or animal bones, artifacts, or pieces of wood during the course of an extensive program of roadbuilding....

On June 16, 1931, a human skeleton was found in Minnesota.... We believe this skeleton represents glacial man in America.

ALBERT ERNEST JENKS,
Pleistocene Man in Minnesota,
Minneapolis, 1936

We are today justified not only in assuming and considering possible but in regarding as virtually certain the existence of a genuine American Protolithic age of bone-cultural character which goes back at least to the last interglacial.

OSWALD F. A. MENGHIN,
Acta Praehistorica, I, p. 25,
Buenos Aires, 1957

EVER since Neanderthal man was discovered in the year 1856 we have known that human beings lived in Europe during the Ice Age. The Peking finds of 1929 introduced us to the Ice-Age inhabitants of Eastern Asia. Only in very recent years has the curtain risen on a vast new prehistoric stage occupied by the glacial inhabitants of America, beings far older than anyone had ever dared to dream.

For decades, the American scientists held that their continent remained uninhabited until comparatively recent times, but it has gradually emerged that there is no such thing as a New World on our planet. Leading American authorities on prehistory assumed that men did not set foot on their continent until after the last Ice Age, in about 8000 B.C. It was thought that these men had belonged to the Mongol race and that they brought their culture, which corresponded roughly to a transition from the Upper Paleolithic to the Lower Neolithic, with them when they migrated. Then, so the theory went, they became subdivided in the course of a few millennia into a large number of separate peoples—the American Indians.

All that subsequently came into being on American soil, sedentary life, agriculture, primitive cattle breeding, ceramics, weaving, metalworking and the great advanced cultures with their monumental buildings—all this was supposed to have originated independently. To oppose this form of cultural isolationism was to risk being ridiculed in some American academic circles. The idea that inventions can travel or that the fruits of culture can be transmitted across continents and even across oceans was denied acceptance, at least where America was concerned. Any resemblances between phenomena occurring both on American and Asian soil—apart from the primitive early cultures of the subarctic regions of Siberia and Alaska—were described as independent developments. It was postulated that because he shares his fundamental disposition or "elementary ideas" with others of his species man will always, under a set of given conditions, do and produce the same things. The opposite view, diffusionism, stresses the greater likelihood that similar forms and similar ideas have radiated from a common center, especially in the case of cultural assets which display more complex characteristics. The diffusionists have now largely prevailed over the so-called independent inventionists.

In the old days, anyone who objected that numerous similarities existed between the Old and the New Worlds was referred to the theory of "elementary ideas" and "accidents." The first half of this theory implied an identical impulse to invent, and the second an inexplicable, unexpected and equally identical response to a similar situation. It cannot be denied that accidents and elementary ideas occasionally beget the same results in quite different parts of the globe; but by and large, cultural similarities surely occur far more rarely because of this than for reasons of historical contact. Only those who close their eyes to historical development and regard the condition of a particular tribe at a particular point in time from a purely static point of view, only those who remain blind to hundreds of thousands of years of human migration, blind to the inescapable exchange and dissemination of cultural assets and ideas and blind to the interrelationships of the men and races of this world, can believe in a wide application of the theory of accident and elementary ideas. No theory which looks upon the American continent as entirely isolated can be tenable, and it may be said that this view has now been superseded.

The true facts are quite different. We now know for certain that men set foot on American soil as long ago as the last phase of the Ice Age (Pleistocene). It is even probable that they were there much earlier than that, during the last interglacial period. There were many prehistoric migrations to America, but probably each originated in Asia.

It has been asked why people should not have crossed to America from Europe long before the Vikings and Columbus. True, a few authors, mainly fantasts and fiction writers rather than experts, have assumed the existence of such prehistoric European-American migrations, but almost certainly all belong in the realm of fable. Atlantis was not a continent which lay between America and Europe and was engulfed by a flood. Platos Atlantis, if it had any reality at all, was more likely a city somewhere to the west of the Straits of Gibraltar; perhaps, as the student of prehistory and archaeologist Adolph Schulten assumes, the city of Tartessus, which stood in the estuary of the Guadalquivir in southwest Spain and was founded in 1150 B.C. Nor have the Ten Lost Tribes of Israel anything to do with America. They vanished into the continent of Asia, not America. It is almost certain that none of the truly historical peoples—Pelasgians, Phoenicians, Basques or Celts—ever reached the shores of America. Again, there is no evidence to support a theory of a prehistoric migration from Australia to America via the South Pole. This is just another of the misguided theories which even serious scholars invent from time to time. America, as far as scientific indications go, was in contact only with Asia during prehistoric times and remained so, discounting an unimportant Viking precedent, until the advent of Columbus caused the gigantic continent to reorient itself and become a receptacle of Western culture.

Like Europe and Asia, the New World experienced four Pleistocene glaciations which roughly corresponded in time to the equivalent glacial periods in the old continents. North American scientists have named them after four of their states. In order of decreasing age, they are: Nebraska, Kansas, Illinois and Wisconsin. Between these Ice Ages lie the three warmer or interglacial periods known as Afton, Yarmouth and Sangamon. The fourth Ice Age, Wisconsin, was succeeded some 8,000 years ago by the postglacial, Neothermal or Holocene period in which we are still living today.

During glacial periods the waters were drained from the world's oceans and deposited on the mainland in a frozen state. In the last Ice Age, for example, the level of the sea dropped by more than three hundred feet. In the Bering Straits a drop of only 120 feet would be sufficient to form a small bridge of land, so it may be assumed that during the last Ice Age a land mass some hundreds of miles wide came into being in the Bering region, enabling animals and human beings to cross from Asia to North America. Once man had arrived in the new continent, vast areas lay open to him. More-over, a milder climate must have prevailed on the southern margin of the thawed land mass than would have been possible even during the interglacial periods, for if the Arctic Ocean was cut off from the Pacific the coasts of Asia—and America, too—must have been lapped by warm Pacific currents.

What could have impelled the people of the Wisconsin Ice Age to desert Asia for America? The earth was still largely unpopulated, so it can scarcely be supposed that these journeys into the unknown were occasioned by pressure of population. Indeed, pressure of popu-lation would have been the last reason for such a movement in those northern regions.

Anyone who has roamed the unexplored areas of the world knows that the best plan is to follow game tracks. Siberia's primitive peoples still use them as roads today. It is probable that Ice-Age man, who was a food collector and, above all, a hunter, followed in the wake of his game. Huge herds of animals may have wandered across into North America, principally herbivorous species who were lured by the American grasslands. The American scientist Loren C. Eiseley goes so far as to speak of "grass bridges": "It must have been by way of an alley of grass that the passage was achieved, and the abundance and advanced evolution of tall, middle and short American grass must have been an immediate and fertile stimulus to southward migrants from over the Asiatic bridge during the Pleistocene." The cold-steppe bison, the woolly mammoth, the tundra-loving musk ox and llama-like camels wandered across, followed by the men who hunted them. Cultural remains of these men have often been found with fossils belonging to their quarry. Ice-Age Americans lived principally on game, so they pursued the animals as they made their way into the wide plains, feeding on grasses and treading the game paths with a million hoofs.

It may be conjectured that these migrations usually followed the Yukon and then led through the valley of the Mackenzie, both of which rivers were partially free of ice even during the glacial periods. American carbon-14 datings of the most widely disseminated remains of human culture in the New World generally indicate a period lying between ten and twelve thousand years in the past. By that time, the close of the last Ice Age, the "paleo-Indians" had penetrated to southern Patagonia. The bearers of these cultures belong to the Homo sapiens type. The skeletal remains of numerous late Ice-Age inhabitants of America have already been unearthed, though lack of space forbids one to mention more than a few examples from North and South America.

The skeleton of the so-called Minnesota man, found during excavations by a road-construction gang in 1931 in the neighborhood of Pelican Rapids and written up by the American ethnologist Albert E. Jenks, probably belongs to the end of the last Ice Age. The designation Minnesota man is misleading, for the individual in question was a girl. The skull is broken but otherwise in a remarkably good state of preservation. It has a high forehead, while the lower half of the face is somewhat protuberant or prognathous and displays a set of fine and exceedingly powerful teeth. Some authorities believe that they can detect Mongol characteristics in the Minnesota girl, whereas others have tried to prove a resemblance to the Ainu type.

Since this almost complete skeleton was found in the sedimentation of a glacial lake, it may perhaps be surmised that its owner, who was about fifteen years old, met her death by drowning. The objects found lying near her do nothing to contradict this, for they were obviously all things which she wore on her person. From the site where the skeleton lay were unearthed fragments of a fresh-water mussel (*Lampsilis siliquoidea*) and a sea snail (*Busycon perversa*). In the upper edge of this shell, which hails from the area of the Gulf of Mexico, are two holes. These may, of course, be natural, but it is also possible that the shell was worn as an article of jewelry. We can at least deduce from its presence that the Minnesota people of that era were in contact with the Gulf of Mexico and carried on a form of trade by barter. Sixty fragments belonging to a tortoise shell some eight inches long may indicate that the girl wore it on her person as a container or rattle. Also found was a foot bone, .28 inches long, belonging to a diving bird which still nests in north Minnesota and may be seen as far north as the Canadian tundra. This bird flies south annually, but never farther than north Minnesota. Finally, twelve very small birds' foot bones were also discovered near the dead girl, together with a wolf's incisor.

Another exceedingly interesting find was a dagger made from the antler of the Canadian deer (wapiti) which now measures about eight inches and must originally, when undamaged, have been ten inches long. In the handle is a hole which the Stone-Age craftsman had made by boring through it, not very accurately, from both sides. It appears from the position of the dagger that the girl wore it around her neck. The nature of these articles encourages one to assume that the girl was carrying them because of their magical properties. The bird, the rattle, the wolf's tooth, the mussel-shell jewelry, the piece of stag's antler—all these are in some degree reminiscent of paleo-Siberian cultures.

In 1933 the fossil remains of a man were unearthed in a gravel bank near Browns Valley, also in Minnesota. The man's grave was outlined with red chalk, and near him lay burial gifts in the shape of some carefully made stone points. He must have been between twenty-five and forty years old when he died. His skull is long and narrow and corresponds to that of some of the North American Indians. Describing this find in 1937, Jenks estimated its age at about 12,000 years.

The Tepexpán man, discovered in the Valley of Mexico by the American anthropologist Helmut de Terra in 1949, probably lived 11,000 or 12,000 years ago. Radiocarbon tests of peat from the layer in which the fossils lay gave a date of 11,003 ± 500. De Terra even thinks he has established that Tepexpán man died by accident, perhaps while pursuing a mammoth, for stone tools and mammoth bones in the same formation only a mile south of the Tepexpán provide evidence that man and mammoth were living in the same area at the same time.

Finds made at certain places in the Argentine Pampa also go back to the end of the last glacial period. In 1881, near Fontezuelas in the region of the Arrecifes River (Buenos Aires Province), Santiago Roth dug up a human skull on top of which lay the bony armor of an extinct armadillo called the glyptodon. The circumstances of the find were such as to banish any doubt that the man and the armadillo were contemporaries during the last Ice Age.

While the ethnological status of human fossils found in North America still poses many unsolved problems, all anthropologists concur in ascribing the Fontezuela skull to the high-skulled and graceful Lagoa Santa people, in whom some authorities perceive similarities to the Melanesian race. We shall be dealing with the Lagoa Santa site and its discoverer later in this chapter. Suffice it here to say that this race composed a considerable share of the early population of America. There is, however, no justification for designating it as *the* paleo-American race, especially as paleo-European types were more strongly represented in paleolithic America.

In addition to human skeletons, large numbers of campsites dating from the close of the Ice Age have also been discovered. In 1926 a Negro cowboy came upon the bones of an extinct species of bison in the neighborhood of Folsom, New Mexico. It was only after this Stone-Age hunter's haunt had been excavated by paleontologists from the Natural History Museum of Denver and strangely shaped stone points had been found in the company of animal fossils that American students of prehistory began to countenance the possibility that American man was older than had been previously imagined. The celebrated Folsom projectiles known as "fluted points" are on average only two inches long and leaf-shaped. Miss H. M. Wormington, famous American prehistorian, describes them in her book *Ancient Man in North America* (Denver, 1957, p. 27) as follows:

They are pressure flaked and of excellent workmanship. They have an average length of two inches, are thin, more or less leaf-shaped, with concave bases, usually marked by ear-like projections. There is frequently a small central nipple in the basal concavity. The lower edges and base normally bear evidence of grinding. The most important characteristic, however, which usually distinguishes the Folsom is the removal of a longitudinal flake from each face. This produces a fluted point with grooves or channels extending from one-third to almost the entire length of the point. Most Folsoms have a hollow-ground appearance when viewed in cross-section. Rare examples ... have been found with only one grooved face, and there are some points of the same shape as Folsoms that are ungrooved.

It is highly probable that the Folsom points were spear points, i.e. missiles used for big-game hunting. Various explanations have been offered for the groovelike recesses on one or both faces of the points. The theory that these furrows were intended to make the projectiles lighter and give them greater range does not seem logical. If Folsom points were merely spear points, this infinitesimal decrease in weight would not have exercised any significant effect. Bow and arrow had not yet been invented, and it is unlikely that the Folsom points were launched on their own as small free-flying projectiles. Again, the theory that Stone-Age man grooved his points bayonet-fashion to ensure that his quarry bled more freely also seems farfetched, as does the suggestion that the broad furrows were added for aesthetic reasons. It is far more likely that the spear points were flaked to make them fit the shaft better.

Similar artifacts have been discovered at many places in the Great Plains. Between 1924 and 1934, Folsom points were found at a Stone-Age campsite twenty-eight miles north of Fort Collins in northwest Colorado. Most of these pieces lay on the surface. The owner of the land, William Lindenmeier, consented to more extensive excavations, and these were carried out by Major Coffin and Judge Coffin, as well as by Colorado's Museum of Natural History under the direction of Figgins and Cotter. The remains of nine bison (*Bison taylori*) dug up there were of exactly the same species as that which had already been identified at the Folsom site. When a stone point was discovered in the spine of one of these bison it became clear that the extinct species of bison and the man who had manufactured stone points of this type must have been contemporaries. Fluted points were later found as far afield as the Rocky Mountains and the Atlantic seaboard, Canada and the Gulf of Mexico.

There are several varieties of fluted points. The finest type, as found at the Folsom and Lindenmeier sites and at many other places in the United States, is more recent, while the elder, which is coarser and longer, not so finely retouched at the edges and equipped with a shorter groove, is known as a Clovis point. Apart from this, large numbers of other shapes and missile points are attributable to the hunters of the late glacial period, notably the leaf-shaped type and others equipped with tongues for attachment to a shaft. To generalize, spear points are far more abundant and diverse in America than in the Old World, and in North America constitute the most important legacy left by Stone-Age man. Stone spear points of comparable age have also been found in Central and South America.

For an immense period, therefore, fifteen thousand years and probably far longer, spears equipped with stone points remained the chief weapon of the paleo-Indians of the American double continent. In order to give smaller spears greater velocity and range, they frequently used a spear sling or throwing stick known to archaeologists by the Mexican name *atlatl*. Naturally, most of the spear shafts have fallen away to dust, but a few remains have been found here and there: in the Gypsum Cave, Nevada, painted spear shafts and leaf points; in the Leonard Rock Shelter, also in Nevada, a decorated atlatl spear; in Fort Rock Cave in southern Oregon, the fragments of a wooden spear sling and numerous sandals made of hide and dating from the early postglacial period.

America also possesses some late glacial stone industries which are devoid of spear points. These are characterized mainly by various sorts of coups de poing. Menghin surmises that the American core-tool cultures are connected with those of the Old World. While it has not yet been ascertained by what route they traveled from

Southern Asia to America, it is noteworthy that a glacial core-tool culture has recently come to light in Japan. This has effectively reduced the cultural distance between Asia and America.

At Lindenmeier, hunters left behind the remains of an entire banquet. They had obviously roasted and eaten their prey on the spot where it had been killed, for many of the bones were charred and several of the stone missiles exhibited traces of fire. The Lindenmeier site also yielded some foot bones belonging to a camel (*camelops*), together with the remains of other mammals' bones and a fragment of mammoth tooth. All these have been scientifically examined and described in the fullest detail by the archaeologist Frank H. H. Roberts, Jr., one of the foremost authorities on paleo-Indians. Among the finds were about six hundred stone implements, fluted points, snub-nosed scrapers, side scrapers, end scrapers, a variety of cutting edges, drills, flakes with small, sharp points, rough-flake knives, fluted knives, large blades, sandstone shaft polishers and rubbing stones of the same material, not to mention pieces of bone with scratched ornamentation and fragments of tools manufactured from animal bone. The abundance of the finds leads one to suppose that the Folsom people used the site as a camping ground all the year round and over a long period of time.

Kirk Bryan and Louis L. Ray of Harvard University have devoted an immense amount of exhaustive research to ascertaining the period at which Folsom man occupied the Lindenmeier camp. The Wisconsin Ice Age was long past its peak but it was not yet over. A sub-arctic climate must have prevailed at the time and the mountains were still covered by ice. According to radiocarbon dating, the Folsom man of Lindenmeier lived between nine and ten thousand years B.C. The site at Lubbock, Texas, has been dated at 9,883 ± 350.

The sites which have yielded Clovis points are older. To these finds belong the stone points unearthed from 1932 onward between Clovis and Portales in New Mexico, where two hand-fashioned pieces of bone were also found at a later date. These discovery sites are situated close to the Texas-New Mexico border. In 1936 and 1937 John Lambert Cotter discovered two grooved points at Clovis. One lay about an inch beneath a mammoth's rib, the other between

[18] Taken more than 1,200 miles from its mouth, this photograph illustrates the enormous width of eastern Siberia's largest river, the Lena.

[19] When the *Graf Zeppelin* flew over this remote river in the year 1929 a cyclone towered up in its path, creating a scene of eerie and almost unimaginable beauty: soaring, circling clouds, jet-black but flecked with light on their billowing flanks, racing above the eternal darkness of the forest; unearthly gusts of wind catching the tops of the trees below and wresting them to the ground; sudden flashes of lightning illumining the Tunguska as it writhed in its forest bed far beneath and turning it, for seconds on end, into a ribbon of molten silver.

[20] Swamp taiga, a perilous and inhospitable expanse stretching for as far as the eye can see. The Russians call these marshy basins *totchki*.

[21] Endless and oppressive enough to daunt the stoutest heart, these taiga marshes are deathtraps which take days to cross.

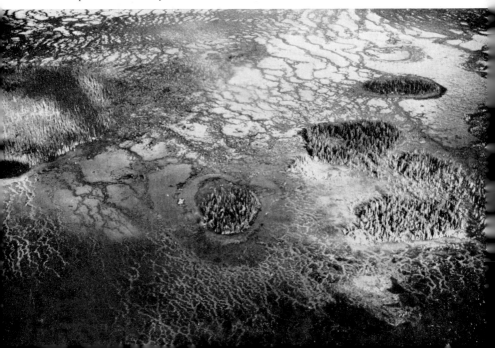

[22] An Orochon in hunting garb. The Orochi are breeders and hunters of reindeer whose nomadic culture and economy are based entirely on that animal. Even their name reflects this. (*Oro-chon* means "reindeer-man.") On the left is an old musket, on the right a *palma*, the wooden shaft surmounted by a blade with which the Orochi formerly hunted bear.

[23] I encountered this old Orochon and his wife on the borders of the taiga near the Amur River. They had adopted a form of Western clothing.

24] These five young Orochi belong to the same family. The eldest girl is already allowed
o smoke a pipe.

[25] Various stages in the construction of an Orochon tent. A framework of thin branches is covered with birch bark and later secured by a few external poles.

[26] A river spanned by the wickerwork weir baskets in which the Tungus catch fish.

[27] This Manego, whom I met on the banks of the Amur, had spent his whole life in the depths of the taiga. He used to make his way to the river every five years or so to barter his skins against ammunition and other necessities.

[28] Orochon women seated before a tent in a forest clearing. Though slightly built, they are endowed with an amazingly strong constitution. Their skulls are round, their faces brown, their eyes small, dark brown or black, and narrow-lidded. Their faces reveal surprisingly little of the hardships of their nomadic existence. Orochon women are fond of smoking, and the Tungus in general seem to take only too readily to any form of Western drug. This picture clearly shows how tents are faced with strips of birch bark about two feet wide and twenty feet long. The material is impregnated with natural juices before use.

two of the animal's leg bones. The geologist Ernst Antevs set their age at between ten and thirteen thousand years. Powerful missiles up to six inches long, they were presumably spear points used for hunting mammoth.

Finds made at Naco in Arizona indicate that the Stone-Age inhabitant of America did not confine himself to spear points of especial length when hunting mammoth. In 1952, at Greenbush Creek, a mile west of Naco, eight spear points were dug out of chert and dark gray felsite. They were lying among the bones of a mammoth (*Parelephas*) which was still fairly young—between twenty-five and sixty—when killed. The Naco points belong to the Clovis fluted type and range in length from about 2¼ to 4½ inches. None of the missiles was actually embedded in bone, but their position indicated that they had caused the animal's death. Dr. Ernst Antevs has established that the Naco finds belong between ten and eleven thousand years in the past.

Controversy surrounds the age of finds made near Lewisville in Denton County, Texas, where excavations have brought to light nineteen fireplaces, the remains of extinct bison, elephant, horse, camel and smaller animals. The largest fireplace contained a Clovis point and a large piece of charred wood. It was thought that if the age of the charcoal were first established this would automatically shed light on the age of the Clovis point which occupied the same layer. Accordingly, the charred piece of wood was handed over to the Humble Oil Company's laboratory for radiocarbon dating. It appeared that the charcoal's age was greater than could be ascertained with the laboratory's existing technical equipment, whose maximum range was in the region of 37,000 years. All the archaeological circumstances discourage one from believing that the Lewisville finds are really as old as this, and doubt has been cast on the accuracy of these tests. Even though examination of charcoal from another fireplace near Lewisville also indicated an age in excess of 37,000 years, the case is at present regarded as inexplicable.

One of the most interesting sites in America is the Sandia cave near Albuquerque, New Mexico, which was excavated from 1936 onward and written up by Frank Hibben in 1941. Beneath a layer containing Folsom artifacts and separated from them by a sterile stratum were some roughly fashioned silex points which exhibited surface retouching on both sides and a lateral groove at the lower end. These Sandia points were found in company with elephant, horse, bison, wolf, sloth, camel and mammoth fossils. The Sandia culture must, from its geological circumstances, be considerably older than the Folsom site. Hibben estimated its age at about 19,000 years. A few fragments of ivory from the Sandia layer were handed over to the University of Michigan for dating by the carbon 14 method. The results indicated an age in excess of 20,000 years, according to H. R. Crane.

Substantially older finds are known in America. The Shasta Caves in California have yielded bone implements which hail from the last interglacial at the very latest, and stone implements of the same period have been found in sedimentation at San Diego (G. F. Carter). The primitive stone implements of Thule Springs, southern Nevada, must also be of very great age. Hearth sites were also found there, and Willard F. Libby's 1955 tests of carbonized remains gave a result of 23,800 years. This seems to show that Paleolithic contemporaries of the Neanderthal man existed in America.

Where did the manufacturers of the fluted points come from, or the men whose silex points with surface retouching on both sides were found in the Sandia Cave, or the people of Thule Springs, the Shasta Caves and San Diego?

It cannot reasonably be supposed that the hunters of twenty or forty thousand years ago were capable of traversing the huge watery expanse of the Pacific. The only remaining possibility is that many successive waves of men migrated to North America across the Bering Straits. Admittedly, it is surprising that none of the Paleolithic Siberian cultures bears a resemblance to the Folsom or Sandia implements, but there is no lack of ready explanations for this. It should not be forgotten, on the one hand, how little we still know of the Ice-Age cultures of Siberia, and, on the other, that the American cultures of which we so far have knowledge are probably the result of indigenous developments whose course is as yet unexplored.

There is evidence to suggest that Folsom man was already in

Alaska, that is to say, in the area most nearly contiguous with the continent of Asia. Edward G. Sable found a Folsom point, identified by Frank H. H. Roberts as paleo-Indian handiwork, on the Utukok River north of the Bering Straits at about the 70th parallel, a region entirely dominated by the Arctic Ocean. At Cape Denbigh on Norton Sound, the American prehistorian J. Louis Giddings, Jr., came upon a cultural layer containing flint implements, notably burins and fragments of Folsom projectiles. The burin is a specifically Old-World form which does not occur in America except in the Far North. It may reasonably be supposed, therefore, that these and similar discoveries made in Alaska and Canada provide a pointer to man's route from Asia into North America, at least during the early postglacial period. The migrants would naturally have kept to the center of the peninsula and followed the valley of the Yukon, for Alaska, like northeast Asia, was only ice-bound in the mountains, even at the height of the late Pleistocene glaciation. Pushing farther eastward from the Yukon, the wanderers would have entered the basin of the Mackenzie, skirted the foothills of the Rocky Mountains, and eventually reached the broad plains of the Missouri and Mississippi.

But this, as we have mentioned, applies only to the Upper Paleolithic period. Exhaustive research carried out in the past few years has increased the likelihood that the existence of man in America goes back much farther than was originally supposed. The fact that no fossils belonging to the Pithecanthropus or Neanderthal type have been found in America does not disprove the existence of Lower Paleolithic inhabitants. We now know that there were Upper Paleolithic presapiens forms whose appearance approximated far more closely to modern man. Added to this is the possibility that many paleoanthropological finds have been and are still being lost to science because they owe their discovery to inexperienced individuals and are not brought to the attention of experts.

More than a century ago, the Danish zoologist P. W. Lund dug up numerous fossil animal and human bones in the Sumidouro Cave near Lagoa Santa in the Brazilian state of Minas Gerais. The human remains belonged to about thirty individuals of all ages and consisted of some thirty mandibles, fifteen skulls in varying states of preservation and many smaller bones. Unfortunately, Lund himself published no precise account of these discoveries, and later researchers were forced to rely on his correspondence alone. The material, which is preserved in the Zoological Museum at Copenhagen University, was re-examined by the Viennese anthropologist Hella Pöch in 1938. She made several noteworthy observations. Among the skulls were two which exhibited a much higher degree of petrification than the others and were also distinguished by other special characteristics. The low forehead was peculiarly receding and the nasal cavities extremely wide. Lund himself spoke in his letters of skulls which were differentiated from the others by their primitivity, but his remarks were entirely ignored by later researchers until Hella Pöch resurrected them and deduced from the existing evidence that the two fragmentary skulls hailed from an older geological layer than the rest of the human remains, which belong to the Lagoa Santa (lagid) race.

It seems that whole skulls of this type were brought home by Lund, only to be later lost. During the last century, scientific institutes were not always ideal places in which to store antiquities, and many modern archaeologists would do better to "dig" among the mountains of cases in museum vaults than in the field.

Since the two disputed skull fragments from the Sumodouro Cave displayed no protuberances above the eye cavities, Hella Pöch ascribed to them a primitivity of a special sort. Nothing was yet known of the presapiens type or she might perhaps have associated them with it, but she did draw attention to their resemblance to the modern Botocudos. Menghin has questioned whether the Argentine authority José Imbelloni's "fuegid" race, which is represented principally among the western Indians of Tierra del Fuego but also among the Botocudos and other American tribes of extremely primitive culture, might not be a late and naturally very adulterated branch of this ancient racial type. It is worth noting in this connection that H. Gross, the well-known glacial research expert from Königsberg who now lives in Bamberg, ascribes the very controversial skulls from Melbourne and Vero on the east coast of Florida, both of them undoubtedly of the sapiens type, to the last interglacial period because the large armadillo, wolf and tapir found in the same bone bed have always been regarded as interglacial forms.

Be that as it may, the bulk of archaeological evidence makes it extremely probable that the earliest human settlement in America dates back to the last interglacial period and is at least 100,000 years old, since which time various races and tribes have migrated into America across the Bering Straits. It is also likely that any surviving remnants of the oldest human types are to be found mainly in the most southerly part of South America and in Tierra del Fuego in particular, because, as the millennia rolled by, they were pushed ever farther to the south.

CHAPTER 6

NEVER A TIME WITHOUT HISTORY

The fact that the universal idea of history first took root in the soil of Judaeo-Christian religion does not absolve science from an attempt to verify that idea.... The idea need not be erroneous or perverse simply because it is religious in origin.

WILHELM KOPPERS, *Das Problem der Universalgeschichte im Lichte von Ethnologie und Prähistorie,* Anthropos 52, 1957, p. 371

The modern historian knows that if only he had the capacity he could become the interpreter of the whole past of mankind.

R. G. COLLINGWOOD, *The Idea of History,* Oxford, 1951, pp. 25–26

TO A cosmic geographer with a purely objective interest in man, our species would appear as no more than a highly organized form of skin cancer which is destroying the earth's surface with ever-increasing rapidity. So writes Carleton S. Coon, the eminent American anthropologist, and the British prehistorian O. G. S. Crawford further observes that microbes and bacilli do not look upon the diseases which they produce as anything bad. Everything, therefore, depends upon one's point of view.

However magnificent we consider our achievements to be, humanity may well have experienced its finest hours during the last interglacial period, or between seventy and eighty thousand years ago. Man's freedom was probably greater the farther back in prehistory he lived. The "golden ages" are always old. Homer knew of them; Hesiod recalled them some 800 years before the birth of Christ; they were extolled in the early legends of Africa and by the Indians of ancient times. The tradition of Paradise and the Fall has been disseminated in one form or another among virtually all the races on earth since time immemorial. It should not be forgotten that the idea of evolution is only a thing of yesterday, unconnected with the thoughts and verbal traditions of past peoples and periods and diametrically opposed to the ideas of primitive races still alive today.

We may perhaps be forgiven for having come to believe in our infallibility, considering our achievements in the scientific field. But our spheres of knowledge are only component parts of a whole bound together by a spiritual nexus which we are even farther from comprehending now than we ever were. The true mysteries of human life, of man's earliest existence on this earth, of anthropology and prehistory, cannot be tackled by modern rationalistic and scientific methods alone.

As children who have been expelled from the paradise of timelessness, we have a deep yearning to discover and explore the past. But if we do so, our researches must embrace the whole of the past, for only a view of the world which goes back to the origins of man can truly be termed universal history.

As has been said, by "history" we mean what has been transmitted to us via written sources. While these written traditions have greatly enriched us, they have also induced a sort of myopia, and we find it difficult to recognize the significance of the much larger span of time known as prehistory. Menghin is right when he says that we must reach much farther back into prehistory if we want to get to the root of things and arrive at a full understanding of the present. Written history lies so close to us that its five or six thousand years amount to no more than a day in the life of mankind. Being children of our time, we tend to think almost solely in terms of written history, even though it is really the prehistory of mankind which has made us what we are. We, with a recorded history of about six thousand years, are only the infant children of forefathers at least six hundred thousand years old. Only they could explain to us how the animate biped with the upright stance has managed to survive for several hundred thousand years. In order to grasp the mystery which is man we must trace his life through every epoch. He has always been active, never merely dormant, always in contact with a chain of events which has never once been broken. There never was a time without history.

If man's spiritual and moral strength had not been greater than his technical, inventive abilities during the Paleolithic Age, the biped with a capacity for abstract thought would never have survived until now. Today, our technical achievements soar into the stratosphere and beyond, while our moral and ethical strength sinks to the ground like a pricked balloon, weighed down by the philosophy of despair. That is why it is so important to form even a shadowy impression of the infinitely long and painful road which man has so far traveled and to realize that he has reached us not with the aid of stone implements but by means of other, imponderable resources which belong to the sphere of soul and intellect.

The very muteness of archaeological finds encourages us to underestimate the men who made them. But coup de poing and stone blade bear testimony not only to a life of articulate speech, laughter and tears but also to a vast multitude of intellectual achievements. They bear testimony to millions upon millions of conversations, to hunting calls, cries of victory and the groans of dying men. But, lying mutely there before us, they tell us little of the age-old spirituality of man.

Is there any way of drawing aside the curtain of prehistory and seeing more? Is there any possibility of dispelling the cold rigidity of these stones and making them talk?

If the cultural remains of prehistoric man are compared with the activities, ideas and general culture of such primitive peoples as still exist today, whole new vistas open up before our eyes, worlds to which we should never otherwise have had access. Because the cultural history of mankind is one large unity, prehistory and comparative ethnology are closely linked. Ethnology is concerned with the culture of living or recently extinct peoples. A great deal of what prehistory leaves unexplained becomes evident from the observation of primitive peoples. This is our passport to the hinterland of prehistory.

Ethnology can provide us with a great deal of information about our Stone-Age ancestors and supply the essential details of the spiritual culture of early man, while prehistory has been responsible for demonstrating that "even the earliest scientifically tangible man must have been a full and truly human being." Thus two sciences bring us closer to the emotions, intellect and soul of primeval man, while a third, anthropology, will do the same when it has matured enough to grant scientific recognition to the existence of the soul.

We moderns are so engrossed in thoughts of progress that we confuse good with new and old with bad. Europeans of the last century, for instance, imagined that after eighteen hundred years they had finally grasped the doctrines of Christ and were entitled to preside over all races from the throne of world history, loftily differentiating between good and evil, primitive and progressive. The status of the "savage" or "uncivilized" barbarian was regarded as nearer that of the beast than of the enlightened European.

In prehistoric times and among the so-called savages, it was alleged, polytheism predominated, whereas the West had only one god. Yet the belief in a single god is very much older than the recorded memory of man. Ethnology can "manufacture" history. Basing his conclusions on an immense number of ethnological comparisons drawn from every quarter of the globe, Wilhelm Schmidt has identified the earliest form of religion as a belief in one god. We now know, as a result of Schmidt's comprehensive research, that the first religion was always and everywhere traceable to a supreme being, and that far from exalting this idea the passage of time has only brought about its descent from a higher to a lower plane.

It was assumed in the last century that the "historyless" races almost invariably practiced polygamy, whereas Europeans had evolved the "progressive" practice of monogamy. In fact, there are reasons for believing that monogamy originated in the distant days of prehistory. Henri Breuil, after devoting a lifetime to the study of the early Paleolithic period, arrived at the conclusion that Stone-Age men's daily need to defend themselves, assist each other and ensure supplies of food for all could have been met only by the maintenance of strong family ties. Man or woman alone would never have survived. The same applies, as the Austrian anthropologist Wilhelm Koppers has constantly emphasized, to the majority of primitive peoples today.

The zoologist Ernst Heinrich Haeckel, the most ardent follower of Darwin's theory of evolution in Germany, who lived from 1834 to 1919, tried to prove that man evolved from the ape, via Pithecanthropus alalus and Homo stupidus, into Homo sapiens. Like Darwin's theory of human development or evolution, Haeckel's was immediately transferred to the fields of philosophy, morals and religion. The utensils of the early inhabitants of our earth and the difficulties which attended their invention were grossly underestimated. Again, it was believed that our forefathers must have gone about naked several tens of thousands of years ago, and that it was a sign of progress in the nineteenth-century European to muffle himself from the neck downward. Yet the men of the Aurignacian did not use their awls and needles on thin air sixty thousand years ago, but sewed clothes together from animal skins.

The early history of man's intellectual development does not reveal anything like the "rough, crude common sense" which the English anthropologist Sir Edward Burnett Tylor postulated. Tylor believed that throughout the long span of its existence the chief efforts of human society have been directed toward changing "from a savage to a civilized condition." The whole of nineteenth-century ethnological literature is contaminated by the use of this term "savage." There are no "savages" among the primitive peoples. Even "primitive" is a dangerous expression to use, for many so-called primitive peoples possess a remarkably subtle and variegated world of ideas, not to mention moral standards which are frequently much higher than those of the West.

Exactly the same applies to prehistory. Who knows if the maker of coups de poing and flake blades saw Tylor's "civilized condition" merely in terms of improving those tools, or whether he was indifferent to such things and strove to achieve progress and self-advancement in the maintenance and improvement of moral standards? The truth is that we are still proceeding, even today, on the idiotic and vain assumption that man has gradually raised himself from barbarism to advanced civilization. There is absolutely no reason to conclude that, because their tools were simple, people's customs were gross, their language undeveloped or their religion primitive.

Technical development is far from being a criterion of the moral and social level of a race. Every culture has its spiritual and moral as well as its material side and seems to share this dichotomy with the universe, which would be inconceivable without some sort of creative and spiritual impetus. These two aspects of culture, the material and the spiritual, can grow at quite different speeds, and a high degree of one does not by any means presuppose a high degree of the other. Extremely primitive tools may well have been used by people of extremely high moral caliber, for material and spiritual cultures are not linked by communicating doors. Indeed, great refinement in material things is often a symptom of the morally brittle society.

There never has been such a thing as a "prelogical" or "alogical" human being, and the French sociologist Lucien Lévy-Bruhl, who invented this creature in 1910, repudiated his brain child several decades later. K. J. Narr says: "The specifically human intellect was in operation at the beginning of the period traditionally covered by prehistory, and has been sufficiently demonstrated by extant remains." We must therefore assume a basic correspondence between early and latter-day human nature. There is a unity in human nature, an identity of species between the human intellect of prehistoric times and that of the brief epoch during which man has been writing and recording actions and events in the form of history. Where the existence of tools has been positively established, there, too, is proof of the existence of a complete human being, however old his artifacts or cultural remains may be.

Hobbes, Morgan, Tylor and Spengler saw man as a predator which had become tamed and refined in the course of history. They regarded primitive requirements such as shelter from the elements, protection against wild animals and an adequate supply of game as the sole motive forces of evolution. All stimuli were attributable, in their opinion, to natural causes. Spengler took the laws of natural science and applied them to history as a whole. Following nature's example, Spengler postulated general rules for the course of history just as a man might predetermine the growth and development of a plant which he has already studied. In the end, he came to believe that he could predict history. As H. Kuhn wrote in a review of Arnold J. Toynbee's *Study of History*, in *The Journal of Philosophy*, 1947: "The biological analogy holds undisputed sway in *The Decline of the West*. For Spengler, cultures, each a living entity by itself and essentially unrelated to other specimens of the same genus, seem to emerge out of the Boundless, run their fated course, and relapse into the original abyss 'according to the order of time' like the successive worlds in Anaximander's cosmogony." This naturalistic conception of history, in which human beings are merely objects, in which there is no creation and no god, came naturally to a man who had passed his civil service examinations in zoology, botany, physics, chemistry, mineralogy and mathematics!

Were libido, hunger and cold the only things which actuate human beings, their cultural development would have been constant and equal at every stage and in every place. Were they so actuated, we should be able to believe Toynbee when he asserts that six of his twenty-one "civilizations"—Egyptian, Sumerian, Minoan, Chinese, Mayan and Peruvian—"grew directly out of a primitive living-standard." In fact, of course, modern research is still far from advanced enough to enable us to determine—one might say "dig out" —such transitions and derivations, and lack of knowledge or adequate research does not entitle anyone to conclude that a culture originated independently and spontaneously. R. G. Collingwood, in *The Idea of History*, comments:

> One forgets that the historical fact, as it actually exists and as the historian actually knows it, is always a process in which something is changing into something else. This element of process is the life of history. In order to pigeon-hole historical facts, the living body of history must first be killed so that it may be dissected.... Toynbee regards history ... as cut up by sharp lines into mutually exclusive parts, and denies the continuity of the process in virtue of which every part overlaps and interpenetrates others.

The unity of human nature and the constant, uninterrupted flow of human experience weights the odds far more strongly in favor of human cultural unity than of parallel development. The Austrian ethnologist Robert Heine-Geldern has become convinced, after many years of research, that the more advanced cultures represent a fundamental whole. If we proceed on this assumption we gain an entirely new insight into the over-all development of human civilization and enter upon a train of thought which takes us immeasurably farther into the history of mankind, leading us eventually to its beginnings and turning the historian into the "backward-facing prophet" of Friedrich von Schlegel's ideal.

If we concede the unity of human nature, the constant flow of human experience and finally the unity of human culture, we must also concede the existence of a universal history which, in association with ethnology and prehistory, embraces the whole earthly existence of man.

The moral consciousness of primeval man must already have resembled our own, even though the beginnings of his material culture create a very primitive impression. This can be seen in the case of some primitive races today. Morally, ethically and religiously, they are on a high plane; materially, they resemble people of primeval times—a fact which even Tylor recognized.

As has been said, it is these present-day "savages," these primitive peoples, who offer us the best opportunity of reliving the dawn of mankind and disclose how illuminating a collaboration between prehistory and ethnology can be. There are remarkable parallels between the Paleolithic and the ethnologically primitive races. It is a long and arduous journey from stone implements, fire and slaughtered game to a comprehension of the actual life of a prehistoric race of men, yet it can be made not along the dark roads of prehistory but the lonely and often difficult paths of ethnology.

We shall go among races who live in the northern part of the earth, in regions where man has had to come to terms with the cold, where a large world of ideas is dedicated to the bear, where the reindeer dominates whole cultures and where a thousand small details remind us of the connection between people of the Stone Age and men still living today. These regions are the vast tracts inhabited by the Arctic peoples of North America and northern Siberia.

In visiting these ancient races we shall attempt to rediscover the footsteps of God, obliterated as they have been by the aeons of time which have elapsed. If there ever was such a thing as a primordial monotheism, if belief in a supreme being formed the earliest stage in man's religious development, then the whole evolutionistic conception of religion is doomed to destruction. Strangely enough, the majority of people alive today believe in such an evolution and in the development of religious knowledge. We of the West regard faith in a single supreme deity as the highest stage of religious development. Since we normally imagine ourselves, with varying degrees of conviction, to be at this stage, it follows that things must have been different or more primitive in earlier times. In fact, we are still in the throes of polytheism. Christ's call has held this tendency in check, but two thousand years after His Sermon on the Mount we are still crucifying, still dancing round the Golden Calf, still paying homage to a miscellany of cure-all doctrines, worshipping pictures and making obeisance to the photograph, a form of effigy greatly feared by primitive peoples and one which threatens gradually to replace the whole of our real life.

Contemporary man regards his era as the zenith of wisdom and generally considers that every religion stands a little higher than its predecessor. This view springs from an observation of the strides made by technology. Our whole mental equipment is tending to operate more and more on technical lines, with the result that we transfer the truths of technology to every other sphere of life until we imagine that we are to be congratulated on having "invented" monotheism. The fallacy reposes in the fact that technique alone progresses and that only technique can be evolutionary.

The ancient peoples of the circumpolar regions teach us something quite different. They teach us that man's spiritual and moral attributes have scarcely progressed at all, that the soul existed from the very first and that buried in this amazingly exalted beginning is the mystery of God.

If we examine the divine beliefs of the most ancient primitive races, it is not beyond the bounds of possibility that ethnology may one day lead us to a primordial manifestation of God. In other words, it may supply us with historical evidence of the Supreme Being. That ethnologically ancient races believed in a supreme being and that this faith became stronger the farther into prehistory its traditions extended is important because our Western culture depends solely on the supremacy of the spirit. God, as the supreme supersensual idea, represents the strongest foundation of the Western will to spirituality. God is the beginning and the inspiration of

Western culture; without Him it would perish. It is an old adage that all culture depends on divine belief and that it can arise only where man is aroused and inspired by deep genuine faith.

Why should we not pursue our search for the Supreme Being when we attempt to analyze the structure of the universe and set no limit on our technical undertakings? If we devote so much money and scientific endeavor to cosmic research and journeys into space, why should our efforts to identify God among the last surviving primitive peoples lag behind?

Our first visit will be to the erstwhile masters of the American continent, and our first task to inquire after the origins of religion among the surviving remnants of the Indian tribes there.

CHAPTER 7

THE ORIGIN OF AMERICAN INDIANS

Of great interest to students of prehistory in America is the problem of man's migrations from the Old World to the New. It is virtually undenied that as far as we know, prehistoric man entered America from Eurasia.

RALPH S. SOLECKI, *Archaeology and Ecology of the Arctic Slope of Alaska.* Annual Report of the Smithsonian Institution, 1950, p. 469

FROM the Arctic Ocean to Tierra del Fuego, the original inhabitants of the American double continent present an extraordinary mixture of racial types. While their hair is usually straight, some tribes are curly-haired. Again, some American Indians are very light-skinned and others extremely dark. In many areas their noses are aquiline, in others narrow and prominent, and in still others flat and broad like those of many Siberian tribes. Cheekbones display varying degrees of prominence, as does body hair, which is generally sparse. Quite similar conditions prevail in Siberia. There, the longer one lives among the primitive tribes, the more distinctly one notices ethnological differences and the more confused one becomes by the multiplicity and variety of North Asiatic faces. One also recognizes that among the paleo-Asiatic types there are some which are more reminiscent of the Ainu than the Mongol.

The theory that America's earliest inhabitants belonged to the Mongol race does not seem logical. There is really no such thing as a unified Indian race, and the Indians do not represent an offshoot of the Mongoloids. By and large, European physical traits are at least as strongly represented among the aboriginal inhabitants of America as Mongolian.

The heterogeneity of the American tribes is so great that it does not seem possible that it could first have developed in the New World. Countless racial groups of varying sizes migrated across the Bering Straits in the course of thousands of years, and the ancestors of the American Indians must have brought their individual characteristics with them to the New World. At the time of Columbus, about a million Indians lived in America north of Mexico and there were about three hundred different tribes. Today, the number of Indians in the United States, Canada and Alaska is only about half a million. On the other hand, some tribes, notably the Navaho, Sioux and Cherokee, have grown in size.

Joseph B. Birdsell, American professor of prehistory, has postulated an interesting but controversial theory. He regards the human fossils of Chou-k'ou-tien and, in particular, those belonging to the sapiens type in the Upper Cave, as a cross between the Amurian type and ancient Mongoloid types. The Amurian type belongs to the eastern branch of the Caucasian race, and Birdsell believes that these Amurian people, primitive Caucasian ancestors of the Ainu, were the earliest migrants to reach America.

It is doubtful that this view can be entirely accurate, but the oldest group of Asiatic migrants to arrive in America—apart from the bearers of early Paleolithic cultures—were certainly Europid-Caucasian in type. They were followed at the close of the Ice Age by the Lagoa Santa race. The blood of the yellow race was a much later admixture, for the Mongol migrations probably did not occur until 2000 B.C., and then only partially via Siberia. They may have come to a larger extent across the Pacific. So, as Menghin expresses it, "a light Mongolian film spread gradually across every tribe of early American inhabitants." It is because of this very late admixture of yellow blood that the various tribes of America create a Mongoloid impression which has given rise to their erroneous classification in the Mongol race. For many tens of thousands of years, the early inhabitants of America were the descendants of paleo-Europid peoples who had also occupied Siberia. The Mongol in them is only about four thousand years old.

The age of American man may also be the reason why it is almost impossible today to relate any of the Indian languages to any Eurasian linguistic group. The differences are so pronounced that a homogeneous and comparatively recent settlement of America is quite improbable, if only from the linguistic point of view. The eminent anthropologist Dr. Franz Boas demonstrated in 1933 that most of the

Indian languages could not be traced back to a common origin. On no other continent on earth are so many different languages spoken, and it is impossible to identify any structural or phonetic characteristics which are common to all the American languages. One can only try, as American philologists do, to classify the Indian languages in groups, e.g. Tlingit, Haida and Athapascan under the name Na-Dene, and Shoshonean, Nahuatlan, Piman, Tanoan, Kiowan, Penutian, Mayan, Totonacan and probably others, in the Uto-Aztecan group. Fifty-six linguistic families have been identified in the United States and Canada, twenty-nine in Central America, and no less than eighty-four in South America—and this despite the fact that many languages had become extinct before anyone had a chance to study them.

In recent years, American authorities have regrouped the languages of the northern half of their continent in seven linguistic families: Eskimo, Athapascan, Algonkin, Siouan, Uto-Aztecan, Iroquoian and Muskhogean.

It does not follow that because American tribes possess similar cultures they also speak the same language, and peoples who speak related languages, like the Hopi in the Southwest and the Paiute in the West, may easily possess quite dissimilar cultures. The Hopi are agriculturalists and the Paiute hunters and food gatherers.

Does this mean that there are no links between the Asiatic languages and those of America?

Chukchee and Eskimo vary in structure but exhibit certain conformities. The manner in which thoughts are verbally expressed is similar, but the methods and expressions themselves are different. Similar relationships have been ascertained in the languages of the Chukchees, Koryaks, Kamchadals, Aleuts and Eskimos, so a common linguistic origin may be attributed to several of the circumpolar races of both the Old and the New Worlds. Robert Shafer drew attention in 1952 to certain resemblances between Athapascan and Sino-Tibetan.

At all events, the existence of circumpolar relationships since the end of the last Ice Age (8000 B.C.) cannot be denied. If these remain difficult to prove linguistically, some of the cultural conformities are so striking that they can scarcely be accidental. The North

American hunter-fishermen, Algonkins, Athapascans and Eskimos, and the Indians of the Northwest, Tlingit, Haida, Tsimshi, Wakash, Salish and others, bear a strong cultural resemblance to the primitive peoples of northern Asia.

The tents of various Siberian tribes, structures consisting of a single wooden pole and sheets of birchbark arranged in a prescribed way, have their counterpart in the American Indian's birchbark wigwam. Canoes faced with birchbark and receptacles made of folded and shaped sheets of the same material are to be found on both sides of the Bering Straits. The drums of most primitive peoples are tall in format, i.e. barrel-shaped or cylindrical, even when they only possess one drumskin. Siberian and American tribes, by contrast, have flat hoop-shaped drums resembling tambourines. Certain forms of burial, particularly the custom of "high" or super-terranean burial, appear to have come to America from Asia. The postglacial invaders of North America brought sledges and dogs with them, also spears and a form of wooden spear sling still to be seen among the Chukchees of Siberia, though the reinforced composite bow was probably adopted from Asia long after the spear. The shape and workmanship of certain stone tools is of North Eurasian origin, as are tailored garments made of skin. Warm clothing, especially sewn clothing, is not invariable to all dwellers in Arctic conditions. The Fuegians, Alacaluf and Yamana, for example, wore only a form of cape. Finally, the shamanism of the New World betrays many striking resemblances to that of the Old and is probably of North Asiatic origin. Ideas of cosmogony in Europe and Asia and related ideas in northwest America so often correspond that the adoption of this whole store of conceptions by the New World from the Old is as good as proved. One very typical tradition which could scarcely have arisen independently on both sides of the Bering Straits is the bear cult.

American scientists gladly concede all these early cultural debts. It is only the much later similarities which many authorities have attributed to man's inventive capacity, pointing to the lack of vital thought, utensils and foodstuffs which prevailed before the arrival of Columbus as evidence of the New World's complete subsequent isolation.

In reality, there were many connections between Asia and America and large-scale adoptions of customs, ideas, technical methods, styles and ornamentation even in the late period; that is to say, roughly between 2000 B.C. and A.D. 1000. The bronze cult vessels of China's Shang Dynasty (1766–1122 B.C.) carried early pictorial symbols which preceded the advent of writing proper, and their reliefs and pictures illustrate the religious practices and precepts of the Shang and pre-Shang periods. Karl Hentze, a leading authority on the civilization of the Shang Dynasty, has demonstrated many connections between Shang culture and the high cultures of pre-Columbian America. He has shown that the development of the pictorial world of religious symbolism on ancient Chinese ritual vessels is similar to that of pre-Columbian Central America and shares certain characteristics with Peruvian pottery painting and textile design. The earliest bronze cult vessels of China approximate in their religious representations to the same stage of development as that of the painted vessels of the Chavin, Paracas and Nasca cultures of Peru or the Mayan culture of Central America.

What complicates the question is that one cannot just assume the occurrence of Pacific crossings without more ado. If sea traffic between Asia and America was possible, why did not Indian corn—originally a Mexican plant—or cultivated beans and melons reach the Old World? Why did not wheat, barley, millet, rice or any domesticated animals (with the exception of dogs) find a new home on the American continent? The reason why the wheel was not used in America may, as Dr. Gordon F. Ekholm of the American Museum of Natural History has so illuminatingly pointed out, be that it was not in widespread use in Asia either. The paleo-Indians' commonest mode of transport was the travois, a device consisting of two shafts attached by a belt to a dog's back. The ends of the shafts were left to trail along the ground, and the load was suspended between them. This method of transportation probably reached the American continent at the same time as the introduction of the dog. Apart from that, races such as the peoples of Mexico had evolved other practical ideas which made the wheel superfluous.

The adoption of an idea or an article may well justify one in assuming the existence of cultural contact, but the nonadoption of some article or invention is no reason for repudiating it. We have only to consider all that our own excellent means of communication are transporting across oceans and continents in our own day and remember the difficulty Diesel experienced in getting his motor accepted by the world at large. Why is the soya bean cultivated in such small quantities in Europe even though it can withstand harsh climatic conditions? The sweet potato, which was introduced into the Polynesian islands, presumably from America in the first millennium A.D., still finds no place on the menus of most European countries today.

Judging by certain cultural parallels between the Old and New Worlds, seagoing boats must have been in existence by the first pre-Christian millennium at the very latest, for not everything could have come across the Bering Straits. If we tend to underestimate the possibility of prehistoric sea voyages in, say, the second millennium B.C., and if we fail to find evidence of sea-borne migrations or exchanges of knowledge between neighboring continents, this may be due in part to the fact that sea voyages leave no trace unless they are recorded in writing, and that primitive boats scarcely ever survive, from the archaeological aspect, for periods lasting thousands of years.

Agriculture, pottery and sedentary habits appeared in Mesopotamia in about 5000 B.C., in India in about 4000 B.C., in China in about 3000 B.C., and in North and South America in about 1500 B.C. There is a pattern distinguishable here, and it was in accordance with this pattern that cultures spread slowly across the world and crossed the Pacific Ocean. Ekholm asks why, if it was an independent American invention and did not arrive in the New World as a result of diffusion, agriculture did not begin on the American continent in 5000 B.C.

American scientists have divided the principal forms of cultural life in North America into six so-called "culture areas." This creates the impression that the development of North American Indian culture took place in various geographic units which flourished side by side. Anything which occurred before the beginning of sedentary life and thus constituted true prehistory was normally designated as "marginal," and little importance was attached to it, since it was long thought that America was not settled until relatively late, or about eight thousand years ago. Actually the culture areas only acquire validity after the advent of indigenous agricultural settlements. Historically, their importance is limited because they do not extend anything like far enough into prehistory. It would be more organically correct to follow Menghin's suggestion and classify the cultural domains of America's primitive peoples according to their mode of life: lower hunters and food collectors, big-game and steppe hunters, hunter-fishermen, hunter-cultivators, lower cultivators and, finally, members of the high cultures. One group did not exist in America, nomadic cattle breeders or warrior herdsmen like the Turks and many of the Mongols, and its absence did much to differentiate the New World from the Old.

CHAPTER 8

AMERICAN INDIANS AND
THE SUPREME BEING

*The Deity of the Pawnees is Atius Tiráwa (father spirit). He is
an intangible spirit, omnipotent and beneficent. He pervades the
universe, and is its supreme ruler. Upon his will depends everything that happens. He can bring good luck or bad; can give success or failure. Everything rests with him. As a natural consequence
of this conception of the Deity, the Pawnees are a very religious
people. Nothing is undertaken without a prayer to the Father for
assistance.*

GEORGE BIRD GRINNELL, *Pawnee Mythology*,
Journal of American Folk-Lore, VI, 1893,
p. 114

AMONG the native peoples of the American continent, a firmly
anchored belief in the supreme being exists principally among races
whose culture has preserved its ancient cast. These are the tribes of
hunters and food collectors who have failed to share in certain aspects
of progress and who, being gradually forced into the outskirts of
their continent, have remained the more strongly dominated by
their ancient traditions. Magnificent legends have survived among
the ancient peoples of America, amazing verbal traditions whose
roots must lie buried deep in human history. Hundreds of thousands
of years may have obliterated the traces of God and much may have
been lost of the directness, profundity and truth of the earliest faith,
but something of it still survives.

Among the oldest races in North and South America are the
Algonkin tribes, the people of central California and the Fuegians.
They have preserved their ancient cultural values, and it is among
them that the primordial faith in a supreme deity lives on.

Many of these people died out long ago, but undaunted efforts
by scientists have often helped to win the race between death and
knowledge, as in the case of a small and now extinct tribe called
the Wiyot-Wishosk. The remnants of this people, who lived on the

coast of California north and south of Humboldt Bay, were exhaustively studied by A. L. Kroeber.

In the myths of the Wiyot, the supreme being was known as Gudatrigakwitl. Alfred L. Kroeber, famous American anthropologist and ethnologist, an authority on the culture of the North American Indians, writes: "Perhaps the most marked characteristic of these myths is the important role assigned to the creator and supreme deity, Gudatrigakwitl, 'Above-old-man.' It will be seen that he represents a well-developed idea of true creation." The supreme god of the Wiyot needed no sand, earth, clay or sticks for the creation of man. God merely thought, and man was there. The first man was called Chelkowik, and God thought a woman for him. But the first men were bad, and so they had to die. "God still lives today," said the Wiyot. He cannot be attacked by any disease, is immortal and will continue to exist as long as the world endures.

In about 1870, St. Powers wrote about the Mattole, a small tribe which also lived on the California coast. By 1910, only ten pure-blooded members of this tribe were still alive, and it has since died out entirely. In the religious tradition of the Mattole, God (described as "Great Man") provided the earth's surface with only one living creature, a lonely Indian who went his solitary way through the black, silent, frosty wastes. Not until a great storm had occurred was the world finally completed. Like many primitive American peoples, the Mattole were also familiar with a Flood legend.

The god of the Sinkyone was the Great Wanderer. Known as Nagaitso, he was also called simply Spirit or, in the language of the Sinkyone, Kojoi. He created the earth and human beings. His adversary Coyote assisted him, but simultaneously introduced evil and death into the world.

Another now extinct tribe was that of the Kato, the most southerly Dene tribe on the west coast of North America. Pliny E. Goddard, Curator of Ethnology at the New York Museum of Natural History from 1909 to 1928, collected their myths, and so we know that they regarded Tsenes (the Thunderer) as the true creator, while Nagaitso (the Great Wanderer) only assisted in the act of creation. The creation of all things and all living creatures was portrayed with remarkable strength and grandeur in the myths of the Kato. God first made the heavens, the firmament, and mankind. Then he brought into being rain, wind, sun and moon, beasts of the sea, springs, streams, plants and land animals. Finally, the Thunderer made a tour of the world. "Follow me, my dog, let us look." The plants had grown, fish swam in the streams and the rocks had waxed large. "I shall try the water once. You drink also," said the god of the Kato. "I made the earth good, my dog. Quick, go, my dog."

How did the story of the Flood reach America? For it was pre-served in the myths of many races in the American double continent for thousands of years before the first Christian missionaries arrived. Did America, too, experience a flood about ten thousand years ago, at the close of the last glacial period, or were tidings of the great watery death brought across from Asia?

We do not know, but we certainly meet the "American Flood" in many of the new continent's myths. The Kato, for instance, de-scribed it as follows: "It rained, it rained every day. Every evening, every night, it rained. It rained too much, people said. They now had no fire. The streams filled, the water rose in the valleys, the water surrounded them on every side. All people went to sleep. Then the sky fell down. There was no more land. The waters of the ocean covered the whole earth. All the grizzly bears died, all the elks drowned, all the panthers drowned, all the deer drowned—all animals drowned."

It is interesting to note that in the ancient myths of the primitive peoples of America, just as in the portrayals of the Book of Genesis, the first human beings had to die because they were evil. In the myths of the East Pomo, who lived in northern California, the supreme being was called Marumda. He lived alone in a house of clouds in the North. After creating the earth, the god of the Pomo made deer, birds, rabbits, women (out of four feathers) and men (out of his own hair). But the first generations of men were evil. They acquired too much power: they could fly. So Marumda sum-moned the great waters to cover them, and only a few families escaped the flood. Marumda bade men do better in future. Marumda's creatures still possessed the power to be either man or beast, but they once again violated the laws of marriage, hunting and fishing. Marumba therefore sent a raging fire across the whole earth. Many people tried to seek escape in the seas but the water began to boil and they died. Others climbed tall trees, but the trees caught fire. When Marumda had destroyed all the living creatures whom he considered evil, he removed man's power to determine his own shape. From that time forward men remained immutably men and could no longer become animals, and animals became true animals and could no longer be men.

According to the ideas of the Miwok (Moquelumnan), who belong linguistically to the Penutian family, the world was populated six times. The last creation of mankind was effected by Coyote. The myths of the Miwok also contain references to a Flood, but they combine Coyote and the supreme being in a single person.

Kroeber proved that all the peoples of central California believe in a creator of the world, the maker of men and their material surroundings. They usually picture him as an exalted, grave and kindly figure. However, this beneficent and truly divine being is often associated with a second, Coyote, who partly collaborates with the supreme god and partly works against him, inducing imperfections in the world and mortality among men. The Creator is seldom alone, and this may conceivably indicate that a weakening, adulteration or deterioration of the supreme god idea has taken place in the course of thousands of years. Coyote works against the deity and is the cause of all the evil and imperfections which threaten to spoil the Creator's plans. In other myths, the supreme god and Coyote, who is also associated with human guile and merriment, have become merged, but the legends of central California normally draw a clear distinction between the two.

Doubts are often voiced as to whether the supreme deity of many American peoples might not have been incorporated in their religions by Christian missionaries. Because the Salishan-stock tribes from the upper reaches of the Frazer River in Canada and its tributary the Thompson were converted to Catholicism by French missionaries at an early date, some authorities hold that their belief in a supreme being was not originally their own but could be traced to Christian influence. All the three Salishan tribes who live by these rivers, the Thompson Indians, the Lillooet and the Shuswap, have a profound belief in the supreme being whom they refer to as the Old One or Old Man. This faith in a supreme deity is most firmly and explicitly preserved among the Thompson Indians who dwelt in the center of the whole area.

A distinguished scholar named James Teit devoted years of his life to a study of the Salishan tribes, during which time he mastered their language and constantly tried to help them. It is Teit whom we have to thank for the knowledge that the Old Man was an integral part of the ancient religion of this race and had been so long before French oblates arrived to preach the God of Christianity. Teit eventually came to the conclusion that the Old Man, far from being a white man's god, was an original feature of these Indians' mythology. The Old Man was also called Great Chief or Mystery. It may have been a relic of Asiatic influence tens of thousands of years old that the dwelling place of the Old Man was assumed to be in the highest mountains, but prayers which were no doubt addressed originally to the Old Man alone were later directed to the mountain peaks themselves.

Even if we know that the religion of the Thompson Indians, as far as James Teit's research indicated (*Traditions of the Thompson River Indians of British Columbia*, 1898), was uninfluenced by Christianity, it is nonetheless interesting to find that this ancient American race believed in a Resurrection. The Old Man says to Coyote: "Soon I am going to leave the earth. You will not return again until I myself do so. You shall then accompany me, and we will change things in the world, and bring back the dead to the land of the living."

The Viennese ethnologist Josef Haeckel attaches great antiquity to a belief in a supreme deity among the fisherman tribes of America's northwest coast, i.e. the Tlingit, Haida, Tsimshi, Bellacoola (Bilqula) and Kwakiutl.

The Bellacoola call their supreme god Aelquntäm. Since this name is derived from the expression for "chieftain," Aelquntäm must be the chief of all supernatural beings. Although he possesses certain human attributes, he existed before all other living creatures, guiding the sun and determining the movements of the moon, of coming and going, ebb and flow. Aelquntäm bade four wood carvers whom he endowed with infinite power to make a number of human beings. People who possess the ability to carve animals and men out of wood enjoy the same respect and veneration among the Indians of the northwest coast as they do among the Gilyaks of the Amur estuary and other Siberian tribes. So the four master craftsmen carved animals, birds, trees, flowers, fish, mountains, rivers—everything which goes to make life on earth. Powerful is the man who can make effigies of nature, say the Bellacoola, but all his power comes from Aelquntäm.

The Tsimshi, northern neighbors of the Bellacoola, call the supreme being Chief of the Air. Like the Haida who live on Queen Charlotte Island, the Tsimshi closely associate their supreme being with the sky. Indeed, the Haida describe their deity as Sinssganagwai, which means "Power of the Shining Heavens."

The supreme being of the Tlingit, a race living on the coast of southern Alaska, does not live in the sky but at the beginning of all things, in the world of darkness, in a house by the source of the Nass River.

Haeckel concludes that the idea of a supreme being was already a spiritual possession of the coast cultures when the Bellacoola migrated from the interior to the sea, and that the coastal tribes owned a very ancient store of common myths which they had probably inherited from the ancestors of the inland Salish.

It may thus be assumed that the tribes of the Northwest have believed in a supreme being for a very considerable length of time. The origins of this belief repose in one of those basic cultures which can be disclosed only by ethnological and prehistorical research. The problem is an important one, for on its solution depends the answer to whether the ancient peoples of America only evolved their belief in God at a late stage or even adopted it from European missionaries, or whether it is an age-old and factual tradition. Did God exist, in fact, or was He invented?

The area inhabited by the large Algonkin group extends across the whole eastern half of the north of North America. Owing to the influence and pressure of several neighboring races, the Algonkin split up into numerous cultural, economic and religious units, but they were originally hunters. A few of their component tribes specialized in gathering wild rice in the area of the Great Lakes and in making sugar from the sap of the species of maples. Agriculture developed in the south.

The Great Spirit of the Algonkin, Kitshi Manitou, is the supreme god of ancient times, although, once again, it has been questioned whether this belief always existed among the Algonkin by those who allege that Manitou was first introduced by Christian missionaries. Some authorities believed that Manitou was the name of an old magical power which assumed divine form in the course of Christianization. Curiously enough, E. B. Tylor subscribed to both theories. In his main work, *Primitive Culture,* published in 1871, he wrote that Manitou could not be a deity of alien origin because he differed essentially from anything the Algonkin could have been told about God by missionaries and colonists. In his treatise *On the Limits of Savage Religion,* on the other hand, he traces the belief in the Great Spirit back to the teaching of Jesuit missionaries.

Fortunately, we know from Andrew Lang that prior to 1633 and before the commencement of any missionary activity the earliest European students of the Algonkin had already recorded the Indians' faith in a supreme being. Master Thomas Heriot was an extremely erudite mathematician who was as proficient in the Indians' language as in his own. He lived in Virginia for many years and eventually left the country on June 18, 1586. "They believe," he reported, "that there is a Supreme God who has existed from all eternity."

William Strachey, who sailed from England aboard the *Sea Venture* in 1606, was shipwrecked off the Bermudas and finally reached Virginia in 1610 in a small boat put together from the wreckage of the original vessel. He served the newly founded colony as first Secretary of State to the Governor, Baron De La Warr. Strachey told of the great god of the natives who controls the world, makes the sun shine, created the moon and stars, and rules the earth.

Edward Winslow accompanied the first American colonists to land at Plymouth Rock after their voyage aboard the *Mayflower.*

On March 22, 1621, he was authorized to negotiate with the Indian "king" Massassoit and conclude a treaty, and in July of the same year he set off to meet the Indians at the head of a deputation. It was the first attempt by the English to explore the interior. When Winslow told the natives of the God of the Christians they replied that this was very good, because they believed the same things of their own god, Kiehtan. Kiehtan made all other gods. He was the creator of all things and dwelt far away in the western skies. He also created one man and one woman, and through them the whole of humanity, but it was not known how mankind had become so widely scattered.

Andrew Lang's evidence of the southeastern Algonkin's faith in a supreme being is based on testimony which dates from the arrival of the first white men in the years between 1586 and 1633. A belief in Manitou existed and the god of the Algonkin was alive before any European set foot on the new continent. David Zeisberger, an exceedingly active missionary from Zauchenthal in Moravia who compiled numerous dictionaries of Indian languages, was the author of several grammars and translated Biblical texts for Algonkin tribes, commanded not only the Delaware and Onondaga tongues but also Mohican, Monsey-Delaware and Chippewa. He wrote in about 1779: "They believe and have from time immemorial believed that there is an Almighty Being who has created heaven and earth and man and all things else. This they have learned from their ancestors." John Heckewelder, Moravian missionary in the late eighteenth century, assistant to David Zeisberger, and author of several books on the Pennsylvania Indians, added more details in 1818: "Their Almighty Creator is always before their eyes on all important occasions. They feel and acknowledge his supreme power." William Penn, in a letter dated as early as August 16, 1683, said: "They believe in a God and Immortality, for they say, there is a King that made them, who dwells in a glorious country Southward of them, and that the Souls of the Good shall go thither, where they shall live again."

To repeat: was Manitou an indeterminate magical force or was he the supreme being? Was Kitshi-Manitou, the Great Spirit, an undivided god?

The Great Spirit stood at the head of religion, but he was not its focal point. He occupied an exalted position far above the world which he had created, and cared little about the progress of his creation or the petty doings of mankind. Ancient American Indian legends still tell of the Great Spirit's intercourse with mankind. He manifested himself to them at the quarry of Coteau des Prairies, the common mecca of many Sioux and Algonkin tribes.

Of the central Algonkin tribes, it is the Ojibwa who have supplied scholars with most information about Manitou. Because Manitou could appear in many guises, he has always been a difficult subject for research. Ideas of him varied in complexion because the secret rites practiced by his adherents in themselves presupposed a large number of different manifestations. In accordance with the precepts of individual totemism among the Ojibwa, as among many American Indians, all young men had to spend a period in solitude, meditating, doing penance and fasting. This lasted until Manitou appeared to them, after which he became their tutelary spirit. It was because Manitou could adopt so many shapes when appearing to young men in solitude that ideas of him became so remarkably diverse.

W. J. Hoffman, who lived with the Ojibwa from 1887 to 1889, persuaded the shamans of that tribe to give him precise information about their secret societies and rites. He has recorded many interesting details about Manitou. In his work *The Midewiwin or Grand Medicine Society of the Ojibwa,* Hoffman wrote: "The Ojibwa believe in a multiplicity of spirits, or man idos, which inhabit all space and every conspicuous object in nature. These man idos, in turn, are subservient to superior ones, either of a charitable and benevolent character or those which are malignant and aggressive. The chief or superior man ido is termed Ki'tshi Man'ido—Great Spirit—approaching to a great extent the God of the Christian religion." If only because Kitshi-Manitou itself means "Great Spirit," therefore, the chief god should be thought of as a personality.

The traditions of the Ojibwa also make mention of a heroic figure who exhibits certain characteristics reminiscent of our Noah and Moses but is also capable of unscrupulous dealings, a figure who mediates between Kitshi-Manitou and mankind. This mediator is

called Nenebojo, Nänibozhu or Minabozho, and it was through him
that the Great Spirit imparted the secret rites of the Midewiwin or
secret society to mankind. Nenebojo and his twin brother were born
simultaneously of a virgin. Although the girl had been warned by
her mother not to walk into the west wind, she did so, and thus
became the mother of twins. Nenebojo's brother was killed by water
spirits who, when Nenebojo took vengeance upon them, dispatched
floods of water which engulfed the whole earth. Nenobojo fled to
a mountaintop and built a raft, taking with him one pair of every
kind of living animal. When he judged that the flood was drawing
to a close he sent out an otter and then a beaver, instructing them
to dive and bring up some earth. The first to reappear was the musk-
rat, which succeeded in bringing up some sand in its mouth and
claws. From this Nenebojo fashioned an island which grew and grew.
Then he sent out a raven, and the raven did not return. Finally he
dispatched a hawk and a reindeer to find out if the earth was big
enough.

Nenebojo or Minabozho (the word means "Big Rabbit") was very
popular with the Indians. Alanson Skinner collected many anecdotes
about him from the Plains Ojibwa in Manitoba, and Paul Radin,
gathered Nenebojo legends from the Ojibwa of southern Ontario.
He is supposed to have performed many of his deeds in the vicinity
of Lake Superior, and his grave is said to be on the northern shore
east of Thunderbay Point. A tricky individual, Nenebojo was capable
of deceiving people, annoying them and confounding them with
unexpected feats of cunning. However, the Indians do not appear to
have endowed him with these characteristics until a fairly late date,
for in very ancient times he was innocent of such hobgoblin-like
peculiarities and the Indians regarded him as helpful and benevolent.
Indeed, they believed that they owed their lives and all good things
to his kindly intervention. Not only had he given them the rites of
the Midewiwin, but he was also the servant of the Great Spirit and
an intercessor for mankind. Nevertheless, Kitshi-Manitou was always
invisibly present whenever rites were performed and his name was
uttered only with the utmost reverence. William Jones, too, has
stressed this in his "Ojibwa Tales from the North Shore of Lake

[29] Everything worn by the Orochon comes from the reindeer, from skin cap to moccasins. Outer garments are richly decorated, stained with vegetable dyes and sewn together with reindeer hair.

[30] Several hundred Golds still survive in the region of Khabarovsk on the Lower Amur and in Manchuria. They used to be hunters but have become peasants and cattle breeders in the last fifty years. These two women are wearing clothes which exhibit a strong Chinese influence.

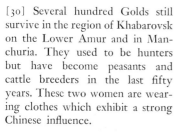

[31] Among the Reindeer Tungus of Manchuria girls are regarded as marriageable from the age of seventeen onward. This Orochon girl already possessed an illegitimate child, an asse which substantially increased her *kalym* or bride-price.

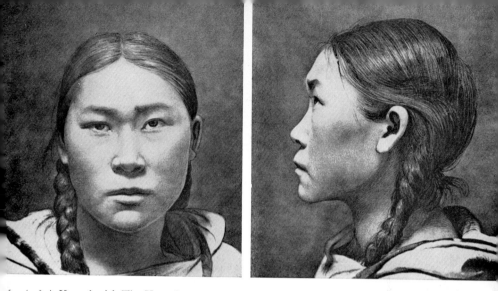

[32/33] A Koryak girl. The Koryaks are a proud and high-spirited but extremely hospitable tribe which has always tried to maintain its independence. According to Jochelson, they are immune to panic and have no fear of death.

[34] Koryak reindeer-drawn sledges. The animals are harnessed in oblique formation by traces of varying lengths. Although each sledge is normally drawn by three to five reindeer, it can only cover between fifteen and twenty-five miles a day and in summer even less.

[35] Sunken hut belonging to Sea Koryaks. Large dwellings like these were unearthed by Jochelson at Gishiga Bay. This particular hut was occupied by fifteen people. Even though the poplar-wood ladders gradually grow black with soot and grease, the Koryaks climb up and down them with great agility carrying heavy loads, buckets of water or cauldrons of hot swill for their sledge dogs. Being a "sky pillar" and a tutelary symbol, the ladder is regarded as sacred and its tip carved into the likeness of a human face.

[36] Covered with skins and strong enough to withstand the most violent gales, this large tent belongs to Reindeer Koryaks. On its roof can be seen three reindeer sledges which have been used to weight it down.

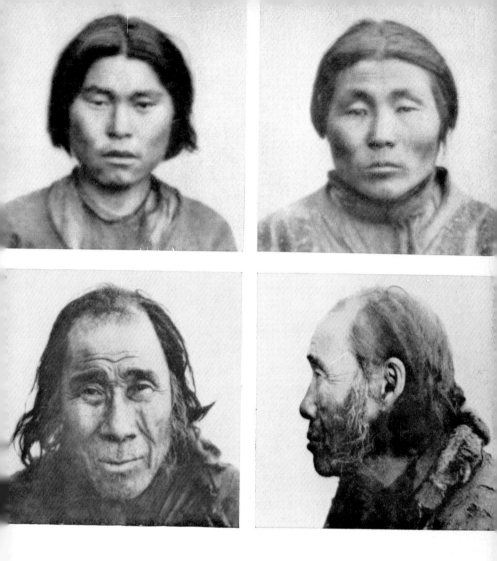

[37-40] Three Yukaghirs, members of an
almost extinct tribe renowned for its
honesty, hospitality and fearlessness but
one which has been almost wiped out by
hostile Chukchees and diseases such as
smallpox. The last of the Yukaghirs now
live by the Arctic Ocean in the estuary
of the Kolyma and on the river Alaseya.

[41] No child of the Tundra Yukaghirs ever falls out of these saddles. Reindeer are entruste[d]
even with cradles containing young babies.
[42] The body of a Yukaghir girl on its way to a tundra funeral, drawn by reindeer.

[43] The face of a Yukaghir woman, furrowed by hardship, experience and the elements. Pure-blooded Yukaghirs have almost ceased to exist, and this woman has a high proportion of Tungusic blood.

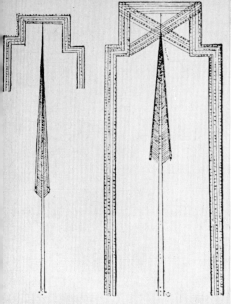

[44] Love letter "written" on birch bark by a Yukaghir girl. The slender arrow on the left represents the man of her choice and the broad arrow on the right the girl herself. He is standing in an almost dismantled house, which denotes his imminent departure, while she is enclosed by a complete house. The oblique beams signify grief and sorrow. Free translation: "You are going away, leaving me here alone. I weep and grieve on your account."

[45] An old Yukaghir woman in front of her tent on the upper reaches of the Kolyma. The tent is covered with skins and has the usual smoke vent at its peak.

Superior," *Journal of American Folklore* (1905). "In the first place the term manitou is a religious word; it carries with it the idea of solemnity; and whatever the association it always expresses a serious attitude and kindles an emotional sense of mystery."

Anyone who wants to explore the religious history of America's early cultures must make his way into the last outposts of her ancient peoples. These include the Fuegians and Patagonians and certain tribes of the Chaco region. In the remote solitude of South America, much has survived of the age-old Eurasian cultural waves which once crossed into North America and gradually, in the course of tens of thousands of years, found their way down into the Antarctic islands at the continent's southern extremity. Here can be found Indian beliefs which have elsewhere become extinct.

The earliest cultural drift brought into the southern triangle bounded by Arica, Chaco and the Straits of Magellan several elements which have become diffused over almost the whole of the Araucanian, Patagonian and Fuegian regions. J. M. Cooper, the priest and anthropologist who died in 1949, concluded from the nature of these cultural assets and from their widespread presence in the southern areas of the double continent that they formed part of the life of the earliest immigrants. These ancient appurtenances include sling and club, spear and harpoon, the hairbrush, ball game, fur cloak and short cape. Clothing, as can be seen, was quite scanty, and no covering was worn on the feet even during the icy winters. However, even these earliest Americans were accompanied on their southward journey by dogs. Smoke signals were made, and a belief in the supreme god already existed. The prehistory of southern South America makes a particularly helpful contribution to the study of the early history of American man in general. Once investigations have been conducted on more systematic lines, a clearer and more distinct picture of life in the America of long ago will emerge. The late priest and anthropologist John Montgomery Cooper and Kaj Birket-Smith, the Danish ethnologist, recognized this. The famous German ethnologist Walter Krickeberg wrote:

And because the earliest, subarctic culture in America is only a ramification of the same Eurasian cultural layer, and could retain its life and purity only in the seclusion of Antarctic South America, those modest remains will also contribute, as Schiller delineated the task of ethnology in his inaugural lecture at Jena, to the re-creation from this mirror of the lost beginnings of our race.

Alcide d'Orbigny, a French paleontologist, published two extremely interesting works in the years 1835–1844 and 1839, and the Englishman G. C. Musters amplified his research in 1873. Both men undertook extensive journeys through Patagonia, and both displayed a keenness of observation and a talent for accurate reporting.

Musters recorded that the Patagonians believed in a great and good spirit who created both animals and the Indians themselves. If this good and omnipotent being was not pictured as paying overmuch attention to mankind, it proves only that the Patagonians' idea of the universe and its master was appropriate to people whose night skies are cold, clear and starry. Musters reported that the supreme deity was not accorded a cult, but that magical rites were performed for the benefit of malevolent natural forces and the spirits of the dead.

D'Orbigny likewise recorded that the Patagonians believed in a supreme deity and that this single god created the world and mankind. Of the Araucanians of the Argentinian Pampa, the French scholar wrote that they believed in a creator of all things, a beneficent being who gave them everything and protected them when they were in danger without insisting that men, in their weakness, must please their god in return. The Araucanians asked their god only for bare necessities, for man is the master of his fate and God, who controls the whole universe, provides him with all that is needful in any case. The Puelche, another Pampa tribe, also believed that the exalted and kindly being would give them all that they desired without having to be asked. Both the Araucanians and the Puelche had, in addition to their supreme god, a number of evil spirits.

The Argentinian scholar F. P. Moreno wrote in 1879 that the kindly god of the Patagonians was called Sesom. This name resembles that of the high Pategonian deity Setebos, whom Pigafetta and

Fletcher mentioned in the sixteenth century, as well as Settaboth in Shakespeare's *Tempest*. T. Falkner recorded in 1774 in his *Description of Patagonia* that the Puelche called their supreme god Guayavacunnee, or Lord of the Dead, and that the Araucanians knew their deity as Tequichen, or Lord of Men, while the Taluhet and Diuihet called him Soychu, The Lord that Dwells in the Land of the Strong Drink. In his history of the Apipones, written in Latin and published at Vienna in 1783, M. Dobrizhoffer noted that Soychu was a being who dwelt outside the earth, invisible and worthy of the highest veneration. The Land of the Strong Drink is the world to come, in which the dead dwell in a state of perpetual inebriation. Christian influence was apparently responsible for the Araucanians' renaming their supreme god Guenechén (Lord of Men) or Fuchá Huentrú (Great Man).

Throughout South America, more peoples believed in one supreme god than was at first imagined. The inaccessibility of immense tracts of primeval forest, the lack of written sources and the difficulty of "looking into the soul" of South America's primitive races often led scholars either to overlook their faith in a supreme being or to underestimate its importance because the high god was invisible and thus never seen in effigy. Alfred Métraux, the brilliant authority on American Indian religions, has recorded the various names and forms under and in which these primitive peoples knew their God in "Religion and Shamanism" (*Handbook of South American Indians*, 1949). He concludes his study with the following remarks (pp. 559, 563):

The number of High Gods in South America was certainly larger than this summary indicates, but in most cases our information is either scanty or unreliable. Both the nature and the functions of these High Gods require more detailed investigation.... The tradition of a Creator or Great Ancestor, who made the world and mankind and who set men on their way to civilization, is probably general throughout South America. Because of the contrast between the loftiness of this figure and the insignificance of his active part in religion, which has often been pointed out, there is a tendency to consider him to be no more than a mythical character. Nevertheless, even though the Creator or Culture Hero usually keeps aloof from human affairs, his remoteness is less absolute than our imperfect knowledge of the Indian religious systems may lead us to suppose.

CHAPTER 9

THE DEATH OF THE YAGHAN

All is over! They have all been annihilated by the insatiable greed of the white race and the fatal effects of its influence. The Indian world of Tierra del Fuego is gone beyond recall. Only the restless waves round Cape Horn thunder out an everlasting threnody for the Indian dead.

MARTIN GUSINDE,
Urmenschen im Feuerland,
Vienna, 1946, p. 388

THE Portuguese navigator Fernão de Magalhães (Magellan) was a self-willed individualist who did not take kindly to advice and could rarely be dissuaded from anything once he had set his mind to it. Had this not been so, he would not have discovered the straits that connect the world's two largest oceans, the Atlantic and the Pacific. Charles V commissioned him to find a passage from the Atlantic to the South Seas which would enable him to approach the Spice Islands (now known as the Moluccas) from the west and claim them for the Spanish Crown. Magellan planned to sail around the southern tip of the American continent with five ships and thus reach the sea which Balboa had been the first European to sight from Panama in 1513. It was Magellan who first christened the vast new ocean El Mar Pacifico.

On October 21, 1520, the squadron sighted a promontory or, more precisely, a flat sandy spit of land which Magellan named Cabo de las 11,000 Virgenes (Cape of the 11,000 Virgins) in honor of Saint Ursula and her companions, October 21 being her saint's day. To the south of this cape, the sea appeared to run deep into the mainland.

Ordering the *Trinidad* of 110 tons and the even smaller *Victoria* to drop anchor at the entrance to this bay, Magellan dispatched the *Concepcion* and the *San Antonio* westward to ascertain whether the inlet was only a bay extending into the mainland or a passage leading to the South Seas. When he learned that what confronted him was the southern passage to the unknown ocean, Magellan boldly led his squadron into the uncharted channel which still bears his name today.

As they sailed through the cold and inhospitable region, the sailors sighted burial places not far from the shore, as well as a dead whale and whale bones. At night, on the southern shores of the channel, Magellan saw large numbers of fires, and this prompted him to christen the strange land Tierra del Fuego. After twenty days, Magellan had sailed 375 miles along a channel which varied between 20 and as little as 2½ miles in width. Yet, throughout the whole of the voyage to the Mar del Sur, not a single native was sighted. The campfires and smoke signals which the daring navigator saw in the distance were the first and only signs of life which Europeans had ever received from America's ethnologically oldest inhabitants.

Four Indian races live or lived on Tierra del Fuego: the Chono, who are long extinct, the Yaghan (Yamana) in the extreme south, the Alacaluf who adjoin them in the southwest, and the Selknam (Ona) who inhabit the northeast corner main island.

Early seafarers who dropped anchor off these inhospitable islands were immediately struck by the small build of the Yaghan and Alacaluf. The average height of the Yaghans is 58.3 inches for men and 56.8 for women. The Alacaluf are smaller still, the men being 56.8 inches tall on average and the women only 55.7. Both these pygmoid races are water nomads. They have also been called "canoe Indians"—an appropriate description, considering that they spend a large proportion of their lives on the countless channels which turn their world into a patchwork quilt of land and water.

The northeastern racial group is composed of the taller Selknam. They are landsmen who own neither canoes nor horses, and are consequently known as "foot Indians." The Selknam belong to the Patagonian group and their language may be classified among the Patagonian "Chon" languages. The Yaghan and Alacaluf, on the other hand, bear no physical or linguistic resemblance to any other South American tribe, and their own two languages are entirely dissimilar.

For centuries, very little was known about these peoples, and the few expeditions which visited them brought back vague and conflicting reports.

During the years 1828–1830, the 235-ton brig H.M.S. *Beagle* slowly sailed the seas of the world under Captain (later Admiral) Robert Fitzroy, who had orders from the British Admiralty to explore the coasts of Patagonia, Tierra del Fuego, Chile and Peru. He did so, discovering the Fitzroy Canal (named after him, but more usually shown on modern maps as the Canal de Beagle) and the so-called Otway Water. In the years 1831–1836, the worthy captain was dispatched on another voyage round the world, once more aboard the trusty *Beagle*. His route again included the southernmost islands of South America. The famous scientist Charles Darwin, only twenty-two years old at the time, took part in these voyages, and the observations which he made exercised a decisive influence on all his subsequent research.

Regrettably, Darwin made some false inferences which had unforeseeable results. Of the Indians on Tierra del Fuego he wrote in *Journal of Researches into the Natural History and Geology* (1860 edition, pp. 205, 206):

> I could not have believed how wide was the difference between savage and civilized man: it is greater than between a wild and domesticated animal, inasmuch as in man there is a greater power of improvement.... The language of these people, according to our notions, scarcely deserves to be called articulate. Captain Cook has compared it to a man clearing his throat, but certainly no European ever cleared his throat with so many hoarse, guttural, and clicking sounds.

Darwin's discoveries are sadly overshadowed by his fallacies. In his day, primitive peoples were always dismissed as "savages," and it is only a small step from false evaluations of this type to anthropological errors of crucial importance.

During his voyage to Tierra del Fuego in 1828–1830, Captain Fitzroy picked up two Yaghan men, a young boy and an eight-year-old girl, and brought the four back to London with him. The boy, who had been traded in exchange for a mother-of-pearl button, was nicknamed Jimmy Button. Fitzroy took good care of his protégés while they were on board and observed them closely. He wrote: "Far, very far indeed, were three of the number from deserving to be called savages—even at this early period of their residence among civilized people."

One of the men died of smallpox on arrival in England. The three surviving Indians were taken back to Tierra del Fuego in 1831 and put ashore there, but not before experts in London had submitted them to such psychological tests as were considered appropriate at the time. Little of the "savageness" of these exiled children of nature can be gathered from the report of this examination.

"Fuegia Basket," by this time a girl of ten, had a most affectionate disposition, became passionately angry when provoked, and often displayed considerable mental agility. Unrapacious and honest, she possessed a good memory, a talent for languages and a strong sense of the Supreme Being. The following, unnerving, extract from the examiners' report might well be deemed more applicable to a criminal than to the child of an alien but morally superior civilization: "It would not be difficult to make the girl into a useful member of human society in a short time, for she learns easily." Darwin himself had a high opinion of the little Yaghan girl. In his *Journal* (p. 208) he wrote:

> Fuegia Basket was a nice, modest, reserved young girl, with a rather pleasing but sometimes sullen expression, and very quick in learning anything, especially languages. This she showed in picking up some Portuguese and Spanish, when left on shore for only a short time at Rio de Janeiro and Monte Video, and in her knowledge of English.

Even after 1855, when missionaries had established contact with the southernmost inhabitants of Tierra del Fuego, no details of their religious beliefs came to light. The English clergyman Thomas Bridges first set foot in the southern islands when he was only thirteen, and began to study the Yaghan language at a very early age. In the year 1861, he was entrusted with the spiritual care of the natives and immediately started to record their language in writing. By 1863 he had already compiled a dictionary of seven thousand vocables. In 1868–1869 the mission was transferred from Keppel Island to Ushuaia, the most central point in the Yaghan area. Here

Bridges continued to work tirelessly at his dictionary, and by 1879 he had recorded the immense number of more than thirty thousand Yaghan words.

This caused a sensation in Europe, for people found it hard to grasp that a primitive race should possess such a rich store of language and even harder to understand that these ancient American tribes were not, in fact, primitive but had brought an amazing wealth of spiritual culture with them when, many thousands of years before, they traveled half the earth to find their last home in the southernmost tip of the "new" continent. Bridges wrote in 1886: "My dictionary of Yaghan has 1,081 pages, each averaging 30 words which multiplied make 32,430 words." In reality, he had overestimated the number of words in his dictionary, but that does not detract from the magnitude of his achievement. Bridges' unique manuscript, which is now of incalculable scientific value, was at long last published in printed form by Martin Gusinde. J. Alden Mason said of the Yaghan language in 1950: "The tongue is said to be markedly euphonic, soft, melodious, agreeable, with a rich vocabulary."

Bridges never enjoyed a thorough education. He tended to be narrow-minded and slightly intolerant, and he was definitely not the sort of man to comprehend or appreciate the spiritual culture of the Yaghan without applying European criteria to everything they said and did. It was the fashion in his day either to obliterate or radically transform any element of the "foreign" or "exotic."

A missionary in the Yaghan area for twenty-five years, he compiled a grammar in addition to the dictionary which was his magnum opus. He spent the last ten years of his life at Puerto Harberton, where he had built a farm. On April 28, 1898, he died, a tough, unbending pioneer and a student of people with whom he never really established friendly relations. By that time the decline of the Yaghan was as far advanced as it was irresistible.

Bridges' successor, the Reverend John Lawrence, worked at Punta Remolino until he died in October, 1932, after sixty years on the Canal de Beagle. However, the mission station had been closed long before that date. P. W. Schmidt's factual research contains all the tragedy of a dying race: "In Christmas 1912 thirty-six adult Yamana arrived in Punta Remolino. A special service was held for them at which five children were baptized. That was the mission's last sign of life, and in 1916 it was completely abandoned."

The missionaries demonstrated not only that it was possible to live among the natives of the Fuegian islands without constant danger to life and limb but also that Europeans could survive the harsh climate. It was not the Europeans who were in danger, but the natives, for as always missionaries endeavored to wean these children of nature from their ancient ways and to Europeanize them by destroying their birthright. The fact that such a remodeling of the Fuegian Indian culture would eventually mean its death was lost on these well-intentioned men of God. Martin Gusinde, renowned Austrian ethnologist and anthropologist who for several years was professor of anthropology at the Catholic University, Washington, D.C., foremost authority on the Tierra del Fuego Indians, says: "All the mischief which forms the calamitous accompaniment to Europeanism inundated it and delivered its national characteristics, together with its once numerous supporters, to premature destruction."

The crux of the European fallacy was, and still is today, a failure to recognize that all ancient primitive peoples believe in a supreme being, and so there is no need to convert them to a god which we happen to call by a different name, no need to eradicate "ancient superstitions" and introduce a new god, and no need to burden and corrupt alien races with the whole ballast of our own culture, a culture which embodies quite as many disadvantages as that of any other race.

Thomas Bridges could converse fluently with the natives, yet he never realized that the people of Tierra del Fuego possessed a genuine idea of God and that they had been aware of Him long before the first missionary arrived in Keppel Island and Ushuaia.

At the time of the first European voyages to Tierra del Fuego the Yaghan numbered about 3,000, the Alacaluf 5,500 and the Selknam 4,000. By 1924 these figures had dwindled to 70, 250 and 260 respectively as a handful of white settlers had dispossessed the ancient tribes of their land, slaughtering the "unwanted savages" without scruple. Seafarers visited the islands in search of riches and adventure, bring-

ing alcohol and syphilis in their train. The Alacaluf suffered especially from these innovations. Other concomitants of the Christian
invasion were diseases which had never before existed on Tierra del
Fuego, such as tuberculosis, measles and influenza, ailments which
wrought particular havoc among the Yaghan. John M. Cooper
reported that only forty Yaghan were still alive in the year 1933,
and in 1948 Mason estimated their number at barely twenty.

In 1919 Martin Gusinde undertook an expedition to the Yaghan
and Selknam. A second expedition followed in 1920, and in 1922
Gusinde set out with Wilhelm Koppers on a third journey to the
dying races in whom he had developed so great an interest. In 1923–
1924 Gusinde visited the remote island world for yet a fourth time.
The ancient races on the southern tip of America had at last become
the subject of competent research. If Koppers and Gusinde had not
preserved the material and, more especially, the spiritual culture of
the Fuegians for science at the very last moment, they would have
died out before we had gathered any essential information about
them.

That was what happened in the case of the Chono, the vanished
race of canoe nomads who lived in deep fjords and winding waterways in the hilly islands of the South Chilian archipelago. Captain E.
Simpson met one surviving Chono family in the Puquitin Channel in
1875. Since that time, nothing more has been heard of them. We
know almost nothing about the Chono, even though they existed in
considerable numbers only four hundred years ago. Apart from the
name Chono, only three words of their language have survived, and
these are merely the names of birds which we cannot even identify.
Cooper has carefully assembled all the information about them given
by Spanish priests in the eighteenth century and by the crew of the
ship *Wager*, which came to grief off the Guaitecas Islands in 1741,
but it amounts to pitifully little.

Now, the bell has tolled for the Yaghan and Alacaluf as well. The
last members of their kind are now the southernmost aborigines in
the world. They themselves have a tradition that their ancestors were
the first men to set foot in their labyrinth of islands, and science has
recognized in these Old Fuegians not only a very ancient but perhaps

the earliest ethnologically identifiable migration into America. Forced farther and farther southward by various tribes from the north, their forefathers must have wandered the length of the continent, traversing unimaginably vast and desolate expanses in the course of fifty or a hundred thousand years until, between about 1,300 and 2,600 years ago, they found dubious asylum in their windy, cold and rain-swept islands. The date of their arrival has been estimated by S. K. Lothrop from the middens of the Yaghan culture on the Canal de Beagle. Dr. Junius S. Bird of the American Museum of Natural History reckons that the Yaghan reached Tierra del Fuego about 1,800 years ago. Somewhere in the middle of this period, perhaps 1,000 years ago, the Yaghan culture adopted the conical tent of the Selknam, who followed them into the area at a later date.

Some of the basic characteristics of the Yaghan and Alacaluf are reminiscent of the very ancient Lagoa Santa race. This is probably because the same human type advanced slowly from northern Asia across the Bering Straits, down the two Americas and into Tierra del Fuego, continuously mingling with other races on the way. It has frequently been surmised that the Fuegian Indians are the earliest inhabitants of America.

Blood-group research sheds an interesting light on these ancient ethnic relationships. In the heart of Asia, e.g. in the areas of Tibet, Turkestan and Sinkiang, group B predominates, while the Mongoloid inhabitants of northeast Asia are normally group O. The Yaghan and Alacaluf belong mainly to group B, which is rarer among the Indians of North America, whereas the Selknam generally come under group O. Ashley Montagu, the American anthropologist, points out that the Tungus and the Eskimo are particularly strong in group O and suggests that the erstwhile B group traveled from central Asia, crossed America and found its way down into the south polar regions. "We may take it as highly probable that the Yaghans represent if not the oldest living population of America, then certainly one of the oldest, and possibly constitute the surviving descendants of the original refugees from Asia."

The Yaghan used to paddle ceaselessly from shore to shore, feeding on mussels, crabs, fish and birds' eggs of every description. When fish lurked too deep to be reached with ease they ordered their womenfolk to dive for them, on the grounds that they could stand cold water better than men. At night they would lure cormorants with flaring torches and club them to death. Sea lions, seals and whales were dispatched with spear or harpoon. All these forms of food are exceedingly rich in oil, fortifying and protective against cold. They were almost always eaten baked or stewed, the method of boiling in water being unknown. Fish and eggs were also baked in hot ashes.

Once a family had landed at a favorable spot they quickly constructed a shelter out of a framework of sticks covered with sea-lion skins. Inside this modest hut a fire burned continuously. The Yaghan's sole protection from cold, wind and heavy rain was a cape of otter or sea-lion skin, but once inside their huts or while performing any heavy manual labor they always threw this off. At night they slept huddled together on the ground.

The Yaghan's physique has been affected by a mode of existence which makes comparatively little use of the legs but demands great exertions of the trunk and arms during hunting, fishing and paddling. These boat nomads have spindly legs, a thick torso, almost no waist, and powerful arms. Their heads are large, their features broad and flat. Indeed, their external appearance was such as to encourage early seafarers and adventures to describe the Yaghan tribe as peculiarly repulsive. Once again, this is an overexaggeration, for all primitive peoples display a certain grace when seen in their natural surroundings and undistorted by the system of tubes and sacks which constitutes the European idea of clothing. Liquor, disease, European clothing and the unequal battle between bullet and arrow all combined to bring death and destruction to this race.

It is unfortunate that, despite his excellent knowledge of the Yaghan tongue, the leading missionary on Tierra del Fuego should have had such a remarkably superficial notion of cultural research. To quote Thomas Bridges' own words: "Most of their superstitions are childish and unworthy of notice."

Thanks to the thorough and exhaustive work of Koppers and Gusinde, science has for the first (and the last) time learned something of the lofty edifice of this people's spiritual culture. Both men, Gusinde and Koppers, were themselves admitted to the Yaghan tribe and were eventually initiated into its secret male rites.

The Yaghan's most important ceremony was that at which boys and girls were initiated into religious life at the age of puberty and received instruction in behavior and tribal customs. They were taught to honor old age, be unselfish, peaceable and industrious, and on no account to spread rumors. Depending for its authority on age-old tradition, this ceremony took place at the behest and, as it were, under the eyes of the unseen supreme being. It was a kind of prehistoric Confirmation Service. The scene of the ceremony, known in the Yaghan language as the *ciexaus*, was a large oval hut consisting of a framework of thin branches covered with moss and grass. Boys and girls had to prepare themselves for the occasion by fasting, sleeping little, working hard and bathing daily in ice-cold sea water. They were only allowed to drink through a narrow, hollow bird bone. Boys were tattooed for the occasion, but only lightly and without lasting effects. The custom of tattooing is very ancient, for tattooed figures can be seen in certain wall paintings in glacial caves in southern France and northwest Spain. The word itself, being derived from the Polynesian expression *tatau*, is much younger, and appears for the first time in Captain Cook's dispatches.

No women or strangers were permitted to attend the male rites of the Yaghan, which were known as the *kina* and always took place under the guidance of a shaman. The kina had its origin in an extremely interesting myth. Once upon a time, it appears, women had complete mastery over men, who were compelled to do woman's work and obey while the female sex ruled the roost. Then came an uprising in which many women were slain by men and others transformed into animals. Only girls under the age of eighteen months were spared. Until this juncture women had maintained their sovereignty by painting their bodies and wearing masks in order to simulate spirits and keep the men cowed and submissive. It was only when men accidentally discovered this ruse that they appropriated it themselves and thus gained the upper hand. Consequently, when performing the kina rite, Yaghan men used to paint themselves and mime spirits by wearing masks of bark or sealskin which looked not unlike sugar loaves. Thus disguised, they sang, danced and ritually bullied the women into submission.

The kina rite was far from being the religion of the Yaghan, who had believed in a supreme being from time immemorial. It is now clear that they did not adopt this belief in God from Christian missionaries but very probably brought it with them from Lower Paleolithic Eurasia, as John Cooper has rightly surmised ("The Yaghan," *Handbook of South American Indians*, 1946):

> In view of these archaisms in the complex, of the many distinctly native features (e.g. master, owner, not creator or maker), of the absence of all characteristically European or Christian conceptions, and of the express and emphatic statements by the natives whose memories or whose knowledge from their elders reached back to the premissionary days, there can be no reasonable question but that Yaghan theism is aboriginal, and not the result of missionary influence.

Koppers and Gusinde also mention that Yaghan men and women rejected any suggestion that they had borrowed their faith from Europeans. There is absolutely nothing reminiscent of Christianity in the prayer forms of worship of these primitive people. Archaistic turns of phrase testify to the antiquity of their beliefs. Even the English missionary John Lawrence, who succeeded Bridges at Punta Remolino, found it impossible to refute Koppers' and Gusinde's statement that the Yaghan's faith in a high god was an ancient racial heritage. Their religion is devoid of the Christian concepts of a Last Judgment and a Resurrection. The Yaghan always spoke of Watauinewa, The Great Spirit Up There, convinced of his omnipresence, his inaccessible greatness, and the impotence of mankind. The name of their supreme being meant, roughly, "old—very old," but they also described him as Hitabuan, an expression compounded of the words *tabuan* ("father") and *hi* ("my").

The Anglican missionary John Lawrence, who lived among the Yaghan on the Canal de Beagle for sixty years, had a son named Frederick. Frederick wanted to marry a Yaghan girl, but she had to live in an annex of the Lawrence farm for fifteen years before the missionary consented to the match and his son could marry the girl of his choice. Koppers tells us that she made him an affectionate wife and handled the white servants in the house efficiently. From her, Gusinde and Koppers learned many details of her race and its spiritual culture. "One cannot call her a Christian," Koppers wrote, and quoted her as saying: "We have our Hitabuan, that is enough for us."

In the Yaghan tongue, Frederick's wife was called Wiyina Makalikipa. Knowing how attached she was to the religious beliefs of her race, her husband decided not to try to shake them, but his elderly father never really established a friendly relationship with her. Wiyina Makalikipa was known as Nelly at home. When she heard the captain of a Chilian cutter complaining about the weather, she observed that such a thing had been unknown among her people in earlier times and that the habit of grumbling at the weather had first been introduced by the Europeans. Sometimes there was too much wind for them, sometimes too much rain, sometimes too much snow and too little sun. One ought to take the weather as it comes, she continued. Complaining about it only made it worse, for Watauinewa is naturally annoyed by such criticism.

Most of the missionaries who devoted their life's energies to the conversion of the Fuegians were probably guilty of not inquiring first whether these ancient American peoples believed in God already, or at least in a supreme being to whom no nationality could be attributed. Gusinde says that the natives were unanimous in stating that the missionaries had never questioned them about such things. "How were we to tell them of Watauinewa without being asked?" The Yaghan probably guessed that, when the English spoke of "Our Lord," they meant the same as they themselves did when they referred to Watauinewa. The idea of God was already there and did not owe its propagation to any missionaries. A true mission's first task should have been to revive the Yaghan's fading recollections of their Supreme Being.

The Yaghan's Flood myth may hold a key to the catastrophe which actually occurred between eight and ten thousand years ago. Their legend tells of unutterable cold, towering masses of snow, the freezing of great waters, and many deaths from starvation and exposure. After a very long time the sun began to shine strongly, a great thaw set in, and people crept out of their huts and caves once more. The Yaghan were aware that many glaciers date from this period.

A variant of this Yaghan myth has it that mankind met destruction not because of cold but because of the immense floods caused by melting masses of ice. People fled to the mountains, but many were drowned because only five mountain peaks projected above the water. The battle for man's liberation from woman was supposed to have taken place during the great freeze, and by the time the floods were over woman's power had been broken. It is very probable that the end of the last Ice Age really did lead to vast inundations and a rise in the level of the oceans, between eight and ten thousand years ago. There may also have been inundations of this sort during the interglacial periods, tens of thousands of years ago. In any case, it is certain that the Flood legends of every race are not imaginary but based on the actual occurrence of vast natural catastrophes.

Extremely interesting parallels can be drawn between the Yaghan and the primitive peoples of Siberia. Like the primitive peoples of Siberia, the Yaghan regard the *kos-pix,* or what we should call "soul," as an incorporeal being which roams during sleep. In the view of many Siberian and American peoples, the soul can reach the Land of the Dead. Both in northern Asia and America the shaman is said to send out his soul to fulfill determinate and often difficult tasks. Both the ancient races of Siberia and the tribes of America believe that it is dangerous to wake a sleeping man whose soul is "in transit." The soul subsists in a man's breath and exhalation. When he dies, he "breathes out his soul." Such ideas are as ancient as their presence among the prehistoric circumpolar races is certain.

CHAPTER 10

THE ALACALUF: EARLIEST OF ALL AMERICANS

*Surely they are worthy of some little heed before they vanish
for ever from our view; a race whose past is the tale of a continent,
and their future—silence.*

W. S. BARCLAY, *The Land of Magellanes*,
Geographical Journal, 23, 1904, p. 79

THE Alacaluf are very like the Yaghan in their way of life. They too were water nomads, roaming the narrows of their island world unceasingly in bark canoes. Like the Yaghan, they originally drank nothing but water and never tried to ameliorate their uncomfortable, unpretentious mode of existence. In this, they observed an important but usually unheeded rule for survival. Man should accustom himself to the preservation of his material culture only in so far as natural forces do not destroy the complex of his inventions. With the arrival of Europeans in Tierra del Fuego, the three Indian races were weaned from their hardy way of life and thus lost their powers of resistance in a world which continually robbed them, in an abrupt and unexpected manner, of the protection of their borrowed civilization.

The area inhabited by the Alacaluf formerly extended from the Gulf de Peñas to the Canal de Beagle and their hunting grounds included the whole jumble of islands which straggle along this Chilean coastal strip. Today they are only to be found around the shores of Eden Bay in Wellington Island—the site of a Chilean army post—and in the vicinity of a lighthouse on the island of San Pedro. J. Emperaire established in 1953 that only 61 Alacaluf were still alive. Save for two families who were still trying their luck as canoe-borne hunters, the Alacaluf had abandoned their nomadic habits altogether.

How can we explain the constant dwindling of the Alacaluf as a people, now that they are no longer being exterminated by the whites?

Some of the Alacaluf migrated to larger towns such as Punta

Arenas, Puerto Natales or Puerto Montt, and were thus lost to the tribe. When children of nature like these adopt urban life and abandon their old living habits, degeneracy sets in. The results are disease and death or intermarriage with the alien townsfolk. Some of the Alacaluf–Emperaire counted 41 cases among 396 members of the tribe—perished by drowning, a common hazard in the lives of southern canoe Indians, who have had to pay tribute to their dangerous home waters from time immemorial. Others were killed by their own countrymen in retribution for theft or as a result of feuds. Infant mortality was very heavy, too, but the physical decline of the tribe was accelerated mainly by the apathy and demoralization which followed the abandonment of nomadic life. The evil effects of European clothing, too, have been greatly underestimated.

The Alacaluf used to display extraordinary powers of resistance to cold and other climatic extremes. Dr. Junius Bird recorded (in "The Alacaluf," *Handbook of South American Indians*, 1946) the following interesting observations: "Children, barely able to walk, were seen seeking mussels on the rocks immediately in front of the hut. With one or two clutched in their hands, they crawl back into the hut to roast and eat them. By the age of four, children cook nearly all the shellfish they consume, and begin to handle the shellfish spears" (Bird, 1946). Emperaire observed in *Les Nomades de la Mer* (p. 101):"In a country where it rains 280 days a year and where strong winds blow almost unceasingly, an artificial layer of grease on the naked skin and a few animal-skin wraps are better than perpetually wet or damp clothing." I, too, have been able to observe the ill effects of alien clothing on primitive peoples in northeast Asia, especially among peoples such as the Golds, Udehe and Daurs, who have come under particularly strong Chinese cultural influence.

When once a primitive race has reached the conclusion that an alien way of life is superior to its own traditional customs and habits, this is usually the signal for its irresistible decline. When the Fuegians realized that sailing ships and motorboats went faster than canoes or hollowed tree trunks, when they saw that wooden huts and houses offered more protection from the elements on their stormy islands than their ancient windbreaks, tents and conical frameworks of branches, when they knew that matches were a more reliable means of obtaining fire than pyrites and flint, when they noticed that bullets killed more efficiently than arrowheads of slate, bone or pebble chips, they began to lose confidence in their own culture and found it less trouble to beg a few Western necessities from passing ships than to go on using the many products of their own invention.

The one thing they never grasped was that material change would impair their own spiritual strength. Like ourselves, they have never understood, and never will, that men can survive the passage of time no better in weatherproof houses than in primitive windbreaks. This lack of comprehension is not their fault. Technical progress and an inherent tendency to expand is something which few races survive.

The most dramatic change wrought in the primitive peoples is that they have lost their own high god and cannot understand ours. Yet God is and has always been a supermundane, indivisible unity. Admiral Fitzroy, who had been captain of the *Beagle*, himself wrote of the Alacaluf who inhabited the maze of islands at the southern tip of South America. Observing how, on certain occasions, the natives used to gaze up at the sky with reverence, he realized, as a widely traveled man of equally wide interests, that this upward gaze was directed toward a supreme god. He also heard from Captain Low that the Alacaluf believed in a good spirit and that they prayed to him when breaking their fast after a spell on short rations.

Martin Gusinde, Wilhelm Koppers, Junius Bird and J. Emperaire have all given detailed reports about this most mysterious among the Fuegian tribes, and we now know that the Alacaluf believed in a supreme being whom they called Xolas or Kolas. The word Xolas means "star." Stars being, in a sense, the eyes of God, it is highly probable that this collective idea was the origin of their term for Him.

The Alacaluf's supreme being is a pure spirit. God, who has never possessed a body, existed before the creation of the world, plants, animals and human beings, and is an independent, self-sustaining spirit. The Alacaluf believed in the perpetuity of this supreme being and in his fundamental kindliness. Because God was never anything but good and because it was not in His nature to give mankind anything but the best, there was no need to pray to Him. However, the supreme being of what is perhaps the oldest of all American Indian peoples could also punish a man who disregarded the commandments of the spirit who lived above the stars. Should such punishment be meted out, there was once again no need to pray. Affliction had simply to be endured and could be neither diverted nor evaded.

The surgeon August Bier believed that the soul represents the animating principle of an organism and that it escapes as soon as it leaves the body. This assumption accords with the ideas of the ancient circumpolar races as well as with those of Tierra del Fuego. However, Bier unfortunately saw the soul in a strictly biological light, so he believed that it inhabited every living organism in the plant as well as the animal world. This failed to take account of what is, apart from man's body and intellectual faculty, his most important attribute. The idea of the soul as a "breath" conferred by the act of creation, that it is somehow independent yet belongs to individual human beings, is one that was widespread among the earliest primitive peoples.

Most ethnologists now assume that the Fuegians, and the Alacaluf in particular, are remnants of ancient northern races. If that is so, the earliest religion was pure monotheism, and the belief in souls or spirits which reside invisibly in men or material objects did not develop until much later. The Alacaluf held that the souls of the dead journey to Xolas, the supreme being, to the place where Xolas dwells in spiritual and incorporeal isolation on the other side of the stars. There they remain, never to return, never to descend to earth again and never to be feared by man.

Fear of spirits or of the souls of the dead is widely disseminated among the circumpolar races in the northern regions of the world. The Alacaluf, too, retain an early form of this ancient religion, a recollection of the time when souls remained with the supreme being in the sky. It seems that, as human faith dwindled and the memory of a single god which man retained from the time of his creation faded, so the substitute gods or substitute spirits increased in number until they developed into the astrology of the advanced Oriental cultures and the horoscopy of our own day.

CHAPTER 11

THE SELKNAM AND THEIR GOD TEMAUKL

The Ona had a very clear belief in a Supreme Being whom they called Temaukl.... He lived above the stars, far from the world and in most respects was rather indifferent to worldly affairs.... Gusinde's large monograph, Die Selknam, *contains practically all that we know of Ona culture.*

JOHN M. COOPER, "The Ona," *Handbook of South American Indians,* Washington, 1946, Vol. I, pp. 109 and 123.

WE KNOW today that of the three Fuegian races the last to arrive in Tierra del Fuego were the Selknam, also known as the Ona. Selknam was their own name for themselves, while Ona or North People was what they were called by the Yaghan. The Selknam lived on the Isla Grande in the extreme north of the area, and bear a closer linguistic, ethnological and anthropological resemblance to the Patagonians than to either of the other two surviving Fuegian peoples. They were nomadic hunters who went after the cururo and guanaco with bow and arrow. Cururos lived in large numbers in the north of the Isla Grande. They are steppe rodents about the size of the gray rat, gray-black in winter and gray-brown in summer. The guanaco, more common in the south of the Isla Grande, is known to zoology as *Lama huanachus,* and was the only member of the South American camelidae to reach the extreme south of the continent. During its long travels in an everlasting quest for new feeding grounds, the guanaco has been known to swim salt-water straits, and has even reached the Isla Navarino, southeast of the Tierra del Fuego group.

The Selknam had many admirable characteristics. Cooper in "The Ona," *Handbook of South American Indians,* lists some of them:

Hospitality to a guest was given as a matter of course. A guest on entering kept silent, without looking around curiously, and only after a while began to tell his story. Eating gluttonously or hastily, especially when on a visit, was disapproved.... It was bad form to mention the names of neighbors, and particularly to mention the names of the deceased in the presence of their relatives.... Hunters from other families and territories could be received as guests and could hunt with and at the will of the members of the particular family. Such a guest, if short of food or other raw material which he needed, would ask permission and only in the rarest cases would be refused.... Stealing from fellow Ona was severely reprobated, and was actually very rare.... There was no incentive to accumulate wealth, and no prestige attached to possession of wealth.

The Ona families were always on the move. Possessing no canoes or horses, they combed their domain on foot, continually changing camp in the course of their nomadic hunter's existence. For this reason they are also called Foot Indians, to distinguish them from the water-borne Yaghan and Alacaluf on the southern tip of the continent. The Ona differ from the other two peoples in yet another respect. They are unusually tall and their bodies are well proportioned. In reality, they represent a group of Patagonian extraction which has penetrated southward. Their language, too, belongs to the Patagonian Chon family.

According to the accounts of Gusinde and Cooper, the Selknam are confirmed monotheists. The more elderly among them, who largely held aloof from the white intruders, spoke of their high god with deep sincerity and great conviction. They called him Temaukl, a name of great antiquity whose origin Gusinde was unable to discover. The supreme being is also known as the One in Heaven or That One There Above. He is referred to with great respect, has neither wife nor children, and is always alone. Being a spirit, he requires neither food, drink nor sleep, just like a human soul after death. Temaukl is above the firmament and beyond the stars, never comes down to earth, yet knows all that happens. He created the earth and the empty void, but the various forms of existence were created by the first man, K'enos.

The high god of the Selknam gave his people laws, precepts and commandments which were transmitted to them by K'enos. Temaukl is kind and loves mankind, but he can also punish men with disease and death. After death the soul travels to heaven and remains there, in the abode where God dwells and to which his first man, K'enos, was summoned. Souls can never return to earth. Only the spirit of a sorcerer remains in this world, roving restlessly about until a new young shaman assimilates it into himself.

The Selknam frequently used to offer their god a small piece of meat before beginning their evening meal, even though they knew he had no need of it. When morning came, this primitive sacrifice had always disappeared. During very cold winters and snowstorms the womenfolk throw a piece of burning wood out of the hut as an appeal to the invisible god for clemency and good weather.

The Selknam's mythology has it that language, marriage, family life, upbringing and the duties of members of the tribe were all handed down from the Supreme Being in primeval times. All men's subsequently acquired knowledge and abilities were transmitted to them by K'enos.

The pygmoid Yamana and Alacaluf were certainly driven into the southern tip of South America earlier than the Selknam. The Alacaluf are probably the oldest of the three human types, for their material culture is more rudimentary than that of the two other races. Spiritually, the Yamana and, even more so, the Alacaluf are closer to the Supreme Being than the Selknam, for among the canoe Indians the supreme being is perfectly monotheistic in conception, whereas the Selknam possessed a mediator in the shape of K'enos.

The Yamana did not regard their god as the Creator, and Selknam considered that the supreme being only made heaven and earth, while K'enos ruled the world and created mankind. Only the Alacaluf, probably the most ancient tribe of all, regarded the Supreme Being as the sole creator of heaven, earth, and humanity.

Let us remember that the oldest American evidence of this belief in a high god is being buried at this very minute, and that it will not be long before the few surviving Alacaluf families take the secret of their belief irrevocably to the grave. Let us reflect that while we may be "progressive" enough to have reached the moon, a dramatic story is almost imperceptibly drawing to a close here on earth.

CHAPTER 12

PALEO-ASIATICS AND TUNGUS

The culture of all these Paleo-Siberian people is extremely archaic. They had scarcely emerged from the neolithic period when the Russians arrived.

ROMAN JAKOBSON, *The Paleo-Siberian Languages, American Anthropologist,* Vol. 44, 1942, p. 607

IF AMERICA'S most ancient races are to be found at its southern-most tip, those who want to find the oldest races in Europe and Asia must search the remote border regions of those continents.

So many ethnic displacements and interminglings have occurred among the denser populations of Europe that very ancient peoples have managed to survive intact only at a few isolated points. Not only have such races preserved their ancient languages, but their physical build has remained virtually unaltered in the course of hundreds, if not thousands, of years. Among them are the Basques of the Pyrenees, the Brythonic-speaking Celts of Brittany and Wales and the Goidelic-speaking Celts of western Ireland, the Isle of Man and Scotland. The Lapps, whose domain once extended much farther southward, have been compressed into the northern borders of Sweden and Finland, while the Samoyeds have been pushed back to the coasts of Northern Siberia by the Scandinavians and Russians.

In northeast Asia, the displacement of Siberia's oldest peoples is even more manifest. The remnants of such tribes now live on the extreme edge of the continent, some along the shores of the Arctic Ocean, others on jutting peninsulas, like the Chukchees on the Chukchee Peninsula and the Itelmen on Kamchatka, and others on islands, like the Gilyaks and Ainus on Sakhalin. It is interesting to note that languages survive longer than physical attributes. Despite intermarriage and despite the modification of their way of life, customs and ideas, people retain an obstinate hold on their language, while their physical appearance changes much more rapidly over the years through intermarriage with neighboring tribes. For instance, it is already difficult to distinguish a Gilyak from an Olcha, and a foreigner will perceive little outward difference between a Korean and an Ainu, yet all these people speak quite dissimilar languages.

Physically, Siberia's oldest peoples often exhibit great similarities, but linguistically they can be regarded as isolated North Asiatic groups. Among these isolated border races are the Gilyaks, Ainus, Kamchadals, Koryaks, Chukchees, Yukaghirs and Chuvantzy, and related to these pockets of Asiatics are the geographically and linguistically isolated peoples of northwest America, the Aleuts and Eskimos. It is correct to call all these outcasts "border" races, even though they include the Yenisei Ostyaks of the Siberian interior. The latter, too, live on the borders of large and geographically determinate areas, so border races need not always be coast dwellers.

Ousted by more numerous, vital and conquisitive tribes, older races were forced to flee to the extremities of their respective continents, as the now-extinct Tasmanians did when they almost reached the Antarctic and the Fuegians when they sought refuge in the southern tip of South America. The displacement, linguistic isolation and generally dwindling numbers of these ethnic groups all indicate that they are marginal tribes or remnants of large, extensive and ramified peoples. The distinguished scholar Leopold von Schrenck christened the oldest peoples of northern Asia "Old" or "Paleo" Asiatics.

Because the border peoples of northern Asia were frequently swamped and oppressed by the Mongols and because intermarriage with Mongols occurred on a large scale and over a considerable period, the skull formation, features and physique of the Paleo-Asiatics display many Mongol characteristics. It should, however, be noted that the Mongol admixture is for the most part very recent, being only one or two thousand years old. People who were forced on to islands, e.g. the Ainus, found it easier to preserve their racial integrity. In their case, the Japanese overlay is only superficial and did not occur until very late.

The Eskimos were probably expelled from Asia altogether. This theory was espoused by Venjaminov as early as 1840. The name Eskimo is the French form of an Algonkin word meaning "raw-meat-eater." The Eskimo's own name for his race is *innuit*, which simply means "men." The Eskimos crossed the Bering Straits and Alaska to reach the sparsely populated North of America, and this eastward migration has survived in their legends, which tell how they once lived in a western country under milder skies but were ousted by other peoples and forced to leave their home. Being bold and skillful watermen, the Eskimos succeeded in crossing the straits which divide Asia from America. Gilyaks, Ainus, Kamchadals, Koryaks and Chukchees were pushed eastward and in their turn forced the Aleuts onto their chain of islands and the Eskimos across the Bering Straits into North America. Since both the Eskimos and Aleuts are very ancient peoples whose forefathers may even have lived in Europe during the Ice Age, many authorities count them among the Paleo-Asiatics. After comparing Stone-Age Siberian skulls with those of Eskimos, the eminent Danish anthropologist Jörgen Balslev Jörgensen stated in 1953:

It is in Asia then that we must seek the origin of the Eskimos. And it now turns out that the prehistoric Siberian crania, of all the crania used for comparison, are those that come nearest to the Eskimos.... We must, judging by the archaeological conditions, assume that the Eskimos originate from Asia, more precisely from the areas round the great Siberian rivers, from where they have wandered to America during the last millenniums before Christ.

The second large group worthy of attention is that formed by the Tungusic peoples. While their ramifications extend across immense areas of Siberia and northern Manchuria, only in the North Manchurian area, in the Argun-Amur region, have they preserved their ethnic purity. There in the taiga of northern Manchuria their ancient traditions, their religion and their whole culture have found an asylum whose exploration is truly worth while. Like the Fuegian Indians, they, too, have reached the end of a long journey in time. Before the soul of the last Tungus returns to the Lord of Mountain and Forest, we shall take a last look at this ancient race, its hunting and riding, its eternal wandering and tent building, its forms of marriage and burial and, above all, its belief in the divine.

CHAPTER 13

THE TAIGA

*Scarcely anyone succeeds in penetrating the inmost depths of the
taiga. It is too vast for that.*

VLADIMIR K. ARSENYEV, *In the Wilderness
of Eastern Siberia*, p. 291

I CAN still hear the song of the eternal forests, the howling of wolves,
the roar of great rivers hurrying on their way. I can still hear the
laughter and the cradle songs of the Tungus, the hoofbeats of their
reindeer, the crackle of their fires. I can still see the woodcutter
deep in the solitude of the forest who asked me: "Lord, is it war
again? I have heard it said that they now have huge birds made
of steel, eagles of world destruction, on which they fly even to
the moon. Is it just a tale, or is it true?" That man still lives in the
taiga, still unaware of the existence of ocean liners, concrete super-
highways, skyscrapers, cinemas, television, and people who have
no time. . . .

Taiga is the virgin forest of Siberia. But it is more. Taiga is
wild, uncleared terrain, mostly forest but also composed of open
ground, swamps and barren hillocks. Taiga is what the Russian
peasant calls the land that begins where his tillage ends.

Russian geographers borrowed the word *taiga* from Paleo-Asiatic
languages to describe a particular type of forest region which creeps
low across the ground for hundreds of miles, broken by miles-wide
tracts of starved and frozen land, eventually to drown in vast marshes.

Taiga means forests of larch, spruce, fir, birch and aspen—a few of
them giants but most of them stunted by short summers and long
winter nights, by icy winds from the Pole and eternal frost beneath
their roots.

Taiga means death, danger and decay, swarms of stinging flies and
gnat-ridden swamps. Taiga means miles of impassable country where
death seems to have gained the upper hand and no high ground
rejoices the eye, where roots do not strike deep into the ground but
weave and wrestle wildly on the surface, barring any would-be

traveler's path. And wherever the forest ends there, suddenly, is an infinite sea of sinister swamp stretching to the horizon, dotted with small grassy hummocks which offer no sure foothold, a vast natural discord, a landscape such as might be imagined on some alien planet.

Taiga means charred forests, a myriadfold maze of dead, gray, bark-bereft, almost branchless trunks pointing rigidly at the sky as though some divine architect had played a monstrous joke with telegraph poles. Although forest fires develop intense heat here they cannot consume the sap-filled trunks, and so they gnaw them away, reducing them to an army of gray, bleached ghosts. It is impossible to tell where a fire has begun or ended, and at times the plumes of smoke from these taiga fires rise above hundreds of square miles of land.

Taiga can also mean spruce and fir trees packed together so densely that only their tips are green, while everything in the darkness below is a withered gray or rust of dead needles. Taiga is an immense, melancholy and comfortless land which yet possesses its own beauty.

The widest belts of taiga are situated in east and west Siberia, narrowing as they cross the Urals and approach Europe but running northwestward into the forests and swamps of Karelia. The true heart of the taiga is the forest country between the rivers Lena and the Yenisei, between the 58th and 64th parallels, from the region of the Aldan, via the Middle Lena to the Yenisei and on to the Ob, and consists of dense coniferous forests of larches, European and Siberian firs mixed with white fir or *pichta*, aspens and lindens. Here hundreds of watercourses twist and turn in immense spirals through the otherwise uninterrupted taiga. Here and there, moribund and half-choked waterways cut black, serpentine convolutions into the expanse of treetops, until the taiga gradually gives way to swamps and isolated patches of forest.

The greater part of northern and central Siberia, from the Tass to the Ob and down to the Urals, is swamp taiga. The largest marshy area in the world, it stretches for hundreds of miles and consists of stagnant lakes and boggy pools of glistening green water interspersed

Map of Northern Asia. Manchuria lies between China, Korea, Siberia and the Mongolian steppes. Manchuria today belongs to China; the former inhabitants of the area, the Manchurian Tungus, are nearly extinct. Moho is the northernmost Chinese point in the Far East.

with myriad tufts of grass. The basin of the Ob is a gigantic collection of such marshy pools, and is completely impassable in summer.

Southeast of the Upper Lena and north of Manchuria, the taiga comprises immense rolling larch forests from which project the barren heights of the Yablonovyy Range, bare and treeless rock dotted with occasional subalpine bushes. Primor'ye, the southern

125

portion of the Russian Pacific coast, contains huge osier-filled valleys, with scrub forest and large marches to the east of the Lower Amur. West of the Amur lies Manchuria, the northern parts of which are also taiga and a still largely unexplored region.

I was determined to go into the vast land of the taiga, to live there and to know its people.

At the beginning of the last war, Manchuria was occupied by the Japanese. Nobody was allowed to enter the uncharted area of the Amur Bend, nobody was permitted to find out what went on there. No foreigner had ever entertained such a plan, and "Besides," said the sons of Nippon, smiling and bowing, "it is impossible to get there."

Impossible? Why?

Because there were no roads, because no railways had yet been built, because the northward route was blocked by huge marshes, because the whole region was unknown, because no maps of it existed. Of course, I could try to reach the most northerly point in Manchuria, right on the Russo-Manchurian frontier. I could travel up the Amur to the remote village of Moho, but it was dangerous. When the Russians caught frontier jumpers they summarily hauled them off to Siberia and nothing more was ever heard of them. Nevertheless, if a man managed to travel up the Amur, he might be able to penetrate the last remaining areas of unexplored taiga.

I spent a whole year assembling permits, passports and papers, surmounting one obstacle after another. Then I traveled the entire length of the Amur, reached the northernmost point of Manchuria safely, lived in the trackless taiga and got to know its primitive peoples.

I remained in the forests of Manchuria and the steppes of Mongolia for some years, but it was not until later that I began to relate what I had seen and heard with what is known of early humanity, aided in my work by ethnologists, anthropologists and prehistorians from many countries.

In northeast Asia I learned something of shamanism, of magic and the religious ideas of the circumpolar races. I tapped sources which have since dried up, probably forever, because all access to them is now barred and the ancient races are rapidly dying out.

I attempted to explore what still seems to me to be the most important question of our time: Was the biped, whose brain suddenly began to function with such remarkable efficiency, alone? Did he develop a soul without the participation of some outside agency? Or was the distinguished archaeologist W. F. Albright right when he wrote in 1946 that "man has not raised himself by his own bootstraps"?

A great truth revealed itself to me in the unexplored forests of northeast Asia. I realized that the Tungus, Gilyaks, Ainus and all the people whom I came to know there, far from being liars and fantasts, seemed to have been aware of God's existence for an incredible length of time.

There was a time, probably a million years ago, when man was not yet man, but God was already God.

The Amur is one of the most magical of all the world's rivers, a river of eternal forests, clear waters and infinite solitude. It is the cradle of shamanism, the highway of the spirit world of northeast Asia, an ever hungry, ever rapacious Black Dragon among rivers.

From the source of the Onon to the sea, the Amur measures some 2,750 miles. It is almost three times as long as the Rhine and would, if superimposed on the Atlantic, stretch from England to Newfoundland. The Sungari, its largest tributary, flows past Harbin at a summer rate of nearly 650,000 gallons per second, reaching 945,000 at full spate, but that is little in comparison with the volume of the Amur itself, which at high water passes Khabarovsk at a rate of no less than 13,000,000 gallons per second. Aptly called a traveling sea, the Amur drains all the swampland in the Siberian taiga. It occupies eighth position in the list of the world's rivers after the Missouri-Mississippi, Nile, Amazon, Ob, Yangtze, Congo and Lena, but its basin is immense even by Asiatic standards: nearly 800,000 square miles, as compared with those of the Yangtze and Volga, which drain some 700,000 and 560,000 square miles respectively.

The Amur collects its waters from the mighty forests and bogs of the North Asian taiga belt and flows as clear as crystal, quite unlike the rivers of the Mongolian steppes or the Chinese loess. This is why the Chinese christened it the Black River, to distinguish it from its yellow brothers, the Yangtze, Hwang Ho and Sikiang. The

Tungusian for Black River is Hara Muren—hence the Russian contraction "Amur"—while its Chinese name is Hei-Lung-Kiang, or "black-dragon-river."

All the rivers of Northern Asia flow northward into the Arctic Ocean. Although the Amur lies to the south of the Yablonovyy and Stanovoy ranges, it, too, flows northward from Khabarovsk for 600 miles, counter to its own tributaries. In this northward path are the seeds of a geographical tragedy. Khabarovsk is only 230 miles from the open sea as the crow flies, but the Lower Amur's northerly route steers it into the inhospitable Sea of Okhotsk and, worse still, into a corner of the sea which is masked by the island of Sakhalin and has thus become a shallow sandy sleeve particularly susceptible to early freezing. For this reason, the Amur remains an eternal prisoner of the Asian continent and the North Asian taiga and has never become an arterial link with the Pacific like the Yangtze. Although there are thousands of miles of navigable water above Khabarovsk, Khabarovsk will never become the Hankow of the North, nor will Nikolayevsk ever rival Shanghai. No Singapore or Hong Kong will ever arise on the bleak and ice-bound Shantar Islands in the eastern corner of the Sea of Okhotsk. For with the coming of winter, the Amur freezes over and its tributaries coagulate, effectively barricading the whole of Siberia behind a back door of ice. Being ice-free for only about 185 days out of 365, the Black Dragon falls into the same category as a cold Arctic river like the Dvina, which remains open for between 163 and 190 days each year.

Although the warm Kuroshio Current flows through the Pacific past the Aleutians to Alaska, it bypasses the Sea of Okhotsk and leaves it the refrigerator of northeast Asia. No wheat grows in the North Manchurian taiga, no vegetables or potatoes. The ground never really thaws out. All in all, it is a place where man is only grudgingly tolerated, the natural domain of the shaggy-coated bear, the wolf and snow leopard.

This corner of the world has no links with Europe, for it was entirely unknown to the geographers of antiquity. Alexander reached the Indus and Justinian's galleys sailed to the River of Pearls and Canton, but the Yenisei, the Lena and the Amur remained as far

[46] This was the view that met the eyes of hunters 70,000 years ago as they looked eastward from the mouth of the Drachenloch cave. The cave, which was probably inhabited only during the summer months, lies at a height of 8,000 feet, above the village of Vättis in the Tamina-Calfeisen Valley, Switzerland.

[47] Here, high in the mountains, Stone-Age man sacrificed to God. The dotted line shows the ascent to the Drachenloch, hidden away among a confusion of rocks. It is now regarded as certain that the caches of bears' skulls and bones found in this cave were sacrifices testifying to a high degree of spirituality among the men of the Paleolithic Age.

[48] A limestone missile, probably used by Neanderthal man, discovered at La Quina, Charente, France.

[49] The celebrated Neanderthal skull from La Chapelle-aux-Saints. The careful arrangement of his grave indicated that this man believed in a life after death. Reaching their prime in about 70,000 B.C., the Neanderthalians gradually declined in numbers until, in about 30,000 B.C., their race became extinct. Neanderthalian remains have been found not only in the Feldhofer cave (in the Neanderthal) between Elberfeld and Düsseldorf but also in Le Moustier, La Chapelle-aux-Saints, La Ferassie, Palestine, Uzbekistan and other places.

[50] A male skull from La Ferassie, Dordogne.

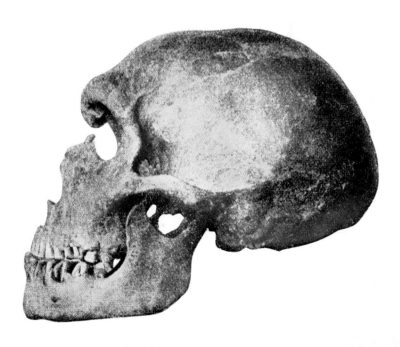

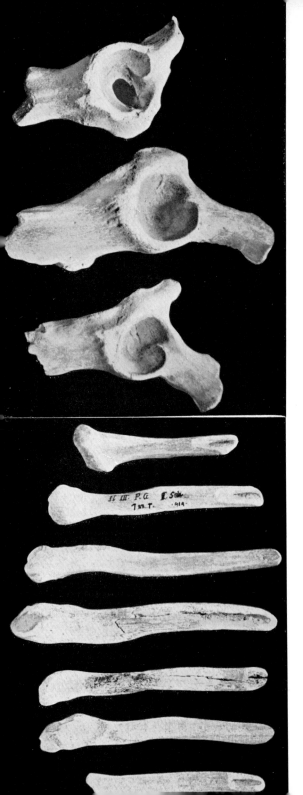

[51] The hip-joint sockets of cave bears found in the Drachenloch are noticeably worn around the edges. They were probably used for tanning purposes, from which we may deduce that man wore skin clothing 70,000 years ago. Hip-joint sockets would also have lent themselves for use as bowls, cups or oil lamps.

[52] These bone tools from the Drachenloch were used for skinning game and for preparing and smoothing pelts. The unmistakable polish on the ends of the bones could only have been produced by some human agency.

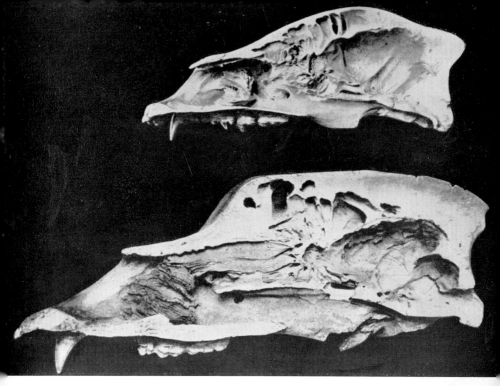

[53] Two bisected skulls, one of our own brown bear (*above*) and the other of the extinct cave bear (*below*). Comparison shows how powerful the cave bear was, how impressive his olfactory equipment and how acute his sense of smell. Seventy thousand years old but complete in every detail, this skull has aroused the admiration of many zoologists.

[54] These cave bears' claw marks may be as much as seventy thousand years old. They were found deep in the interior of the Drachenhöhle near Mixnitz in Styria, in whose narrow defiles Stone-Age hunters set their traps over a period which lasted from the Upper Mousterian to the close of the Central European Aurignacian. The marks were made by desperate animals as they clawed the bare rock in an attempt to escape the hunter's net. The remains of 50,000 bears were found in this cave alone.

[55] Cave bear's jaw, and beneath it a skinning tool of the same material showing distinct signs of use.

Skinning tool manufactured from part of the upper jaw of a cave bear, complete with rear molar.

Portion of a cave bear's skull with rounded edges. This could only have been manufactured deliberately by human beings who lived 70,000 years ago.

These completely alien white pebbles were brought into the Drachenhöhle by Paleolithic man, obviously from some distance away and possibly as pieces used in some form of game.

[56] Fragments of iron pyrites and limestone found near the hearth in the Drachenhöhle which may well have been used for kindling fire.

Remnants of charcoal from the hearth in the Drachenhöhle.

Charred pieces of bone, also from the Drachenhöhle.

An extremely rare find made at Appenzell, Switzerland, this tapir's jaw belongs to the Middle Tertiary and is thus 30,000,000 years old.

[57] These sizable fragments of cave bear's marrowbone from the Drachenloch served as skinning knives and smoothing implements. Their broken edges clearly reveal traces of wear.

[58] The only complete cave bear's skeleton in existence (*Ursus spelaeus Blum*) was unearthed nearly five thousand feet up in the Wildkirchli cave in Switzerland and now reposes in the Heimatmuseum at Saint Gallen. The cave bear probably carried its head lower than this reconstruction suggests. It was the skull and marrowbones of such mighty creatures (this one is nearly nine feet long) which men sacrificed to their supreme god 70,000 years ago.

[59] From left to right: R. A. Dart and R. Broom, the celebrated authorities on Australopithecus africanus; Abbé H. Breuil, the foremost living prehistorian; and C. van Riet Lowe (1894–1956), leading expert on African archaeology.

[60] (*Above, left*) P. Wilhelm Schmidt, who was born at Hörde near Dortmund in 1868, won great acclaim for his research into Australian, Asiatic and Oceanian languages. He was the author of definitive works on the linguistic families and regions of the world and one of the greatest ethnologists of our century. In his multivolume work on the origin of the idea of God he proved that even the earliest men believed in a supreme deity. Schmidt died on February 10, 1954, at the age of eighty-six, leaving behind a life's work of almost unbelievable magnitude. (It comprised no less than 658 separate publications.)

[61] (*Center*) H. V. Vallois, France's leading paleoanthropologist and long-time Director of the Musée de l'Homme.

[62] Pierre Marcellin Boule (1861–1942), a French scholar of world-wide repute whose works on fossil human remains are an integral part of the history of anthropology.

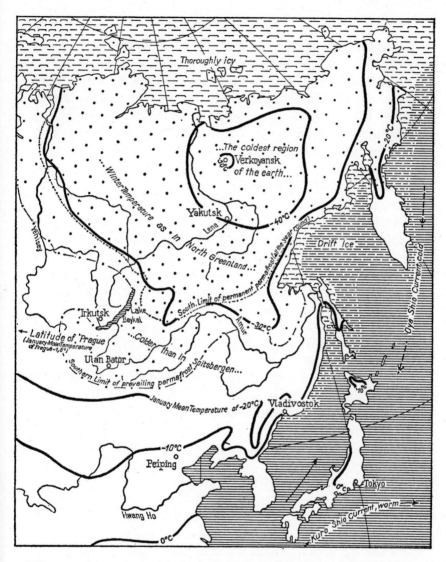

Winter weather map of northeast Asia. At the northern Amur Bend there is, even in summer, a constant frost three to six feet beneath the surface. The area is so cold because the warm Kuroshio Current is deflected toward the east by the islands of Japan. The cold Oyashio Current enters the Sea of Okhotsk from the north. Verkoyansk, the coldest spot in the world, lies at the northern Amur Bend.

beyond the ken of the West as if they had been on another planet. Even today, this northern region is Asia's Ultima Thule and the Black Dragon remains, in the Chinese imagination, the keeper of the North. Few ships ever land on these northern coasts. For Asia, the Amur is a line of demarcation, a border between Manchuria and Russia. No bridge crosses it and the Manchurian peasant looks upon it as the frontier of his world.

In wandering through the taiga I sought something which many have dreamed of: a chance to look beyond the horizon and catch a glimpse of times long past, times in which men lived as a few Tungus, Gilyaks and other primitive peoples still do today in the last un-explored corners of their remote world. I tried to draw near to them and slough off the cultural heritage of the West in which I was raised.

I sought to return to the time when man confronted nature hun-dreds of thousands of years ago, without hearth or hut or any but his own puny resources.

My yearning to experience the Stone Age in person had already brought me a long way from the continent of Europe, but when I reached the Amur it was as if I was a million miles from the bustle of daily life in the immense cities of Europe and America and from the amorphous masses who, unaware of their past and indifferent to their origins, are sentenced to live in concrete cells, doomed to an everlasting round of toil and haste, melancholy and feverish enjoy-ment.

By the time I reached Moho, 375 miles of Amur lay behind me. Moho, the northernmost point in Manchuria, is a remote and insig-nificant village which knows nothing of the world and of which the world knows less. Yet this speck on the map was to be my gate into the lost and now-forbidden world of the Orochi, the Manega and Gilyaks.

South of Moho lies the impenetrable Manchurian taiga, almost half a million square miles of uncharted forest wilderness, an area of primeval forest which fills the greater part of the mighty northern bend of the Amur and forms the continuation of the Siberian taiga, unknown, trackless, and virtually uninhabited.

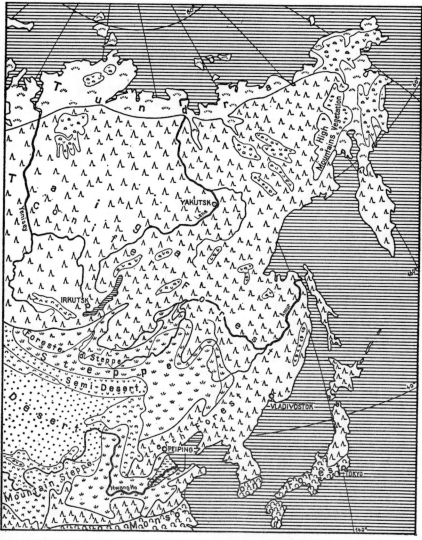

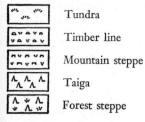 Tundra			Steppe
Timber line			Partial desert
Mountain steppe			Desert
Taiga			Flood area
Forest steppe			Monsoon forest

Here in northeastern Asia are the largest evergreen forests in the world. There is a clear line of division between the different types of vegetation, from the arid desert area to the taiga to the polar tundra. This vegetation is totally uncultivated.

CHAPTER 14

THE WOLF HAS AN "EVIL HEART"

It has been shown that the sharp line of demarcation which we draw between mankind and lower animals does not exist for the savage. To him many of the other animals appear as his equals or even his superiors, not merely in brute force but in intelligence.
J. G. FRAZER, *The Golden Bough,*
Part V, Vol. II, p. 310

IN MY TRAVELS in the taiga I learned, by observation and from the peoples with whom I made friends, much of the animals and the beliefs surrounding them.

The Ugicha, a tributary of the Albasiha, which itself is a tributary of the Amur, flows through a dark and gloomy valley thickly populated with huge larches and firs. The lighter birch does not thrive there, unlike the beech with its dark red foliage. The Ugicha is a paradise for the wild boar. Here they can roll in the autumnal bogs to their heart's content, rooting about with their snouts, sharpening their tusks, grunting and rubbing themselves pleasurably against cedars and larches. The rutting season lasts from November to January, and the sow carries for about eighteen weeks. Then, in April or May, she seeks out an inaccessible hiding place. Pushing leaves, dry grass, small branches, bark and sticks together into a large heap and boring a passage into it with her body, the sow builds a nest with only one entrance and there deposits her litter, which may vary in number from six to twelve.

Wild boar have no enemies in the taiga apart from the Tungus, and even the Orochi seldom venture into their boggy domain except in winter, when snowshoes give the man advantage. The boar quickly scents danger and he runs, first cantering and then breaking into a gallop. The Tungus will follow a herd relentlessly until the massive creatures tire and slow down. Once they are exhausted they must either fight or die, and this is the moment when their tusks can prove exceedingly dangerous.

Bristly animals whose powerful bodies crash through the forest like mobile hills, wild pigs are not only enormously strong but cunning, extremely cautious and brave. Many Tungus showed me scarred relics of wounds which had been inflicted by the tusks of this dreaded beast.

Wild-boar hunting is a very ancient pursuit. During the inter-glacial stage of the Protolithic period, boar lived in the forests of Central Europe, but later, during the glacial period that ensued, they retreated southward into the erstwhile forests of Spain. W. Soergel alleges in *Jagd der Vorzeit* that Paleolithic man did not attack wild boar because tuskers and carrying sows were so adept at defending themselves. Judging by what we know of these dangerous and power-ful animals today, this does not seem unlikely. Against this, there are the finds made at Taubach near Weimar, where individual bones be-longing to various kinds of game—among them fossils of wild pig—were unearthed from a layer of volcanic limestone. These discoveries belonged to the Mousterian; that is to say, to the period between 70,000 and 80,000 B.C. The manner in which many of the bones had been broken indicated that man had been at work and that he was trying to extract the tasty marrow. The limestone also yielded flint tools and traces of charred wood, so it must be assumed that man roasted or boiled his food there. On the walls of the Cueva del Charco del Agua Amarga, a Spanish cave, some man of the Miolithic period has left a memento of wild-boar hunting, a work of art depict-ing a fugitive boar and a hunter in pursuit. The latter has hurled his spear at the animal and has evidently wounded it.

The Tungus of northern Manchuria look upon the wild pig as an intelligent animal and accord him a certain measure of respect be-cause of his lightning-like speed in attack and his ability to take on even the tiger successfully. That is why they speak to these valiant warriors of the forest and watch with bated breath as their black flanks pass by. That is why, too, they never place overmuch reliance in a single bullet or even in the palma, which a boar can scythe through like a thin twig with one sweep of his tusks.

Every evening the taiga echoes to the plaintive calls of deer. These animals found sanctuary in the taiga in distant times and have sur-vived there since in the untouched forest areas. Finds of bones be-longing to the deer family date back to the Eocene period, or more than fifty million years ago. The giant deer of the Ice Age, however, is extinct. It is certain that Ice-Age hunters were not responsible for its disappearance because very few bones of the giant deer have been found among fossils of many other types of game. In fact, remains of the giant deer have nowhere exceeded two per cent of the entire yield from any one site. Kurt Lindner adopts the view that the chief cause of its disappearance was not man's hunting activities but the abnormal relationship between the size of its body and its antlers, which grew more and more disproportionate. No species of animal could have existed indefinitely under such conditions, and the giant deer died out completely, whereas elk and fallow deer have survived into our own day.

Red deer, on the other hand, formed one of the staple sources of game in the Ice Age and were much favored as models by the cave artists of eastern Spain, an area where these animals could roam the vast forests as their inclination took them. The cave pictures of Cueva de los Caballos, Cueva de la Vieja, Alpera and Cogul testify that red deer were successfully hunted at the time, mainly with bow and arrow. We do not know for certain whether nets and traps were used in the Stone Age, although a cave drawing at La Pasiega portrays a deer covered with a crisscross web of lines, but it is probable that Stone-Age man organized large battues in eastern Spain.

Larger than the Canadian wapiti, the deer of the North Manchurian taiga is a vivid red in summer and a yellowish, brownish red in winter. The Russians call it the *isyubr*. The rich, free life of this king of the forest is menaced on every side. A thousand enemies surround him, not least the forest fire. Isyubri lead a quite unique existence and one which is extremely difficult to explore in detail. Abnormally acute hearing, a fine nose and good eyesight make the isyubr virtually unapproachable, for the deer of the taiga never relaxes his vigilance for a moment. His caution and timidity prompt him to move to high ground in summer so that he can keep an eye on the surrounding countryside. He dislikes direct sunlight, preferring undergrowth, shadow and forest gloom. He likes to linger in secluded spots in the forest which he knows well, places which offer plenty of tree and shrub foliage, forest herbs, lichen, mushrooms, grapes and cedar cones. The taiga is crisscrossed by a whole system of deer paths which can be followed for miles through otherwise impenetrable forest.

In September, the does gather in herds of between six and a dozen, avoiding the stags until the strongest seeks out the herd and takes possession of it. From then on, the dominant male drives his wives along as the whim takes him. They drink from the river when he drinks and follow him into the undergrowth when he makes for the woods. For his part, he drives them hither and thither and cows them into submission, disciplining them with his antlers and sometimes goring a particularly disobedient consort to the ground in fury. The less fortunate males follow the herd at a distance, their only alternative being to wait or fight.

The Chinese call the isyubr *ma-lu* (the elk is *to-lu* or *kan-ta-han*), and their hunters hunt it principally for the sake of its antlers which the deer lose each winter and start to grow again in spring. By May, they have almost attained full size but are not completely hard and still contain blood vessels. These young, blood-filled and not yet horny antlers are highly prized by the Chinese and form the basis of numerous greatly esteemed medicaments. Very high prices are paid for them, and with good reason. Whereas the ancient circumpolar races have always submitted docilely to the natural laws governing life and death, the high cultures of the Far East have been trying for thousands of years to discover the "medicine of life," a remedy which will prolong the brief span of man's existence.

Young ma-lu antler was an elixir of life much prized by the emperors of ancient China, though its discoverer is unknown. Up to a thousand yuan can be paid for an immature antler of this type, which, when ground into a powder, represents one of the treasures of the Chinese apothecary. An old man, so the Tungus informed me, should take a dose of five grams night and morning. If he does so, warmth will course through his old frame, his blood will circulate more vigorously, his face will gain color and his body take on new youth and virility. "And what if a young man takes it?" I asked a Tungus. "Ma-lu antler is only good for old people," he warned me. "The young can become deaf and blind. Even a royal antler only takes fifty days to grow each year, and these days are the days of the ma-lu's greatest strength, a strength which suffices for a whole herd of ma-lu females. Ma-lu antler is life."

When I knew the North Manchurian taiga, it was an area where the Tungus lived in complete freedom. The forests and marshes around the Amur were so inaccessible that no form of authority, control or political system, whether Japanese, Chinese or Russian, found it practicable to lay the bony hand of bureaucracy upon them. It was here I knew the Orochi, the reindeer-men.

In the language of the Orochi, *oro* means reindeer and *chon* is a man. The regions where *chon* still rides his *oro* in peace are among the last surviving reminders of paradise on earth.

Evamatu is a typical Orochon. He rides his reindeer along narrow game paths, up steep and thickly wooded mountain slopes, across clearings and through difficult marshes. Reindeer are amazingly sure-footed. Their gait is light and elastic, unhurried yet swift. The taiga is their domain, and their agile hoofs will carry them across broken rocks, low bushes, fallen trees, snarled roots, seething rivers and sullen swamps.

A reindeer's back is extremely mobile, so the rider sits on the shoulder blades of the forelegs, grasping a halter which runs around the cheeks and the bridge of the nose. There is no bit, so the rope cannot be used to guide the animal. A rider guides a reindeer with his legs, which hang free, and unless the possesses a good sense of balance both he and his saddle will hit the ground before he has gone a few yards. Evamatu says firmly that men have owned reindeer, "ever since trees have had leaves and the sky has had stars, ever since the Evenki have roamed the forest: that is to say, from times immemorial to men or Tungus." There must be an element of truth in this. The reindeer is not a wild animal which has been caught and broken in, but a beast of burden bred by generation after generation. The whole culture of the Orochi, everything they own or do, stems from or refers to the reindeer. Even their language shares this association, for it contains countless expressions which simultaneously embrace the world of the reindeer and the world of man.

The Tungus' reindeer are white, smoke-gray or black. Brown

animals are rare. The back and the upper part of the legs are dark, the belly and lower part of the legs usually white. Antlers, which often exceed thirty pounds in weight, begin to sprout during the first autumn, and reach their maximum weight and size during the fifth autumn, after which they decrease from year to year. Reindeer cast their antlers in the first half of April. Growth soon begins anew, though it develops slowly until August, by which time the antlers are covered with a soft, thick skin. At the beginning of September, this skin falls off or is scraped off on trees by the animals themselves. Since blood often continues to circulate beneath the skin until this time, animals may occasionally be seen with trickles of blood running down their foreheads. This seldom happens among domesticated reindeer, however, because at the beginning of September the Orochi normally saw off the antlers with a small bone-handled iron saw, binding them at the base to prevent bleeding or cauterizing them with a hot iron. The removal of the antlers is not only painless, but also necessary, because it prevents breakage and injury.

A swath of fine white hair extends from the reindeer's throat to its chest. The Tungus believe that an animal will die if this hair is cut off, and so, because it is much in demand as a decoration for fur bags, the Orochon women pluck it out hair by hair. Reindeer hair is very short but dense. It falls out in spring, usually in bunches, leaving large bald patches of skin, but the hide becomes evenly covered with new hair at the beginning of autumn.

Wild reindeer, which the Orochi call *sachoi*, are only to be found in any numbers on the Upper Vitim and in the Muya district, although there are signs of an increase in their numbers in the Yakutsk area. They are dark brown in color, black and white being an exclusive feature of domesticated strains.

Reindeer feed principally on lichen, known to the Orochi as *laucta* and to the Yakuts as *labykta*. They also eat fungi, berries and young tree shoots, but without lichen they do not thrive, which is why they live only in areas where lichen is available in large quantities. That means the taiga and the section of tundra forming the northern region which lies between the Yenisei and the Bering Sea.

Reindeer moss or laucta is pale green in color. It carpets forest clearings in a subdued and agreeable shade which fades away to a whitish gray in the gloom beneath the trees. Laucta will also grow on poor soil, roots, rocks, scree and branches. This is important, because snow often lies so deep in winter that reindeer cannot dig down far enough and have to make do with what grows above-ground. The Orochi frequently cut down small lichen-covered trees to help their animals graze.

Reindeer are very fond of salt, and Orochon women always carry some in a *dayasuruk* (*dayasun* = salt) or small leather pouch in order to tempt the animals when they summon them with their reindeer-hoof clappers.

The average dead-weight load a reindeer can carry effectively is two *pud*, about seventy-two pounds. A horse can carry far more, but it is unsuited for crossing the sort of wild country where reindeer will happily carry a load or a rider. Seventy-two pounds is no great weight, but dead weight is harder to carry than live. The Orochi are a small, fine-boned race, and Orochon women seldom weigh more than ninety-five to a hundred pounds. Carrying two pud of dead or live weight, reindeer will cover twenty or thirty miles of the most difficult terrain in a single day, and in winter, when two or four animals are harnessed to a sledge (*narta*), they are capable of doing forty-five miles or more. It should be mentioned that the Orochi of Manchuria do not use sledges.

Reindeer are tended and milked by the womenfolk. Their milk is sweet and thick but poor in fat. Almost everything the Tungus wears is made of reindeer hide: the stout moccasins which protect his feet, his trousers, his Tungus apron, his jerkin, his cap and, unless they are made of blue squirrel skin, his thick gloves.

Orochon families usually roam in groups of three or four, their reindeer forming communal herds which are left to graze and find water for themselves. Reindeer leave camp during halts to look for pastures which are generally many miles from their owners' resting place, sometimes returning in the evening and sometimes staying away for days on end. However, they have a standing inducement to return to the world of human beings: their eternal foe the wolf.

Wolves become a terrible menace during the cold of the winter, often cutting down half a herd.

At mating time, the male reindeer try to drive a few does out of camp into the taiga. Since that would put them at the mercy of wolves, the Orochi build a sort of corral called a *kure* into which they drive the does. The womenfolk also take an active part in building this enclosure, inside which the does suckle their young. During this period, the males mill wildly around outside. Their neck and the upper part of their chest swell up, the skin on their temples grows taut and hard, they paw the ground, butt each other with the stumps of their antlers and rear up on their hind legs, trying to wound their enemies with their hoofs. If their antlers were not sawed off they would injure each other fatally. The most savage of them are loaded down with a heavy wooden yoke which restricts their freedom. The mating season lasts until mid-October, when the sexes settle down to a new spell of tranquil coexistence.

A reindeer herd generally comprises two or three bucks, about twenty-five gelded males, twenty-odd does, ten to fifteen young does of breeding age, and about thirty calves. Roughly half the animals die before reaching sexual maturity, for reindeer are extremely susceptible to infections, particularly pneumonia. Flies and mosquitoes are their greatest source of annoyance in summer. If the weather is hot, small horseflies try to deposit their larvae in the animals' nostrils, causing the maddened reindeer to snort and stampede. The larvae develop in their palates and are either coughed out in spring if an animal is strong enough or, if it is too weak, remain there to gain a hold and eventually kill it.

On summer days when the air is still, every reindeer is surrounded by a huge cloud of gnats which float above it, and swarms of gadflies which lay their eggs in the hairs of the animal's back. Only a drop in temperature, a bath or a brisk canter into the wind can relieve the reindeer of their summer torment. The Orochi kindle large fires and the reindeer station themselves in the protective cloud of smoke to evade their torturers, their antlers protruding in ghostly fashion from the haze. Sometimes, maddened by stinging flies, they even plunge into their masters' tents.

There are only a few reindeer in the North Manchurian taiga, probably a few hundred in all, but the number in Siberia, where they still play an important role as beasts of burden and draught animals, is estimated at 1,200,000.

The Soviet Department for the Arctic (Glavesevmorput), which administers the whole of northern Siberia from the sixtieth degree of longitude eastward across the breadth of Irkutsk, has tried to increase the number of reindeer by encouraging farming and establishing veterinary stations and schools for reindeer breeding. Mobile schools are being used to "liberate" the reindeer herdsman from his illiteracy. Institutes for the study of Arctic agriculture and cattle breeding have been set up at Obdorsk on the lower reaches of the Ob, at Igarka on the Yenisei and at Yakutsk on the Lena, while Leningrad boasts an Institute of Reindeer Industry. All these measures are inspired by a desire to turn the nomads among the sixty nationalities in the Russian Arctic into sedentary citizens. This means that the nomad is being wrenched from his own way of life and familiarized with modes of existence which are often physiologically detrimental to him. In many areas, the result has been tuberculosis on an appalling scale. Centrally heated institutes are no substitute for the store of experience which Tungus have accumulated in thousands of years of nomadic life.

The Chinese have never been good cattle breeders, and are infamous for their cruel treatment of their horses. But the Tungus loves his animals and sees more in them than mere chattels and objects of exploitation. The Orochon needs no stick or whip to drive his reindeer. They obey his word of command alone. Each reindeer has a name of its own—Onyikan, Ogdikan, Buyudikan, Nuktukan—and comes when it is called.

The deepest affection has always existed between oro, the reindeer, and orochon, his master. This is one of the most enchanting discoveries any visitor to the taiga can make. And every Evamatu who rides through the taiga dreams and sings of his reindeer, the friend on whom he is dependent and whom he guards and cherishes.

In view of the Tungus and other primitive Siberian peoples, an animal which defends itself, which can be killed or provides particularly good meat, has a "good heart." One such is the stag, for he is among the most highly prized of all game. He is spoken of with respect and no harm must ever be inflicted on his soul.

The wolf, an eternal enemy of all circumpolar races, has an "evil heart." He cannot be tamed like the dog. He is hard to hunt and cowardly, and not much is known about his soul in the forests of the North.

Since the people of northeast Asia believe that no living creature can rise from the dead unless his bones are unscattered and undamaged, and since it is considered improper to prevent such resurrection, many taiga and tundra folk take the bones of deer, elk or other game carefully into the forest and lay them out on raised platforms or hang them from trees. I have even heard of Tungus in the taiga who bury wolf bones in this manner, a custom which Uno Harva, Professor of Finno-Ugrian Religions at Helsinki, recorded among the Yakuts as well. All this stems from these tribes' conviction that the spirit of an animal is similar to the intelligence of a man, that man and beast both possess an immortal soul, and that soul, spirit and body will reunite as long as the skeleton survives.

CHAPTER 15

THE TUNGUS: A DYING RACE

After four hundred years, during which European influence has been exerted on all the other peoples in the world, not a single large race or racial group has become Europeanized.

ANDREAS LOMMEL, *Der Cargo-Kult in Melanesien, Zeitschrift für Ethnologie*, 78, 1953, p. 18

AT ONE TIME the whole of northeast Asia was Tungus country. The Tungusic nomads roamed, at a period as dark and remote as the floor of a Siberian forest, from the bleak and melancholy waters of the Yenisei to the Bering Straits and Kamchatka, from the Arctic Ocean to Manchuria and the borders of Korea, an area as unimaginably vast as its climate, fauna and flora are varied.

We must try to rid ourselves of the idea that nomads are either savages, backward or primitive, nor should we regard nomadism as merely a halfway house on the road from food collection to agriculture. Nomadic life is a highly specialized form of existence which demands a comprehension of and feeling for immense tracts of territory, an abnormally well-developed topographic and climatic sense, and an ability to forecast, often from far away, where the best pasture land lies. Nomadism is an everlasting trek to more favorable hunting and grazing grounds, a journey into the best spring and summer pastures and back into regions which will permit men to survive the winter. Nomadism demands highly developed techniques in the handling of animals and extensive knowledge of the living habits and adaptability of grazing animals. Nomads are expert at solving difficult transport problems in the most impassable country and must always be ready to meet and combat the danger of a surprise attack. It took many tens of thousands of years before men learned how to maintain themselves in the steppes and forests, and they brought with them a rich store of spiritual culture dating from very ancient times. The Tungusic reindeer riders, who also keep the reindeer as a milch animal, carry about with them a whole world of inherited and acquired knowledge and a many-sided spiritual and material culture which it is difficult for us to comprehend in its entirety. The life of the nomad demands, as Ellis H. Minns has so well described in "The Art of the Northern Nomads," a great deal of skill, courage and endurance. On the other hand, the nomad does not have to bend laboriously over his furrows in the dust and heat. He lives in an ever-changing landscape, lives and has his being in wide-open spaces.

But, wherever the nomad has won over the townsman or agriculturist, he has turned the urban culture which is past his comprehension into ruins and grazing land. The story is an old one. One day, the nomad stormed to the attack with his newly forged sword and reduced Babylon to shards which bespectacled scholars carefully put together again two thousand years later. As first the angry man of the wilderness bars the trader's path when he tries to enter the steppes or the taiga. Then he goes looking for him, his mind filled with thoughts of destruction. One thing he never succeeds in doing, however, is to turn the agriculturalist into a nomad. No sooner have wars, famines or floods driven the peasant from his home than he settles down on another patch of land with a few goods and chattels and plows new furrows. This is the story of the world's river valleys, the story of the Hwang Ho and Yangtze, the Euphrates and the Nile. Once men have become sedentary nothing can turn them into nomads again, but the townsman can put the nomad in chains, compelling him either to adapt himself or perish. Whole continents have been wrested from nomadism in the course of history, North America from the American Indians, Australia from its two roaming aboriginal races, and vast tracts of central Asia from the Scythians.

Whenever the Chinese peasant has worked his way forward with the plow and pushed the taiga back a little, he usually tries to make the Tungus sedentary, too. It is an old and only too human trait to try to wean others from their own way of life. The man of the West takes this for granted. Only his own mode of existence seems sensible to him, which is reasonable enough as long as he does not try to impose it on others. But, even if most cultures are incapable of thinking except within their own limitations and according to their own scale of values, it is nonetheless surprising that today, when we are supposed to have so many modern scientific methods at our command, we are still unable to rid ourselves either of our ethnologically ant's-eye perspective or of the erroneous belief that a primitive people's only prospect of development and progress is to adopt what we ourselves possess.

The Russians have succumbed to this very human but no less primitive fallacy on a grand scale, particularly the modern Russians who are working indefatigably toward the "enlightenment" and "civilization" of the Siberian races. Any Tungus who fails to share the views of the Russian ruling class is by definition backward, even though he and his culture have already survived for several thousand years.

"The October Revolution," wrote the Soviet scientist A. F. Anisimov in 1936, "found many races in formerly Czarist Russia, especially the aboriginal inhabitants of the extreme North of our Union, at a very humble stage [of development]." He went on to infer the necessity of assimilating these people, whose development was a thousand years behind the times, into the Socialist culture. Explaining that the peoples of the North stood, economically, culturally and politically, at a very low ebb, Anisimov drew attention to their limited Neolithic techniques and called the Tungus' nomadic economy semiprimitive and backward. On the other hand, he did recognize that assimilation could be dangerous for the nomads and urged that at least some regard should be paid to the forms of the old nomadic life, a feature lacking in the measures undertaken hitherto.

In his book *The Golden Stream*, the Soviet author N. Yakutski gives an idyllic picture of life as it is lived among the Tungus of modern Russia:

In the morning, when the sun's radiance illumines the snow-covered forests and blue hills, the inhabitants of the Tshagda settlement are awakened by the whistle of the district power station. In all the erstwhile nomad camps, bluish smoke rises skyward from the chimneys of solidly constructed wooden houses. There are no nomads on the Utshur any more. The hunters' families live in clean, cozy houses heated by tiled stoves. They no longer sleep by the open fire with their children clasped to their breasts, but in beds, and they like to dress well. A man who cannot read or write has become a rare phenomenon. All the children learn. The young Evenki [Tungus] are producing large numbers of specialists these days: teachers, doctors, engineers, mine technicians, geologists, experts on fur-bearing animals and skillful hunters. The young Evenki know the bad old days only by repute.

The bad old days? They were the days when the Tungus were still allowed to lead a nomadic life, the days of free hunting and free roaming through tundra and taiga, the days, in short, when Tungus were still Tungus. For the people who live in clean, cozy houses and sleep in beds are not Tungus. Their culture has been taken from them and, with it, their existence. The Tungus are losing Siberia just as they have already lost Manchuria (apart from the northern bend of the Amur) and as Inner and Outer Mongolia are being wrested step by step from the Mongols.

The Finns and Turks, the Mongols and the Mongol-speaking inhabitants of central Asia, the Tungus of northern Asia and the Samoyeds in the extreme north of Europe are all classified as "Altaic" peoples. Reduced to a simple formula, the Altaic peoples comprise Turks, Mongols and Tungus, a classification more easily comprehended in linguistic as opposed to cultural terms, so that one can also talk of the Turko-Tatar, Mongol and Tungusic linguistic groups. These linguistic groups exhibit certain similarities. The word "hill," for instance, becomes *tebe* in Osmanli-Turkish, *uba* in Tatar-Kazan, *tube* in Tchuvash, *dobo* in Mongol and Buryat, and *dube*, in Tungus. To give an example of one expression which is similar in all the Finno-Ugrian tongues, here are the various versions of the word for "fire": *tuli* (Finnish), *tulle* (Estonian), *tolla* (Lappish), *tul* (Mordvinian, *tuz* Magyar) and *tu* (Samoyed). It should be noted that certain words in these languages bear no resemblance to each other whatsoever. Johannes Benzing, professor of Altaic philology, has pointed out that the connection between the Altaic peoples and languages is much harder to delineate than the connection between the Indo-Germanic or Semitic languages, which are clearly distinguishable from other linguistic groups and from each other by their type and common vocabulary. While the relationship between the Turkish and Mongol languages must be assumed, it has not yet been proved, and S. M. Shirokogorov, outstanding Russian ethnologist who is an authority on the Tungus, considered that more evidence of the common roots of the Turkish, Mongol and Tungusic languages is needed. The existence of a common origin or mutual borrowings is always difficult to establish.

The term "Altaic peoples" is derived from the Altai Range, although their original home may well be much farther to the east. The Altai Range forms the focal point of the vast Eurasian land mass. It begins south of Novosibirsk and Barnaul and stretches deep into Mongolia until it reaches the trans-Altaic Gobi.

The Tungus are not so much "a people" as "peoples." There is a northern and a southern Tungusic group. Linguistically, the northern group comprises Evenki, Orochon, Managir (the language of the Manega), Solon, Negidal and Lamut, and the southern group Manchu, Gold, Olcha, Orokian and Samagir.

Geographically speaking, the Tungus' domain includes taiga, steppe and tundra. Even today, it covers the eastern bank of the Middle Yenisei, the basins of the twin Tunguska Rivers in Siberia, the basin of the Upper Angara, Manchuria, Russian Primor'ye and the bleak plains and wild mountains around the Sea of Okhotsk from the Amur to Kamchatka. On ethnological maps, therefore, the name Tungus extends across a very wide geographical area.

In reality, however, the Tungus are dying out. In 1897 there were 62,028 genuine Tungus. According to the Soviet census of 1926 their numbers had by then been decreased to 37,546, and Hans Findeisen, the leading expert on the peoples of Siberia, estimates their present numbers at between twenty and thirty thousand. It seems fairly certain from this that the Tungus are on the way to eventual extinction.

That is precisely why I explored the forests of the Amur Bend. There in northern Manchuria, the Tungus still maintain their ancient hunter's and reindeer breeder's culture almost intact. It is hard to determine exactly how long they have been breeding reindeer. According to research conducted by Levin and Vasilyevitch, reindeer breeding was introduced toward the close of the first millennium A.D., when the Tungus came into contact with Mongol tribes in Transbaikalia, learned the art of horse breeding from them and applied this knowledge to the breeding of reindeer. Levin and Vasilyevitch conclude from this that the Tungus also adopted numerous Mongol terms dealing with the handling and harnessing of horses and transferred them to their own field.

Be that as it may, cultural exchanges between the peoples of Siberia and central Asia have always taken place, and the borrowing of terms or expressions does not necessarily entail the borrowing of material objects. Apart from this, herds of reindeer were being *accompanied* by man a very long time ago, as far back as 8000 B.C., and it is not such a big step from leading or driving reindeer to taming or domesticating them. Few would care to say when the Tungus first began to live with reindeer, when they gave them up or when they rediscovered them. According to U. T. Sirelius, the reindeer was known in Finland as a draught and riding animal as long ago as the Stone Age. It is certainly very doubtful whether the domestication of reindeer in historical times was merely copied from the southern practice of breeding horses and cattle. There is plenty of historical evidence for the appropriation of other races' cultural values or habits, but cases of imitation are very rare. Vladimir G. Bogaras, a Russian ethnologist who was exiled to the Far North in his youth for revolutionary activities, became interested in the life of the aboriginals and was thus launched on his scientific career, cites the fact that while the North American Indians adopted cattle, sheep and horse breeding from the whites, no Indian ever considered using cowboys' methods for breaking in the indigenous bison.

Bogaras believes that the northern practice of keeping reindeer is extremely ancient. In his opinion, it began shortly after the last glacial period, when reindeer, accompanied by hunters, moved northward. The process of domestication took place during these migrations. Thus the breeding of reindeer by the Tungus as riding animals for use on hunting expeditions can, as Bogaras says, be regarded as the earliest form of reindeer domestication. The Chukchees and Koryaks do not call the Tungus "reindeer-men" without good reason. Franz Hancar, professor of prehistory at the University of Vienna and a specialist on east Europe and Asia, estimates the date at which reindeer were introduced into the hunting economy as beasts of burden at between 5000 and 3000 B.C., and the beginning of reindeer breeding proper at between 3000 and 2000 B.C. The domestication of reindeer was probably an original idea, and reindeer may well have been the world's first domesticated animals.

The fact that reindeer were not domesticated by the Indians of North America has no bearing on the age of reindeer nomadism, as the Russian ethnologist Waldemar Jochelson has pointed out. If the absence of reindeer breeding could be regarded as evidence that reindeer breeding in Europe and Asia was of recent date, other similar but patently erroneous conclusions might be drawn. For instance, some of the Siberian peoples own reindeer herds, but others, such as the Kamchadals, never adopted reindeer breeding even though they knew of it. The Kamchadals' failure to adopt the practice is not attributable to the nonexistence or late appearance of reindeer culture, but to quite other reasons. The Kamchadals, coastal Chukchees and Koryaks simply found that they could obtain an adequate living from the rivers and sea without having to resort to the difficult and arduous practice of keeping reindeer.

The Eskimos of the Chukchee Peninsula did not adopt reindeer breeding from the Chukchees until 1915–20, by which time the seas had been severely depopulated by white whalers and a shortage of food had arisen. Similar motives prompted the United States' authorities to introduce the Siberian reindeer into Alaska. Hunters had destroyed large stocks of fish and game; gold prospectors, miners and adventurers had brought the natives' economy close to collapse; and there was a risk that thousands of Eskimos would perish. It was in order to improve conditions among the aboriginals that the Americans introduced the Siberian reindeer into Alaska and other regions adjoining the Bering Sea, with the result that the Eskimos could begin a new but still-nomadic life.

Wherever nomads—and that includes the Tungus—have become sedentary, their ancient freedom has vanished, for a reindeer economy is by definition nomadic.

The conquest of Siberia by the Russians spelled doom for the Tungus because they opposed the invasion and a whole series of tribes were wiped out in the fighting which ensued. When armed resistance proved hopeless the Tungus changed their tactics, submitted to foreign control and offered their services to the Russians as guides. They suffered a great deal in the process, not least from the avarice of fur traders, large and small, the drunkenness and injustice of officials and the brutality of convicts.

After the revolution the land was split up into districts and national areas. Some five hundred schools are instructing youthful Tungus in things for which they have no conceivable use. Children who have learned how to hunt, build tents and look after reindeer naturally lose these important skills when they are forced to sit on school benches for any length of time. As long as the Tungus are nomads, their children cannot receive a state education except in boarding schools, and education of this type militates against all the rules for survival which nomadic peoples have acquired in the course of thousands of years. It is well known that Eskimo children from the Canadian Arctic who have spent several years in boarding schools often cast a heavy burden on their hunting and fishing relatives when they return. In Siberia, the Tungus have been given law courts, the vote, and the doubtful privilege of leadership by Party functionaries —all from a wish to make the taiga folk "productive" and wean them from the old nomadic ways which are natural to them. Whether the Siberian Tungus are strong enough to resist these innovations remains to be seen, but it is improbable.

In Manchuria, the Tungus are as good as extinct. Such of the Orochi and Manega as still live in the forests of the Argun and the Amur Bend can be reckoned in hundreds, while the rest of Manchuria contains another few thousand Tungus who are becoming or have already become sedentary: the Solons, Daurs and Golds.

CHAPTER 16

THE TUNGUS' ORIGINAL HOME

Anyone who has covered large stretches of taiga in bitter cold or knows the extreme difficulty of crossing its soft ground and marshes in the chill of autumn will tell you that clothing should be light and allow a maximum of mobility.

SHIROKOGOROV believes that the Tungus' ancestors were early inhabitants of China who lived in the valleys of the Yellow River and the Yangtze and were forced to move northward by pressure of population from the west. On reaching the Amur region, Transbaikalia and the coastal areas of Eastern Siberia, they encountered the ancient Paleo-Asiatic peoples who had been living there since prehistoric times, adopted some of their living habits and ultimately evolved a forest culture of their own in the Siberian taiga.

Almost all Tungus wear, or used to wear in earlier times, a peculiar type of garment whose significance is not immediately apparent but which one comes to regard in quite another light after spending a little time among the Tungus. This garment remains open in front and is curiously reminiscent of a frock coat. The opening is covered by a long apron, fastened at the neck and waist, which many authorities have described as a doublet or stomacher, though this gives a false idea of its length.

It might be supposed that such light clothing must have originated in the south, since it does not appear to be warm enough for a northern race like the Tungus. Koppers, for example, has compared the Tungus' stomacher with the aprons of the Miao women.

The Miao were an early Chinese people remnants of whom are still to be found in the southwestern provinces of Kweichow, Yunnan, Kwangtung and Szechwan, as well as in Tonking and Annam. Many of the Miao's customs and cultural traditons appear to have come from the north, and the Tungus have adopted certain traditions from the south. Apart from this, the Miao and the Tungus exhibit anthropological resemblances. Among the peoples of Asia, the Tungus constitute an independent linguistic group. The language of the Miao is equally independent, and cannot be related either with Chinese, Siamese, Tibetan or Japanese. The Tungus are hunters and reindeer breeders. It is hard to say for certain when they began breeding reindeer, but they were originally hunters and food gatherers. Tradition has it that the Miao were not always agriculturalists and cattle breeders and that they were once hunters who lived farther north. Finally, both Tungus and Miao used bow and arrow in earlier times.

Citing all these similarities, Wilhelm Koppers considers it possible that an age-old connection between the Tungus and the Miao may once have existed. There are, however, many indications to the contrary. The word *miao* means "sons of the soil," and Chinese script conveys it by placing the symbol for "grass" above the symbol for "field." This would indicate that Miao agriculture is very old. In fact, the Miao appear to possess a very ancient agricultural tradition, and it is unlikely that such long-time agriculturalists are related to people whose whole being is rooted in nomadism.

Many ethnographic factors suggest that the Tungus originated in a milder climate, i.e. in a more southerly region than Manchuria, but these indications may be of recent date and have stemmed from the extensive conquests of Chinese territory made by the Manchu Tungus. Moreover, light clothing is not an invariable sign of southern origin. Anyone who has covered large stretches of taiga in bitter cold or knows the extreme difficulty of crossing its soft ground and marshes in the chill of autumn will tell you clothing should be light and allow a maximum of mobility. Very warm and therefore heavy clothes would be quite unpractical.

The Tungus are extremely fast travelers. Their secret, which any visitor to the taiga quickly copies, is to wear clothes which do not restrict movement. They are experts at husbanding body heat, generating it by traveling at a near run when on the move and maintaining it when resting by warming themselves at the fire, with which they still have a primeval, even magical relationship. All Tungus, provided they are still nomads and have not become degenerate, possess a unique skill. They are past masters of the art of squatting, and can survive even the coldest nights huddled up in that position, especially in an emergency, when for some reason they have been unable to kindle a fire. I have often observed and admired this facility among the Tungus. Their "frock coat," too, is a brilliantly devised traveling outfit, and anyone who accompanies these swift-striding nomads through the taiga will quickly discover it to be the only appropriate form of dress. Up in the forests of northern Asia one does not get the feeling that this walking costume must have originated in the south—not that this is the only thing which militates against Shirokogorov's theory that the Tungus' original home was in China.

The Russian prehistorian A. P. Okladnikov assumes that during the Neolithic period, or between 6000 and 2500 B.C., the Tungus resided in Cisbaikalia, the region dominated by the Angara and Upper Lena. In support of this, the burial ground of Ust'Uda on the Angara yielded a female skeleton on whose ribs lay the remains of some piping which could have bordered the stomacher of a Tungus shaman's costume but certainly showed that the open coat and stomacher were worn in this region during the Upper Neolithic period. The animal-sinew piping, which had survived the passage of time, clearly outlined the cut of the garment it had once adorned.

Did Tungus live there, and were they already wearing the coat we know today? It is quite possible, in view of other discoveries of more recent date—diadems, pendants of animal teeth, boats made of birch bark, lures for harpoon fishing—all of which were found in graves of the second century B. C., and all of which are reminiscent of Tungusic culture.

The Russian scholar M. G. Levin opines that the Tungus had two points of departure, one in Cisbaikalia and the other in Transbaikalia, —that is to say, the regions to the west and east of Lake Baikal respectively—and he assumes that these two groups, which resembled each other culturally and anthropologically, subsequently linked up.

A number of philologists and prehistorians think it fairly certain that the Amur area was not the Tungus' original home. Against this, the Finnish scholar Uno Harva suggests that the Tungus' migration followed an east-west route and that its point of departure was the Amur valley. Uno Holmberg of Helsingfors University and von Schrenk also regard the territory surrounding the Amur as the original home of the Manchu Tungus.

We should, of course, be very careful when talking about "original homes," for most of them are a great deal older than we suspect, and scientists tend to conclude that they have plumbed the origins of something when more remains to be discovered. The more prehistoric finds from a particular district are associated with a particular people, the more prone we are to assume that we have identified an original home. But the number of prehistoric finds depends to a large extent on the amount of digging undertaken and on the more or less haphazard insertion of a spade at one particular spot, and it is abundantly clear that the mounds of debris and human relics which have so far been excavated are exceeded a millionfold by those that have not. Far less digging has been done in Transbaikalia and northwest Manchuria than to the west of Lake Baikal, and, as far as I know, no one has ever conducted any excavations at all on the Russo-Manchurian border to the right of the Amur.

Today Manchuria is Chinese territory, but once upon a time, toward the close of the first millennium A.D., before the plough had driven its first furrow or the soya-bean fields stretched for mile after mile, when the whole of Manchuria was still taiga, a mighty host of Tungus erupted onto the stage of world history and poured southward.

CHAPTER 17

THE BEAR KNOWS ALL

By day and by night, in cloudy weather or bright, his big damp nose told him most of what he needed to know and dismissed what was unimportant. He came to rely upon it more and more. Even when his eyes and ears both informed him of something he would not believe it until his nose had confirmed it. But man cannot understand this because he has sold the birthright of his nose for the privilege of living cooped up in towns.

Adapted from ERNEST THOMPSON SETON,
The Biography of a Grizzly

THE bear possesses a soul just as the human being does. The Orochi are as steadfastly convinced of this as they are of the idea that there is a girl carrying a pail of water on the moon. No Tungus ever kills this largest and most powerful predator in the Siberian forests without a compelling reason. Yet it is not the bear's strength which fills the Tungus with such awe and respect nor the elemental power of the mighty beast which makes them tremble. There are deeper reasons for their dread of the bear's soul. A bear's facial expression can be extraordinarily human at times. A bear can walk upright on two legs and when skinned bears a gruesome resemblance to a man. Finally, there is an ancient belief that the bear is in communication with the Lord of the Mountains and with the sky, and certainly he has from time immemorial been surrounded by an aura which enjoins caution and respect.

Very large numbers of brown bear live in the North Manchurian taiga. There is *Ursus arctos,* which inhabits the densest forests of central and northern Asia, Eurasian Russia and the coasts of the Sea of Okhotsk. I also saw the massive gray bear, the largest surviving predator on earth, which resembles the grizzly or giant bear of Alaska or *Ursus arctos horribilis,* the Kodiak bear. This animal has been described as bulky, clumsy and awkward, but sharp, curved claws, immensely powerful masticatory equipment and bunches of neck and shoulder muscle make even the heaviest bear an agile climber and allow him to haul his massive body up trees by the brute force of his arms and legs. It is true, of course, that the struggle for existence cannot be maintained indefinitely by brute force alone, and that is probably the reason for the dying out of the cave bear, a gigantic and excessively heavy creature which ultimately found itself with no enemies save man and may have become extinct because of a lack of natural selection. Some day the brown bear and the grizzly will also roam the burial grounds of the taiga for the last time, lay themselves down in some lonely cave and send their souls winging to the stars.

Bears are strange animals, and often act in such a human way that one is tempted to credit them with a considerable reasoning power. They hoard their food in the ground and establish caches of provisions. Sometimes they dig up a dead animal, carry it to another place and bury it again—and they never seem to forget the spot. Being relatively slow-moving, they can prey only on small animals, carrion and fish. The bear is however an excellent swimmer and fisherman. Apart from live prey, the bear also eats plants, being especially fond of berries, mushrooms and acorns. And bears especially love honey. No tree is too high or cliff too steep to climb if a honeycomb is at stake.

Generally speaking, bears do not attack human beings unless their own lives are in danger. They can scent man from so far that it is almost impossible to stalk and intercept them. One can come across fresh tracks or find heaps of dung still steaming in the cool gray light of dawn, but the bear's unrivaled sense of smell will have warned him of one's approach in ample time. By nature cautious and wary, he generally regards discretion as the better part of valor. Orochon women going unarmed into the depths of the bush to collect bilberries often hear the snorting and grunting of a bear enjoying a snack of the same forest fruit. Tungus girls seldom show any alarm at the approach of a bear, well knowing that his sole motive is to steal the fruit which they have already gathered. Accordingly, they either gather up their things and move on or shout at the animal to scare him away.

Mother bears with young, on the other hand, are aggressive and nervous, constantly on their guard and easily aroused. In my experience, they are more dangerous when they sense a danger which they cannot recognize than when they can hear and see it distinctly. Bear cubs are blind and remarkably tiny when they arrive in the world. They are usually born in January, after a gestation period of seven months, and by spring are able to accompany their mother on journeys in quest of food. Even at this stage if a she-bear is attacked or one of her cubs wounded or killed she will try to come to grips with her adversary.

When Tungus are not actually hunting bear and only want to drive them away, they wave their spears, bang guns or pieces of wood against a tree, and shout at the top of their voices. Even females generally pay attention to this warning and retreat without attacking.

It is extraordinarily difficult to kill bear, for they will often stop several bullets with scarcely a blink. I heard of one bear in the taiga who took thirteen bullets in the body and still showed fight. A bear is truly vulnerable, especially to primitive weapons, only when he rears. As a rule, however, he only rises to his feet at the last moment, when he gets to close quarters in order to strike with his forepaws, so the Orochi encourage him to rear prematurely by jumping and waving their arms in the air.

In former times, the Orochi used to hunt bear with the palma, an extremely dangerous undertaking because the spear had to be thrust into the animal's heart from close quarters. The procedure was to induce the bear to rear and, when he came to grips, level the spear at his heart so that he ran onto it. What made things even more difficult was that the palma had to be kept out of sight until the decisive blow was struck because a bear was always capable of brushing it aside with his forepaw at the last moment.

Some Siberian tribes used to tackle bear with knives. The hunter's left arm and hand were thickly swathed, while his right hand held the weapon, a long blade. This method resembled that used by gladiators in Roman arenas. Lastly, bear were also hunted with the ax, though to lay one of these primeval giants low with such a weapon was an art in which the chances of survival were never more than fifty-fifty. Even when the Orochi did possess firearms they were so old and unreliable that many men never returned from bear hunts.

The bear senses everything, hears everything, knows the activities and intentions of human beings and, above all, remembers everything. All Tungus believe him to possess uncannily fine instincts. In fact, the bear's scent and hearing are much more highly developed than his eyesight, which is why, when the Tungus are asked how a bear knows when he has met you once before, they answer: "He smells it." It is quite astonishing how surely the bear can scent things from a great distance. He can spot the presence of an enemy or the slightest change in his hunting preserves, which he knows down to the last detail. His scent and hearing endow him with powers of observation so acute that he invariably reacts quickly to human intentions. When he is hunted he only shows himself at night and always keeps close to cover. When he is well treated, as in the United States' national parks, he becomes extraordinarily trustful.

The question of whether a particular bear has encountered a hunter on some previous occasion is considered extremely important by the Tungus. They insist that the animal knows when a man has harbored evil designs against a bear or has already been attacked or touched by one, and believe that it will make a point of attacking him. Hence, it is better not to go hunting with such a man. Objects which have been touched by a bear can also be dangerous, so Tungus avoid coming into contact with them. Once a hunter has killed a bear he would be better advised never to hunt another. All this is a symptom of the widespread fear of natural vengeance which the Tungus have passed on to the Siberian Russians. The converse applies, too. Anyone who is on good terms with bears will seldom be harmed by them, and the inhabitants of Siberia can tell countless stories of grateful bears who have repaid one good turn with another.

When a bear dies the soul leaves its body and is then capable of harming the soul of a man just as any liberated soul can. A bear's soul must therefore be treated in a proper manner and its meat eaten in a strictly prescribed fashion—above all, not in the presence of women. It is exceedingly important to keep the bones to one side so that the bear's skeleton can be deposited in a tree or laid out on a platform high above the ground. No bones must be missing, or the bear's soul will never rest. The head is cut off and either laid on a slab of wood supported by posts or hung up in a tree. Many Tungus, though not the Orochi, hang the whole skin up in the forest. Since the bear's soul is carefully watching all this, it is advisable to talk loudly of its maltreatment by some distant tribe so as to delude it and ensure that it will not persecute its real murderers. Live bears are especially dangerous because they can hear and scent everything. Consequently, the Orochi never speak openly of a particular animal which they have seen or whose hiding place they have discovered. As a general rule, all talk about a bear which one intends to kill should be avoided, and if a Tungus finds a cave or lair in the rocks he does his best to indicate it to the others by means of gestures alone.

I never heard the Orochi describe bear in any but circumlocutionary terms such as "the black one," "the ugly one," "the honorable one," "grandfather," "grandmother" or "big baby." When they see a bear emerge suddenly from the undergrowth, they call: "Go back where you came from. We shall do you no harm." The Tungus believe that "the honorable one" thinks like a man, and when one sees this morose and incalculable creature with its half-open jaws and lolling tongue sitting manlike on a fallen trunk and calmly regarding its foe, one is tempted to agree.

More legends and anecdotes are told about the bear than about any other animal in the Siberian forests. No other animal has so much power, even when it is dead and its soul has left its body. Its paws, claws and teeth are all regarded as talismans with tutelary properties. The people of eastern Asia are familiar with countless medicaments made from various parts of the bear's body, and anyone who visits an apothecary in the Far East will discover how expensive these exotic remedies can be.

CHAPTER 18

AN OFFERING OF BEARS' SKULLS

*We discovered that, even in the snow-covered tundras of North-
ern Siberia and Northern Canada and on the most inhospitable
coasts of the Arctic Ocean, an avowedly monotheistic religion was
embraced with reverential faith and a warm heart by the peoples
who had been there longest.... Especially prominent among the
sacrifices offered to the Supreme Being are the skulls and bones of
slaughtered game, because they ... thereby acknowledged God as
absolute master of their sustenance and, with it, of life and death.*

P. W. SCHMIDT, *Der Ursprung der
Gottesidee*, Vol. III, p. 563

WHY is bear medicine of such great value? All the Tungus of Northern Asia, the Manchurian Chinese, the Buryats, the Mongols, the
Koreans and all the inhabitants of China set great store by medicaments which have been prepared from various parts or organs
of the bear's body. The only things held in comparable esteem are
the tiger, the young antlers of the isyubr deer, known as *panty*, and
the root of the ginseng plant. The idea that curative effects can be
derived from the strength of a bear or tiger or the vitality of a
deer's antlers is something which originated in a hunter's world
such as that of the Tungus. That is why the shamans of some Tungus
tribes wear a headdress of stag's antlers when performing rituals,
while others model their clothing on the bear's external appearance.
Whether dried bear's gall ground into a powder and mixed with
water is a genuinely effective remedy for inflammation of the eyes,
and whether it originated in the Chinese or Tungus' store of medical
experience is something I was unable to establish conclusively.

The roots of the ginseng plant which grows in the forests of the
Russian province of Primor'ye, North Korea and Manchuria, bears
a remarkable resemblance to a human being. As we have already
seen, a skinned bear is also reminiscent of a human being, so it is
evident that the Tungus regard both plant and animal as possessing
a soul very like that of a man. In fact, they speak to both of them
as though they were addressing human beings. The Tungus talk to

all animals, plants and natural phenomena, it is true, but their relationship to the ginseng plant and the bear is more personal, stronger and more active. It is a mixture of sometimes genuine and sometimes feigned affection and solicitude, respect and awe.

The ancient Finns believed that a human soul resided in the bear. Professor Kaarle Krohn of Helsinki writes of the songs which the Finns sang when feasting off a bear's head and ceremonially depositing its skull in a sacred tree. "O God, thou who has given what is not to be eaten without song and whose head must be laid in a tree." The most valuable and efficacious parts of a bear are its head, skull and leg bones. Since a bear's skull contains the most tasty part of the animal—its brains—and since the leg bones contain the delicious marrow, the Tungus have always, from very early times, sacrificed them to their god. When I questioned some Orochi and Manega about this, they said that they always buried a bear's skeleton to pacify the animal's soul but that it was an age-old tradition to place the skull of a slaughtered bear in a tree as a sacrifice to the supreme god. The practice of laying out the skeleton on a platform aboveground was a form *of burial*, but the exposure of the head must have been a form of *sacrifice*. The Tungus are quite explicit about this, even today, when they owe allegiance less to a supreme god than to a "lord of the forest and mountain."

This was not always so. The lord of the forest only gained in importance as the age-old faith in a single supreme god declined. The fact that the ancient custom of sacrificing a bear's head, skull and leg bones is no longer observed and is even sinking slowly into oblivion is just one of the many symptoms of a dying race. First, the ancient faith vanishes, and with the waning of a belief in God, which among the Tungus was a belief in a single supreme deity, comes the disappearance of the conviction that Heaven sustains and protects its own. Waning faith is linked with the decline of a culture and ultimately of the men who sustained it.

The Tungus call God "Boa." At least, that is how the ancient name sounds when pronounced by the Orochan, though Shirokogorov also writes "Buga." The Orochi call the Spirit of Heaven "Dagachan." It is hard to ascertain from them whether Dagachan and Boa are one and the same, but all the Tungus who I met during my travels on the Manchurian side of the Amur Bend still had an inherent knowledge or idea of the supreme being, the great God of the Sky. This god remains eternally invisible and is aware of all that goes on in the world and the universe. The Tungus have no conception of a God of Wrath. God has no Hell at his disposal and could never banish a man to a place of purgatory or damnation. God is always kind, always beneficent, and never punishes by dispensing evil. I even doubt whether the Tungus would accept the suggestion that God sometimes takes away their luck at hunting, though many authorities—Shirokogorov among them—assume them to believe that God punishes by withholding His gifts.

Neither the Orochi nor the Manega have ever tried to portray their invisible supreme god in visible terms. The strange little wooden figures which the Orochi and Manega carve on trees or occasionally display on wooden altars are effigies of a forest spirit whom they call Bainaca. Bainaca is lord of wild animals and holds the destinies of hunters in his hand, from which it follows that God is not responsible for dispensing good or ill fortune where hunting is concerned. The Tungus of the North Manchurian taiga offer small quantities of all kinds of food to the spirit of the forest, putting aside a little of what they have prepared for a meal on a small pedestal or framework of planks. There is a practical side to these offerings, too, for the lonely traveler may use them to still his hunger in an emergency provided that he replaces them at the next opportunity. This, at least, is how it was in northern Manchuria. The spirit of the forest is a subordinate being and has no connection with the Tungus' high god, who is invisible because he is one with the weather, the sky, the sun and the whole universe, and because he alone stands above the mysteries of infinite space and infinite time, not subject to these powers and therefore incapable of suffering harm or destruction by their agency. Although Shirokogorov speaks of the Tungus' supreme god, Buyam, Boya or Boga, he mentions nothing about the sacrifices made to him and refers only to the modest offerings set aside for Bainaca: horsehairs, scraps of food and small birch twigs. The Orochi and Manega both told me, however, that

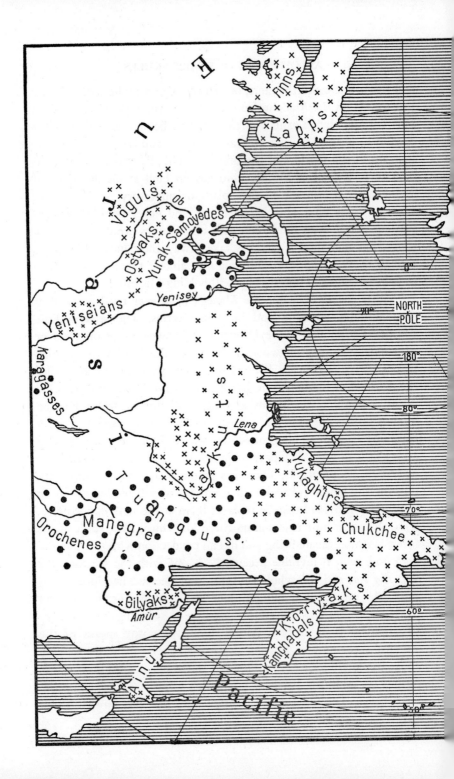

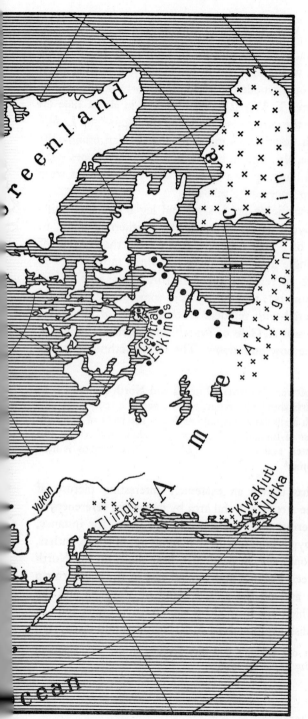

Head, skull,
and bone sacrifice

Bear cults
and bear caves

The people who since
the Stone Age have
believed in a supreme
being and have sacri-
ficed bones and skulls
live on the arctic coast
nearest the North
Pole. Bear cults, how-
ever, originated in a
younger, subarctic cul-
ture and are found in
regions farther south,
for example Lapland
and Hudson Bay.

their fathers still practiced the custom of sacrificing bears' heads to the supreme god, wrapping them in birchbark and putting them high up in a tree or on a wooden scaffold. This corresponds exactly with what the explorer T. W. Atkinson observed in about 1860 on his journeys through the country surrounding the Upper and Lower Amur, and also with descriptions given by the Russian ethnologist Miss M. A. Czaplicka, although in her version the bear's bones were placed in a sack and hung up in a tree. As usual, the Tungus were careful to see that no bones were missing.

The practice of sacrificing head, skull and leg bones was transmitted by the Samoyeds in the west, via the northern Tungus, to the central Eskimos of North America. Apart from the concept of sacrifice and of a single god, these races had three more things in common: they were all reindeer breeders (or, in the case of the Eskimos, reindeer hunters); they all lived, as some of them still do, in conical tents covered with reindeer hides or sheets of birchbark; and they all, as Professor A. Gahs of Zagreb, an Austrian ethnologist, has stressed, used the bow and arrow. The Danish ethnologist Birket-Smith writes:

> The cultural link between Northern Eurasia and North America is so close that the two parts should be regarded as a single circumpolar cultural district in which a similar environment forms the basis of common development. The test of human intelligence throughout the Arctic and boreal regions is winter, and the vital problem in these regions is how winter can be overcome.[1]

Professor Gahs has drawn an extremely interesting picture of divine worship in the Arctic cultural area by compiling references to sacrifice from numerous different sources. We learn, for instance, that the Yurak Samoyeds built sacrificial mounds out of sticks, antlers, bear and reindeer bones and, in particular, bear skulls on the North Siberian coast between Pechora and Yenisei east of the southern tip of Novaya Zemlya and on the sacred island of Vaygach and the Yamal Peninsula, which are formed by the Obskaya Guba and the Kara Sea. The Swedish explorer Nils A. E. Nordenskjöld discovered

[1] Über die Herkunft der Eskimos und ihre Stellung in der zirkumpolaren Kulturentwicklung," *Anthropos* 25, 1930.

on the northwest coast of the Yamal Peninsula an altar built of reindeer bones and about fifty bear skulls, some of which were hung on sticks. Close by was a hearth containing the ashes of a recently extinguished fire, and near it Nordenskjöld saw numerous reindeer bones, clear evidence of a sacrificial feast, as he noted in the report on his expedition to Novaya Zemlya and the Yeniseyskiy Gulf.

The Russian scholar B. Zitkov, describing a journey to the Yamal Peninsula in 1913, refers to a sacrificial mound composed of polar bears' skulls. He learned that the Samoyeds had been accumulating bears' skulls on this spot for over a hundred years. The Samoyeds' supreme being is called "Num," and it was to this single deity that the skull sacrifices had been offered. Like Boa, the god of the Orochi and the Tungus in general, the Samoyeds' high god is all-embracing. He is earth, sky, the whole of nature and the universe in its entirety. The fact that the Samoyeds also recognize numerous spirits does not change their conception of Num as an invisible being of un-equaled sublimity who loves men and gives them good hunting by dispatching spirits whom he has entrusted with its bestowal.

The Samoyeds are a fast-dying race of whom little is known today. Let us take a last look at these people who have for so long believed so implicitly in a single, supreme deity, who have sacri-ficed to him, trusted him, relied on his omnipotence and, confident of his good will, have carried their culture from one age to the next on swift sleighs which skim through the northern forests and across the wintry grandeur of the wide tundra.

The Samoyeds' own name for themselves is Nyentsi, or "men," which is what the Russians call them today. In Russian, Samoyedi means "self-eater." The Samoyeds have never been cannibals, how-ever, and it is very doubtful whether the name is Russian at all. It is more probably of Finnish derivation and may be connected with the indigenous term for Lapland, Sameandna, or that for Finland itself, Suomi.

The Samoyeds spend the whole of their life on the move and take all their possessions with them: tents, sledges, boats and dogs. They harness three or four reindeer to each sledge, the lead animal a little in front and the remainder behind in an oblique formation which looks superb when the team is traveling at speed. Guided in this way, they traverse the gleaming surface of the snow as lightly, swiftly and weightlessly as birds on the wing.

The sledges are small but as stoutly constructed as only the Eskimos, with their ancient store of experience, can make them. Dogs are never harnessed to sledges but run alongside, pale yellow, incredibly hardy animals who bark unceasingly and snap greedily at the raw fish which forms their staple diet.

The Samoyeds themselves live on reindeer meat, although they never drink reindeer milk. A Samoyed is really herdsman, hunter and fisherman all in one. Reindeer are the principal form of capital, and the more head a man owns the happier he is. The northern herdsmen are constantly preoccupied with a quest for better pasture, and this makes their life a wearisome and arduous one. In spring and summer they move northward, in autumn and winter southward, their whole existence spent in avoiding flies and finding the best grazing land, keeping their herds together, counting them, cutting out sick animals and, last but not least, protecting them from wolves, which are as much a menace in the tundra as in the taiga. So the Samoyed skims along on his smooth-gliding sledge, controlling his herd with dogs, changing their direction, catching animals with his sixty-foot lasso and training them in the difficult art of sledge pulling.

It is no simple matter to be herdsman, fisherman and hunter all at once. The Samoyed must be able to construct tents, sledges, boats and fishing tackle; he must know a multitude of hunting secrets, have countless tricks at his command, meet the perpetual severity of nature with a degree of patience quite alien to Western cultures, possess superhuman powers of endurance and be capable of withstanding plagues of insects and the harshest climate in the world. All this presupposes a great, very ancient and time-tested culture, and we can tell by studying these people that the men who preceded Ur and Babylon and the beginning of our recorded history were far from savages. Accustomed to the unceasing vicissitudes of fate, the Samoyed never complains, never expects too much of life and is convinced that he must master it on his own. He asks for help only in an emergency, repays a loan at the first opportunity, and has never learned how to beg or steal.

We owe a great deal of what we know about this almost extinct race to the outstanding work of the Finnish scholar T. Lehtisalo, who conducted an expedition to the Yurak Samoyeds of northern Russia and northwest Siberia in the years 1911–1912. He traveled by water to the estuary of the remote rivers Tass and Pur, accompanied reindeer breeders on a trip to the Sjoida, carried out scientific research at Oksino in the Pechora Delta and spent days, weeks and months with impoverished Samoyeds who, having already been robbed of their nomadic liberty, were living in small villages. Then, in the year 1914, once more sponsored by the Finno-Ugrian Society, he explored the domain of the Forest Yuraks on the Irtish. Lehtisalo amassed a great deal of invaluable information about these Arctic people, and all that has since come to light, even in very recent times, is merely a repetition of what he has already told us.

The famous explorer De Dobbeler, who carried out exhaustive research into the Samoyeds in about 1885, wrote:

The Samoyeds believe in a Supreme God, the sky. He is good and, as such, will not do them any harm. Since God is the sky and the sky is God, both are known by the same name: Num. God is worshipped on sacred mountains. When the Samoyeds climb such a mountain after a long journey they slaughter a reindeer, eat it and hang the animal's head either in a tree or on a stake driven into the ground. Before throttling it, they look up at the sky and say: "God, we have led it hither," and, when they have put the noose round its neck: "Do you see, God, what we are doing?" During the killing, they cry: "O-ho-o-o-ho" and "U-hu-u-u-u," and after it they say: "God, take this."

G. M. Vasilevich wrote in 1956 that the Yenisei Tungus look on the bear as a hero who sacrificed himself in order to provide mankind with reindeer. In the extreme east of Siberia, fragments have survived of a myth which tells how a girl gave birth to a bear cub and a baby. It seems that when the brothers grew up they engaged in mortal combat, and the man was defeated.

The mere existence of such a legend indicates how deep and time-honored is the reverence accorded to the bear. The Evenki have more than fifty different names for the animal. When one has been killed it must always be skinned and gutted by a member of another tribe so that its soul will not know who the real hunter was. Vasilevich records that the eastern Tungus used to preserve the head and other bones of a slaughtered bear carefully. The head was then hung from a tree and the bones deposited nearby, either high up on a broad branch or on a wooden platform in the taiga.

P. G. Pallas, who undertook a journey through various Russian provinces between 1768 and 1773, told how the Karagasses used to lay the head and heart of a slaughtered bear on a sheet of bark, raise it to heaven and pray for a continuance of good hunting. Uno Harva's reference to the fact that the Karagasses do not eat the brain is extremely interesting. Apparently, they are reluctant to break the animal's skull. Since, as mentioned before, the brain is considered the most valuable and tasty part of a bear, we may regard their abstinence as a sacrifice intended for the high god.

A belief in a single supreme deity and creator prevails among all the ancient peoples whom we are presumptuous enough to call primitive. Waldemar Jochelson says that he has established this in the case of the Tungus, Yakuts, Koryaks, Yukaghirs, Kamchadals and Aleuts.

Even as late as the last century, Western science credited humanity with an upward trend in religion, an evolutionary chain which began with dark superstition, sorcery and magic and ended in monotheism. The more man developed, so the theory ran, the more clearly he recognized the falsity of magic until he eventually reached the highest religious level, monothesim, or a belief in one god.

Yet magic and monotheism have always existed side by side and still do today. And most students of ethnology are now convinced that the earliest religious concept was a belief in one god, and that this "primitive" monotheism deteriorated as animistic ideas clouded its purity. It was only later that magic gained a hold. The weaker the faith in a high god became, the more magical formulae were called in to supply the deficiency.

Jochelson conducted research into the Yukaghirs in the years 1895 and 1896 and later in 1901 and 1902. And in his writings refers to the high god, known as Pon, to which the Yukaghirs sacrificed reindeer. In ancient times their offerings used to include dogs and, so tradition has it, an occasional human being. Human sacrifice was not, however, destined for Pon but for the spirit of the elk. It was the custom to sacrifice a girl who had set eyes on the head of a slaughtered elk—an act which signed her death warrant—together with two puppies, a male and a bitch.

Uno Harva supplies some really startling information. He learned that in the Turuchansk district the Tungus used to keep not only the skin of bears' heads but also the scalps of enemies whom they had killed. It is known that the Ostyaks (who are related to the Finns) and, of course, many American Indian tribes made a habit of scalping their enemies, so that it is not surprising that the same custom existed in Siberia. When the chieftain of a Yukaghir tribe died, the flesh was stripped from his corpse with bone knives and dried in the sun. To avoid physical contact with the dead man, the Yukaghirs wore gloves and masked their faces. The flesh was put into a sack and hung on stakes or deposited in a tree some feet above the ground. The Yukaghirs then distributed the dead chief's bones among his relatives, who wore them as amulets and consulted them whenever an important problem came up for discussion. The head itself passed into the possession of the tribe's oldest member.

It is evident that the skulls of dead men once played at least as great a role in religion as bears' skulls. If we go back three or four hundred thousand years in time to the human skulls which were found at Chou-k'ou-tien near Peking, we must consider whether they fulfilled the same purpose as the bear skulls of Siberia—whether, in fact, the human skulls of Chou-k'ou-tien may not have been intended as a form of sacrifice.

In earlier times, the Yukaghirs inhabited a huge area which extended from the Lena to the Kolyma and the Arctic Ocean to the Verkhoyansk Mountains. They now live eastward of the lower reaches of the Indagirka and are in grave danger of extinction. Their environment is ruled by the harshest climate in all Siberia and they are continuously exposed, usually without shelters adequate

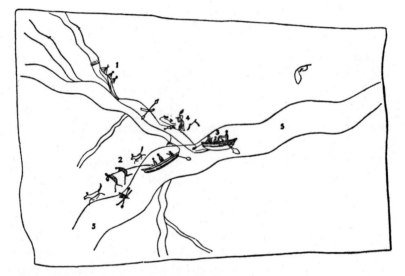

This Yukaghir picture-letter shows the Kolyma (5) and its tributary the Nelemnaya (1). Three tents can be seen on the banks of the Nelemnaya and above
them a weir basket. A boat is being towed upstream by two men (2) accompanied by two dogs. The boat on the Kolyma (3) is being steered toward a
hunter on the bank (4), who is carving up a reindeer.

to the sharpest of north winds since their home lies close to the
coldest regions in the world.

The name Yukaghir is probably Tungus in origin. Many of the
Orochi's tribal names end in ghir, and the word Yuka itself has a
Tungusian ring. The Yukaghirs call themselves *odul*, which means
"strong" or "mighty," though it seems almost self-derisory when one
considers that defeat by the Chukchees, smallpox, taxation, exploitation and measures aimed at "civilization" and "enlightenment"
carried out first by the Imperial and more recently by the Soviet
Russian administration have all but wiped the tribe out. The few
hundred Yukaghirs who still survive have extensively intermarried
with Yukaghirized Tungus.

Jochelson records that the Yukaghirs have a strong aversion to the
smells peculiar to members of other races or tribes. According to
them, the Lamuts smell of squirrel, bear and rotting reindeer meat,
the Yakuts of old fish liver and cow dung, and the Siberian Russians simply of stale air. It may be added that Jochelson himself

Yukaghir picture-writing on birchbark. Letters of this kind were left behind on trees as a means of communicating hunting news and information to fellow members of the tribe. (1) Hunters pursuing wild reindeer. (2) Two hunters with snowshoes and guns. The hunter in front is resting his gun on a stand and has hit one of the reindeer. (3) Three conical tents, men, a dog and sledges, and behind them two Tungus aprons. (4) A hunter stalking on all fours toward a tree in which two birds are sitting.

suffered from the odor emanating from the Yukaghirs' own garments, which were made of fishskin!

The Yukaghirs spend the summer fishing from riverbanks. They never bathe, however, and their hair is perpetually infested with lice. When Jochelson told them that his own head was free of lice they gazed at him sadly and remarked: "We have observed that lice leave a man's head only when he is on his deathbed."

Yukaghir girls and women are of an exceedingly nervous disposition, as were the Orochon women whom I observed at first hand.

Any sudden mental shock reduces them to a state of tremulous anxiety.

The Yugaghirs are an honest and uninhibited people who innate sense of pride forbids them to beg food from neighbors even in time of famine. They were probably very courageous, too, though this virtue may well have hastened their end, as courage unsupported by adequate technical resources often does.

Hospitality was an invariable characteristic of the Yukaghirs, just as it is of the Orochi and Manega and all the ancient peoples of Siberia. On reaching sexual maturity, girls are allotted a tent of their own, and since intercourse with the young men of the tribe is permitted there is a certain amount of nocturnal wandering from tent to tent. Neither the Yukaghirs nor the Tungus in general see anything amiss in this practice. None of these tribes steals, cheats or deceives, which accounts for their constant exploitation by foreigners. They are honest and helpful by nature, and their life is a mixture of high morality and practices which we should ordinarily describe as hopelessly immoral. The fact is, of course, that theirs are very ancient cultures which cannot be judged by our own standards.

A stranger is always invited to share a girl's bed, not necessarily so that he can enjoy her company at night but because two sleep more warmly than one. The Tungus are amazed to hear that this is considered immoral, their attitude being that since strange hunters usually come from far away it is only natural that they should be offered the best quarters and the greatest hospitality.

The so-called primitive peoples possess a spiritual culture and a delicacy of thought and feeling which we have always underestimated, particularly during the last century.

"Once upon a time I thought I knew the meaning of the word savage. Since then I have dwelt among people who dress in skins, live mainly on raw meat and are as alien to and untouched by the European world as can possibly be conceived. The term 'savage' has now lost its validity for me." These words were written by Vilhjalmur Stefansson in 1925, after years spent among the Eskimos. The Eskimo's domain stretches for some six thousand miles from the Aleutians and Alaska in the west to Greenland in the east. Indeed, a small number of Eskimos still live on the easternmost tip of Asia, on Capes Deshnev, Chukhotsk and Ulakpen. The total of the Eskimo population throughout the world today is roughly 43,000.

In the year 982 the Icelandic chieftain Eric the Red founded the first Scandinavian settlement on the coast of southwest Greenland. A daring seaman of Norwegian descent, Eric also dispatched the first expedition to North America. His Norsemen somewhat scathingly christened the Eskimos "Skraellinger" or weaklings. Torfinn Karlsefne encountered a few Eskimos on his voyage to America in 1003–1006. Some two hundred years later, in about 1200, the Eskimos began to attack the Scandinavian settlements in Greenland, and the Norsemen, who had by that time lost touch with the land of their origin, were eventually defeated by the "weaklings." They may have been either entirely exterminated or, as Fridtj of Nansen believed, assimilated by the Eskimos. It was not until the fifteenth century, during attempts to find a northwest passage, that the Eskimos were, so to speak, rediscovered. When Martin Frobisher landed on the Greenland coast in 1578 he found no Viking descendants left, only Eskimos. All traces of the erstwhile pioneers had been wiped out.

1933 saw the death of a man to whom we owe most of our knowledge of the oldest Eskimos. Knud Rasmussen was born in Jakobshaven, Greenland, in 1879. His father was a missionary and his mother the child of a Danish father and an Eskimo mother. Rasmussen was eternally proud of his Eskimo blood and had learned the Eskimo dialect of his homeland before he could speak a word of Danish. The Greenland Eskimos' name for Jakobshaven is Ilulissat, "the icebergs," and there Rasmussen and his brother played exclusively with Eskimo children from an early age. In 1910 Rasmussen collaborated with Peter Freuchen in founding the Arctic station at Thule in Greenland, the northernmost settlement in the world. In the course of his seven "Thule Expeditions" he visited nearly all the surviving Eskimo tribes, discovering in the process that his native Greenland dialect was comprehensible by Eskimos throughout the immense area they inhabited. He lived with the Eskimos like a brother, and a spirit of understanding for this great, lonely world and its people colors every line of his fascinating reports. In his *Report of the 5th Thule Expedition* (Vol. 9, *Intellectual Culture of the Copper Eskimos*, p. 120) he writes:

> It is not much that Netsit and I have to say to each other; there is nothing to encourage communicativeness, and so evening arrives on the first day out, and we find a convenient snowdrift where we can build a house for the night before we really get to know one another. I have preserved a few cigarettes for consumption on special occasions, and in the evening after our caribou-meat stew and a welcome cup of coffee, I feel that the time has arrived for luxurious excess, so I light a cigarette and give one to Netsit. To my great surprise he does not light it, but wraps it up in a rag. I do not know that anyone else but just we two, after about ten hours' struggling forward through the cold wind, would think our snow hut warm; but to us the effect of the little blubber lamp with its golden light is that it spreads such warmth around us that we really feel quite comfortable, and give way to an inner feeling that we ought to get something out of our evening. We boil an extra cup of coffee, and I prompt Netsit to tell a tale or two. To carry our luxurious enjoyment to the utmost, we have crawled into our sleeping bags, after having sealed the doorway of the hut and buried the snow blocks entirely under a thick layer of loose snow.

Rasmussen spent a lifetime listening to the Eskimos' myths and folk tales and committed them carefully to paper. Many of the ancient stories, though strangely beautiful, were rather bizarre and had no point in the Western sense. Rasmussen once asked Netsit, who was his favorite storyteller: "Now what is the point of that story? I think it has such a queer ending." Replied Netsit: "It is not always that we want a point in our stories, if only they are amusing. It is only the white men that want a reason and an explanation of everything; and so our old men say that we should treat white men as children who always want their own way. If not, they become angry and scold" (*op. cit.*, p. 124).

Rasmussen wrote of Sila, the supreme being of the Reindeer or Central Eskimos. He heard references made to this god everywhere, even on the Island of Nunivak in the Bering Straits, in the extreme west of the Eskimo world. When he asked an Eskimo shaman called Najagneq whether he believed in any one of the powers of whom he spoke, Najagneq replied: "Yes, I believe in a force which we call Sila and which is not to be explained in simple terms, a powerful spirit, the sustainer of the Universe, the weather—indeed, of the whole of earthly life, so vast that his speech to men is not couched in ordinary words but in storms, falls of snow, showers of rain, tempestuous seas and all the forces of which men stand in awe. But he has yet another way of manifesting himself, in sunshine, calm seas or little, innocently playing children who understand nothing. . . . In good times Sila has nought to communicate to mankind. He vanishes into his infinite Nothingness and remains there as long as men do not abuse life and respect their daily bread. No one has ever seen Sila. His abode is so mysterious that it is at once near us and infinitely far away."

Diamond Jenness, author of *The People of the Twilight*, established that the Copper Eskimos also believe in Sila, "The Being who dwells in the sky and makes the sun go down," and Rasmussen again heard of Sila from the Iglulik Eskimos during his Fifth Thule Expedition, this time described as "a great, dangerous and divine spirit who lives somewhere up in the air, out there in the Universe between sky and sea" (*op. cit.*, p. 71).

William Thalbitzer, another distinguished authority on the Eskimos, observed in 1928 that Sila's name reflected an age-old conception of life which had maintained a particularly strong hold on the Caribou Eskimos. Sila, they held, embodied the wide-open spaces, the air, the weather, the world and, apart from these, intelligence and sagacity. Rasmussen established that the Eskimos of King William's Land never ate the marrowbones or brain of reindeer. After stripping them of meat, they used to sink the heads of slaughtered reindeer in a river. These are genuine primitial sacrifices of the sort found in many ancient Arctic cultures, sacrifices which comprise the most prized part of an animal, the brains in its skull and the marrow in its bones.

The explorer Nils A. E. Nordenskjöld records something of even greater interest. In the eastern extremity of Northeast Asia, on the isthmus which links the mainland with Irkaipi, he came upon some ruined Eskimo earth huts which had once been inhabited by a tribe of Eskimos called the Onkilons who were ousted by the Chukchees in about 1750 and forced to flee to distant islands in the Arctic Ocean. The Onkilons' former dwellings, which were constructed of driftwood and whalebone and had at one time been faced with earth, were connected by long tunnels. Nordenskjöld writes in *The Voyage of the Vega Around Asia* (1881):

> At several points on the mountainside we found large collections of bears' skulls, most of them overgrown with moss. They were either lying in a circle facing inwards or compositely arranged with reindeer and walrus skulls and upright reindeer antlers. Near the reindeer antlers lay the skull of an occasional elk or other species of deer, also complete with antlers. Numerous seal skulls were also in evidence, although other bones belonging to that animal were entirely lacking. No human fossils were found in the vicinity of these collections of bones, which the natives [Chukchees] alleged to date from the Onkilons' time, so it can probably be assumed that these were the sites of early sacrifices.

So many distinguished field researchers have given credible accounts of the preservation of the skulls and bones of game animals as a form of sacrifice to the supreme being that it is difficult to understand how an eminent ethnologist like Ivar Paulson can disregard or even dispute the fact. It is undeniable that the Eskimos conceive of an immense number of good and evil spirits, but there is more to their religion than this. J. W. Bilby, author of *Nanook of the North*, says in his *Among Unknown Eskimos* that it consists in a "belief in one Supreme Spirit, of whom no fear is felt because he has no evil intention towards man. Man was made, indeed, by the Great Supreme Spirit."

The home of the peoples who sacrificed or still sacrifice skulls and marrowbones extends far up the northern coasts of Europe, Asia and America. These are isolated parts of the world where ancient customs and age-old religions were mostly likely to survive, boreal regions which were least accessible to the influence of later eras. It is important to recognize, as Gahs, the American ethnologist A. J. Hallowell and the Danish prehistorian G. Hatt were the first to do, that while skull and marrowbone sacrifice spread to the Arctic coasts of the extreme north it survived in its purest form some distance from the Bering Straits; that is to say, some distance from the bridge between Asia and America.

That area is the home of something quite different, the bear cult or bear ceremony which we shall describe separately in another chapter. There is, therefore, an older Arctic culture which sacrifices skulls and marrowbones to the supreme being and a younger, subarctic culture which performs bear ceremonies. It is undeniable that the reindeer peoples' custom of sacrificing to their supreme deity originated in very ancient times.

Why should so infinite a conception of God have survived in the Arctic cultural zone, away from the Bering Straits? With his habitual respect for the unfathomable, Pater Wilhelm Schmidt has admitted his inability to suggest a cause. Nature may harbor a deeper reason for this enigma, but the days of sacrifice, of a knowledge of the supreme god and of the great truths which we call miracles are not yet gone. "Miracles happen daily on the coasts of the Arctic Ocean," wrote the Arctic explorer Stefansson. "The Eskimos are men like any others, with this difference, that the civil virtues are more highly developed among them than among us Europeans. Their hard struggle for existence has educated them in peaceful coexistence."

Earlier ethnologists' fundamental error in failing to recognize the intellectual and religious attainments of so-called primitive peoples coupled with an insufficient correlation of ethnological and prehistorical information has led us to underestimate the intellectual life of Paleolithic man. Only when we understand that, despite their hardships and their everlasting struggle for self-preservation, the boreal races have always cherished thoughts of something higher; only when we know of their reindeer and bear sacrifices to the supreme god; only then can we gain a true picture of life in Paleolithic times.

CHAPTER 19

GOD AND WORSHIP SEVENTY THOUSAND YEARS AGO

Commenting on the Drachenloch in 1941, P. W. Schmidt called it not only the most extensive but also the richest Lower Paleolithic cult site because these early men had expressed their worship of and thanks to the supreme creative being for the bestowal of food by making entirely individual, primitial offerings of game.... It was not, therefore, a question of worshiping the bear itself but of using sacrifice to worship and secure the favor of an abstract deity.
　　　　　　　　　HEINZ BÄCHLER, *Urgeschichte der Schweiz,* p. 438

It can be said that the Drachenloch supplies the first evidence in man of an already awakened higher spiritual life which belongs in the realm of spiritual culture.
　　　　　　　　　EMIL BÄCHLER, *Das Drachenloch,* p. 110

A STRANGE creature walked the earth in about 70,000 or 80,000 B.C. Short, but with a fairly large skull, he had a receding forehead and jutting, protective brows. Although the lower part of his face was prominent, his chin almost nonexistent and his orbital cavities extremely large, his features were far from animal in cast. He was clumsily built, and it is probable that, although he was extremely well muscled, he seldom exceeded five feet four inches in height. The first trace of this peculiar being was a skull which came to light in 1848 during chance diggings in Forbes Quarry, north of the Rock of Gibraltar. In 1856, workmen excavating a quarry came upon some obviously human remains in the Feldhofer cave at Neanderthal between Elberfeld and Düsseldorf in Germany. These remains, which were passed on to Dr. Johann C. Fuhlrott, German anthropologist, comprised the vault of a skull, two femurs, a shoulder bone, a radial bone and other fragments. The mysterious creature was thenceforward known as Homo neanderthalensis. Gordon Childe, the English anthropologist, archaeologist, author of *What Happened in History,* among other books, suggested that apart from carrying his head low Neanderthal man also walked with a shuffling gait, but this is not accepted today. Childe's view was probably based on an old and erroneous reconstruction, for Neanderthal man's hunting habits presuppose a high degree of mobility.

Neanderthal man had a cranial capacity of between 1,200 and 1,600 cubic centimeters. Not too much reliance should be placed on conclusions based on the volume of a single skull, of course, for skulls vary in size from man to man, and several are needed before one can obtain an idea of average capacity. Fortunately, a sufficiently large number of Neanderthal skeletons have been unearthed, e.g. in Germany, Moravia, France, Belgium, Spain, Italy, the Crimea, Palestine, Uzbekistan and even in Africa (in Rhodesia), and it was early recognized that several different Neanderthalian races must have existed. The human remains found at Krapina in Croatia, for instance, vary quite considerably from the "classical" Neanderthal type, both in cranial index and formation of the lower jaw.

A great deal is now known about Neanderthal man, his anatomy, his mode of existence and his implements. The fossils of Peking man's contemporaries, the Pithecanthropus erectus of Java or Heidelberg man of Germany, have largely been ground to dust in the course of hundreds of thousands of years by the action of rivers, landslides and geological subsidence. But there is still another reason why Neanderthal remains are fairly plentiful. As man began to visit caves more often, so his skeleton was more likely to survive the passage of time. Having about a hundred complete or fragmentary Neanderthal skeletons in our possession, we are in a position to assess his average cranial capacity as 1,400 cubic centimeters. Taking into account all the races of men in existence today—non-European included—the modern average is 1,200 cubic centimeters for women and 1,300 for men. Neanderthal man therefore had a larger cranial capacity than the normal man of today.

Professor Franz Weidenreich, the famed German anthropologist, concludes from this that the human brain grew to the size of Neanderthal man's and then gradually decreased again. Of course, the volume of a man's brain has no direct bearing on his intellectual ability. (Anatole France and the celebrated French statesman Gambetta had cranial capacities of only 1,100 cubic centimeters, whereas those of Jonathan Swift, Lord Byron and Turgenev are alleged to have been far above average.) It can, however, be said that the human brain has not exhibited any increase in mass since the time of Neanderthal man, or about 100,000 years ago. More important than its volume is a brain's shape, and in this respect Neanderthal man's brain was considerably flatter than that of modern man.

Despite all we know about him, Neanderthal man remains an enigma because, although he inhabited vast areas of the world and evolved a remarkable culture of his own, he ultimately disappeared entirely. According to radiocarbon (C 14) dating, Neanderthal man still lived in North Africa in 30,000 B.C. and may have survived even longer in Ethiopia. Although he was a nomadic hunter like his forefathers, he had a preference for living in caves. He survived immense changes, but was probably driven to seek shelter in caves more and more as climatic conditions deteriorated under the onset of the last glacial period 120,000 years ago. Evidently, nature proved more than a match for him, because he failed to survive the height of the last Ice Age.

Neanderthal man's tool industry is known as the Mousterian, from the site of its discovery in the Dordogne area of France. He was the sole exponent of this culture and the inventor and preserver of the way of life which we have christened after the cave of Le Moustier in the valley of the Vezère, where the French paleontologist Édouard Lartet and the English prehistorian Henry Christy undertook excavations from 1863 onward. The "warm" Mousterian fell in the intermediate period which preceded the fourth and last Ice Age, while the "cold" Mousterian extended into its first half, so Neanderthal man must have waged a determined struggle for self-preservation in conditions of ever-increasing cold.

So remarkable are the evidences of his existence that the ziggurats of Mesopotamia, the pyramidal tombs of Egypt, the temples of Greece and the circuses of Rome pale into insignificance. Magnificent tokens of high culture though these are, they date—in the broadest sense—from our own era. For what are six or seven thousand years

compared with the almost inconceivably distant heyday of Neanderthal man, seventy or eighty thousand years ago?

Neanderthal man was familiar with the practice of burial. He dug
pits and laid his dead to rest in a prescribed manner. It has now been
definitely established that such cavities are of artificial origin and
that they were sealed with large bones or boulders. Graves of this
type have been found at Le Moustier, La Chapelle-aux-Saints, La
Ferrassie, Carmel in Palestine and Teshik-Tash in Uzbekistan.

In 1908, an artificial pit was discovered sunk into the original floor
of the cave of La Chapelle-aux-Saints. Buried beneath archaeological
strata of dust and earth and hidden by an accumulation of rubble
and fallen fragments of rock, it turned out to be a place of human
burial. It contained only the skull of an old man, but this skull proved
to be the finest specimen of the Neanderthal group yet discovered.
The depression which had served the old man as a last resting place
was about four feet six inches long, forty inches wide and a foot
deep. This grave testified to the care which Neanderthal man already
lavished on his dead, but it was a token of something more. Would
the dead have been accorded so secure, indestructible and durable
a grave had there not existed a firm conviction that there was a life
after death? Certainly the idea that death may not be the end of all
things seems to have been in evidence here. Man's conviction that
there is a life after death expresses itself in the stones which he
erected to protect his dead from the pressure of the surrounding earth
seventy or eighty thousand years ago. La Ferrassie in the Dordogne
even contained a small cemetery where one of the large stones used
to seal a grave exhibited some small artificial recesses which had
probably held food intended to sustain the dead man in the next
world. On the other hand, one of the corpses had simply been laid
out on the ground and—if Menghin's supposition is correct—covered
with branches and earth.

One noteworthy feature is that these graves were almost invariably
sited in a west-east direction like our own churches, so that a dead
man's head usually pointed westward and his gaze was directed
toward the rising sun, source of the light which would awaken him
to new life. Even when the corpse lay on its side with knees drawn

up, it was still placed so that its eyes would catch the awakening light.

Man of the Mousterian period already had a genuine death cult, and his belief in an afterlife or resurrection shines with almost disconcerting clarity out of the endless twilight of primeval times. He sent his dead into the next world equipped with flint tools and supplies of food. He also scattered their bodies with ocher, whose reddish color—as we learn from primitive peoples still alive today—assured the departed of breath, warmth and life. Blood is red and so is the fireball of the sun when it seems to leap the horizons of the boundless seas and plains. Not only had Neanderthal man mastered the art of body painting but he probably believed in a single all-powerful god.

Once upon a time vital and remote, great and all-embracing, this single god seems to have degenerated in the course of hundreds of thousands of years, degenerated because man's technical progress has made him increasingly aware of the passage of time, and, as his sense of time has developed, so his memory has deteriorated. Ever since man learned to record his thoughts in writing, the memory of his hundreds of thousands of years' apprenticeship to life has been fading. Memory has been replaced by the library and the electronic brain, and with the waning of memory has come a paling and blurring of the wealth of his experience, a diminishing awareness of all that the biped with the strangely well-developed brain once underwent. As he learned to forget the primeval forces which repose in the eternal forests, wandering glaciers, mighty mountains, river and oceans, so man must have lost his god. But certainly in the beginning he believed there was *one* creator, not a polytheistic menagerie.

Neanderthal man dwelled not only in wide plains but in mountainous areas and even on islands. The Stone-Age discoveries made at Mont-Dol near Saint-Malo in Brittany are, as the French prehistorian A. Vayson de Pradenne has pointed out, typical of the Mousterian—that is to say, of the Neanderthalian—culture. Today, Mont-Dol is a hill set in a plain, but when it was inhabited by Neanderthal man, it was an island separated from the coast by nearly two miles of sea. It is certain that contemporary man had no boats, but he must have been able to wade across to the mainland from time to time, for the island could scarcely have provided an adequate supply of food. The reason for Neanderthal man's sojourn on this sea-girt islet remains shrouded in mystery.

In the rocky fastnesses of the Alps, we once more pick up the trail of Neanderthal man. High in the majestic mountainscape of Switzerland, in the cantons of Saint Gallen and Appenzell, are three caves which have yielded some amazing discoveries: the Wildkirchli, the Wildenmannlisloch and the Drachenloch. The Drachenloch cave extends into the rock for 230 feet and comprises six chanmbers. Near the entrance the cave walls are clothed with cave mosses and lichen, a beautiful glowing green which reaches far into the fading twilight of the vaulted interior, where the light of day scarcely penetrates. Fighting a desperate battle for survival, plants suck greedily at the faint rays of light which help them to manufacture the chlorophyll that gives them color.

Though unknown to the world at large, the Drachenloch has provided the key to innumerable secrets. Its discoverer, Emil Bächler, spent a lifetime fighting for scientific recognition of his cave. His realization that, seventy or eighty thousand years ago, man had been doing sacrifice there, opened a chink in the thick and all but impenetrable curtain which had hitherto denied us a glimpse into the spiritual life of Stone-Age man. Also in the Drachenloch were found a number of stone kists or chests. When the side wall of one large kist was removed, seven well-preserved bear skulls were found in the cavity, carefully piled on top of one another with their muzzles pointing toward the cave's exit.

The stone kists found in the Drachenloch are probably the earliest man-made constructions in the world. All three caves yielded large numbers of bear skulls, some of them scattered about but others carefully arranged in piles. Portions of cave bears' skeletons were also found neatly laid out in layers, sometimes side by side and sometimes superimposed. Thirty broken fibulas were found stored on top of a large slab of rock, their jointed ends all facing one way and their broken ends the other. In another place, a bear's skull was found ringed by small slabs of stone, each about the size of a man's hand, which followed the outline of the skull precisely. In the Drachenloch, small stone walls had been erected about eighteen inches from the wall of the cave itself. Here, too, fragments of cave bears' skeletons were discovered together with complete or partial skulls, some of them pierced by holes. Several skulls lay in niche-like recesses in the rock walls or between fallen boulders.

Apart from this, many extremely diverse types of tool were found, most of them flake tools like flat shells or broad, roughly fashioned blades. I have examined these tools very closely for myself. Although they are generally quite small, many of them being only an inch long, they reveal the formative intervention of the human hand and eye. Many of them, too, are handsomely colored. There are flakes of jasper, brownish red like coagulated blood, other flakes of green quartzite, chips of green flint, and the cores from which the blades were originally detached. It is evident that the stone blades were chipped by means of a hard quartzite hammer. Their cutting edges are crude and irregular, and almost all the blades show signs of heavy wear. The inhabitants of these caves did not worry about the aesthetic appearance of their tools, probably because they were birds of passage and only used such raw material as was available, whatever its inadequacies, in order to manufacture enough tools for their immediate requirements. Moreover, they apparently only needed simple tools, probably because they possessed other implements with which they were more familiar and which seemed more appropriate to their purposes.

These were the bones of the cave bear. Almost all the unbroken cave-bear skulls found lacked a lower jaw, and this lower jaw was used as a percussive implement, one of the canines being retained for splitting purposes. Hip-joint sockets were used for scraping hides, as one can deduce from the pronounced signs of wear apparent on their edges. It is clear that tanning was practiced here, and we thus know that men were wearing skin garments about eighty thousand years ago. Weigh one of these hip-joint sockets in your hand, and you will at once realize that it could have served other purposes. For instance, its concave shape would have made it an excellent drinking vessel. I cannot personally imagine what other cups Neanderthal man would have drunk from, if not these natural bone vessels. The depths

The cave bear was Europe's largest Ice-Age predator. It penetrated the Alps and was hunted by the people of the Mousterian and Aurignacian periods. Neanderthal man used to sacrifice the skull and marrowbones of the cave bear to his god. The reasons for its eventual extinction are unknown.

of his cave dwellings were dark, and hip-joint sockets may also have solved the lighting problem. At any rate, they would have made extremely practical bowls for oil lamps. Every conceivable kind of tool was manufactured out of the bones of the cave bear—possibly arrowheads, too, though this is very dubious. In general, we can only wonder that men succeeded in hunting this dangerous creature at all. Perhaps they used only the corpses of animals which had died from natural causes—though the *haut-goût* would have deterred the average modern!

Many bones displayed cutting marks which Emil Bächer, discoverer of the cave, mentioned but did not illustrate in his published works. Being aware that some authorities have leapt to the conclusion that no signs of damage were evident on them at all, I consulted Bächler's son. Heinz Bächler wrote me the following reply:

I examined a large proportion of the material the year before last and found a number of cutting marks which are definitely distinguishable from more recent damage, principally on the articular protuberances of the occipital bone, the first two cervical vertebrae and on the shoulder and hip joints. By no means all the well-preserved bones bore these scratches and cuts, but, judging from my own practical tests conducted on fresh cow bones with original stone tools, this is understandable, for

Tiny splinters were removed from a stone blade in this manner to give it a sharp cutting edge. This process is termed "retouching."

considerable pressure must be exerted before one damages the tough and slippery periosteum, and with a little practice one can sever the muscles and sinews of a joint without scratching the bone at all.

It may also be conjectured that Neanderthal man purposely avoided damaging skeletons because he wanted to commit them to eternity intact.

The weapons of the contemporary hunter were very primitive. He may either have driven his quarry into the interior of a cave, held it at bay there and attempted to kill it with heavy wooden clubs, or ambushed it on a game path and hurled his spear from a vantage point such as a rock or tree. Some bears' skulls found in the Drachenloch exhibited half-healed fractures which suggest that man was not always successful in his dangerous pursuit.

In each of the three caves which have been mentioned, the Wildkirchli, Drachenloch and Wildenmannlisloch, the skeletal remains of some thousand bears were found. Bächler assumed that all the bones discovered in the Drachenloch and Wildenmannlisloch had been brought there by Stone-Age hunters, for bears do not appear to have used them voluntarily as places of refuge. On the other hand, Wildkirchli may occasionally have been used for hibernation, but it certainly was also frequented by human beings from time to time. No animal could have accumulated these hoards of hunting trophies, nor could they be a freak of nature. Only a deliberate act on the part of early man can account for them. One of the jawless skulls in the Drachenloch, for instance, posed an almost insoluble problem. Another bear's femur had been driven through its right cheekbone in such a way that it could only be removed by means of a fairly complicated maneuver. Only a human intelligence could have been responsible for this. Nature does not build rectangular chests out of flat slabs of stone, nor does she spirit seven bears' skulls into them.

No one would have guessed that traces of Neanderthal man would be found at such an altitude. Wildkirchli lies at a height of nearly 5,000 feet, Wildenmannlisloch in the Churfirsten is more than 5,300 feet up, and Drachenloch above Vättis in the Tamina Valley no less than 8,000.

How did Neanderthal man reach these altitudes, what induced him to brave the hardships and dangers involved in such an ascent, and why did he transport such large quantities of bears' bones into the solitude of the mountains? Why were fragments of cave bears' skulls piled so neatly on top of one another, and why were the outer edges of the bone cups so highly polished, as though they had been worn away by generation after generation of human hands? Were they Neanderthal man's drinking vessels? What was he looking for so far above the tree line, when he could only have visited these caves in spring or used them as a hunting base in summer?

In the Drachenloch, beneath the entrance leading from the first chamber into the second, Bächler came upon a layer of coal-black material containing ash and the remains of burnt wood. In the center of this hearth he found a quantity of small bones and stone fragments, some charred and others only scorched. The earth beneath the fireplace had been reduced to red, powdery dust. Examination of the carbonized remains revealed that Neanderthal man had used pinewood as kindling. Apart from this open hearth, a fire pit was discovered in the entrance leading from Cave II to Cave III. This was covered by a flat stone slab about eighteen inches square. Perhaps seventy thousand years old, the hearthstone's reverse side was stained with smoke, and the fire pit beneath it contained ash, the remains of charred wood, and burnt bones. Having explored different possibilities of making fire in the Drachenloch, Bächler established that smoke was carried away most effectively when fires were kindled beneath the entrances to the various chambers.

Close by the fire pit was the "bone altar" on which lay the cave bear's skull with the femur through the aperture in its cheekbone. Emil Bächler explicitly used the term "bone-altar," and it would appear that fire pit and place of sacrifice were in some way connected.

The Drachenloch cave is the most interesting and perhaps the most important cult site in the entire history of mankind, a place where, more than seventy thousand years ago, thank offerings were being made to the supreme creative being. They were thank offerings for the bestowal of game, but they may have had an even more important significance, for the Drachenloch cave contains the oldest stone structure of religious significance in the world; indeed, it is the earliest stone monument to the human past and the earliest visible expression of man's regard for an invisible god.

Some scientists are hard to convince, however. The Swiss paleontologist F. E. Koby, for instance, has questioned whether the bears' bones display any signs of human workmanship at all and disputes that the caves reveal any traces of Paleolithic man. He suggests that bears were considered too dangerous to hunt at the time and describes the dry-stone wall, upright stone slabs, bears' skulls and marrowbones in the Drachenloch as "fortuitous," attributing the signs of wear on the tools found there to the trampling of bears' feet.

Most of the objects found in the Drachenloch, Wildkirchli and Wildenmannlisloch caves are now in Saint Gallen's regional museum. I have devoted a great deal of time to these finds, have examined them closely, and cannot agree that Roby is correct. No one has yet disproved Bächler's dating of his finds, and it seems that the Drachenloch must have been inhabited by Neanderthal man during the last interglacial, that is to say, in the warm period which preceded the last Ice Age when temperatures may have approximated those of our own day. Certainly neither beast nor man could have existed at or even reached such an altitude during the height of the Ice Age. The primitive stone and bone tools found in the Drachenloch best lend themselves to classification in the Mousterian, i.e. in the Neanderthalian culture. The primitive substage of the Mousterian, the pre-Mousterian, represented by the Drachenloch finds discloses every aspect of Neanderthal man's tenacious struggle for self-preservation, yet it must have had its lighter moments, for the Wildenmannlisloch yielded thirty small, white, almost circular quartzite pebbles which were geologically alien to the cave and must have been brought there by Paleolithic man. We do not know what they were meant to be or what purpose they fulfilled, but it is probable that they were accumulated simply because of their aesthetically pleasing shape, possibly even as pieces for some form of game.

No human bones were found, although human fossils would have have survived quite as well as animals'. One explanation of this may be that man disliked living so close to his dead and was afraid of them. Fear of the dead was not uncommon at this period, as the bound corpses found in other parts of the world prove. Again, burial places have been identified in caves situated at lower altitudes. Perhaps this is an individual case in which the absence of human fossils can be attributed to man's unwillingness to turn his living quarters into a burial place, or to the fact that he never remained here for long and the probability of death during residence was thus correspondingly less.

All in all, the caves remain an unsolved mystery, as Bächler himself admitted. How, for instance, can we explain the discovery, in a carefully protected niche in one of the chambers of the Wildenmannlisloch, of a small figure resembling a female sculpture? Made out of the lower jaw of a cave bear, it may be either an artifact or a freak of nature. One thing is certain: the flattened planes of its "head" were rubbed smooth by some human agency; perhaps, as Emil Bächler suggests, because the bone was originally used as an instrument for smoothing animal skins. This may also be the reason why certain portions of the so-called "pseudo-Venus" appear to have been polished. Bächler is of the opinion that the figure came into being

Wildkirchli, Wildenmannlisloch and Drachenloch are three Swiss caves which have yielded the most interesting discoveries of cave bears' bones yet made. Traces of fire were found at all three sites. According to Heinz Bächler, the charcoal in the Drachenloch is the oldest legacy from Stone-Age man ever to be dated by the radiocarbon method, and goes back at least fifty thousand years. The cave bears' skulls and marrowbone sacrifices in the Drachenloch indicate that as early as seventy thousand years ago man believed in a single god. The Drachenloch also contained stone chests or kists which are the earliest man-made structures yet found.

accidentally, as a result of continual friction due to use, not as a deliberate attempt to reproduce the shape of a human head. I have examined the figure closely. The closed eyes, delicate mouth, small forehead, slim neck and back all convey an impression of careful workmanship. A second "Venus" discovered in the same hiding place has smooth patches but no recognizable head.

Even if the pseudo-Venus was not actually made by Stone-Age

man, the cave dweller must have noticed its resemblance to the figure of a girl. Why else would he have put it to one side and preserved it so carefully? The prehistorian Friedrich Behn, in his book *Vorgeschichte Europas*, asserts that the people of the Neanderthalian race were lacking in any form of artistic impulse. The celebrated Venus statuettes of the Stone Age belong to the Aurignacian, a far later period. The pseudo-Venus may, therefore, be unique in its period, the earliest portrayal of the human figure known to have been made, or at least recognized as such, by man. It is probably the most remarkable evidence of prehistoric activity or comprehension in the world. Between four and five inches tall, the Venus was found on October 21, 1926, and reposes today in the Heimatmuseum at Saint Gallen, a Paleolithic Sleeping Beauty waiting to rejoice the eye of the occasional visitor.

Evidences of Paleolithic bear sacrifices have also been found outside Switzerland—so far afield, in fact, that the idea of sacrifice appears to have been common to numerous Middle Paleolithic people and not merely the prerogative of a few individual magicians or priests. Traces of ritual burial or sacrifice were discovered in the Petershöhle near Velden (Central Franconia in Germany), in the Teufelshöhle near Pottenstein (French Switzerland), in the Kitzelberghöhle in the Bober-Katzbach Mountains, in Cabrerets (in the Department of Lot in France), in the Caverne des Furtins (Saône-et-Loire, France), and in alpine and subalpine cave sites in Yugoslavia. Cave-bear skulls, other bones and Mousterian tools were "found in such a peculiar position that they are quite irreconcilable with natural precedents."[1] In the Salzofenhöhle, more than six thousand feet up in the Totes Gebirge not far from Aussee in Austria, the paleontologist and paleobiologist Kurt Ehrenberg found three cave bears' skulls which had been accurately ringed with stones. In all three cases, charcoal remains were discovered beside or beneath the skulls. In the Petershöhle, bears' skulls had been carefully deposited in small holes and niches. In a cupboard-like recess in the rock wall, four feet above the floor of the cave, five skulls, two femurs and a humerus were

[1] S. Brodar, "Zur Frage der Höhlenbärenjagd und des Hölenbärenkults in den paläolithischen Fundstellen Jugoslawiens," *Quartär*, Bd. 9, 1957, pp. 147–159.

found, all belonging to cave bears. The skulls fell to pieces in the diggers' hands during removal. The man responsible for exploring the Petershöhle, K. Hörmann, declared: "These skeletal remains could not have got up there or in there by any natural means." It seems probable therefore that they were a conscious committal to eternity and a deliberate sacrifice, not a fortuitous act but a calculated gesture toward an exalted and timeless power.

A large quantity of bear fossils were found near Mixnitz in Styria, Austria, in a cave known as the Drachenhöhle. Man had taken refuge there from time to time and cave bears had also lived deep in the interior, though it is improbable that man and bear occupied the cave simultaneously.

Near a spring two hundred yards or so from the entrance to the cave, living quarters and a fireplace were identified, together with artificially arranged stones, bones displaying traces of fire and large numbers of utensils. The large eyeteeth of cave bears had been fashioned into tools, weapons and scrapers, the latter having been used principally to remove sinews from fat.

The discoveries made in this cave surpass one's wildest imaginings. The remains of no less than fifty thousand bears have been counted there, although the place was frequented by these animals for such an immense span of time that this works out at only a few bears per annum! Far in the depths of the cave are a number of very narrow passages formed by huge blocks of stone which had fallen from the walls and roof, and on the sides of these passages can be seen the marks of bears' paws, so distinct in places that the five furrows made by one set of claws can easily be counted. It is immediately apparent that the animals were in dire straits, probably because they had been trapped and were exerting every ounce of energy in a desperate attempt to escape.

Scratch marks of this type were identified at several points in the cave's interior, but always where the walls narrowed. Sometimes vertical and sometimes horizontal, they are visible evidence of a dramatic fight for freedom, escape and survival. Adolf Bachofen von Echt, Austrian paleontologist, surmised that snares had been laid in these defiles, a laborious task, considering that the everlasting

[63] The so-called "marriage of death," a double grave discovered in the Grotte des Enfants at Grimaldi. The two bodies had been buried on top of a disused hearth and covered with slabs of stone. The only explanation of the old woman's cramped attitude (*left*) is that she was tied up before rigor mortis set in. Both she and the youth on the right were buried at the same time, and it is possible that the people of the Aurignac culture provided dead men with wives who could serve their needs in the world hereafter.

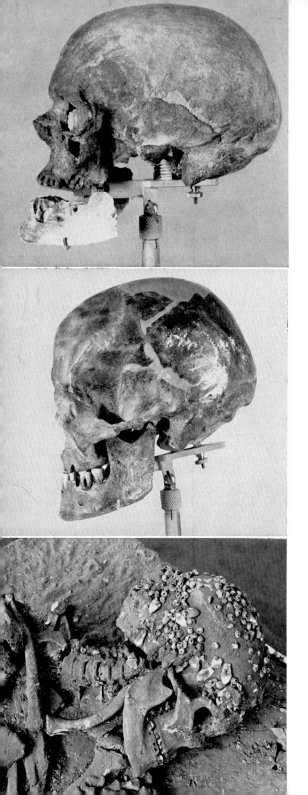

[64] This old man's skull was found by chance in the Cro-Magnon cave near the railway station of the small town of Les Eyzies, Dordogne, in 1868. It gave its name to the Cro-Magnon race which began to displace the Neanderthalians in about 60,000 B.C. The Cro-Magnids are members of the Homo sapiens group to which modern man belongs.

[65] Discovered at Chancelade near Perigueux in 1888, this skull has given its name to the Chancelade people who appeared in about 60,000 B.C., at the same time as the Cro-Magnon race. They too belonged to the Homo sapiens type.

[66] This Cro-Magnon skull from the Cavillon cave (Grimaldi) near Menton reveals that the people of the Aurignacian used to wear caps made of leather or skin. The trimming of varicolored shells is still lying in its original pattern on the dead man's skull.

[67] The earliest representation of the human figure so far discovered. It may have come into being either deliberately or accidentally, as a result of manual wear, but the cave dweller of 70,000 years ago certainly recognized its human characteristics, for he carefully stuck it into a fragment of cave bear's mandible. This mysterious little human effigy is known as the "pseudo-Venus," and was found in the Wildenmannlisloch cave on October 21, 1926. It is now on display in the Heimatmuseum, Saint Gallen.

[68] The famous *tête à la capuce* or hooded head of Brassempouy was found in 1894. It is made of ivory and stands only one and a half inches high.

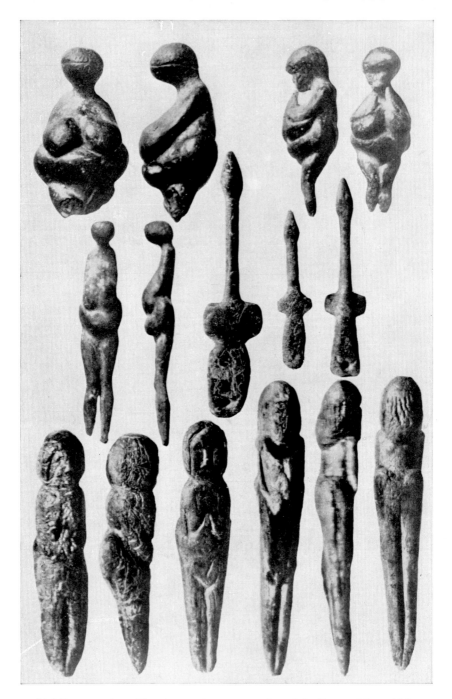

[69] Statuettes from Gagarino on the upper reaches of the Don and from Malta in Siberia. Only some of these small Venus figures are obese, but all are of ivory or bone and belong to the Aurignacian.

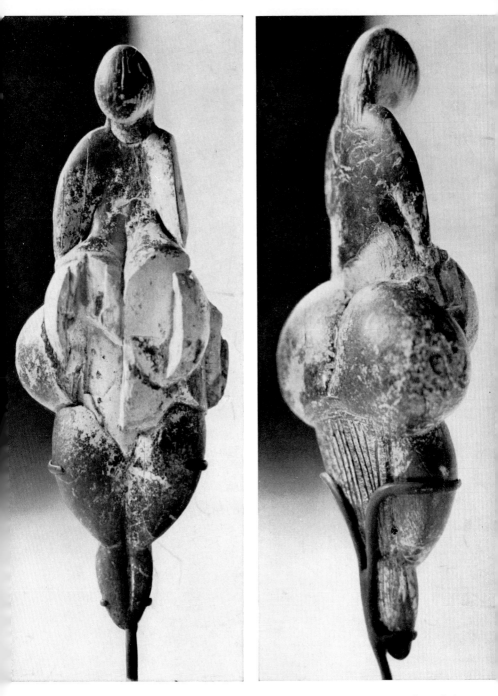

[70/71] The finest Upper Paleolithic statuette in our possession. Front and rear view of the Venus of Lespugue, found in the Grotte des Rideaux (Haute-Garonne) in 1922. It dates from the Upper Aurignacian.

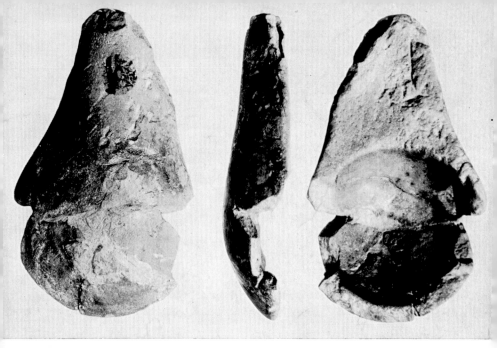

[72] Stone-Age man illuminated his cave with this lamp, which was fueled by animal fat. Found at Lespugue in the Grotte des Scilles. (Front, side and rear view.)

[73] Two white owls with their young. A Magdalenian drawing found in the Trois-Frères cave.

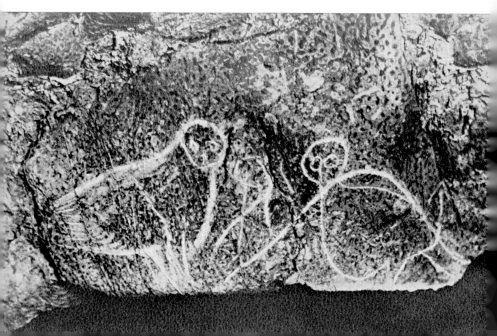

[74] The Gilyaks who inhabit the lower reaches of the Amur hold a river festival when the ice thaws after the long winter. This *tol-nir* or bird-shaped bowl is used exclusively on such occasions.

[75] *Lankh-chonsh-charsh* or wooden club used by the Gilyaks for killing seal.

gloom of the cave's interior could have been only sparingly illumined by oil lamps. When a bear was trapped, man would creep up and try to kill it with his primitive stone weapons. The snares were probably made out of bear's sinew, which meant that the animals fell prey to the unyielding strength of their own tough fibers.

Man must have laid his traps before a bear entered the cave to hibernate. Then, perhaps carrying a flaring pine torch in one hand, he slipped into the cave in the animal's wake. It must have been an exhausting and dangerous business, following the great beast as it retreated ever farther into the depths, clambering up steep walls of shelving rock until it reached the defile and was caught. Then came the animal's struggle to break loose, the hunter's wary approach, his darting attacks and withdrawals as he tried to deliver the *coup de grâce*. The only way to club a bear to death was to aim for the base of its snout, no easy matter with an animal of the cave bear's elemental strength. Healed fractures in some of the skulls found testify that the hunter occasionally missed his mark during these life-and-death encounters, allowing the bear to break away. One skull, dug up at Brno in Czechoslovakia, had a complete flint embedded in it, which indicates that man used his primitive weapons on the awesome predator at quite close quarters.

Many types of bear were found in the various layers in the Mixnitz cave, among them truly gigantic beasts with skulls two feet long. Skulls of other specimens varied in width from very broad to very narrow. The cave was occupied for a remarkable length of time, perhaps a hundred thousand years, which would explain the enormous quantities and wide variety of remains discovered there.

And in one fairly secluded side passage were found seventeen bears' skulls, all placed carefully in an upright position. We are again reminded of the Swiss and Franconian cave sacrifices.

All sacrifice presupposes a deity. If I had not been told repeatedly by the Tungus of the North Manchurian taiga that the time-honored practice of offering the skull and marrowbones of their quarry was a sacrifice to the supreme god, I should be doubtful about this, but the sacrifices of the Siberian peoples in the Arctic cultural zone are definitely directed toward an invisible being who is the sky and light and universe—in a word, God. Thus I believe Stone-Age man's mysterious doings in the caves of Saint Gallen, Franconia and Styria were directed toward God and His worship alone. And I further believe that like the peoples of Siberia, the men who killed cave bears and sacrificed the choicest parts of their carcasses believed in a supreme being. "This," to quote a remark made about the Drachenloch by the eminent prehistorian mentioned before, P. Wilhelm Schmidt, is as archaeologically certain as anything of the kind can be."

The people who lived nearly a hundred thousand years ago looked upon one god as the creator and sustainer of the world. Everything seems to indicate, as Genesis records and Saint Paul claims in his Epistle to the Romans (i, 20), that man's knowledge of God dates from the Creation itself.

CHAPTER 20

CRO-MAGNON MAN

He almost certainly compensated for his inability to read and write by having a better memory. A recollection of perhaps hundreds of thousands of years lay open to him, vast spans of time which are now lost to our view.

ACCORDING to H. Obermaier, famous German professor of prehistory (1877–1946), the Upper Paleolithic period lasted from 30,000 to 10,000 B.C. At the beginning of that epoch Europe must have witnessed a frightful tragedy: the extinction of the Neanderthalian race. In endless, thawing plains, amid huge glacial masses left behind by turbid waters, near emergent seas and rivers and in still ice-bound mountains and highlands, Neanderthal man died a mysterious death. His caves lay abandoned, his hunting cries died away and his culture perished. But it was not a sudden process. Neanderthalians were still living in Ethiopia in about 30,000 B.C. and perhaps even later.

As early as 60,000 B.C., however, other men had appeared on the scene. They arrived quickly and in large numbers. Swarming across the whole of Central Europe, Italy, Spain and the Near East, they laid claim to a vast expanse of territory. The fact that they succeeded the Neanderthalians so ubiquitously and so thoroughly is in itself an argument against their having evolved from the older race. The first discoverable traces of these new people are at Jabrud on the eastern slopes of the Anti-Lebanon mountains in Syria and on Mount Carmel in Palestine.

The Cro-Magnids, as the newcomers are called, were taller than the Neanderthalians, their adult males attaining a height of between five feet seven and five feet eleven. They had strongly developed muscles and short, broad features. The term "Cro-Magnon man" comes from the cave of the same name near the railway station at Les Eyzies, a small township in the Dordogne of France. It was there that Olaine Laganne and Louis Lartet unearthed five skeletons, one belonging to an old man, two to adult men and the remaining two to a woman and a child. The elderly man must have been nearly five feet ten. The woman had been wounded in the temple, possibly by a stone weapon which was found lying close by. Hundreds of sea-snail shells lay near the bodies, all drilled for stringing as a form of jewelry. These shells hailed from the Atlantic coast and must have been imported by the Cro-Magnids, either as spoils acquired on hunting forays or by barter.

The remains of typical Cro-Magnids were also found in the caves at Baoussé-Roussé in the Menton district. The so-called Grotte des Enfants in the Grimaldi cave near Baoussé-Roussé is of particular interest because it contained the skeleton of an old woman, arranged in a squatting position, and just behind her that of a youth with his knees slightly drawn up. Both bodies lay on their right side and had been buried in a single grave, so close together that the youth was embracing the old woman from behind. The fact that all their bones were found in strict anatomical order suggests inescapably that they had been buried at the same time.

The Indologist O. Schrader christened burials of this type *Totenhochzeiten* or "marriages of the dead," but it is doubtful whether Otto Tschumi's use of the expression in this case is correct because the woman was much older than the man. There is, however, another explanation. It may have been the custom to put a woman into a dead man's grave to ensure that he was well cared for in the next world. The woman may even have been given to him in marriage posthumously, so that she could accompany him on his journey into death. It is also possible that the woman was sacrificed, for she appears to have been tied up before rigor mortis set in. Another extremely interesting point is that the dead couple were lying on top of a fireplace. Like the bears' skulls in the Drachenloch cave, this is yet another reminder of the age-old connection between fire and mortality, living flame and the cold rigidity of death. The fire pit was scattered with ocherous earth, the red pigment which was supposed to sustain life in the world hereafter. The custom of sprinkling ocher, which we have already met in the case of Neanderthalian burials, was always associated with the idea of afterlife and is not, as the Soviet scientist M. S. Pliseki suggests, to be compared with the profane use of ocher by the Tasmanians, who mixed it with fat and rubbed it into their bodies as a protection against cold.

Each of the bodies mentioned above had been adorned with necklaces and bracelets of pierced snail shells, mussel shells and deer's teeth. The young man was provided with some flint blades, and the snail shells found on his skull indicate that he was wearing a net, cap or headband of some sort. Also by his head was a bone dagger, possibly placed there for his protection in the next world just as the warriors and tyrants of old used to put a sword beneath their pillow before going to sleep in order to defend themselves in an emergency. In all, sixteen skeletons were found in the Grimaldi cave. Some scholars claim to have identified Negroid skulls among them belonging to a race older than that of the Cro-Magnids, but it is probably that these are merely varieties of the Cro-Magnon type.

Chancelade man, too, has long been regarded as representative of a separate race. He was shorter than the Cro-Magnon people, attaining a height of only five feet three to five inches, but his cranial capacity was 1,700 cubic centimeters, or more than that of the average modern European (1,350–1,500). His body has also been sprinkled with ocher, yet another illustration of the importance which the people of the Upper Paleolithic period attached to the custom of coating their dead with red earth and the conscientious care with which they carried out a procedure designed to ensure the continuance of life after death. It is interesting to note that as early as 1766–1788 the explorer Jonathan Carver had discovered the connection between red pigment and burial while visiting an Indian tribe in what is now the state of Iowa, and it was Carver's research which inspired these lines in Schiller's *Nadowessisches Klagenlied: "Farben auch, den Leib zu malen, steckt ihm in die Hand, dass er rötlich möge strahlen in der Seelen Land."* ("Put ye colors in his hand, too, to paint his body so that he may shine redly in the Land of Souls.")

Chancelade man's knees were tightly drawn up in a manner which indicated that he had been bound, not for execution but probably soon after death had taken place, to compel him to rest in peace and prevent him from avenging himself on the living.

Many scholars, among them Gervais, Boule, Testut and Hervé,

have compared Chancelade man with the modern Eskimo of Labrador and Greenland, and have established the existence of great similarities between them. H. V. Vallois rejects these arguments, but it is nonetheless possible that Chancelade man and Eskimos are descended from a common Asiatic stock. Certain comparisons can be drawn between the Cro-Magnids, the Ainus and the skeletons found in the Upper Cave at Chou-k'ou-tien near Peking. Weidenreich does no more than state that the Paleolithic population of western France—Cro-Magnon man, Chancelade man, who was dug up only a few miles away, and the Grimaldi people—all exhibit an already substantial variation in type.

Another Cro-Magnid skeleton was found buried at Les Hoteaux in the French Department of Aisne, also in a hearth grave and also, it is interesting to note, covered with a layer of ocher. One illustration of how difficult it is to differentiate between the various Cro-Magnon people or compare them with modern races is provided by the skeleton found by O. Hauser, a Swiss dealer in antiquities who undertook several excavations, in the rock shelter roof of Combe Capelle (Perigord, France) in 1909. Mochi regarded this skeleton, which belongs to the Aurignacian, as "Ethiopid," whereas Weinert compared it with the Eskimo and Von Sergi christened it "Mediterranoid." This serves to show how extraordinarily difficult it is to classify a find this old in terms of the modern human race. The Combe Capelle man had been buried in a squatting position. In the grave with him were found a necklace composed of *littorina* and *nassa* snails, flint tools and the foot bone of a fossil pig, the latter probably intended as sustenance in the world hereafter.

Some 180 whole or fragmentary skeletons belonging to Cro-Magnon man have so far been found. Generally speaking, the Cro-Magnid's cranial capacity was well developed and compares favorably with that of modern Europids. The brain itself was just about as extensive, and Vallois considers that the men of the Upper Paleolithic period were not inferior to modern men in intellectual ability. The French paleontologist Georges Bataille, too, asserts that Cro-Magnon was in no way inferior to modern man except, perhaps, in experience.

I cannot believe this, for experience was very probably the one field in which the Cro-Magnid surpassed us. He almost certainly compensated for his inability to read and write by having a better memory. A recollection of perhaps hundreds of thousands of years lay open to him, vast spans of time which are now lost to our view, whereas we possess only the experience gained during six thousand years of written history. What is more, we are only imperfectly conscious of our heritage. Human memory is stronger than written records and always was so until man substituted tablets and books for his recollective powers and thereby impaired them. It is even a moot point whether we are superior to Cro-Magnon man in technical experience, for the manufacture and use of stone, bone and wooden utensils presupposes an immensely ancient tradition and great manual dexterity which we are only too prone to underestimate. We and our contemporaries belong, scientifically speaking, to the Homo sapiens type. The men of the Cro-Magnon races were also representatives of that type. It is probable that this early Homo sapiens was a bitter foe of Neanderthal man and attacked him with all the weapons at his command, and it is also probable that his main advantage over the older type of man lay in the possession of superior means of destruction.

There is a possibility that the Cro-Magnids defeated the Neanderthalians in a series of wars and eventually annihilated them. Nevertheless, it seems inconceivable that the Neanderthalians vanished completely. However sanguinary the battles that took place, a few Neanderthalians should have escaped and survived, especially as their race was so widely dispersed throughout the world. Yet they appear to have died out, everywhere and entirely.

As for their conquerors or successors, their place of origin remains unidentified. Their culture emerged in Europe with such abundance and strength that it seems impossible to regard it as a development of the Neanderthalian or Mousterian culture. Modern authorities tend to think that the Cro-Magnon people migrated to Europe from an area east of the Urals and the Caspian Sea. Scarcely any traces of their culture have been found in these regions, but this may be because they have not yet been sufficiently explored. As always with such migrations, the newcomers seeped into Europe by several routes and in several different waves.

Some light may have been shed on the beginnings of the Cro-Magnon people and their place of origin by the discoveries made at Mount Carmel, where American and English archaeologists collaborated between 1931 and 1937. Among those participating were the American School of Prehistoric Research, the British School of Archaeology in Jerusalem and the Royal College of Surgeons.

A limestone formation twelve miles long and pierced by a number of caves, Carmel lies immediately to the south of Haifa. In two caves in the southern part of the mountain, just over two miles from the Mediterranean coast, human bones were unearthed. Beneath the rock shelter roof at the mouth of the Mugharet-es-Skhul cave, the fossils of ten human beings came to light—five men, two women and three children. In another cave, the Mugharet-et-Tabun, it was the skeletal remains of a thirty-year-old woman that particularly aroused the interest of the British anthropologist and archaeologist Theodore D. McGown and the anthropologist and explorer Sir Arthur Keith, who reported their findings in *The Stone Age of Mount Carmel*.

The Tabun people bear a resemblance to the Neanderthalians of Europe, while the Skhul types are closer to the Cro-Magnon race. If one regards the people of both caves as members of the same population—that is to say, if one classifies all the Carmel skeletons in a single group as McGown and Keith do—the result is a race which can be described as intermediate between the Neanderthalians and the Cro-Magnids. Each individual betrays a certain amalgamation of the physical attributes of both types, and McGown and Keith therefore regard the people of the Tabun and Skhul sites as members of a single race, not only because they lived in the same place at almost the same time but also because their cultures are very nearly identical and no sharp distinction can be drawn between their teeth. The two scholars unearthed some other extremely interesting facts. For instance, they identified an injury to the hipbone of a powerfully built Skhul man which proved the existence of a spearlike weapon of great penetrating power. Had this weapon been made of bone or stone, the broken tip would have lodged in the wound and so survived like the human bone in which it was embedded, but since all that remains is a splintered cavity McGown and Keith assume that the weapon must have been made of fire-hardened wood which has entirely decomposed during the intervening years. They made some other really remarkable discoveries. The Tabun and Skhul people did not suffer from caries, and very few of them lost any teeth at all during their lifetime. They also appear to have been free from rheumatism, although—or perhaps because—they spent the majority of their life in the open.

In short, the Near East was once inhabited by a man who may be regarded as a forerunner of the Cro-Magnids, and it is possible that he represents the outcome of crossbreeding between the Cro-Magnids and the Neanderthalians. McGown and Keith suggest that, long before the dawn of history, western Asia was the cradle of Europe and the point of departure for a number of races, cultures and languages. On this basis, the routes and connections between western Asia and Europe would seem to be very ancient, and the "Caucasians" who migrated westward into Europe may have exterminated the Neanderthalians just as, in our own era, the white inhabitants of Australia have ousted and destroyed the aboriginal races of the world's fifth continent.

The fact that no fossils of the Neanderthal or Cro-Magnid type have been yet found in the Western Hemisphere cannot be taken as conclusive proof that such remains may not be found in the future. If such a find should be made the new questions it would raise would surely surpass any solutions it might suggest.

CHAPTER 21

HANDPRINTS, STATUETTES, WANDS
AND RELIGIOUS ART

*The main point to establish and remember is that every culture
is traceable to simple initial forms and that cultural history as a
whole goes back to the Lower Paleolithic; that we are, in fact,
standing on the shoulders of primeval man, and that without his
achievements those of later generations and the present day are
inconceivable.*

GEORG KRAFT, *Der Urmensch
als Schöpfer*, p. 89

THE Cro-Magnon people possessed a culture which has been christened Aurignacian, after the site of its discovery in the cave at
Aurignac excavated by the archaeologist Édouard Lartet in 1860.
The Aurignacian is the first stage in the Upper Paleolithic period,
sometimes described as the Mammoth or, later, Reindeer Age, terms
which make up in vividness and impact what they lack in precision.

The men of the Aurignacian period had begun to hunt reindeer.
Their bone spear and arrow points were sometimes provided with
grooves designed to retain poison or allow blood to flow freely. We
can only wonder at the deliberation with which the hunter of the
day tried to ensure that no wounded animal survived. Harpoons
with single and double rows of barbs were used, not only for fishing
but also for hunting large game. Mammoths were either hunted with
spears, as they were in the Mousterian, or trapped in pits. Aurignacian
hunters also constructed and used gravity-operated traps which
crushed animals beneath weights, usually heavy trees. (Tree traps
are still employed by the Tungus and other peoples of the Siberian
Arctic.) It is nonetheless amazing that a massive beast like the mammoth could be felled by a gravity-operated trap. Yet a wall engraving
from Font-de-Gaume depicts a mammoth trapped in this way, and
a stone engraving found in the Johannisburg district of East Prussia
also portrays a mammoth and a gravity trap. The gravity trap depicted in the de los Cantos de la Visera cave resembles, as Kurt Lindner has observed in his book *Die Jagd der Vorzeit,* the tree traps of

the Blackfoot Indians of North America. The German ethnologist Julius Lips, who believes gravity traps originated in Asia, thinks that they traveled across Europe and Spain until they reached Africa, but did not reach northern Siberia until post-Miolithic times. Plausible though it is, this theory has not yet been proved. I personally believe that the trapping technique of northern Siberia is much older than Lips suggests.

The Cro-Magnids had abandoned coups de poing and hand points for long thin blades about three or four inches long, i.e. chips of flint whose edges had been retouched or skillfully trimmed. Their tools, which were generally finer and smaller than those of their predecessors, included keeled and conical scrapers, burins and gravette points. Especially characteristic of the Aurignacian are tools made of bone, ivory and reindeer horn, bone chisels, small hammers of bone or antler, polishers, awls and end scrapers, keeled and otherwise.

The Aurignacian also saw the beginnings of art. Very slowly, the first examples of portable art appeared, the first pieces of sculpture, the first reliefs, engravings and paintings on the cave walls of thirty thousand years ago. The origins of art are shrouded in mystery, but what could be more enthralling and fascinating than to plumb the depths of man's aesthetic sense and trace it back to its rudiments? No one who tries to do so can fail to recognize how deeply, innately and inextricably linked man is with this striving to mold and create.

Man has been possessed by a creative urge since very ancient times. Forever impelled to experiment and explore, it is as if he senses something within him which he must extract and examine so that, seeing it, he will know something of his own personality. And so he starts to create, to express his inmost and most personal thoughts in a free and untrammeled manner. This is where the claim that God created man in His own image finds its truest and most profound fulfillment, for God and man are both creators, one in nature and the other in art. Eons ago, inspired by a God-given restlessness and desire for self-expression, man reached tentatively for materials and began to mold them to his ideas.

The primitive artistic impulse is already recognizable in man-made objects dating from roughly 50,000 years ago. On the walls of numerous caves in Spain and France, among them those of Altamira, Gargas, Trois-Frères, Le Portel, Cabrerets and Font-de-Gaume, can be seen the imprint of human hands. Aurignacian man used to lay his hand against the surface of the rock and spray it with black or ocher, either by mouth or some other means unknown to us, thereby producing a jumble of negative impressions strangely reminiscent of an oath-taking ceremony. Positive imprints also exist. These were effected by spraying or daubing the palm of the hand with color and pressing it against a rock wall. The positive handprints in the cave of Baume-Latrone are more than 250 yards from its mouth. In all, thirteen sites displaying examples of this strange prehistoric activity have so far been identified, three of them in Spain and the rest in France.

Positive handprints are rare and always red, whereas negative handprints are normally black. Furthermore, positive prints are invariably incomplete or faded, which leads one to wonder whether they are older than the negative type and whether they found their way onto the walls intentionally in the first place. It is always possible that they were transferred accidentally while red dye was being used for some unknown purpose, perhaps by someone who had leaned his hand against the wall for support. We know that Aurignacian man sprinkled or painted his dead with red pigment, so he may have left handprints while engaged in this task. Needless to say, this is all guesswork. Many of the handprints found in the Gargas cave in the Hautes-Pyrénées show signs of mutilation. Fingers are missing in part or whole, probably not because their owners had doubled them up in some way but because they were genuinely maimed, probably as a result of close combat between man and beast. Yet another possible explanation is that Stone-Age man cut off a finger or sometimes a whole hand for magical purposes or as a form of sacrifice designed to ensure success in hunting. Perhaps, too, he saw in this self-punishment a means of averting sickness and death. At all events, it is highly probable that the mutilation was of an intentional nature because it is almost always the middle, fourth and little fingers which are involved; that is to say, the fingers which can most easily be dispensed with. Thumb and index finger are hardly ever missing, and the fact that, with a very few exceptions, these most important fingers remained intact immediately suggests the idea of sacrifice. Men gave up the fingers which they could best do without.

R. P. Verbrugge, who has recently produced an interesting work on the subject of handprints in prehistoric art ("La Main dans l'Art Préhistorique," *L'Ethnographie*, v. 51, 1957), believes that dancing, magic or religion were involved in this mysterious practice. Just as many races are firmly convinced that the strength reposing in an inanimate object can be tapped by the laying on of hands, so prehistoric man may have believed that an invigorating or curative power emanated from the walls of his caves and could pass into his body if he pressed his hands against them and left his prints behind. In the Far East the lion is a symbol of strength, and this strength is thought to repose principally in his paws. Hence, almost every Chinese who passed the bronze lion in front of the former Bank of Hong Kong in the Bond at Shanghai used to run a hand lightly over one of its forepaws, slowly wearing them away. Paleolithic handprints are older than cave paintings and date from the beginning of cave art, but, despite all the research which has been carried out, their meaning and purpose has never been satisfactorily explained.

Hand silhouettes dating from much later periods, from historical and even quite recent times, have been left on rock walls by races throughout the world, in South Africa, in Palestine and Mexico, in India and in the Cañon del Muerte in Arizona, by the Worora tribe in the caves at Port George IV in Australia and below the rock paintings on the small islands on the southern shores of the McCluer Gulf in New Guinea. There, so the legend runs, the "great ancestors" came sightless out of the east and groped their way along the rocks. Then, having regained their sight, they made their home there. These imprints seem, however, to hold no significance for the present inhabitants of New Guinea. They were always there, and their original meaning has been forgotten. Hand silhouettes dating from perhaps eight or ten thousand years ago have also been found in Patagonia.

The so-called Franco-Cantabrian handprints in the caves of southern France and northern Spain were not art, but they were something new. They were effigies, two-dimensional representations of a three-dimensional human hand, and may have opened the way to a realization that portrayals of nature were possible. Like a convocation of spirits, the number of positive and negative hand silhouettes grew, mute witnesses of man's yearning and desire to record his existence, his "I was here," on stone.

Perhaps the earliest form of drawing to have been identified so far as what has aptly been termed "macaroni," lines scratched clumsily into the walls of caves and running across them in serpentine parallels. It seems unlikely that these wavy lines, which many authorities regard as the beginnings of art and place in the early part of the Aurignacian, are merely aimless scribbles, for the heads, eyes, legs and tails which were added to them are a deliberate portrayal of life. Nobody has yet proved, incidentally, that this "macaroni" really is the earliest form of drawing, and its early dating is based on evolutionary reconstruction.

As we have already seen, cave bears left claw marks on cave walls. It is possible that man imitated these grooves by drawing parallel furrows in the clay-covered walls with his fingers. Be that as it may, cave painting proper did not appear until the Middle Aurignacian.

How did it start at all? Although his caves often ran for several hundred yards into the living rock, Stone-Age man almost always lived near their mouth, where the smoke from his fire would be most easily dispersed. He had been familiar with the lamp, a hollow stone containing blubber or fat, from time immemorial. Unhurriedly, being a creature with all the time in the world to spare, he began to examine the rock wall by the feeble light of his homemade lamp.

One day he saw something new, something enormous, something which held him spellbound. There, fashioned by nature from the vaulted rock, stood the figure of a mammoth, a horse, or a bison. Taking a stone burin, man traced its outlines. Then he called his companions. They could see it too, now, quite clearly. Their life, the life of the hunter, suddenly emerged in effigy from the stone walls—bison, horses, cave lions, all in profile. And with the tracing of silhouettes the first representational art came into being.

We can see examples of this in many caves, places where natural protuberances in the rock walls have been exploited in order to portray a body, a head or the flanks of an animal. Imagination being what it is, it was not long before man saw the makings of animated pictures in the rock; wild horses galloping, for instance, or reindeer fleeing from a pursuer. The walls in a cave's interior, the mysterious shadows cast by leaping flames which played over the recesses and convexities of the rock, the interplay of Promethean glow and natural stone—all these were magnificent teachers. From the very beginning, before silhouettes, reliefs and paintings had properly evolved, sculpture existed. Although deliberate sculpture is probably no older than two-dimensional representation, man had been fashioning tools from stone long before he ever started to draw and paint, and it was not a big step from tools to sculpture. That is why plastic art co-existed with two-dimensional art from the very first in the shape of small animals made of ivory, bone and stone, the ivory being supplied by mammoth tusk. Discoveries made at Vistonice in Moravia, Czechoslovakia, included a sculpture of a mammoth, animal and human figures modeled and baked in clay, a horse's head, a bear's head, a fox's head, a small figure of a bear and a large number of tools, all of the Aurignacian period. Extensive digging has been carried out there by Brno Museum under the direction of K. Absolon.

The so-called "bird hearth" in Württemberg, Germany, yielded sculptures of a hornless rhinoceros, a horse and a wildcat. Quite astonishing numbers of artifacts were unearthed at Prědmost, forty miles northeast of Brno—a massive collection comprising over fifty thousand tools of various kinds. This site, which was also excavated by Absolon, yielded Aurignacian animal figures as well. Central Europe was probably the first area to produce fine plastic representations of animals, followed by France and the East.

By far the most exciting products of the Aurignacian are the famous "Venus statuettes," made by men of thirty, forty or fifty thousand years ago. They are the earliest positively identified portrayals of the human figure ever discovered. The area of these finds stretches from southern France to European Russia and even into Siberia, though, oddly enough, no Venus statuettes have yet been found in Spain. About 130 examples are known, many of them built on ample lines but all lacking feet. Their legs taper off so sharply that it seems probable that the little figures were intended to be stuck into the ground.

Modern authorities are almost unanimous in denying that the Stone-Age man of the Middle Aurignacian made these statuettes for erotic purposes; nor, it is thought, did they serve purely artistic ends. The present view is that these little figures of ivory, limestone and other material had a religious significance.

The reason why the statuettes were almost always of women may be that they were intended to symbolize fertility, for many of them display very pronounced signs of pregnancy. It may be assumed, therefore, that the statuettes from the Grimaldi cave were associated with some form of fertility cult. Modeled in green or yellow soapstone, green crystalline material or bone, they can now be seen in Saint-Germain Museum in Paris. A figure found at Savignano near Modena, Italy, also reveals that the artist concentrated solely on female characteristics and was less interested in the head and legs. This Venus, which is now in the Museum of Prehistory in Rome, possesses the extremely large breasts and prominent buttocks of what anthropologists term a steatopygous type. One striking feature of the Savignano Venus is her conical coiffure or pointed cap. The central or unmistakably female portion of the little sculpture is strongly emphasized, while the head and feet taper away.

The Venus of Willendorf, which was discovered in 1908 and is now on show in Vienna, wears a peculiar basketlike coiffure, has enormous breasts, hips and thighs, and a protuberant belly. Made of limestone and just over four inches tall, she may have been a goddess of fertility, an early Magna Mater or Earth Mother. The two obese ivory figures found at Gagarino on the Upper Don by the Russian anthropologist Sergei N. Zamyatnin in 1928 are only half as large (2.28 and 2.12 inches high) but are strongly reminiscent of the Willendorf Venus. In 1926 a second Venus was discovered at Willendorf, this time made of ivory and dating from the Gravettian or Upper Aurignacian. Its figure is not as exuberantly feminine as the limestone Venus.

Several very slim figures have also been found, a fact which argues against their association with a fertility cult. In 1928 the Russian geologist M. M. Gerasimov came upon a Paleolithic settlement near Malta, a village fifty-three miles northwest of Irkutsk in Siberia. In the course of excavations conducted between 1929 and 1934 he discovered twenty female statuettes ranging in height from 1.1 to 5.1 inches, all made of mammoth tusk or reindeer's antler and almost all extremely slender. No one looking at these dainty little figures would form the impression that they were intended either to portray worship or induce fertility by magical means. Gerasimov unearthed some other extremely interesting objects, among them the remains of five superterranean huts, four hearths built of stone slabs, a child's grave, large numbers of animal bones, reindeer antlers, the remains of strange animal burials, 2,500 stone tools and about 600 bone artifacts of which 150 displayed ornamentation. One really noteworthy feature is that the huts of Malta seem to have been skin-covered structures of branches with central smoke vents; in other words, tentlike dwellings resembling those of the modern Tungus. An oval grave pit contained the skeleton of a four-year-old child lying on his side with his eyes facing eastward. A headband made of mammoth tusk, neck ornaments and ivory beads, jewelry, flint and bone utensils all showed how implicitly the Upper Aurignacian inhabitants of Malta believed in resurrection and a life hereafter.

The figurines of Malta and Gagarino were found inside the remains of ancient huts, and it could be deduced from their position that they had once been hung up or placed in niches, often near the hearth. They may have represented female ancestors who were deeply revered and possessed great religious significance, or, again, they may have been worshipped in ceremonies whose nature must remain forever unknown. Female statuettes of this type have been found in former dwelling places on Kostienki Island and at Yeliceevici; Mézin, Department of Lot at Garonne, France; Willendorf in Austria; Vistonice and Prědmost in Czechoslovakia; and Mainz in Germany. Upper Paleolithic female statuettes and the nature of the sites where they have been discovered indicate that the people of Asia and Europe may have been sedentary as early as the Aurignacian period or at least that their sojourn in a hunting area was often of long duration. In this respect they differed from the later hunters of the Magdalenian period, who were constantly on the move in search of game.

One unique female head, found at Brassempouy in the Department of Landes, France, by the French prehistorians Piette and Laporterie in 1894, is carved in ivory and stands only 1.18 inches high. Its features are quite naturally proportioned and its lack of mouth and eyes does not detract from its genuine if austere charm. It is surmounted by an intricately arranged coiffure or cap which has earned it the name *tête à la capuche*.

One of the finest of all Aurignacian figures is the ivory Venus of Lespugue in the Haute-Garonne, France, found six inches below the floor of the Grotte des Rideaux by Comte Reneé de Saint-Périer, a French prehistorian, and his wife in 1922. The figure, 5.7 inches high, has oval, stylized features and a gracefully inclined head. Like others of its kind, its central proportions are large and its thighs, buttocks and belly strongly emphasized. On the whole, it seems to belong to the Aurignacian's golden age of human representation, and would scarcely be distinguishable from similar sculptures in a modern art exhibition.

The Austrian scholar Franz Hančar draws attention to a strange kind of apron visible at the rear of the Lespugue Venus, to some equally mysterious, fringelike serrations beneath the buttocks of a figurine from Kostienki, and to what looks like an apron on the second Venus of Willendorf. Zamyatnin thinks that these are meant to suggest animals' tails. Animals' tails also figure prominently in the costume of the modern Siberian shaman, just as they do in the Upper Paleolithic cave paintings of masked magicians. Hančar also reminds us that the reindeer hunters of modern Siberia, Ostyaks, Golds, Yakuts and Chuvashes, make a practice of carving human figures or *dzuli* out of larch and aspen wood. Not only are these figures female but—even more remarkable—the Negidals look upon them as the beginning of human procreation and the source from which their whole tribe is derived. "The Upper Paleolithic Venus figurine provides us with the earliest tangible expression of that undying cultural idea which sees in womankind the embodiment of life's beginning and continuance and the image of the immortality of something which is in itself amorphous" (Hančar, p. 152).

While the majority of Aurignacian statuettes portray women, a number of male figurines also exist. In 1891, an ivory sculpture seven inches high was discovered in a man's grave fourteen and a half feet below the surface of the loess at Brno, Moravia, It had no legs and only one arm (the left), but Breuil claims that this deficiency was deliberate and not due to mischance or breakage.

Another interesting piece is the Negroid head in soapstone from the Grimaldi cave which can now be seen in Saint-Germain Museum. This was found by Dr. Julien in 1885 and reconstructed from fragments, no easy task, considering that it was only an inch and a half high. It probably dates from the Upper Aurignacian and is thus about thirty thousand years old.

Among the discoveries made by Absolon at Prědmost in Moravia was a man's head carved in mammoth's tooth. A rather sinister round face just over two and a half inches deep, it dates from the Solutrean or Lower Magdalenian and is thus between twenty and twenty-two thousand years old. Vistonice, also in Moravia, yielded a prehistoric "Leonardo da Vinci" in the shape of a long and strongly individual face which Absolon has dated a thirty thousand years, or the close of the Aurignacian. It is a fine and uncommonly expressive portrait, but it tells us as little as any other Aurignacian head about the exact physiognomy of contemporary man.

One still unsolved mystery is the significance of what have been termed "wands." Made of reindeer's or stags' antlers, they were at first unornamented and had a T-shaped end pierced at the point of intersection by one or sometimes two holes. We first meet these strange implements in the Aurignacian. Later, in the Magdalenian, they came to be adorned with designs and engraving of increasing intricacy. Were they really insignia of power and majesty, or were they tent pegs, ritual drumsticks, arrowheads, brooches or objects of religious significance? If these pierced batons formed part of some kind of harness (and I can see them proving useful for guiding reindeer, which will not wear a bit), it would mean that domesticated reindeer existed in the Aurignacian, a possibility which has not been entertained hitherto but is not entirely out of the question.

Even more mysterious are the semicylindrical or, much more rarely, cylindrical batons found at Lespugue, in the Caverne d' Arudy, at Lourdes, Isturitz, Hornos de la Peña and other places. These are about eight inches long and up to three-quarters of an inch wide. Unornamented *baguettes* of this type existed in Hungary and western and southern Germany as early as the Middle Aurignacian. They may have been used in religious ceremonies, but the strange engraving on the ornamented type—loops, circles and spirals—may have contained messages or information like the batons of the Australian aborigines. Piette thought that he had identified genuine hieroglyphs and individual symbols in this ornamentation, by René de Saint-Périer, who discovered two of these small batons in the Lespugue cave in 1927 and devoted an interesting essay to the problem, finds it impossible to determine their exact use.

The early representatives of the species Homo sapiens evolved a rich and extensive culture. Indeed, the first "modern" human beings were so diverse and their mode of existence and industries so various, despite their common basis, that science has subdivided them into several cultures.

A unique, mysterious and still-unexplained culture was unearthed near Solutré in the French Department of Saône-et-Loire. The Upper Paleolithic period is divided into three groups, Aurignacian, Solutrean and Magdalenian, and the second of these tasks its name from the place mentioned above, which is in the neighborhood of Macon. There, jutting in solitary splendor from the hilly *maconnais*, stands a limestone crag of incomparable beauty, in profile resembling a gigantic natural springboard, a comparatively gentle incline ending in a precipitous drop. The hunters of the Upper Paleolithic period used to drive thousands of wild horses up this hill until they reached the summit, when they forced them to leap off into the depts below. It must have been a dramatic spectacle. Assembling at night, the hunters formed huge cordons and drove their quarry together, yelling, brandishing torches and launching spears and arrows at the terrified beasts until they galloped up the hill in frenzied flight. On reaching the topmost ridge the horses reared and made a final effort to escape, but, ringed by relentless flames, they turned once more and plunged into the abyss.

Whole herds of wild horses must have been slaughtered in this way, for tens of thousands of bones were found at the foot of the cliff. This layer of horses' bones is older than the Solutrean and belongs to the Upper Aurignacian or Gravettian. Other fossils found there included those of reindeer, cave bear, wild cattle and mammoth. We do not know whether all these animals leaped to their death from the cliff top or whether some of them were game which had been brought to the place of slaughter from elsewhere, but traces of fire showed that the hunters feasted off their quarry on the spot.

The presence of very finely retouched flint blades shaped like slender laurel or willow leaves and used as spear points or arrow-heads, together with sharp stone knives and other flint tools, proves that some forms of game were dismembered and prepared for eating at the foot of the cliff. The Solutrean culture produced the best flint workers of all time. They must have been true masters of their craft, for their tools look as though they had been fashioned with consummate ease and give an impression of fine workmanship.

The Solutrean culture covered southwest and central France and Hungary, whereas the Late or Upper Solutrean made its home exclusively in northwest Spain. Bone arrowheads belonging to this mysterious culture were found there, finely fashioned blades equipped with a barb and flattened on one side to enable them to be fitted snugly to the shaft. It seems safe to conclude that bow and arrow were used during the Cantabrian period of the Solutrean culture. One important site of Solutrean art is the Roc de Sers near Angoulême (Charente), where a semicircle of fine animal figures can be seen chiseled into limestone blocks. The German archaeologist Alfred Rust poses some interesting questions: whether, for instance, this was the site of a cult, or perhaps a sculptor's atelier.

Apart from the Roc de Sers, the Solutrean period was relatively poor in art. It looks as though the craftsmen of the Solutrean normally confined themselves to making bare essentials, for the task of self-preservation probably gave them more than enough to do. What they did make, however, was so entirely novel and finely fashioned that it put all previous cultures in the shade. They probably had little time for pure art, even as a form of magic, so the Roc de Sers represents a splendid exception.

The Magdalenian culture evolved from the western Aurignacian. During the Magdalenian period we meet a wealth of remarkably animated pictures, polychrome paints, frieze reliefs and animal sculptures in stone and clay. Engraving and painting gradually attained so splendid a prime in the numerous caves now known to us that we are forced to acknowledge that these ancient artists were fully as far advanced as the artists of today. The caves in which man left evidence of his amazingly rich artistic sense are situated in southern France and northern Spain. As a result, Georges Bataille has claimed, perhaps rightly, that in those days the Dordogne was the world's focal point.

How long ago was this? According to H. G. Bandi, Swiss professor of prehistory, Magdalenian culture emerged in about 20,000 B.C. However, the finest paintings in the caves of Lascaux date from between 23,000 and 25,000 years ago, during the Upper Aurignacian or Gravettian. Firm estimates of this sort are subject to certain reservations, of course, for chronological boundaries are necessarily inexact, but ever since some children discovered the almost invisible entrance to the cave in 1940—in other words, ever since the existence of Lascaux became known—the frontiers of cave art have been pushed back by a considerable distance.

The various caves have posed a large number of unsolved and probably insoluble problems. Why, for instance, were the various portrayals of animals orientated in such an arbitrary way? Why did they not share a common horizontal base line? Why were they drawn higgledy-piggledy, often with their legs pointing sideways, although each individual subject was allotted a consistent base line of its own? In the jumbled mass of animals at Altamira in Spain, the base lines of some figures diverge from the horizontal by as much as forty-five or even ninety degrees, and the same phenomenon can be observed at Font-de-Gaume (in the "Salle des Petits Bisons"), in the cave of Niaux and many others.

Portrayals of reindeer, bison, wild horse, mammoth, musk ox, rhinoceros, cave lion, wolf, elk, deer and ibis all betray an intimate and closely observed knowledge of anatomy and movement. Why, then, are there so few portrayals of man, and why is he almost exclusively depicted in sorcerer's costume, with a mask-like face and large, sightless orbs, as though he were unwilling to betray his personal identity? Were the magicians or shamans of this period blind? Was that the significance of the blank eyeballs? And what about the large hooked noses, strangely pointed beards and arms shaped like mammoths' tusks?

Again, why were so many animals drawn or scratched inside or on top of one another in such an apparently aimless manner, and why did man create his finest work in inaccessible corridors, narrow passages and vaulted chambers?

There is only one answer to all these questions: man was not practicing art for art's sake. His drawings, paintings, reliefs and sculptures probably served religous ends, which is why most portrayals of animals and human beings are to be found on walls in the least accessible parts of caves. In the cave of Font-de-Gaume the pictures start 71 yards from the entrance, in La Mouthe 103 yards, in Combarelles 131 yards, in Baume de Latrone 259 yards, in Trois-Frères 550 yards, in Tuc d'Audoubert 765 yards, and in Niaux 874 yards, while the picture galleries in the newly discovered Rouffignac cave lie more than three-quarters of a mile from the light of day. At Cabrerets (Lot), the visitor must crawl through narrow stone passages to reach the large stalactite-filled chamber where the pictures are. Raymond Furon states that this cave was not used as a dwelling place, and the French prehistorian Abbé Lemozi, who explored it, found nothing but a graving tool. The only way to reach the finest chamber in the Font-de-Gaume cave is to creep through a narrow passage whose entrance lies at floor level. Pictures often appear in the most unlikely places, in corners or shallow, cramped vaults where they are extremely hard to see. The bisons of Marsoulas, for instance, were painted on the walls of a low, narrow corridor. As Menghin says, it is almost impossible to conceive how some of these pictures came into being at all. And it

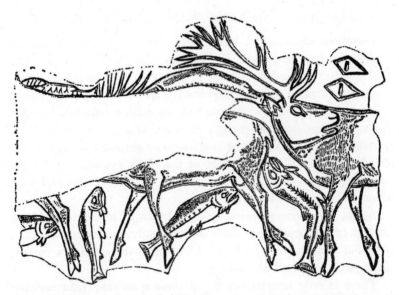

An engraving on reindeer's antler. This fragment was found in the Lorthet cave in the Pyrenees. The trout between the deer's legs may indicate that the animals are wading through water. The stag on the right is looking back over his shoulder in a vivid portrayal of apprehension, probably at some unseen pursuer.

is interesting to remember that approximately the same date (20,000 B.C.) is given to the spear points found in the cave near Albuquerque, New Mexico, and that these points were apparently the highest artistic and practical development of Sandia man.

The first artists, the painters and draftsmen of the Aurignacian, may still have produced their work in inhabited caves, but later, in the Magdalenian, engravings and paintings were executed on the walls of caves not normally used as dwelling places and in remote depths which were extremely hard to penetrate (Raymond Furon, *Manuel de Préhistoire Générale*).

Animals' movements and characteristics were observed with remarkable accuracy. Only highly experienced hunters could have portrayed them in such lifelike detail, as is testified by the numerous corrections visible in some of the pictures. It is no easy matter to scratch a rock wall with a flint burin so that the general impression is one of effortless mastery, yet the animals seem so lifelike and realistic that the sensitivity, artistic comprehension and skilled draftsmanship which they exhibit demand an explanation.

It is well known that primitive races are much more observant than the people of the West. They see more, and they see more accurately. A Tungus would make a far better witness in a court case than any European or American. Our powers of observation have become impaired by a constant flow of impressions and the continuous technical acceleration of the life around us. We simply cannot assimilate all the varied fare offered us by commerce, by cacophonous competition between rival sources of propaganda and publicity, by films, radio, television and a universal hubbub of activity. Our senses can absorb only a part of this. For the rest, speed has made us superficial. In the words of the modern paradox, we shall know less and less about more and more until we eventually know nothing about everything. There is so much in the world to look over that most of it is overlooked.

Good powers of observation belong to life in a state of nature, to technical simplicity. But good or accurate observation does not in itself imply an ability to draw realistically, for sculpture, drafts-

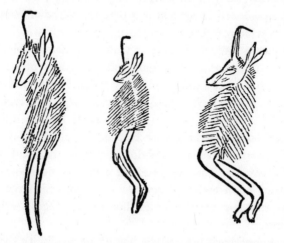

Reminiscent of sea horses, these masked dancers were engraved on bones found at Teyjat, Abri Mège (Dordogne). It is possible that these skin-clad figures represent Stone-Age shamans.

manship and painting presuppose a multitude of physical and intellectual faculties. A long and complex journey must be completed
before a picture can be transferred from the mind's eye to a wooden
panel, sheet of canvas or rock wall, a journey which leads from the
brain, via shoulder, arm and hand to the burin, brush or spatula, a
journey during which, as the German Impressionist painter Max
Liebermann would have said, a very great deal is lost. When acute
observation is coupled with inherited and acquired artistic ability,
the result is skilled draftsmanship. For example, anyone who has
watched Japanese children drawing or painting will know that
their superior gift of observation, inherited sense of form and
rigorous physical discipline—eating with chopsticks, sitting on their
heels, painting written characters—can bear remarkable fruit. Most
Japanese children of eight, nine or ten find it easy to capture a
human model's likeness on paper, and are far more advanced than
Western children in this respect. Stone-Age men did *not* paint like
children—far from it—but, like the Japanese, they were probably
closer to nature from an early age and, like the Japanese, they were
naturally great artists.

Men of the Aurignacian and, more particularly, the Magdelenian
must have possessed an ancient and inherited sense of form. It must
have been widespread, too, or the mastery with which individual
artists depicted individual subjects would be inexplicable. The men
of twenty, thirty and forty thousand years ago probably had a
better eye than we do today, and they certainly had a very delicate
and well-trained touch where engraving was concerned. In his
history of the ancient world (I, 1, p. 245), Eduard Meyer states
that we encounter in the Upper Paleolithic period a culture whose
intellectual content was far superior to that of the Neolithic period
which followed it. The assessment of a culture does not, he points
out, depend upon technical achievements, in which the Neolithic
man was superior to Paleolithic, but on intellectual abilities and
attainments.

I do not consider it beyond the bounds of possibility that the men
who stood on the threshold between Aurignacian and Magdalenian
had already reached the highest stage in mankind's intellectual devel-

opment. In fact, in the religious sphere they were already on the downward path and had abandoned their intimate relationship with the high god in favor of magic.

Once they sacrificed bears' skulls and marrowbones to their single god. Once they were closer to him, but then something new interposed itself between them and their god: art, the religious cult and magic.

CHAPTER 22

THE GILYAKS

"Have you not seen him," a Gilyak asked me earnestly, "the
Nibach on the moon, when it is big? He is a Gilyak!"
VICTOR VASHDAYEV, *In the Nomadic Camps*
of the Gilyak People, Moscow, 1934

IT appears that the religious cult which regards the bear as a mediator between heaven and earth has supervised without interruption
for twenty or even thirty thousand years. It has enjoyed a remarkable life span, and I myself witnessed that it was still alive among
the Ainus and certain Siberian tribes not so long ago. If it were
still possible to roam the northern forests of the Far East freely, one
would probably still come upon remnants of the age-old trinity
composed of man, bear and god.

But the god, for whose benefit the bear cult common to so many
peoples in the northern regions of the world exists, stands on a
somewhat lower plane than the supreme god of the earliest men.
He is only the lord of beasts, mountains and water, a secondary being
quite distinct from the supreme god and one who, unlike him, can
be portrayed in effigy.

A remarkable echo of the cultural activity of men of the Aurignacian and Magdalenian periods of twenty and thirty thousand years
ago, the bear cult's domain embraces vast areas of the Northern
Hemisphere. Among the many races who adhered to this cult only
a short time ago, as some of them still do, were the ancient Finns,
the Lapps, the Ostyaks, the Voguls, the Yeniseis, the Golds, the
Olcha, the Udehe, the Ainus and the Gilyaks.

It has long been apparent that of all these races, it is the Gilyaks
whose life is most intimately associated with the bear cult. For them,
the bear festival is the most important single event of the year and
plays a role in their clan system. Many of their utensils, some of
which are illustrated in this book, bear witness to the extraordinary
significance of the bear cult in the life of the Gilyaks.

The Gilyaks live on the lower reaches of the Amur, around
Udsski Bay, on the coast of the Sea of Okhotsk and—in very small

numbers—in the north of Sakhalin. Together, these small pockets make up an ethnic remnant which is in process of dying out. The Gilyaks resemble the Tungus but are an older race, being genuine Paleo—or "Old" Siberians. Their language differs from other Arctic tongues, and the sound of their speech, with its numerous consonants and sibilants, is reminiscent of certain North American Indian dialects.

The name Gilyak is derived from *kileng*, the word used by the Chinese to describe the native inhabitants of the Amur estuary. Like many other races in the world, the Gilyaks call themselves supply "men" or "people"—*nibach*, in their own language.

The Gilyaks' pigmentation is generally yellowish or yellowbrown, but I have also seen Gilyak girls with white faces and red cheeks. It is understandably difficult to gauge the actual color of these people's skin because their faces are sometimes naturally stained by the smoke from the open fires in their yurts. Yet like all northern races, the Gilyaks have no fondness for dirt and try to keep themselves and their living quarters as clean as possible. For this reason they take air baths in winter as well as summer, a practice which Christian Leden also observed among the Eskimos. They see nothing strange in performing outdoor tasks naked to the waist, even in intense cold, and will happily put on garments which have become frozen stiff while being aired because the donning of these ice-cold clothes hardens their bodies and quickly induces a beneficial glow of warmth.

The Gilyaks have dense, glossy, black hair. Women with long hair wear it in plaits which often reach their hips or, if it is shorter, let it hang loose over their shoulders. Siberian tribes never have curly hair, nor do they find it attractive. Since the men have very sparse facial hair they never cut it off and are extremely proud of their beards or mustaches, even though these are normally sparse. Bald heads are rare, and hair retains its color far into old age. The people of northern Asia are firmly convinced that hair is a repository of strength and that its loss will result in the waning of physical powers and a lack of success in fishing and hunting. This is the age-old idea reflected in the Old Testament by the story of Samson

(Judges, xvi, 19). Because vermin make themselves at home in thick manes of hair, lice are regarded as a sign of health—not that the Gilyaks suffer these pests gladly. The sound of lice and fleas being cracked between strong teeth soon loses its horror for anyone who spends any length of time in northeast Asia.

The common impression that Northeast Asian tribes prefer dull or bleak-looking clothes is quite erroneous. The Gilyaks have always been fond of bright colors. In winter, they wear knee-length furs made of a double thickness of dog pelts. These skins are sewn together with the hair facing outward, and can vary in shade according to the color of the dog: black, white, brown or gray. Every Gilyak wears a belt to which are attached his knife and a few amulets, a wild boar's tooth or a piece of deer's antler. The Gilyak keeps his undergarments on when sleeping and uses his fur as a coverlet. Women wear a knee-length chemise and over it a dress buttoned at the front. Young girls set great store by buttons, which are usually of ornamented and handsomely painted bone. Both chemise and overgarment are adorned with several rows of small brass disks or copper coins which jingle with every step their wearer takes, and women and girls are accompanied by this metallic clinking wherever they go. Dresses are normally made of fishskins which have been tanned, pressed and finely stitched together. They are water-repellent, dark brown or reddish in tone and frequently embroidered in bright colors. The Gilyaks display great inventiveness in devising decorative motifs.

However, it is almost as though the imminent extinction of the ancient Siberian peoples has dulled the colors in their clothing. With the growing adoption of Chinese and Russian dress, the bright colors of their own native costumes have disappeared. Anyone seeing a Gilyak girl of thirty years ago, with fur cap and colorful robe and decorated fishskin boots on her small and dainty feet, would have been amazed by the gay good taste of a people whose life was an everlasting battle against the deadly monotony of their surroundings.

The rigors of their natural environment compel the Gilyaks to build two different sorts of houses. Their winter house, which has to protect them from immense cold, violent storms and flurries of snow, is an earth yurt like a very capacious tent built of wood and half sunk into the ground, lined with thin branches and roofed with timber. An opening in the center of the roof allows smoke from the fire to disperse. Immediately below this vent is the fireplace, where a large cauldron stands, supported by stones. To left and right of the entrance, which is very narrow, are water containers. The floor is spread with brushwood and covered with bearskins. This type of earth yurt must be very ancient, for it resembles the pits unearthed at Kostienki in 1931 and 1933 which turned out to be the remains of oval winter huts dating from the last Ice Age.

One Gilyak yurt often houses three or four families numbering twenty or more people. Sleeping accommodation is disposed around the walls, and at night, when the yurt's occupants sit around the blazing fire on their couches, passing the communal pipe of to-bacco from hand to hand, a congenial atmosphere prevails. This is the moment when the Gilyak's normally a taciturn race, begin to tell stories; and even if drafts creep in at the doorway or the wind sends choking, smarting clouds of smoke billowing around the yurt, even if the roof beams are caked with soot and the fire sometimes goes out, allowing a stream of ice-cold air to descend through the smoke vent, none of this seems to disturb them unduly.

In spring the Gilyaks move house, and move quickly, for the sudden thaw and heavy rainstorms would soon turn the floors of their low-lying winter yurts into a quagmire. Their summer quarters are built on short stakes which hold them off the ground. This protects the yurt from flooding and keeps it dry by permitting air to circulate beneath the floor. In a sense, therefore, the Gilyaks are cave men in winter and lake dwellers in summer, a dual mode of existence which has its roots deep in prehistory.

Although the Gilyaks hunt almost every animal in the taiga, their whole way of life and thought is concentrated on fishing and seal trapping. They are ichthyophagous, born and bred, and there is scarcely any sort of fish which they will not eat. They are probably the world's finest experts on salmon. The men go salmon fishing with nets and boats, leaving their womenfolk to skin the fish and cut them into strips which are either acidulated in pits or strung up on lines and dried in the sun. Dried fish is known throughout Siberia as *yukola*. The Gilyaks call their dried strips of fish *ma*, and ma is to them what bread is to us. Dipping a large hunk of ma in fish oil, they grip it between their teeth and cut it off with a knife close to their lips. Visitors have to get used to ma or yukola, for it is a staple and indispensable form of food during the severe winters. Every day items on the Gilyaks' menu include *ceta* salmon, catfish, eel pout, pike and, last but not least, sturgeon.

When the ice breaks up along the Amur the sturgeon gather in readiness for their voyage upstream. The Gilyaks eat a great deal of sturgeon meat, but they have always sold the celebrated black caviar to the Russians. Though it is greatly esteemed as a delicacy in the West, black caviar loses some of its appeal when it is in constant and abundant supply. The Gilyaks eat their fish either dried or acidulated, never boiled or baked. This is not as strange as it seems. Anyone who eats raw unsalted fish often enough will soon come to enjoy it as much as the Japanese enjoy their delicious *sashimi*. The Gilyaks only cook fishskins, which are regarded as a delicacy when boiled into a whitish porridge and mixed with fish oil and cranberries. The resultant rather glutinous mass, which is called *mossj*, does not taste as bad as one might suppose.

It is interesting to note that the Gilyaks never use salt. In fact, they have an aversion to it. This may be because they assimilate enough salt with their wide range of sea food. Seal meat, like the meat of all mammals, is eaten boiled. The Gilyaks do not think highly of seal meat, although they regard seal fat cut into slices as a great delicacy. Seal oil is used at every meal and also serves to illuminate the yurt. The meat of the white whale, which is much esteemed by the Paleo-Siberian races in general, does not find particular favor with the Gilyaks, even though a well-cooked whale steak has a delicate flavor not unlike veal.

Around the Sea of Okhotsk the seal-catching season begins in April and continues far into August, when the seals migrate to the Amur to feed on ceta salmon. They are hunted either with harpoons or with a weapon consisting of a pole attached to a small piece of

[76] Gilyak cradle, common to almost all the nomadic tribes of Siberia. These cradles are carried on the mother's back or lashed to a reindeer on the march and hung from a branch during halts.

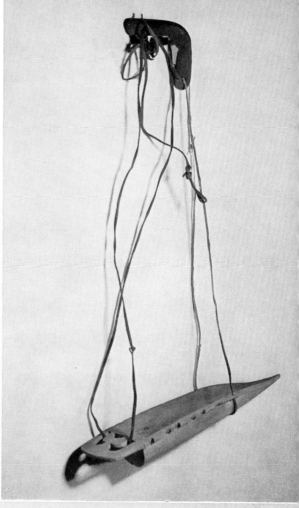

[77] Toy seals carved by Gilyaks for their children.

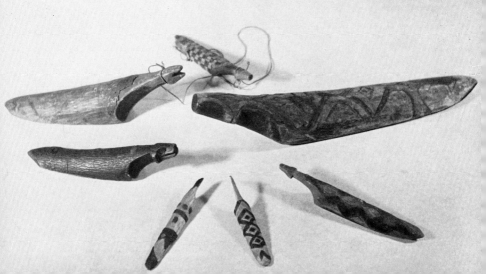

[78] A tall birch-bark box like those used by the Tungus for gathering berries. The primitive peoples of the taiga are extremely skilled at working with this material.

[79] Decorated Gilyak fish tureen.

[80] Almost all paleo-Siberian and Tungusic tribes formerly used eating utensils made of wood, birch bark or fishskin. Here is an ornamented wooden bowl for fish or meat, and a soup spoon.

[81] A watertight dipper made of impregnated birch bark, complete with lip. Like the men of the Stone Age, the taiga and tundra peoples possess a rich material culture of which bone and wooden utensils are part.

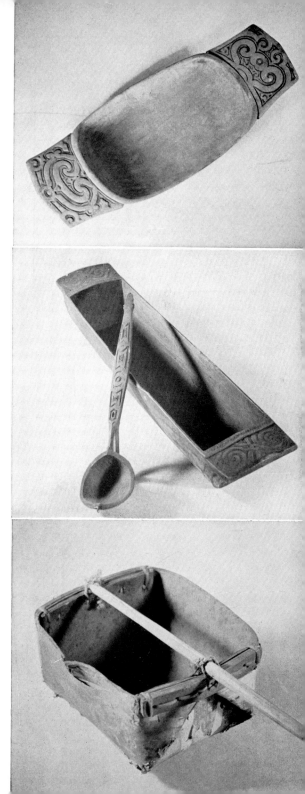

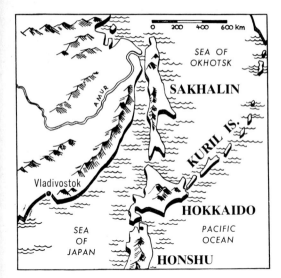

[82] An Ainu girl with her mouth tattooed in the style still popular forty years ago. This strange custom was not, as some authorities used to assume, intended to simulate a mustache but probably served purely aesthetic ends.

[83] (*Above, left*) The last surviving Ainus now live on the island of Hokkaido, in the Kuriles and on Sakhalin.

[84] Evidence of a bear cult 20,000 years ago in the Magdalenian period. Arrows and stones visible on the figure of a bear on the wall of the Trois-Frères cave indicate that it is being shot and stoned to death. Blood is streaming from the animal's snout and muzzle.

[85] The same bear cult and the same ritual slaughter was still being practiced by the Ainus on the island of Hokkaido in our own century. This picture shows a roped bear being shot with arrows.

[86] An amazing similarity exists between bear ceremonies performed some 20,000 years ago during the Magdalenian and the Gilyak festivals of our own era. Deep in the interior of the Montespan cave (Haute-Garonne) Count Bégouen discovered the headless clay figure of a bear. Between its forepaws lay the fallen skull of a real bear which had once been attached to the figure itself. Thirty or so deep circular holes visible on the sculpture are assumed to be traces of spears or arrows used in the bear ceremony of 20,000 years ago. [87] (*Below*) In exactly the same way, the Gilyaks and Ainus tie a bear to a stake and then shoot it with blunt arrows until, finally, the best marksman among them dispatches the beast with a spearthrust or arrow-shot in the breast.

[88] In the course of the bear festival the bear is killed and its soul soars to the lord of the forests and mountains. Although the Gilyaks never portray the supreme god in whom they believe, they do make effigies of Pal Nibach, the lord of forest and mountain, and even wear them as a form of amulet.

[89] Kichikagi, spirit aid of the Gilyak shaman. If one tells the shaman the truth, the bearlike figure remains motionless, but if one lies to him it quivers.

[90] At-Kegn, the "tiger-man" whom all tigers obey. This is yet another being whose aid is enlisted by Gilyak shamans to combat evil spirits. Kegn is reputed to be exceedingly wise but also irascible.

wood fixed with a stone or sharp iron spike. The beasts are transfixed with these and hauled in to be dispatched with blows from wooden clubs. Gilyaks are very skillful at stalking seals, whether swimming or resting on the shore.

The Gilyaks' keelless, flat-bottomed boats are better suited for river work than for the open sea. They are not a great seafaring race and spend their time close to the coast or, better still, paddling the quieter inland waters. I do not know if this was always the case, for the Gilyaks speak of a distant land in the east which they know of only in legend. By the outbreak of World War II all Gilyaks owned firearms, even if mainly of a primitive and old-fashioned type, but in earlier days they used to hunt with bow and arrow or bear spear and lance. As time went by, they became extremely skillful smiths, a craft which they learned partly from the Japanese and partly from the Chinese.

Gilyaks are, by their very nature, tradition and culture, fishermen. If they are also hunters it is principally because they need skins and furs for bartering purposes, although their game, which includes fox, glutton (a voracious weasel-like creature), wolf, sable and deer, provides them with a source of food as well. Although rats are common enough in the Gilyaks' winter yurts, they are never eaten. This does not go without saying, for I have often encountered "cooking rats" in Chinese markets and eating houses. The Gilyaks' favorite meat is bear's meat, and its fat is considered a particular delicacy. As for beverages, the Gilyaks were only introduced to tea and brandy at a late stage, and have no traditional beverages of their own such as other primitive peoples often make from fruit juices, leaves, plant stalks or bark.

All Gilyaks, men, women and children alike, smoke tobacco. It is said that the habit of smoking tobacco was introduced into Japan by the Portuguese at the beginning of the sixteenth century and was later adopted by the Koreans and Chinese. The tobacco plant thrives in Manchuria despite the harsh climate, and I have myself grown it on the banks of the Sungari. The Gilyaks modeled their pipes upon those of the Chinese. They consist of a long brass tube to which is attached or screwed a shallow upright bowl the size of a thimble.

The bowls are so small that they hold only enough tobacco for one or two puffs and must be continually replenished. On taking his place in the yurt, a guest will be the first to receive the pipe from the master of the house.

Dogs play an important part in the life of these people, not only as sledge pullers but also as a source of clothing and food. We meet the practice of eating dog meat among the Eskimos and certain American Indian tribes. The Iroquois used to eat dogs and the Ojibwa feasted on dog meat on ceremonial occasions, as did the Assiniboins during the celebration of the summer dance and the Nootka while performing the wolf ritual. The Eskimos in the southeast of Baffin Island used to breed two kinds of dog, the smaller for eating and the larger for pulling sledges, but the smaller breed has died out.

The Gilyaks' dogs are long-haired creatures with short, pricked ears, and resemble wolves or Eskimo dogs. They range in color from black to red, brown and white, but are mostly a yellowish gray. They are also small, mainly because the Gilyaks have never devoted any time to scientific breeding and consider it too much trouble to select and look after the puppies. Only male dogs are considered suitable for sledge pulling, and bitches seldom get enough to eat. The Gilyaks feed their dogs exclusively on fish, usually inside the yurt. At other times, the dogs spend their leisure hours tied up in the open air, even in the coldest weather, unloved and unloving, predatory by nature and—because they are always fed by the womenfolk—masterless. The Gilyak's dog is a draught animal pure and simple, and the congenial, friendly relationship which we know and value in the West cannot thrive in the harsh environment of the Northeast Asian coastal regions. The fact that dogs are not used for hunting or watchdogs may also explain why the Gilyaks treat them more like cattle and slaughter them for food without giving the matter a second thought.

Dogs are harnessed to sledges in teams of between ten and fourteen. The method of harnessing is simple in the extreme and takes only a few minutes to complete. The animals are attached by their collars to a rope of plaited sealskin, one behind the other on alternate sides.

Because they are harnessed by their necks, there is a tendency for their throats to become constricted, so they tire more quickly than the Russians' sledge dogs, which take the strain with their chests. Whereas bitches are fed only irregularly in winter and are left to fend for themselves in summer, snapping greedily and voraciously at scraps and garbage, male dogs are reasonably well cared for and are never driven to the point of exhaustion. Although they spend the night out of doors, each animal is allotted a small hollow in the snow and bedded down on fir twigs. Every dog is tied up individually to prevent fighting.

Like most of Siberia's primitive peoples, the Gilyaks are monogamous. Cases of polygamy are rare and attributable solely, in my experience, to Chinese influence. A young Gilyak has to purchase his future wife, just as do the Tungus, Ostyaks, Samoyeds, Tatars, Chuvashes and other races of northern Asia. The bridegroom pays the girl's father or her elder brother a price, which in the old days consisted mainly of goods such as spears, metal cooking pots, boats, sledges and dogs.

The average value of these goods used to be in the neighborhood of three hundred gold rubles, a sum roughly equivalent in modern terms to $1,000. A bride could not be paid for by installments. Actually the payment of a bride-price is not an abuse of human dignity and the rights of women, nor does it imply that the bride is being treated like a piece of merchandise. A Gilyak has to put in a great deal of hard work before he is in a position to buy a girl and set up house at all. The fact of purchase is in itself a guarantee of the bridegroom's qualifications, for a man who can earn a bride-price can also feed a family, and immature youths are compelled to wait their chance. Men of primitive tribes who have paid good money for a wife will treat her less harshly, prize her more highly and protect her more carefully than many youngsters of the ostensibly moral West who acquire a wife not only without effort but often with a dowry thrown in. Finally, girls are better reared, fed, cared for and educated by their parents before marriage if there is a prospect of selling them without difficulty and at a high price. Indeed it is debatable which offers the better guarantee of a woman's position in the home, the bride-price of the primitive races or the moral respect accorded to women by the races of the West, for a bride-price must be paid, whereas respect is a normal obligation whose neglect is only one of Western society's many sins of omission.

There is, however, one danger inherent in any system of bride-prices. The young tribesmen of Siberia are often tempted to abduct or carry off the girl of their choice, usually with her consent. It is only natural that a pretty girl will sometimes lend herself to such a scheme if she knows that the man whom she loves cannot produce a bride-price. When this happens, her father and brothers set off in pursuit of the premature bridegroom, often accompanied by the whole village. If they catch him blood often flows, but since all taiga dwellers are fine cross-country runners many a lover succeeds in getting away with his willing victim, in which case the feud remains alive and can drag on for years. I know of Gilyak songs which celebrate the romantic side of such abductions.

Once the bride-price has been paid, a marriage contract is regarded as settled. The man receives his bride and takes her home, which usually means the yurt where his parents and brothers live.

Until the time of their decline under the impact of extraneous influences, the Gilyaks possessed some very admirable characteristics. They were pre-eminent among the Paleo-Asiatic peoples for their energy, moderation, self-control and austere way of life. But with the Russian conquest of the Amur region things changed, though very gradually. Gilyak girls were chaste and unmarried men extremely continent. If a girl gave birth to an illegitimate child, she was thrashed by her mother and her child put to death. Marriages contracted by purchase were usually happy or at least satisfactory, and conjugal fidelity was strictly observed. I never saw a Gilyak kiss his wife in the presence of others, but children were treated with great gentleness and affection. Expectant mothers are not allowed to give birth in the home, and deliver their children in the open air or in a special birchbark tent near the main yurt, as is the custom among many primitive peoples. While this practice may be based on the idea, widespread among primitive peoples, that a woman in child-bed is unclean, it may also be a result of the high rate of infant mortality. Any yurt in which a death has taken place is automatically demolished, which is why Gilyaks carry a dying man into the open air when death appears imminent.

A hundred years ago the Gilyaks still owned slaves, whom they bought from the Ainus or Golds. The nineteenth-century Russian explorer Leopold von Schrenck rightly stresses that these were the only two races to sell their sons and daughters into slavery, but points out that they were people who lived in close contact with the cultural leaders of the Far East, China and Japan, and were oppressed and dominated by them. The Chinese usually acted as middlemen, but the Ainus and Golds also sold their own daughters direct.

The Gilyaks themselves were never sold into slavery, nor would it have been possible for them to enslave members of their own race. Female slaves cost more than brides and were more highly valued than male slaves. They were used like human cattle and performed all the heaviest manual tasks, such as chopping wood, carrying water and feeding dogs. It was considered undignified to keep female slaves as concubines, but marriage between slaves was tolerated, since the owner acquired the children of such a marriage for his "stable" without the necessity for further expenditure.

The Gilyak term for a male slave was *kry ghryss umgu* and for a woman slave *kryghryss utgu*. Koryaks, Aleuts and Chukchees all carried the wives of their defeated enemies off into slavery, fed them and made them perform the heaviest and most menial tasks. Slavery was not a new invention on the part of the primitive Siberian peoples. There is a distinct possibility that slaves existed in prehistoric times, as can be deduced from the fact that bound women were placed in the graves of important men. Certainly, slavery had been customary in China and Korea for thousands of years. Nobody who knows the Far East will find anything very exceptional in the system, considering that just before World War II the vast red-light districts of Korea were populated by thousands of peasant girls whose parents had sold them to the owners of the establishments, who fed them just enough to keep them alive. One should not overestimate the amoral aspect of the Gilyaks' erstwhile system of slavery, for in other respects they are a friendly, extremely hospitable, kind and honest people. Von Schrenck records that the first word for stealing which he learned among the Gilyaks was the Russian expression *ukrastch*, and that only much later on did he become familiar with the Gilyak word *erngarsitch*. He takes this as an indication that the Gilyaks did not learn to confuse "mine" and "thine" until they were brought into contact with the allegedly civilizing influence of the West.

The Gilyaks have always possessed a deep-rooted ability to differentiate between good and evil, honesty and dishonesty, loyalty and disloyalty. Assessed in terms of this inner morality, their culture is an extremely high one. Relying on their clear conception of what is good and on ancient tradition, the Gilyaks regard God as the essence of goodness. They are children of a harsh world in which men have nothing to rely on save their kayak, their physical strength, their wealth of ancient experience and their god. They believe implicitly in a single god, whom they call Kur. Their faith leaves no room for doubt, misery or self-imposed suffering. Everything is clear and straightforward in their minds, so their prayers are usually confined to the simple words: *"Kur pionguchia"* ("O my God, please").

The Gilyaks believe in a single, good, supreme being, an invisible god who cannot be portrayed in effigy. This is not an invention on the part of religiously biased ethnologists, but a fact, for I have witnessed their faith in a supreme being for myself. It is not an invention on the part of Pater Schmidt, either, for long before his time, in 1880, Leopold von Schrenck lived among the Gilyaks and recorded that these seminomads' most ancient religious conception was of God and goodness, and that they worshiped God as the essence of goodness. Leo Sternberg, famous linguist and ethnologist, author of the monumental *Der Ursprung der Gottesidee*, who also knew the Gilyaks well, wrote in 1905 of "Kurn," an expression which not only described their supreme god but embraced the whole world as well. Still more interesting is the age of this faith, which hailed from the most distant past. It was only later that there arose, among the Gilyaks as among almost all Siberian tribes, the idea that other powers may influence the destiny of mankind. Von Schrenck recognized, however, that the Gilyaks' basic monotheism was an echo of something very ancient. What followed belonged to a much later period, and proved incapable either of dislodging or supplanting the Gilyaks' fundamental belief in a single god.

The later importations consisted of several lords of the forest, mountain and sea. These deities are called *nibach*, like the Gilyaks themselves, and resemble men in every respect. The lord of the taiga, the mountains and all the beasts of the forest is called Pal Nibach, while the lord of the sea and all sea creatures is known as Toll Nibach. As fishermen, the Gilyaks are at special pains to maintain contact with the lord of the water, for he is the proprietor and protector of all seals, whales and fish.

The Gilyaks have no idols in the sense of material objects, sculptures or pictures which are directly worshiped as gods. Their wooden sculptures are usually stylized figures of animals, each one of which serves as the abode of a spirit. Being contained by and linked with the figure, a spirit can exercise certain effects through its medium. Almost all primitive Siberian tribes have idols of this kind. The Russians call the tangible figure *lekan* and the spirit which resides in it *chaitan*. Although a chaitan can spread disease, it can also withdraw or, as it were, reabsorb itself. Consequently, special medicinal lekans exist, each inhabited by a chaitan of its own. Lekans may be made of wood, stone, pieces of leather or sometimes a few scraps of cloth. A chaitan does not, however, extend its aid automatically and of its own accord. Elaborate rituals are associated with these idols, which must be given an honored place in the yurt, offered sacrifices and, in some cases, danced to. They can also be chastised, thrown away or burned. The Gilyaks' *kegn* and the *ongon* of the Mongols and Buryats is merely a practical means to a beneficial end. It can be pampered but it can also be deceived; it is never worshiped, and it has nothing to do with the high god.

The Gilyaks' world of spiritual ideas is thus made up of three components: a single and indivisible god; the lords of the mountains, forests and seas; and the idols. These concepts are not a religious trinity but three historically successive ideas. The Gilyaks provide us with a clear illustration of the way in which mankind degenerated from monotheism into worship of "the gods of the high places" and, finally, into idolatry.

CHAPTER 23

THE BEAR FESTIVAL

The Ainus consider that there is One God towering above all, who is the Maker of all others, and to whom all are responsible, for they are His servants and deputies.

J. Batchelor, *The Ainu of Japan*,
London, 1892, p. 248

The Orochi on killing the bear say: "Go fast; go to your master; put a new fur on, and come again next year that I may look at you."

Sternberg, *Gilyaks*, p. 439

science has not yet explained the hominid's transition from concrete to abstract thought. If man did not, in Albright's phrase, "raise himself by his own bootstraps," some other force must have been instrumental.

I am convinced that the oldest races in the world, food gatherers and hunters, originally believed in a supreme being. This is a fact which many leading modern students of ethnology no longer dispute, and one which brings us very close to the oldest races' traditional belief that man's knowledge of God stems from the Creation itself.

If Western culture has not yet fully accepted the modern scientific realization that monotheism came at the beginning of human existence, this is due to the general confusion which prevails in humanity's third religious era, the era of idolatry. We are living in the very middle of that era, at the height of an age that corresponds to the *lekan-chaitan* ideas of the primitive Siberian peoples. This is not to say that the quest for God has been abandoned. On the contrary, it is very much alive, mainly because faith in God has so largely been destroyed by the onset of all-conquering science.

As the knowledge or conviction of a single supreme god gradually waned, so the notion of a lord of the mountains, forests and seas came into being. And the further the supreme god retreated from man's world of ideas and beliefs the nearer to him man wanted to be, in accordance with the age-old belief which has it that absence makes the heart grow fonder. In consequence, he either summoned the effigy of the primordial god of his recollection down from the skies to the mountaintops or attempted to approach the supreme being via a lord of the mountains. But even this was not enough. Man sought a direct relationship with his lost god, a relationship which no abstract lord of the mountains, forests and seas could supply. In search of a mediator, some of the oldest circumpolar races selected a being who could form the desired link, and this being was the bear. The bear has fulfilled this intermediary function for twenty or even thirty thousand years, and still does among certain circumpolar tribes today.

I was able to explore the vestiges of the bear cult at a time when those who believed in the bear's intermediary function were at the point of extinction. Like all facts that are obliterated by the passage of time, customs, cults and ideas are here today, hearsay tomorrow and lost in the limbo of legend and tradition the day after tomorrow. That is how man's knowledge of God became transformed into faith, and why man's faith has declined with each step he has taken down the ladder of religious development. A little while longer, and the bear cult, too, will be legend, but when I knew them the peoples of the North still had a mediator whom they entrusted with a task in the belief that he would fulfill it.

How to build a bridge between the earth and the lord of the mountains? A live bear cannot be sent to the sacred heights, but a dead bear's soul can wing its way to the place where the fate of the Gilyaks is decided. The bear is not, therefore, sacrificed—as he was in the days of Neanderthal man—but dispatched on a mission. He is only the conveyor of sacrifice, not its victim.

This may explain why the bear is so important in the life of the Gilyaks, and why the prehistoric relationship between man and bear played a role whose significance can scarcely be assessed today and is unknown to the majority of our contemporaries.

Capturing a young bear, the Gilyaks take him back to their settlement and keep him in a cage for two or three years. All the members of the clan know that the little bear is destined for the bear festival, so they treat him as an honored guest, feed him with all manner of titbits, take him for walks on his chain, bathe him, and generally take an interest in his welfare.

When the day of the bear festival draws near, large quantities of food and drink are prepared for the clansmen and their guests. Every family in the clan shares in the preparations, arranging the place of execution and making the *inao* or symbolic effigies of mediators between the Gilyaks and the lord of the mountains which are hung on the end of poles in pairs, each pair representing man and wife.

Then comes the festival itself. The bear is taken out of his cage and led from yurt to yurt, being greeted by universal laughter and rejoicing as each family tries to demonstrate the measure of its respect for the animal. However, it is the custom for individuals to tease the growling creature and arouse its fury. A favorite piece of bravado is to grasp the animal's head, kiss it and jump back out of range. If the bear lashes out and scores a Gilyak's shoulder, the wound is regarded as a mark of honor. Finally, the bear is led out onto the frozen surface of the sea or local river to visit the holes where the Gilyaks fish in winter. This guarantees good fishing for the rest of the year.

The bear is led three times around the house of the family which has reared it, after which the master of the house leads it inside, alternately tormenting it with a long stick and addressing it in the friendliest terms.

I assume that this mixture of cruelty and respect is based on the belief that while the animal's flesh has to be tortured and killed its spirit should be treated in a kind and friendly fashion before it sets off on its long journey, because a soul is more easily liberated by torment and agony.

The unfortunate bear is then tied to two posts adorned with inao and left on his own while the Gilyaks go to their yurts to celebrate and the *narch-en* prepare the bows and arrows which are shortly to send the animal on his way.

Who are these narch-en? The bear festival is known by the Gilyaks as "bear play." Alexander Slawik, Austrian ethnologist, records that the participants in a bear festival consist of three clans, each related to the other by a prescribed form of intermarriage. Clan A draws its

wives principally from Clan B and gives its marriageable girls exclusively to Clan C. In this instance, the men of Clan C supply the
narch-en. Assuming that Clan A has reared the bear, the festival will
be given by Clan A, and Clan C will be the guests of honor. Among
the Gilyaks, the bear is always killed by the guests, never by the
animal's guardians. Similarly, it is the guests who actually eat the
bear and take the greater part of its meat home with them.

Clans A and B represent the bear clans in the ceremony, play or
drama, while Clan C represents the human clan. The A and B groups
play the part of bears and the C group the hunters. Leo Sternberg
also confirms that the actual killing is left to the guests, while the
hosts deliberately aim wide of the mark. Alexander Slawik concludes
that the ceremonial killing is a dramatization of the bear hunt in
which the hosts represent the bear clans and the guests personify the
hunters. This seems highly plausible, but why the sharp division of
roles? I believe that it springs from the fear which all northern
tribes have of the soul of a slaughtered bear. The division of roles
is thus a diversionary maneuver in which the hosts are Gilyaks who,
having reared a bear, would never do it any harm, and the guests
play the part of strangers. Thus, a bear is sent on its way still well-
disposed toward its hosts and gives the spirit of the mountain and
forest a good report of the Gilyaks, believing itself to have been
killed by quite another tribe. The Gilyaks feed a bear extremely well
before killing it and entreat it to take the *coup de grâce* in good part.
They also wish it a good journey to its master and express the hope
that it will gain the mountain heights for the Gilyak clan.

Only then is the animal led to the appointed place, attended by all
the male members of the various clans but none of the womenfolk.
The best marksmen fire a few preliminary shots at a chosen target
while small boys pelt the bear with stones. Suddenly, silence falls.
The oldest narch-en, who must also be the best shot, bends his bow,
waits until the beast presents its heart to him, and then lets fly. Immediately, several men step forward and shake the bear roughly. Hallowell suggests that this is to accelerate death, but the Gilyaks told me
that this shaking is supposed to free the soul from the body.

The dead bear is then laid in the snow with its head pointing westward, so that it will not be awakened by the rising sun before it sees the lord of the mountains. The Gilyaks proceed to eat small pouches of food which have previously been hung around the bear's body. There ensues the skinning and dismemberment of the carcass according to a strictly prescribed ritual. The whole skin complete with head is hung up on a wooden framework and food is laid out in front of it in numerous bowls. Meanwhile, the meat is boiled and the entertainment of the narch-en commences. Although the hosts are permitted to eat only the soup from the bear mixed with rice, the guests are forced to eat and drink on a Gargantuan scale, and the feasting lasts for some days. When the narch-en do finally depart, their hosts load their sledges with food and the remains of the bear meat. In return, the guests leave behind gifts for the bear and present their hosts with dogs which are slaughtered and sacrificed in the bear's honor.

Since I met only relatively few Gilyak men who could give me detailed information about the bear cult, I also visited the Ainus. Torii, the famous Japanese expert on the Tungus, believes that the Ainus of prehistoric times were unfamiliar with the bear cult and only adopted it later from the Gilyaks.

The Ainus live in the north of Japan on the island of Hokkaido, but they used also to live on the now Russian island of Sakhalin and in the Kuriles. Their origins are still unidentified, but they are probably an isolated racial group of Caucasian stock, a very ancient human type related to the present inhabitants of western Europe in build, shape of skull and pigmentation.

I have talked with the Ainus on the island of Hokkaido and visited them in their bleak clusters of squat, thatched and wooden huts, villages and townships with names like Horobetsu, Piratori, Nieptani, Chitose, Yurappo, Oshamamu, Shiraoi and Shadai. Looking into their eyes, which are straight and lack the slanting lids of the Mongol, one might almost take them for Europeans, yet there is something Asiatic or even Polynesian about them, particularly the women.

When I say Polynesian I am not referring to the tattooing which Ainu girls have to undergo at a very tender age. This takes the form of a broad stripe above the upper lip which tapers to a point on either side like a mustache. It is not, however, intended to simulate a strong growth of hair on the upper lip, but is merely a form of personal adornment.

Leo Sternberg espoused the view that the Ainus migrated to Japan from the South Seas, basing his theory on various features of their material culture which are common to the Micronesians and other Pacific races as well. The weaver's loom, the outrigger, the bow formerly used by the Ainu, an ancient type of wooden club, the cradle and various forms of ornamentation—all these are enlisted as evidence of the Ainus' Oceanic origins. However, the Ainu race has lived on the Japanese islands for a very long time and seems to have been installed long before any Polynesians or Mongols ever landed there. Indeed, since it once dominated the whole of the Japanese area, cultural elements such as bow and outrigger may well have been adopted, not transmitted, by the peoples of the Pacific. The Japanese scholar K. Koya assumes, probably with justification, that the Ainus were the exiled offshoot of some main European stock. Attention may be drawn in this connection to strange wooden batons which are peculiar to the Ainus and probably hail from the Paleolithic period of the Eurasian mainland. These small sticks are about a foot long and are engraved with double circles (perhaps eyes), wavy lines, stylized symbols reminiscent of animals' heads and intricate patterns. The only things of comparable appearance are the horn batons of the Aurignacian and Mousterian. The Ainus' small pointed sticks, which are objects of great reverence, have been called "beard-raisers," but this description is misleading. The Ainus dip one into a drinking bowl when sacrificing and allow a few drops to fall from it as a libation to the deity. Later, when raising the bowl to their lips, they sometimes use the same small stick to hold their beards away from the rim. Georges Montadon has aptly christened the sticks *baguettes de libation* or "libation wands."

In the seventh century, the Ainus' domain extended as far south as Tokyo, but today they number barely fifteen thousand, all on Hokkaido and most of them intermarried with Japanese. They were still waging a desperate struggle against the Japanese invaders as recently as A.D. 720, but were eventually compelled to withdraw into the colder northern regions of Hokkaido, Sakhalin and the Kuriles. The former masters of all Japan now spend their time carving small wooden bears, stitching the *atush*, a garment made of elm bark, for foreign tourists, and awaiting their final extinction in wretched huts which have been turned into museums for the benefit of ethnologists. The Ainu language is a rich one, and many Japanese words are derived from it, not least the name of their most sacred mountain, the extinct volcano Fuji-no-yama. A large world of ideas, recollections and ancient rites link the Ainus with the bear, to which they attribute their whole existence, their creation and origin. Their name for the bear is *kimum-kamui*, the word *kamui* being almost certainly an ancient form of *kami*, the Japanese expression for divinity. A bear is therefore the "superior being that dwells amid the mountains," and he represents the mediator between this world and the next. No animal could fulfill this function better, for none, in the Ainus' opinion, looks more like man or has a more "human" soul. Consequently, the Ainus' most important festival is the *iomante* or "sending home of the soul."

Like the Gilyaks, the Ainus capture and rear a bear cub carefully. John Batchelor, the greatest authority on the Ainus, said that he at first refused to believe the story that Ainu women suckled young bears but was later forced to reverse his opinion. Writing at the turn of the century, he declared that he had often seen women giving cubs their breasts. On one occasion, he found himself preaching at one end of a hut while five women sat in a circle at the other, passing a bear cub from lap to lap and each giving it a little milk.

At first, the little bear is kept indoors and taken into bed when it cries at night. When it gets bigger, the Ainus put it in a cage until the day comes for its soul to be "sent home." All the inhabitants of the Ainu village and guests from neighboring settlements assemble for the occasion in ceremonial dress. The invitation runs as follows: "I intend to sacrifice the dear little divine animal that dwells in the mountains. Honored friends, come to the feast. Let us unite in the great joy of sending home its soul."

The guests assemble around the fire, drinking in moderation, laughing, dancing and clapping their hands. One of the Ainus then informs

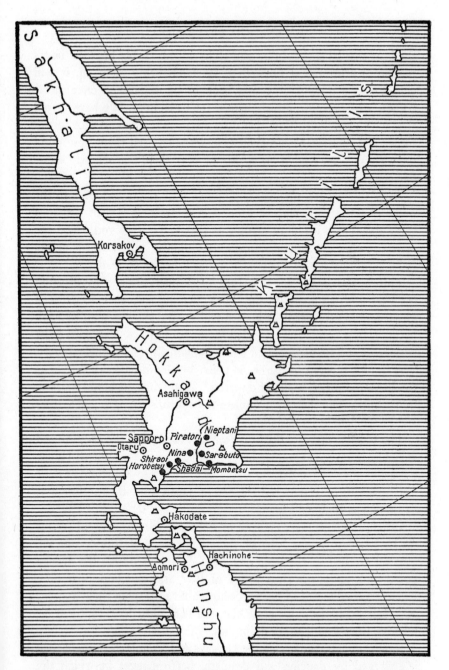

Hokkaido, south Sakhalin and the Kuriles are the only areas where the rapidly dying-out Ainus still live. The black dots indicate villages where the Ainus can be found today.

the bear that its soul is to be sent to its ancestors. He begs the bear's pardon and utters the hope that, far from being annoyed, it will ensure that a good bear comes back to be dispatched once more. "Thou wast brought into the world for us to hunt. We have reared thee with great love. Now that thou are grown, we send thee to thy father and mother. When thou reachest them, tell them how good we were to thee. And come again, we pray thee, that we may sacrifice thee once more."

After this prayer, the bear is pinioned with ropes and led into the midst of the guests, who sit around in a circle. It is then tied to a stake and shot with blunt arrows or thrashed with a rod called the *takusa* so that it becomes thoroughly enraged. This torment at the stake continues until the animal's strength begins to wane.

This is the signal for the best marksman present to dispatch the bear with an arrow in the breast, making sure that no drop of blood touches the earth. It is then laid on the ground with its neck between two beams and throttled for good measure. The dead beast is skinned and its meat boiled and ceremonially eaten amid prayers. The head is severed from the skin and impaled on a stake known as the *keomandemi* or "stake of dispatch." Meanwhile, its blood is drunk by the men, who thereby assimilate the animal's strength and virtues and participate in its dispatch.

The Udehe celebrate the bear festival exactly like the Gilyaks and very like the Ainus. I was told that only two or three hundred Udehe were still alive. These last survivors of a Tungusic-Manchurian tribe live between the Ussuri and the Sea of Japan around the tributaries of the Khor, Bikin and Iman.

When, in December, January or February, the bear's soul set off on its journey to the lord of the mountains and forests and the greatest festival in the year had been duly celebrated, the Udehe could look up at the clear image of Pole Star and hope that they had a good advocate in heaven who would guarantee their hunting and their existence in general. Alas, the bear must have failed in his mission, for the Udehe are dying out.

Harva reports that among the Ostyaks and Voguls the bear festival is followed by dancing and dramatic performances in which the

Ostyak women run about making fluttering motions with their arms and the Voguls dress up as birds of prey. As Harva says, "This symptom of primitive hunter's culture, which undoubtedly goes back to the far-off Stone Age, casts light on the prehistory of human histrionics." We are here confronted by what are probably relics of the earliest form of dramatic art in the world. After feasting off a bear, the hunters place the animal's bones on a raised platform and fire a last shot at the resting place before returning home.

Only about a hundred members of the Olcha, a small tribe which fished and hunted the lower reaches of the Amur between Aofiysk and Bogorodsk, still survive. Both the Olcha and Golds believe that the taiga is inhabited by forest men whom they call *duanteni*. These forest men are lords of the taiga and of animals. The Russian scholar A. M. Zolotarev surmises that the Gilyaks, Ainus, Orochi, Negidals and Olcha all connect the bear festival with commemoration of their dead kinsmen. The Olcha consider the killing of the bear an act of reincarnation, an act which causes the bear, killed in the festival, to go to his parents, the forest men, and bring them the sacrifices of common men.

The ancient Finns used to bid the slaughtered bear: "Tell them, when thou comest to thy forest home, that thou hast not been ill treated here but fed on honey and plied with mead." This and many other passages reminiscent of an erstwhile bear cult are to be found in the ancient Finnish bear songs compiled by Kaarle Krohn.

North American tribes such as the Tlingits, the Kwakiutl, and, above all, the Algonkin celebrate bear festivals much like those of North Asian tribes and are equally careful to adhere to prescribed rituals. This is one of the surest indications that the Tungusic peoples were once linked with the Indian tribes of North America, for the primeval home of all bear cults must undoubtedly have been not North America but Eurasia. There is abundant evidence to suggest that the Algonkin's ancestors were of Siberian origin, and no serious scholar now disputes that the various pre-Columbian migrations to America had their point of departure in Asia. The Wenner-Gren Institute of Anthropological Research in New York has already brought to light interesting information about the transpacific cultural relationships between Asia, Oceania and America, and the Austrian ethnologist Robert Heine-Geldern has demonstrated that the problem of these relationships cannot be solved by rough-and-ready methods like those employed by Thor Heyerdahl of *Kon Tiki* fame. One cannot talk of America and Polynesia *in vacuo* and leave the fact of Asia entirely out of the picture.

As we have seen, the same bear cult can be identified at many points around the Pole, though somewhat inland. Some remarkably interesting comparisons can be drawn between various different peoples. For instance, the inland races of Siberia send a mediator to the exalted being who, as lord of the mountains, stands immediately below God. Not only do we find the same bear cult among the ancient tribes of North America, but we catch echoes of it in the Stone Age.

The Ainus and Gilyaks kill a bear by shooting it through the heart or lungs with an arrow. The wounded bear depicted in the cave of Trois-Frères is spewing blood from its snout and muzzle. The Gilyaks stone a bear before killing it. Small ovals on the bear picture in the Trois-Frères cave show where stones are striking its body.

The Ainus shoots a bear with blunt arrows before putting it out of its misery. The bear sculpture of Montespan exhibits indentations made by arrows of this type or other weapons. The Gilyaks hang the skin of a dead bear on a framework. The same applies to the bear sculpture of Montespan.

It must be regarded as one of the greatest marvels elicited by the modern study of prehistory that both customs—the sacrificing of bears' skulls seventy thousand years ago and the bear cult of about thirty thousand years ago—have been rediscovered in the Stone Age. We have proved that the skull and marrowbones of the bear were sacrificed during the Mousterian. At that time, some seventy thousand years ago, man—probably Neanderthal man—was apparently sacrificing to a supreme god, and sacrificing just as the people of the Arctic coastal cultures still do today, so long afterward.

And in the Aurignacian and Magdalenian, thirty or twenty thousand years ago, bear cult rites were being performed much like those which I have seen at the great bear festivals of the Gilyaks, Ainus and other representatives of the so-called inland cultures.

It cannot be mere chance that the bear cult of our own day and that which we have identified in French caves bear so striking a resemblance to one another. Three hundred thousand years ago in Peking, seventy thousand years ago in the Alps and thirty thousand years ago in southern France (and probably eastern Asia) man believed in a supreme god. There may still be room for doubt where Peking man is concerned, but in the case of Neanderthal man and Cro-Magnon man this faith stands proved, even if the god of twenty or thirty thousand years ago was looked upon only as a lord of the mountains, beasts and water.

CHAPTER 24

SORCERY, MAGIC AND RELIGIOUS CULTS

Everything, however, suggests that we are here dealing with a cult activity of genuinely religious character. . . . The motivation of pictorial cave art corresponds far more closely, in its magnificence, to our conception of the essential nature of art. Nor would it be reasonable if the creative beginnings of art, which we number among the loftiest realms of human activity, sprang from a spirituality not only incomprehensible to us but rooted in error.

A. E. JENSEN, *Mythos und Kult bei Naturvölkern*

No one who stands before these pictures, no one who realizes the loving care with which the deep lines were carved into the rock, no one who has any feeling for the monumental can fail to admire the splendor of these temples of Nature.

LEO FROBENIUS, *Das unbekannte Africa*

MANY races in the world believe not only that the graphic representation of a man reproduces his physical appearance but also that with the capturing of his bodily form in effigy his soul is likewise caught and held captive. Hence their very real fear of being sketched, modeled or photographed. The notion that the fate of a picture may also decide the fate of the man it portrays and that anyone who possesses the former controls the latter is one which has existed from very ancient times.

On the threshold between the Aurignacian and Magdalenian, of about twenty thousand years ago, something must have happened to convince man that any portrayal of his own kind was fraught with danger. With a few isolated exceptions, all the "Venus" statuettes were made during the Aurignacian, and the few that hail from the Magdalenian are largely devoid of artistic merit. It seems obvious that artists no longer dared to portray the human form in effigy. This fear of the human image must have grown up in hunting cultures which had transferred the idea of the danger of pictorial representation to the animal world.

The Tungus used to carve a figure of the animal which they wished to kill and take it with them on hunting trips, on the principle that if the pictorial soul is in the hunter's possession the animal itself will soon follow. The Yeniseis make wooden fish to ensure a good catch. The Ostyaks, Voguls and many other Siberian tribes also try to capture the soul of their quarry and increase their chances of good hunting by means of animal figures, normally carved of wood. An animal is put under a spell through the medium of its effigy, and the soul of a living beast suffers the same fate as the soul of its second self. The animal has, in fact, lost its freedom of action and must eventually succumb to the hunter. A hunter can also portray the death of his game in ceremonial fashion by killing it in effigy, using certain very ancient rituals. This arouses confidence in his ability to triumph over his quarry. Leo Frobenius, famous German ethnologist and founder of the Frankfort Institute for Cultural Morphology, describes the preparations made by Pygmies of the Congo when hunting antelope. Going to a hill before dawn, they drew the shape of the animal in the sand with their fingers. Then, at sunrise, they shot an arrow into the ground so that it stuck in the neck of the animal depicted. After their real quarry had been successfully dispatched with a well-aimed arrow in the jugular vein, they returned to the hill and rubbed a little of the dead antelope's hair and blood into the sand. Finally, the arrow was withdrawn and the picture obliterated.

The premature aura of success derived from this ritual killing tells the tutelary spirits of an animal that they are powerless. This is not sorcery, however. A hunter's concentration on the task in hand, his faith in his future triumph and the psychological presentiment of victory may be actually conducive of success. These are, as Karl J. Narr points out, forms of genuine magical observance which, by intensifying self-confidence, actually influence reality. Pictorial representations of hunting scenes are not sorcery, therefore, but a token of magical activity. Frobenius personally watched the Congo Pygmies during their preparations for antelope hunting. "Anyone who reflects," wrote this eminent authority, "that Spanish rock paintings show animals with hearts drawn in or arrowheads in the region of the heart and anyone who remembers that African and Saharan rock pictures, which are usually of animals, generally appear at points where they are exposed to the first rays of the morning sun must perceive a relationship between the relics of customs still observed by Africans who have been forced into the virgin forests and the relics of Africa's Paleolithic Age."

The exceedingly realistic illustrations of individual animals found in the caves of southern France and northwest Spain may, therefore, have been conjured up on the rock walls as a means of capturing an animal pictorially, of bringing it within a hunter's orbit and then, by the employment of certain magical formulae, of ensuring its death. In other words, what was done to an accurate portrayal of an animal would sooner or later happen to the animal itself. Hence the evident striving in cave painting and sculpture to make any portrayal as lifelike as possible.

Thus, cave art had definite magical connotations, and many cave pictures may have been executed with magic in view. This would explain why individual portrayals are sometimes superimposed on one another, each animal being depicted as a separate creature without reference to an over-all composition. It would also explain the lack of a common base line. Animals are pictured, as it were, *in vacuo*. They are animals per se, portrayed for a magical purpose, drawn or engraved as a means of bewitching them and eventually, after the performance of certain rites, of making them fall prey to the hunter.

But cave art was more than this, as we can tell by comparison with people who still practice the art of rock painting or with places where this form of painting was practiced not long ago. Frobenius writes of the hunters who live in the ethnic basin between the Niger and Lake Tchad in Africa. Among them are a light-skinned type of Magussaua known by the Hausas simply as *mahalbi* or "hunters." The Mahalbi do not allow their young men either to have intercourse with girls before initiation, or to go hunting. The initiation ceremony, which takes place in the bush, is an occasion for much noise and dancing. When the youths have worked themselves into a state of ecstasy, they are suddenly attacked by a leopard or leopard-like being who wounds some of them. They are then obliged to leave the place of initiation walking on their heels. If they trod full on the ground, the savage bush creature would recognize them by their toe-prints and pursue them.

This custom is of particular interest because it has a prehistoric parallel in the Montespan cave, where heelprints of young people were found in the sintered clay floor. These, Narr claims, were left by "men of hunting, sexual and religious maturity" while performing a round dance of a religious nature. This was not merely magic. Twenty thousand years ago, men were sharing in a profound religious experience.

Also of interest in this connection is the art of the bushmen, the South African aborigines who were still painting their black, yellow, red and white cave pictures in our own era and continued to do so until about 1850. Many such bushmen caves have been found near the Cape, and it appears that the art of these pygmoid people can be traced back without interruption to Stone-Age times—in fact, that a genre of painting preserved itself unmodified for ten or even twenty thousand years, only to wane and die in the nineteenth century. The art of these bushmen, who lived by hunting and gathering wild fruits, vegetable materials and roots, like the people of Paleolithic times, is founded on the same spiritual approach as that of the Ice-Age hunters, and its significance is of a magical or religious nature.

The rock paintings of northwest Australia were also cult centers, and had to be repeatedly retouched and refreshed in order to guarantee the continued existence of the beasts and men depicted by them. Strange rock pictures in the hills on both banks of the King Edward River and on the peninsulas enclosing Napier-Broome Bay portray huge mouthless figures representing supernatural beings which control fertility and the propagation of human, animal and plant life. The German ethnologist E. A. Worms, who studied these pictures in 1953 and 1954, emphasizes that the so-called Wondjina paintings have an essentially mythological content, and Adolph E. Jensen, German professor of ethnology, suggested that they were symbolic recapitulations of a primeval occurrence.

If the cave pictures of Southern France and northwest Spain were intended solely to guarantee successful hunting, many details would remain inexplicable. For example, the entrance to the Bernifal cave had at one time been artificially blocked, which suggests that the cave was opened only on certain occasions. The Belgian prehistorian H. Danthine deduces that it cannot have served merely as a place where hunting magic was performed in order to assure a daily supply of food, and suggests that it must have been the site of something much more important, perhaps cult ceremonies held at longish intervals, or places of initiation and worship where communication took place between man and a superior being. The latter would have been a deity who protected animals, dispensed game among hunters and controlled the relationship between man and beast and their natural environment. We must never forget that our Magdalenian ancestors were hunters and that their whole culture was bound up with game. Countless verbal expressions, habits and traditions in each of the five continents testify how deeply this age-old relationship between man and beast still affects our culture in the present era.

If the caves did not serve magical purposes alone, if they were not entered for purely materialistic reasons, if they were really ceremonial chambers in which spiritual contact with higher powers was sought, then the portrayals of wounded animals were probably associated with cult rituals of a religious nature, as Narr suggests. They were an attempt, born of man's continuous connection with hunting, to represent an age-old human victory and symbolize a mythical occurrence. We are still imbued with a primeval urge to express the divinely bestowed element in life through drama, dancing, festivals, ceremonies and the formative arts, just like the men of twenty thousand or more years ago. The dance as a medium of religious expression may be hundreds of thousands of years old, and all such forms of expression or representation culminate in a creative process which strives toward the divine and serves life and its preservation by commemorating its origin.

But life in those days meant an endless round of stalking game and following game paths, of sensing nature's every changing mood. It meant a constantly shifting relationship between biped and quadruped, an everlasting alternation of hunger and satiety, success and disappointment. Anyone who has lived in the taiga for long realizes that in the mind of the Tungus and other Siberian peoples every animal and every natural phenomenon has its own patron and protector, and that because the lord of the mountains and beasts is neither omniscient nor omnipotent the smallest and weakest living creature often escapes death while whole forests perish.

Many primitive peoples have a "lord of beasts" or "protector of game," from the Eskimos of Labrador and the Naskapi to the Quichés of Guatemala and the Caribbean Taulipang in northern South America. Such a conception is common to nearly all the ancient Indian tribes of the American double continent. The Tungus have a lord of the forest called Ure Amaka, a tutelary spirit who extends his protection to animals and mountains and is thought of as a white-haired old man who dwells in the taiga. Samoyeds, Finns, Lapps, Mongols and Buryats are all familiar with the spirit or lord of the forest, a being who speaks in a high, distorted voice, who can call, cry and laugh eerily and is far bigger than common mortals. This giant has found his way into the fairy tales of Russia and the legends of Europe under many different aliases. He probably originated, as P. Wilhelm Schmidt suggests, in the primeval culture of the Arctic and was an offshoot of the idea of a supreme being. He is not God, therefore, but the preserver and patron of the hunting culture, a being who looks after the welfare of animals and apportions game among such hunters as are worthy of his beneficence.

No great art can exist without faith. It was faith that created the pyramids of Egypt, faith that produced the splendors of the Renaissance, faith that sent the cathedral spires of Europe soaring to the skies. No world which is merely an economic system can produce art, and faith must be more than a wish to obtain advantages by magical means. It must be faith in communication with an exalted and intangible being, in communion with a materially disinterested force. Only a heartfelt quest for the unattainable, a desire to bridge the gulf between man and Creation, can lead to the heights of true art. Purely magical beliefs which are dependent upon success alone give birth only to the art of the amulet.

Ziggurats, pyramids, cathedrals and cave paintings, on the other hand, are of quite different lineage. They were born of spirituality and grew from a yearning deeper than that of acquisitive magic, from a dramatic struggle in which the human soul strove desperately to attain the nearness to God which is the hallmark of all great art.

Thus, animals were not painted solely in order to encompass their destruction. At least, not all of them were portrayed for the purpose of gaining power over them, for they were protégés of a father of animals and hunting, of a universal father of nature behind whom, invisible to us and unportrayable by the men of the Stone Age, stood God. This was the idea upon which the cave painter drew for inspiration. Man did not raise art to the remarkable heights represented by Altamira and Lascaux out of selfish and petty motives alone.

If we find it hard to grasp that the hunters of so long ago had more in mind than edible game, we must remember that mankind's spiritual striving has waned as his acquisitiveness has grown. We are far away from Creation, but the men of five hundred thousand years ago were near it. Believing in a single god, they were impelled to build an artistic bridge to him twenty thousand years ago. Today, we are so far from our erstwhile link with the creative force that no bridge can span the gulf.

That the caves were sites not of magical activity but of religious or cult observance is demonstrated by two amazing works ascribed to Magdalenian man. The Montespan cave in Haute-Garonne contains the clay figure of a bear. It is not a particularly beautiful piece of sculpture. The discoverer of the Trois-Frères cave, Count Bégouen, famous French prehistorian, compared it with the sort of shapes children make in the snow. The Magdalenian artist had not displayed any great virtuosity, nor had he produced anything as realistic as the splendid pair of bison at Tuc d'Audoubert. Nevertheless, 170 yards from the mouth of the Montespan cave in the small low-roofed chamber at its far end, Stone-Age man must have had something special in mind. His bear had no head, yet there is absolutely no doubt that figure was planned and executed as such from the beginning. There it lay on the floor of the cave like an unwieldy sphinx with its thick forepaws stretched out in front of it—and between them Count Bégouen found the skull of a real bear.

What was the significance of this? The only possible conclusion was that a real bear's skull was attached to the figure's neck on certain occasions or that it was sometimes draped with a complete bearskin, head included. Count Bégouin established that the convex surface of the sculpture had been worn away as though by friction, which may mean that the process of draping and undraping continued at intervals over a very long period of time. Yet another fact was adduced to prove that the skull lying between the forepaws had really fallen off the sculpture itself. In the center of the abbreviated neck was a triangular depression which may once have held the bone or wooden peg that supported the skull. The hole is so small that some authorities have doubted whether it could have been used for such a purpose, but if the statue was draped with a whole bearskin still attached to the head very little support would have been needed and the small triangular hole would have been entirely adequate. Describing his discovery. Count Bégouin made the following, extremely interesting remark: "We may assume that we found the skull at the spot where it had lain ever since the last ceremony."

But this is not all. The sculpture was pock-marked all over with round, deep holes which looked as though they had been made by fingers or sticks. These thirty indentations suggest that the figure had been ritually speared or shot with arrows.

The Trois-Frères cave (Montesquieu-Avantès, Ariège) was discovered in 1914 by Count Bégouin and his three sons, after whom it was named. This cave contains a great wealth of rock paintings situated more than five hundred yards from its mouth. Among them is one of a bear with a thick stream of blood flowing from its muzzle. The animal is obviously *in extremis*. Its body is dotted with small circles and ovals to represent the stones which have struck it, and it has also been wounded by arrows. One of these must have penetrated a lung, for only this would explain the stream of blood gushing from its snout and muzzle.

The Austrian paleontologist Othenio Abel includes two further portrayals of mortally wounded bears in a group which he ascribes to a single cult, and it is interesting to note that only bears and no other animals figure in this sanguinary type of picture.

The most famous caves in France in which fossils, artifacts and art dating from the Stone Age have been found.

Abel discovered some other strange facts which indicate the existence of a bear cult in the Upper Paleolithic period. There are three
instances in which human heads appear to be depicted wearing bearskin masks and no less than twenty-five examples of bears' heads
on their own.

As we have already seen, Neanderthal man was sacrificing bears'
skulls and marrowbones to his god seventy thousand years ago,
during the Lower Paleolithic. Twenty thousand years ago, in the
Upper Paleolithic, things took quite a different turn. Man was no
longer sacrificing the most precious parts of the bear to his god. The
killing of the animal had become a cult ritual, a bear festival or
ceremony. Although this cult or ceremony must have constituted the
focal point of religious life, man no longer confronted his god face
to face. By now there was a third party, an animal, a very manlike
animal, a creature who was ritually killed and may have occupied the
role of mediator between man and god. The inaccessible position of
many cave paintings and the other facts, mentioned above, which
indicate their religious significance leave little doubt that caves were
the cathedrals of the Stone Age. Frobenius says: "On this basis, each
such site becomes a temple built into monumental natural surroundings and each cave drawing a thing of individual significance."

There was yet another great difference between the activities of
man—i.e. Neanderthal man—in the Mousterian and the mysterious
doings of Homo sapiens in the Magdalenian. Man of seventy thousand years ago was able to converse with God only as Job did, having
not as yet reached the stage of pictorial images. The man of the
much later cave-painting era was using a bridge to approach God,
the bridge of art, but the spiritual imagination of the earlier man who
climbed into the fastnesses of the Alps and sacrificed in the Drachenloch was infinitely greater. We shall never know what he found there
and what he thought, but he was in possession of all the intellectual
and physical powers on which we pride ourselves today. Mankind
lost its original form of belief, which was a knowledge of the
Supreme Being, on the road to so-called civilization. As A. E. Jensen
wrote in explaining the views of Andrew Lang: "In Lang's view,
it was man's indolence which encouraged him to regard it as an

easier mode of existence to commune with corrupt and venal spirits than to live according to the strict precepts of a High God."

But there was yet another difference. The earlier type of man, who believed in one god and made sacrifice to him, was still hunting the cave bear, and continued to do so from the Upper Mousterian until the close of the Central European Aurignacian. At the time when the finest of the Trois-Frères and Montespan pictures came into being, the cave bear was already extinct. All the bears painted, engraved or sculpted during the Magdalenian were brown bears. The cave bear was a far larger and more fearsome beast. We know exactly what it looked like, not so much because of the vast numbers of bones which have been found but because we possess a magnificent drawing of the creature scratched on a limestone slab dating from the Aurignacian. I have seen this drawing in the museum attached to the Geological and Paleontological Institute of Lyons University. The cave bear carried its head much lower than the brown bear and its snout had an upward tilt. Not even the finest of modern reconstructions could have taken the place of this extraordinarily lifelike sketch. The only reason why we can form such an accurate picture of the mammoth, too, is that Stone-Age man embodied the animal in his art. However abundant, the remains unearthed from the frozen soil of Siberia would never have given us a complete idea of the creature as it really was.

As we have already said, there is no art without faith. The animal pictures on cave walls, like the three-dimensional forms of art, all probably sprang from a vigorous and thriving religious life. This is the difference between religious cults and magic. Magic is merely an activity directed toward the attainment of a finite end—in a hunter's economy, the slaughter of game. Cave art was founded on faith, and the greatness of cave art is a measure of the sincerity of that faith. None of this is explicable in terms of development. If, as we like to think, man made his way ever upward, if he evolved spiritually, if each peak he attained lay a little higher than the preceding one, if he began by being as intellectually inferior and semi-bestial as the theory of evolution insists, the cave art of forty, thirty and twenty thousand years ago becomes inconceivable.

This splendid and very ancient form of art presents traditional evolutionism with an insurmountable obstacle, for we have long known that the human intellect basically has neither developed nor improved in the past thirty thousand years. Altamira's art and the religious fervor which it mutely but unmistakably expresses may well have been equaled by the ancient Greeks and the Italians of the Renaissance but was never surpassed by them.

The fact that man possessed the same soul and the same spirituality from time immemorial, that he was, in effect, created in the image of God, is recognizable not only in the traces left by Paleolithic hunters in lofty alpine caves but also in the magnificent relics of Franco-Cantabrian art.

To people who believed in the original concept of evolution the discovery of the caves came as an intolerable shock, and a considerable furore ensued. It was hinted that only the Church could have had a vested interest in demonstrating the existence of spirituality and spiritual life among men at such an early date, and the pictures were dismissed as a pious fraud on the part of Spanish priests. The art of Altamira was discredited and the dark vaults returned to the silence and obscurity in which they had existed for so many thousands of years. When, after decades, it was established that these incomparable expressions of man's spiritual life were not a fraud, the evolutionists tried another tack and described them simply as primitive art.

Today, the spirituality of early man can no longer be disputed. It must be recognized that for both God and man, time does not run up or down; that is, time in reality has no past or future but should be considered as a straight line from above with no beginning and no end.

Paleolithic art, I submit, was never slavishly imitative, never a herdsman's hobby or child's game, and thus never merely "primitive." One has only to look at the Venus of Lespugue to realize this. Human spirituality has been homogeneous at every stage since the moment when it was first called into being by the Creator.

The human race has not reached a zenith. Far too much has hap-

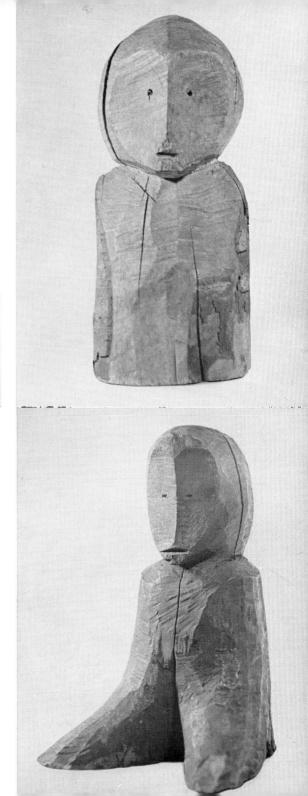

[91] (*Above, right*) The spirit which stands behind the hearth opposite the entrance of a Gilyak yurt and protects the household.

[92] (*Above, left*) Nyokhul-Chsai, a spirit which cures pains in the breasts of old women. The Gilyaks use such figures as pendants and amulets.

[93] Pansh-Omugu, wife of the lord of the yurt. All these pictures of Gilyak carvings are published here for the first time.

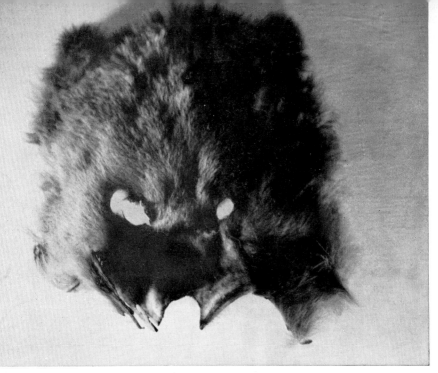

[94] The skin taken from the head of a bear killed during a bear ceremony is used as a dancing mask at the next festival.

[95] After the bear ceremony, the Gilyaks put the animal's skull on the end of a pole and display it at the ceremonial site, preserving it intact in order to ensure the bear's reincarnation. The two hooks on the left are used for hoisting the bear's carcass. In the foreground, a Gilyak bear-spear blade which, like the Orochon's *palma*, was fastened to a wooden shaft.

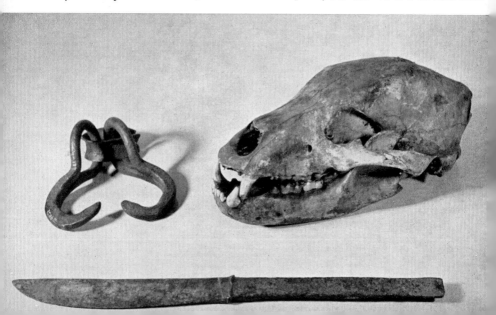

[96] Fragment of root, ending in three bears' heads, used for dividing bear's meat. The Gil-yaks call this implement a *takhai*.

[97] Carved ladle used for serving meat at the bear festival.

[98] Dyed in three colors, this Gilyak tunic is made of fishskins so neatly sewn together that the garment is completely windproof and watertight.

[99] We tend to forget that the peoples of Siberia, together with the Mongols and Buryats, wear extremely colorful clothing. This Gilyak woman's fishskin smock is decorated in blue and red and has a row of brass pendants along its hem. The photograph shows the finely ornamented back of the smock.

[100] This female Orochon shaman had spent a lifetime in the forests of the North Manchurian taiga enclosed by the Amur Bend. The numerous small animal symbols and chains are aids in establishing contact with spirits, while the oval drum serves to heighten the requisite state of ecstasy during which spirits inhabit a shaman's body and his own soul leaves it to roam about the sky.

[101] A Yakut shaman from the district of Verchne-Kolymsk.

[102] Tungusic shaman's drum. The shaman beats his drum in order to capture spirits, enter a state of ecstasy and escape his corporeal bonds. He thereby travels to the center of the world and can, at the same time, rise into the sky. His frenzy communicates itself to his audience. The edge of this drumskin is decorated with pictures of reindeer and the handle of the drumstick is carved into the shape of an animal's head.

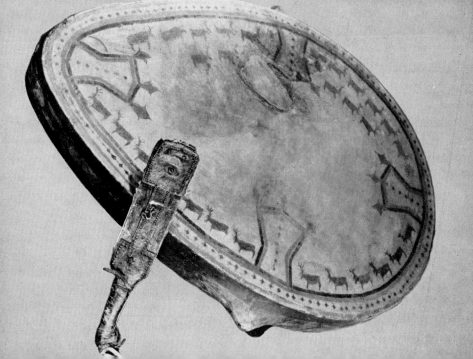

[103] *Oro* is the reindeer and *chon* the man. The Tungus' reindeer are smoke-gray, black or, as in this picture, white. They carry an average load of 80 pounds each and are tended by the womenfolk.

pened and far too many summits of achievement lie behind us for such a theory to hold good. It is absurd to pause on a journey through time which has already lasted five or six hundred thousand years and claim that Heaven is now ours. Man in my opinion was probably far closer to it long ago.

CHAPTER 25

ANIMISM

When the son sneezed his soul sprang from his body and tried to escape through the door, but the spirit stationed there caught it and held it fast, even though the poor soul cried aloud.

From a Buryat story as told by Uno Harva in *Die religiösen Vorstellungen der altaischen Völker*, p. 273

AS THE LIGHT of day fades slowly from the taiga, isolated features remain visible, here a solitary tree, there the roots of another that has fallen spreading its gnarled arms as though in supplication to the darkening horizon. So it is with religion. Dotted over the broad and ancient battlefield of faith lie the still identifiable relics of things which were once young and vital, things which gain in significance because they have reached the evening of their days and will soon be lost in the gathering mists of oblivion.

Among these are shamanism, animism and magic, the last feature visible in the twilight of extinction which surrounds the primitive races of the world. Certainly they were not a beginning, nor were they in any sense predecessors of religion. Indeed, magic is often more pronounced among high cultures than among ethnologically ancient peoples.

Magic is generally described as an activity which releases automatic powers. Its essential characteristic is, in fact, its automatism and mechanical operation. Certain tribes throttle or burn dolls so that the enemy whom they represent will suffer the same fate. Other magical activities are focused not on an effigy but on a human subject whom it is proposed to cure, injure or influence in some way. In many quarters of the world, notably in Asiatic Russia, contact magic is still employed; that is to say, the magical influencing of people by actual physical contact, not excluding the dosing of their food with toxic substances which have been previously bewitched by means of spells. Under this heading come the whole realm of sorcery, the evil eye, spitting as a propitiatory act, the remote-control magic of the Australian aborigines and the injurious magic of the

Chukchis, who bewitch the hair, fingernails or clothing of an adversary in order to bring him *portsha*, the Russian word for "harm." Also classifiable as purely mechanical magic is the shaman's or witch doctor's habit of transferring a disease from a human being to an inanimate object and so of curing him. A good shaman is not, however, a magician.

The wish to exert a supernatural or magical influence not only on living creatures but also on inanimate objects in the external world is present mainly among people whose function or profession depends largely for its success on chance or luck, people such as gamblers, artists, actors, sportsmen, criminals—even not naturally superstitious individuals who are faced by an examination or an important decision.

There is, however, another kind of magic which aims at nothing less than spiritual contact between man on the one hand and a living creature or God on the other. The fact that inanimate objects form the medium of such contact does not transform spiritual magic into mechanical. The Russian scholar S. A. Tokarev, who has very recently published a lengthy discourse on magic, refuses to see more than one side of this idea; namely, the black arts, sorcery and superstitious acts designed to influence objects, living creatures or natural phenomena in a supernatural manner. But not all religious rites can be regarded as sorcery or purely mechanical magic.

In religion, men endowed with freedom of will confront a creative God. They cannot extort anything by religious observance. They can only pray and leave the rest to God. Mechanical magic, on the other hand, demands no good will, no moral preparedness, no religious endeavor. Magic in the primitive sense presupposes no kind of morality, and mechanical magic is never directed toward a spiritual end.

Thus, mechanical magic must be distinguished from genuine or spiritual magic. Spiritual magic does not attempt to provoke automatic changes in nature, but reacts upon the operator. That is why a sorcerer is only a technician, whereas a priest is a man in spiritual contact with God. Communication or communion with the Supreme Being is spiritual magic. The Magi of the West, for instance, were not sorcerers but wise and religiously inspired men who had been drawn to Bethlehem by the spirituality of the Christ child.

If, by compelling spirituality to don worldly garb, one comes to believe that everything harbors a soul or spirit, all objects become animate. I saw for myself how primitive races like the Tungus approach the subject of animism.

I was quite alone, sleeping by my campfire near the banks of the Kumara, when a voice broke suddenly into my dreams.

"I come to you, to see what you are doing." It was an old Orochon. He knelt down, squatted on his heels and regarded me out of his slanting eyes set in a face that was brown, leathery and flat, almost as if it had been modeled out of the soil of the taiga. His hair was short and gray, his build squat and broad.

"And the others?" I asked. "Where are your people?"

"Back there," he said. "Not far off, two or three hours."

Two or three hours was a concrete notion, I knew. It meant anything up to twenty miles, a good day's journey or so.

The trees suddenly swayed and hissed like waves breaking on a pebbly beach. "Old Man Forest a little sad today," said the Orochon in his broken Russian.

"Do you think we're going to have bad weather?"

"Shadows linger a little," replied the old man, "creep a little slowly this evening behind branches, trees and under the ground. Evening come very slow. Tomorrow cold."

"Are you going to sleep now?" I asked.

"You go sleep," he said. "I speak little, very little with fire. Fire not so happy today. Fire bad woman, must speak with her a little."

"Can fire speak, then?"

My new friend laughed. "Nothing greater than fire," he said. "Fire very much power, keep evil spirits away, can drive away dangerous spirits, too. Look close. Outside, fire old woman, white hair, many tongues, talk plenty. Inside, fire young heart, red blood, very strong."

"Can you make old fire young?" I asked.

"Put little bear fat in," said the Orochon. "Then fire red like blood and very happy. Fire always hungry. When she eat plenty, then good girl. Never leave her alone. Fire like company. Leave her alone, then she become angry. If no fat and no wood, then perhaps she go walk, then whole forest burn."

"So you speak with fire?"

"Red woman like to talk. Fire here, fire there, like to talk, like to dance. Give me little fat." He spread it on a small piece of wood and threw it into the flames so that the sparks flew. "Red girl laughing!" The Tungus rubbed his hands.

We sat by the fire for many hours. The longer I was with this man the better I understood his view of the forest. Everything in it was alive, everything was animate, everything had its own soul, everything possessed human faculties; above all, everything was mirrored in the soul, intellect and speech of the Orochon. There was an impressive refinement about a man who was on such intimate terms with every material object and every animal, with sun and wind, storm and loquacious fire. There are few more stupid things on earth than our expressions "savage" and "primitive."

My new friend's name was Sagdikikan. We later encountered each other on several occasions. I learned from him that the sun can scatter golden rain, that water is a temperamental being that weeps, laughs and shouts, that cloud can turn itself into bears, that it tucks in its head and rolls over mountains, that each piece of wood in a fire speaks a different language just as trees themselves do, from black birch and Daurian larch to elm and Amur spruce.

"Amur spruce very simple fellow," Sagdikikan remarked one night when we were once again sitting by the fire. And then he told me what is perhaps the greatest and most important truth I learned on my travels through the taiga. "If there are so many 'fellows,'" I had asked him, "so many respected beings like old trees, angry water, talkative fire, spirits of the dead, carved animals into which the souls of game can creep; if you find it easier to gain power over deer, wolf or bear by using wooden figures like these; if there is so much life everywhere and so many spirits in all things, do you still believe in a supreme god?"

The Tungus regarded me quietly for a moment or two. I could not tell what was going on behind his slit black eyes. All I could see was the firelight flickering on the dark pupils. "Great old Sky-god," he said. "Yes, great old Sky-god always there. He live at top of sky. Highest larch tree cannot reach him. He has sons, seven sons, his helpers."

"And your shaman, your *saman*, is he a god too, or just a helper?"

Sagdikikan seemed surprised at my ignorance. "Saman only man. But saman know human soul, very good doctor. Sometimes, even saman die. Then his soul fly out. Saman can talk with helpers of sky, but this very hard for him. Must suffer much."

I understood. Sky-god and shaman are two entirely different beings. The sky, which amounts to a single god, is high above and inaccessible to the shaman, who is human. Here in the North Manchurian taiga, the Orochi, like all Tungus, believe in a supreme god whom they call the Sky, the Highest, the Sky-god.

The idea that all material objects harbor a spirit or soul, and the habit of talking to thousands of forest creatures and things, are common to all men who live alone in the midst of nature. Half the world believes in spirits, from Africa to the island realms of Melanesia and Polynesia, and from India, Tibet, Turkestan, China and Japan to the taiga, tundra and Arctic. But superimposed on the ideas of these far from simple-minded people whom we so erroneously call primitive is that of the single and indivisible god before whom man fell on his knees hundreds of thousands of years ago.

The realization that body and intellect do not comprise the whole of human personality is equally ancient. People all over the world became acquainted with the soul's existence in sleep, dreams and visions long before the dawn of history. Since sleep divorces a man from his waking self, he came to believe that he could meet his own soul during dreams, that the soul could release itself, roam about, adopt different guises, undergo pleasant or frightening experiences. This belief in dreams is shared by the Orochi, the Tungus as a whole and the tribes of northeast Asia in general, as well as by many of the Indian tribes of North America. To them, the soul is a weightless, winged thing which can go where it will. It is far fleeter than man himself, can plunge into abysses or scale endless heights, tremble and rejoice, laugh, cry or even commit murder. It is a shadowy and intangible thing which leaves no traces, but it can also suffer and experience pain. The sleeper's groan is an echo of the grief and anguish felt by a soul in torment.

Sometimes a sleeping man gets up and goes where his vision directs, following his soul step by step and thus remaining near it. This age-old human experience, which is so ancient that our own span of history shrinks to nothing in comparison, has fostered a belief that something similar occurs in death. The soul abandons the body and goes wandering. And as long as the soul survives, it can see everything and do a great deal, and as long as it lives man lives too. Conversely, if the soul dies man can no longer survive. This is one of the ancient and universal truths of human religion, and another almost equally universal belief is that at the end of the soul's journeying stands God. This train of thought has also given rise to a belief in the transmigration of souls.

In the spiritual world of the Tungus, animals, trees, rivers and all material objects, even stones, possess souls of their own. The marsh has a spirit or soul, as does each forest and mountain. One cannot see these spirits, it is true, but one can hear them speaking in the various tongues. Sometimes, when the spirits of the forest are particularly active, they set upon a man and pull him hither and thither or squat gibbering at his side while he sleeps, so that he wakes at dawn exhausted and depressed. There are countless, innumerable places where the souls of the dead can take up their abode. Since each object has a soul of its own as well, it is wise to engage what we regard as inanimate objects in conversation.

The Latin word for soul is *animus*, hence the term "animism." Animism is not, however, religion, as I learned from Tungus, Polynesians, Melanesians, the Australian aborigines, the Ainus, and the Yaghans, the Alacaluf and the Selknams of Tierra del Fuego. The Japanese, Chinese, Mongols and all the Turkish peoples live, fundamentally, in a world of animate objects, and the same still applies to the Russian peasant household today. Yet all of them believe in one god. When an authority like E. Royston Pike calculates that there are 135 million animists in the world, notably in Asia, Central Africa and Oceania, it is almost as if he were trying to measure the dream vibrations of humanity. Since the whole of our terrestrial and celestial environment is animated and activated by a force beyond our ken, animism is really part of each and every one of us. The closer to nature a man is, the more strongly he feels this. Thus, the number of animists of varying complexions runs not into millions but hundreds of millions.

The term "soul" should not, of course, be thought of here in the Christian sense. The Tungus did not endow their concept of an alter ego with this meaning until they had come into contact with foreign cultures. Their alter ego really is a second self, for they credit a soul with all the attributes of its owner. An able, clever and wise man possesses an able, clever and wise soul, and the soul of such a person knows its way about the world and the universe far better than a primitive soul. It does not blunder so easily, has a better sense of direction and finds its owner again with less difficulty. Being an intangible and imponderable form of life, it can also be envisaged as a puff of breath which is released when a man dies.

These symbols were found on cave walls in the Sierra Morena in southern Spain. Their age is hard to estimate, but is probably in the region of ten thousand years. Although they are not writing, they are a step in that direction. Abbé Breuil believes them to to be connected with death cults and suggests that they portray the condition of the soul after death. The multiplicity of eyes is taken to signify that souls are all-seeing.

Souls like to wander while their owners sleep, so it is dangerous to rouse a dreaming man suddenly in case his soul is too far away to get back in time. Similarly, almost all Siberian tribes believe that a man who is abruptly wakened readily falls prey to madness. Souls also do a great deal of traveling during severe illnesses, which is logical enough when one reflects that severe illness can be a halfway house to death. I met Samoyeds and Chuvashes on the Volga who

were firmly convinced that the soul can be dislodged from its physical habitation by a sudden shock. It need hardly be added that the
dangerous effects of shock are part of our own store of medical
knowledge.

The same applies to shadows. Like his picture, a man's shadow
is part of him. Those who have lived in China know that most
any Chinese would take care to prevent his shadow from being "cut"
by a passer-by, whether driver or pedestrian. On the other hand, if
he is annoyed with his shadow, he will deliberately jay-walk so that
vehicles shave his heels. Car drivers in Shanghai are only too familiar
with this menace.

Shadows can travel at great speed, as everybody knows, and are
expert at hiding themselves, but their main characteristic is that they
always run counter to light. The gate or portal of the soul is usually
the mouth or nose. Through these apertures it wanders forth on its
journeys, and through them it returns to its corporeal abode once
more.

CHAPTER 26

THE SHAMAN'S SECRET

*Shamans are born far in the north at the root of evil maladies.
There stands a larch in whose branches nests are disposed at varying heights. The largest shamans are reared at the top of the tree,
the less large halfway down and the small shamans on the lower
branches. It is said that in the beginning a large bird resembling an
eagle but with feathers of iron flies to this tree, settles itself on a
nest and lays an egg. The bird then hatches the egg out. When a
large shaman is to emerge the bird broods for three years, but
a small one takes only a year to hatch.*

G. V. KSENOFONTOV, *Legendy i Rasskasy
o Shamanach*, Moscow, 1930, p. 60

SINCE the beginning of time, nothing has aroused more curiosity and
awe among men than the starry skies above them. The hunters who
lived hundreds of thousands of years ago enjoyed a far more intimate
relationship with the constellations of the night than the people of
our own day, for modern urban civilizations are blind to the wonders
overhead.

And one place in the celestial vault has always held a peculiar fasci-
nation for men of every era. This is the apparent center of the universe,
the focus of all life and movement in the cosmos. Since the earth
turns on its axis, the stars appear to move in the opposite direction
and a man's-eye view of the whole firmament makes it seem to revolve about a central point which now lies in the region of the
Pole Star.

Especially prominent in the night sky are the seven stars forming
the constellation of the Great Bear, which circles the Pole Star but
never dips below the horizon. Each succeeding generation of men
in the Northern Hemisphere has gazed up at the Great Bear in awe,
but the fact that the Great Bear and all other fixed stars revolve about
the Pole Star has long invested the latter with particular importance.
Many American Indian tribes regarded Polaris as the leader of all
heavenly bodies, the Babylonians saw it as the throne of their god
Anu, and the Aztecs looked upon it as a being superior to the sun.

This belief was not without astronomical foundation, for the Pole Star emits four thousand times as much light as the sun. Given that the sky had a central point and the whole universe pivoted on a single axis, it was only natural that primitive peoples should look for a central point on earth, a place which corresponded to the center of the heavens. And, because it was thought that there must exist a direct connection between the center of the world and the center of the sky, this place became endowed with especial significance. To the Greeks, for instance, the center of the world was Delphi, where stood the ὀμϕλυς Ὠς or "navel of the earth," a conical stone sacred to the god Apollo.

It is interesting to note that Asiatic tribes also believe in a navel of the earth. Their "omphalos" is a sort of paradise, a place of calm and beauty linked by a path with the central point of the heavens. It is this concept which has, from time immemorial, inspired almost every race to try to erect a ladder, pillar, tower or sacred building from the former to the latter, i.e. from the center of the world to the center of the skies, where the "motionless star"—"the nail star," as the Chukchees call it—sheds its radiance. This was why the Tree of Life stood in the middle of the Garden of Eden (Genesis 2, ix), why the Babylonians built their famous Tower, and why the Sumerians erected their artificial mountains or ziggurats, those strange terraced temples of the Bible.

In the view of most Asiatic peoples, the heavens are held together not only by the Nail or Pole Star but also by a huge prop or pillar or, as the Orochi believe, a golden stake. The primitive tribes of Asia symbolize the "pillar of the world" by driving a stake or branch into the ground in the center of their villages and crowning it with "heavenly birds"—polar divers, geese or eagles. The eagle is a sign of heavenly power and a symbol of strength, and the two-headed eagle is regarded by the Yenisei Ostyaks as all-seeing. These ideas are very ancient, but a more recent example of the connection between two-headed eagles and the center of the world can be found in Greek mythology, which tells how Zeus dispatched two eagles to fly around the world in opposite directions. They met again in Delphi, the center of the world, and perched on either side of the celebrated "navel." The Dolgans attach wooden crosspieces to their pillar of the world while Ostyaks adorn theirs with seven sacred heads. The Samoyeds and Ostyaks also make *sjaadais*, sacred figures whose heads taper to a point. The sjaadai, too, is symbolic of the center of the earth or the tree of life, and the Finnish ethnologist T. Lehtisalo records that "long pieces of wood adorned with seven notches are not uncommon." The number seven enjoys the same special significance among almost all Siberian tribes as it does throughout the world, and the so-called pillar of the world is often conceived of as possessing seven stories or steps. For example, almost every pagoda in the Far East has seven floors. It is hard to say why the number seven should be so universally invested with magical properties or religious symbolism, but it may be due to the twenty-eight-day lunar cycle. On the other hand, both the Great and Little Bears are composed of seven stars.

Many races in the Arctic cultural zone have long regarded the sky as a circular tent or, in Uno Holmberg's words, an immense vaulted roof which spans the earth and is pierced by holes (i.e. the stars) through which man can glimpse the universe. The Yakuts believe the sky to be fashioned from an infinite number of tautly stretched skins. When God wishes to see what is happening on earth he opens a few cracks here and there or, as the Chuvashes believe, tears the sky by sending a meteor across its dark expanse. It is a very ancient tradition among the peoples of the North that men can look up through these apertures and see God, and that any wishes they may entertain or express at that moment will be heard by Him.

To nomadic hunters who live in yurts, it seems obvious that a huge tent like the sky needs some form of support, so the notion of a pole or prop is a natural extension of the original idea. What is more, this pole provides a means of reaching the sky, and the man who succeeds in ascending to heaven is the shaman. During shamanistic rites, therefore, a wooden post is erected in the middle of a tent so that its end protrudes through the roof and into the open air. This is the route whereby the shaman's soul soars into the void and reaches the Pole Star or celestial "nail" which forms the entrance to the universe.

The shaman belongs to the spiritual world of the peoples of Siberia, but numerous guesses have been made as to the origin of the term. Some authorities claim that it hails from India and is derived from the Sanskrit word *sraman*, meaning a mendicant friar. While there is little doubt that the native shamanism of Siberia and Central Asia has been subjected to southern influences, it is certainly not a product of Buddhism.

Other names such as the Yakuts' *oyun*, the Turko-Tatars' *kam* or the Mongols' *bügä* or *kami* are not really consistent with the idea of shamanism. Throughout the Far East, *kam* or *kami* means "god" or "lord," but a shaman is something quite different. Scholars of all nationalities have ventured to use the word shaman to describe the sorcerers of many Siberian tribes, but a shaman is not a sorcerer. There is an unfortunate but widespread tendency to use the term shaman as though it were an alternative or synonym for magician, priest or medicine man—none of which have any connection with true shamanism. Hence the cloud of misconception surrounding not only the word itself but the whole nature of shamanism in general.

The only way to get to the root of the word and plumb the depths of the cultural phenomenon which it expresses is to visit Manchuria. In Manchurian and Tungusian, shaman becomes *saman*, and anyone who knows the Manchurian Tungus will realize that here lies the origin both of the term and of the idea. Georg Nioradze, Russian explorer and ethnologist, recognized this, as did the ethnologist Bansarov when he wrote his interesting book *Tchornaya Vera* (Black Faith) in 1846. The Manchurian word *samarambi* means "to excite oneself," "to start up in anger" or "to hit out." The Mongolian equivalent is *samoroj*, while *sam-dambi* is the Manchurian for "to dance."

It is in Manchuria, therefore, that we become acquainted with the essential characteristics of the shaman; namely, his excited condition, his divine frenzy or ecstasy, and his dancing. Whereas the Yakuts and Buryats still call their shamans *bö* (and, as Nioradze points out, their female shamans *ödegön* or *utigan*) the Tungus confine themselves to the expression shaman. The word has passed into our own vocabulary from Tungusian via Russian, but the origins of shamanism lie far in the past and hail from the circumpolar Stone Age, as Mircea

Eliade, a Romanian historian now living in the United States, and other authorities long ago realized.

Like the Tungus as a whole, shamans are facing extinction, and the throb of their ritual drums, their cries and singing will soon fade from the northern forests which have for so long been their home.

A shaman is a man who knows how to deal with spirits and influence them. He is thus a magician. Every shaman is a magician, but not every magician is a shaman. A magician may also be a sorcerer. The essential characteristic of the shaman is his excitement, his ecstasy and trancelike condition. It is because so many scholars have applied the word shaman to the magicians of primitive tribes, who are usually sorcerers and nothing more, that the idea of shamanism has become so vague and distorted. There is no doubt that Tibetan influence traveled across central Asia and penetrated the Siberian taiga belt at many points, but in its purest form, a religious and spiritual magic associated with rapturous exaltation, shamanism is today to be found only among the Tungus of the taiga and other circumpolar peoples.

What constitutes the ecstasy which is the *sine qua non* of shamanism? It is a form of self-severance from mundane existence, a state of heightened sensibility and spiritual awareness. The shaman loses outward consciousness and becomes inspired or enraptured. While in this state of enthusiasm he sees dreamlike apparitions, hears voices and receives visions of truth. More than that, his soul sometimes leaves his body to go wandering.

The Tungus believe in a supreme god, but God is not a shaman nor is a shaman a god. Shamanism is not, therefore, the religion of the Arctic and Turko-Tatar herdsmen, and the authorities of Czarist Russia were wrong to designate it such. Shamanism involves no religious beliefs, no religious rites and—last but not least—no god. Shamanism is a form of activity designed to cure diseases, end cattle epidemics, ascertain the truth or the future and maintain communication with souls and spirits. Thus, although Pater Wilhelm Schmidt rightly points out that it has infiltrated into the religions of most Turko-Tatar herdsmen and hunters, shamanism as a religion by itself does not exist.

All circumpolar races believe that the human soul is imperishable.

They differ only in their conception of the soul's life after death. Some tribes think that it lingers in the grave for a while and others that it leaves a dying man with his last breath, but all of them lay their dead to rest with an eye to the life hereafter, giving them food and utensils, furs to keep them warm in winter and a horse or reindeer to ride. Probably, too, the people of northern Eurasia used in pre-historic times to send male and female retainers to the grave with their master so that they could serve him in the next world, just as the Sumerians did in the royal cemetery at Ur excavated by the late Sir Leonard Woolley during 1922 and 1923, where Queen Shub-ad was found lying surrounded by her whole entourage.

Nioradze records that among the Golds a wife had to share the same coverlet with her dead husband until his burial and was after-ward obliged to sleep by his grave. The few Golds still living on the Sungari in Heilungkiang Province had no recollection of this custom when I asked them about it, but it may well be that in very ancient times they used to kill a wife so that she might be reunited with her husband in the world to come.

The practice of superterranean burial common to so many Siberian tribes may be founded on a belief that the soul remains in the body for some time after death has occurred, and that to bury a dead man beneath the ground is to bury his soul as well. Similarly, to burn his body might mean to destroy his soul. The adherents of Zoroastrian-ism, or Parsees, expose their dead on so-called Towers of Silence and leave them for vultures to devour so that their mortal remains shall not pollute the ground. The tribes of Siberia bury their dead in trees or raised coffins for quite a different reason; namely, in order to preserve the soul intact and facilitate its release from the body.

High burial is especially important in the case of shamans, almost all of whom are laid to rest on a lofty wooden platform or in the fork of a large tree. All their magical implements and ceremonial robes are buried with them, but not before they have been broken or torn to enable the spirits to emerge.

Shamans differ from their fellow men in their ability to commune with the world of souls and spirits, a faculty for intercourse which is far more strongly developed among them than among common mortals. They strive to gain possession of these spirits, and their prestige is commensurate with the number of spirits under their control. The requisite equipment for catching spirits consists of a metal mirror, a drum and a shaman's costume.

Genuine shamanic costumes have virtually ceased to exist among the Altaic peoples, Tungus included, for the ancient mode of life with its sacred forest culture and once strict rituals is gradually passing away. I was unable to find a shaman's costume even among the Orochi, although shamanism still exists in the North Manchurian taiga.

The whole costume, which is worn only on official occasions, is modeled on the external appearance of a bird, reindeer or roebuck. It is made of deer or reindeer hide and hung with a large number of leather thongs, not to mention the diverse magical symbols characteristic of shamanic robes in general. Uno Harva lists many of these appurtenances: for instance, twelve ermine pelts attached to a strap which hangs down the shaman's back, bells beneath his armpits, eagle owl's talons, snakes and iron hands on his sleeves, bear's foot bones on his footwear and iron bear's claws on his gloves and boots. Shamanic robes sometimes varied between different Altaic tribes.

What is the purpose of the shaman's costume and its numerous animal and magical symbols?

Harva stresses repeatedly that its main function is to drive away evil spirits, but the Orochi whom I questioned about the former purpose of the shaman's robe and its many attachments were unanimous in saying that the animal shape and the various animal symbols were designed to help establish contact with spirits. In most cases, a shaman is concerned with winning over, capturing and communing with spirits rather than with driving them away.

My own experience accords with the findings of Mircea Eliade. The shaman's robe represents a spiritual microcosm, an almost complete symbolic system steeped in multitudinous spiritual forces by the act of consecration and inhabited by spirits themselves. By putting it on, the shaman traverses earthly space and starts to establish contact with the spirit world.

The headdress is of supreme importance, as all authorities who have lived among the Siberian tribes agree. The explorer Kay Donner emphasizes that a large measure of the shaman's power reposes in his headgear. The headdress of the Soyotian shaman consisted of a narrow band whose upper edge was adorned with eagle owl's feathers. In the Manchurian taiga and among the Siberian Tungus, many shamans wore reindeer or roebuck antlers on their head, usually forged in iron. Shirokogorov claims that in earlier times antlers were the regular headdress of the shaman.

Metal mirrors are part of the Oriental world of ideas. The Chinese, Japanese, Korean and Tungusic mirror myths are probably based on very ancient tradition. In Japan, the mirror is the senior of the three sacred insignia of state. Made of metal and constructed in eight parts, it is preserved in the inner shrine of Ise in the Dai-Jingu, Japan's most famous temple. The Japanese insist that it is the actual mirror which belonged to the sun-goddess Amaterasu.

The shaman's drum is usually oval in shape. Its rim is made of larch wood, birch or willow, although shamanistic tradition has it that the wood really comes from the cosmic tree. This in itself establishes a link between heaven and earth. By drumming, the shaman magically arrives at the foot of this tree, whence, having reached the center of the world, he can ascend into the sky. The Orochi told me that their drumskins were made of reindeer hide. A shaman uses his drum as a means of capturing spirits, flying through the air, attaining a state of ecstasy and stimulating the senses of his audience. Its most important function, however, is to induce a state of ecstasy. This is not mere hocus-pocus but based on age-old knowledge of the secrets of the human soul and the nature of living things. Not everything is explicable in intellectual terms. The greater and richer world, the world of decision and danger, lies beyond the scope of human thought. It is this world which the shaman must enter. Therein lies his special ability, and therein lie the hazards of his profession.

No one can suddenly decide to become a shaman, for shamans are created by natural intervention in the shape of a sudden and severe illness, spells of fever, demoniacal possession or epileptic fits. Here again, the transmigration of souls plays a part. The Orochi told me that the spirit of a dead shaman roams about for a long while before it settles upon a new human abode. The man in whose body the dead shaman's soul eventually takes up residence then becomes a shaman himself. The process is not a pleasant one. The possessed man is racked with fits, loses consciousness, suffers epileptic spasms, enters a state of trance, and not infrequently dies.

These effects are wrought by spirits which cut off his head, pluck his eyes from their sockets, hack his body to pieces and devour his flesh. The budding shaman can watch this skeletonization with his own eyes, and an elder shaman must have submitted to dismemberment on at least three separate occasions, after each of which the spirits reassemble his bones, replace his eyeballs in their sockets and clothe his frame with new flesh. The shaman experiences this process of death and rebirth with great vividness. He loses consciousness and lies for some days as though dead. Bloodshot patches appear on his body, his clothes sometimes become stained with blood, and gouts of blood discolor his couch of freshly stripped birchbark.

The whole phenomenon is inspired by the idea that a shaman's physical shell must be destroyed before his soul can establish contact with spirits. When this is effected, the spirits move in. Like the bear and other animals, a human being will awake to new life as long as his bones are maintained intact. Early hunters believed implicitly in the resurrection of their slaughtered quarry, hence the solemn nature of the bear ceremony. The bear, too, traverses the supernatural and returns. Its meat is eaten and re-created anew, and exactly the same thing happens to the shaman.

As we have already said, this process is attended by suffering and physical torment, but the tortured man can escape at the height of his agony by using the shaman's most important piece of equipment: the drum. Beating his drum and moving rhythmically, the new shaman sets off on his perilous journey into the supernatural. Since not all spirits belong to one race or speak a single language, a shaman often possesses the ability to talk in strange and unfamiliar tongues. The spirits stimulate his imagination, heighten it, and impel him to speak and act.

A fire burns on the ground. Framed against the night by the red glow of the flickering flames, the shaman begins to move rhythmically, drumming, dancing, leaping and singing. The little bells on his robe tinkle, his iron ornaments clatter, and the Tungus sit there in the dim light, their attention riveted on his every move. The shaman's excitement communicates itself to the circle of spectators, and the larger the audience the stronger the empathy between them and him. They all know each other, being interrelated and members of the same clan. Drawn together by the combination of night and firelight, they allow the monotonous rhythm of the drums to waft them irresistibly away from the everyday world. The excitement mounts, leaping like a spark from one man to the next until all are near ecstasy and each is at once performer and spectator, doctor and patient, hammer and anvil.

When shamanism is used to treat illness, part of its mass-hypnotic effect is transferred to the patient. It has been proved that spiritual forces of this kind can be actually beneficial. I can only confirm Shirokogorov's assertion that those assembled around a shaman experience a satisfaction infinitely deeper than we ourselves do after a musical or dramatic performance.

Little in the world was ever achieved by doubt, but genuine miracles do occur, and these are made possible only by faith. The power that flows into a shaman is the sum total of the faith of all present, and the greater their confidence in him, the stronger the measure of auto-suggestion, the more effective his powers and the greater his ability to hypnotize others. The more excitement and faith a shaman can inspire, the greater his reputation. This is why the greatest shamans are said to "fly," why their audiences can "smell" the spirits they conjure up and why the whole world of spirits becomes "visible." It seems to me self-evident that the medicine men of the Indian tribes of North America, so often described by early travelers and explorers, are in direct descent from the shamans of eastern Asia and through them of the long line leading back to the mysteries of the Mousterian caves.

European scholars who observe shamans with deliberate scientific impartiality often find it difficult to grasp the nature of these inspired and inspiring men, for inflexible scientific objectivity renders it impossible for an audience to be receptive or a shaman to attain the requisite state of ecstasy. The presence of one indifferent, critical or unreceptive individual—even of a stranger—necessarily hampers any shamanic performance. On the other hand, a large and convinced audience can contribute substantially toward curing a sick man and restoring his spirits. One cannot weigh imponderables or pronounce them right or wrong. A shaman must adhere to a certain mode of procedure, and any untoward incident will break the flow. He also has assistants, which is yet another reason why the traditional formula must be observed. It is essential that excitement should mount, that communication between shaman and audience should grow ever closer and that no mistakes or lulls be allowed to break the invisible threads that bind them together.

Every shaman of repute is an expert judge of human nature and a gifted psychologist. In my experience, the Tungusic shaman is far superior to our own doctors in this respect. Although he cannot, of course, rival the Western physician as a specialist in clinical treatment, he possesses brilliant powers of observation and is normally a first-rate diagnostician. There is, moreover, one field in which he enjoys a great advantage over the erudite men of the West. He can fill the lacunae in his knowledge by intuitive means. His patients are firmly resolved to obey him and be influenced by him, whereas the Western doctor has the much harder task of curing skeptics who often think they know more about medicine than he does himself. Indeed, the expression "medicine man" is a far more appropriate description of our own doctors than of the shaman, who has a mental and spiritual mission to fulfill.

I believe that shamans are among the few genuine thought readers, that only shamans are capable of giving telepathic treatment through dreams, of stimulating the emotions and focusing mental vibrations on a given individual. I believe this because only life in unspoiled natural surroundings can bring such powers into being and allow them to function, and because even the light of the sun is a disturbing element, let alone the soulless glow of electric bulbs.

It is impossible to demonstrate the power of shamanism scientifically, nor are we fully acquainted with the nature of its effects. Nevertheless, modern man must always guard against dismissing the possibility of everything that lies beyond the capacity of our intellect to grasp or prove in rational terms.

Shamanism is immensely ancient, and goes back far into the pre-history of mankind. If, as I believe, the magician of the Trois-Frères cave was a genuine shaman, shamanism must be at least twenty-five thousand years old and probably far older. Since humanity survived for six hundred thousand years without the benefits of modern medi-cine, shamanism is a much more ancient branch of knowledge. It is an older and greater mystery, a thing linked with magic and thus closer to the sky, the universe and the truths that defy human com-prehension.

Shamanism derives from man's preoccupation with the sky, but the germ of the idea in its original form may be hundreds of thou-sands of years old. For, long before shamans first practiced their magical arts, a belief in one god existed. Man tried to communicate with this supreme heavenly being, striving to regain something which he dimly felt that he had once possessed but later lost. At the moment of creation, the moment when mind was implanted in matter and the bipedal creature called Homo became capable of abstract thought, man still possessed an immediate awareness of God.

The shamanistic idea of spiritual ascent into the sky is founded on the knowledge or suspicion that this link between God and man, earth and sky, once existed. It is, in the last analysis, a means of assuaging the desire to reach God's presence once more.

CHAPTER 27

SHAMANISM TWENTY THOUSAND
YEARS AGO

*They attempted to find a way to reach the transcendental world
by releasing their souls from their bodies, seeing the bird as a
symbol of untrammeled flight and deliverance from earthly bonds.
By so doing, they hoped to reach their god and the lords of forest,
mountain and sea, or, if this were impossible, at least to establish
contact with disembodied souls.*

THE world's greatest mysteries are still very far from solution. Like
ants endowed with astonishing technical ability, most of us live in
towering, sprawling urban complexes. But, like ants, we have little
idea of what came before us, and none whatever of what will come
after us or what is above us. It may be presumptuous to wish to throw
more light on the seemingly impenetrable darkness of an era that lies
twenty thousand years or more in the past, but it is equally presumptuous to preen oneself on having reached the peak of wisdom
and the zenith of religious knowledge when man may well have once
been far, far closer to the inscrutable mysteries of the world and the
universe.

We do not know what the man of twenty thousand years ago
looked like or what color his skin was. We can only try to ascertain
what he believed in and what his thoughts were when he first began
to portray himself in effigy. The bones which we unearth today
were once clothed with flesh and skin, and without flesh, skin and
hair no exact idea of physiognomy is possible. Even now, after hundreds of thousands of years of interbreeding, the various races still
exhibit differences and may still be diverging. Yet, anatomically and
intellectually, all living men are extremely similar, and spiritually
they are identical.

Of the examples of Franco-Cantabrian art in our possession, approximately 160 sculptures, reliefs, drawings and paintings depict men
or manlike beings. Disregarding a few Venus statuettes such as the
"*tête à la capuche*" from Brassempouy, the "Negroid" head from

Grimaldi and the "Leonardo da Vinci" from Vistonice, we are left with a strange collection of ghostly creatures, men with birds', lions' or ibexes' heads, two-legged beings that are half man, half animal, heads with curiously vacant eyes, massive noses, huge beards and grotesque skulls. The schematic and bizarre portrayals of the human face are not attributable to any lack of artistic ability, for man was quite capable of expressing what he saw in pictorial or plastic terms at least fifteen or twenty thousand years ago and probably earlier. The animals of this era are drawn and painted with a realism and gift of observation which have seldom if ever been equaled.

This realism did not, however, extend to man's own physiognomy, activities, body and gestures. He hid them behind masks, disguised them with inexplicable, almost childish simplifications, tried to turn himself into an animal—even combined the physical attributes of several animals in a single picture, transforming his appearance or bewitching himself in order to disguise his real identity and remain undiscovered at all costs. Thus, despite their remarkable artistic gifts, our ancestors never passed on an accurate idea of their features and confined themselves instead to portraying magicians or similar beings. Of course, it is possible that the Stone-Age artists, draftsmen and engravers really were portraying themselves, but in something more than human shape, in the guise of intermediary beings who were stronger than common men and able to penetrate more deeply into the mysteries of fate, that unfathomable interrelationship between animals, men and gods.

The circumpolar peoples tell us that the road to supernatural powers is easier to follow in animal shape and that spirits can be reached only with an animal's assistance. It is not implausible to suggest that the same intention may have prompted the exponents of cave art to portray themselves in animal guise, ecstatically or—one might almost say—shamanistically.

When dealing with religious or magical concepts, one must think in terms of immense spans of time. Distance has never been any obstacle to the transmission of sacred traditions, and our vaunted advances in technology and communications do not seem to have improved the exchange of spiritual or religious beliefs to any substantial degree. In fact, the existence today of ideological "forbidden zones" probably means that spiritual communication between Siberia, southern France and northwest Spain were better fifteen thousand years ago than they are now.

On September 12, 1940, four French boys aged between fifteen and eighteen found the cave of Lascaux near Montignac-sur-Vezère in the Dordogne. There, in a twenty-five-foot cleft in the "Sixtine Chapel of the Aurignacian," as Breuil christened it, diggers came upon a strange sight. On the wall just above the floor of the shaft could be discerned pictures which had been drawn in black on the yellow and brown limestone. A massive bison stands there, severely wounded by a spear. Entrails hang from the wound, and the hairs on the frenzied beast's back are bristling with rage. In front of the bison lies a man, stretched out stiffly with his arms flung wide. He has four fingers on each hand and a birdlike head. The drawing of this figure is extremely simple, childish or primitive. Also visible in the picture is a rhinoceros, a spear and a stick with a bird perched on top.

The bison and rhinoceros are both drawn in a very naturalistic manner, especially the bison, whose entrails have evidently been wrenched out by the spear's ugly-looking barb. There is something uncommonly dramatic yet natural about the way in which it has turned to inspect the mortal wound. As for the outstretched man and the bird, the artist's evident intention was to capture an idea—but the idea was apparently insusceptible of expression in visual terms.

Many scholars have pondered over this scene, but their attempts to explain it are widely divergent. Abbé Breuil's interpretation of the picture runs as follows: a hunter has wounded a bison with his spear, only to be killed by the rhinoceros which can be seen striding slowly away to the left.

Another expert, Leroi-Gourhan, thought that the schematically depicted man was dying from wounds inflicted by the bison, and conjectured that a Paleolithic grave would one day be found beneath the wall drawing.

If the cave draftsman's sole intention was to portray a fatal hunt-

This strange picture was found in a shaft in the cave of Lascaux. It shows a severely wounded bison, a supine or falling man, a bird on a stick and a rhinoceros slowly walking away; Abbé Breuil believes that the scene depicts a hunting accident, but H. Kirchner and other authorities interpret the mysterious drawing as a shamanistic scene. There are resemblances between the Lascaux culture and the shamanism of circumpolar races still living today.

ing accident, three facts remain inexplicable. Why was the supine figure given a bird's head, what does the bird on the stick mean, and why should the man have been depicted so unrealistically—almost as though he were a pictographic symbol—when the rest of the picture has artistic pretensions?

If we join Breuil in regarding the cave of Lascaux as a "Sixtine Chapel of the Aurignacian or Perigordian," we must agree that the artist could not have meant merely to depict the death of a bison hunter or a man who had unsuccessfully attacked a rhinoceros. It is incompatible with our experience of the ideas expressed by Franco-Cantabrian cave painting that this picture should have been intended to portray a dramatic prehistoric event.

I prefer to adopt the German prehistorian Horst Kirchner's interpretation of the drawing as a shamanistic scene in which the bison is a sacrificial beast, the outstretched figure that of a shaman wearing a bird mask and lying on the ground in a trance, the bird the shaman's tutelary spirit and its perch a "grave stick" or "sky pole." We already know that among many circumpolar peoples wooden bird effigies on poles symbolize a shaman's spiritual journey, and that wooden bird figures are attached to poles near a shaman's last resting place. Finally, there is the idea of a path to heaven symbolized by an upright pole and the belief that a bird can carry a shaman's soul into the sky.

In a book on the Yakuts published in 1896, the Russian scholar Seroshevski describes how he saw an ox sacrificed during a shaman's spiritual "ascent." For this purpose, three stakes were driven into the ground and their tops adorned with carved wooden birds. The Swedish ethnologist Gustav Ränk also mentions that the people of northern Eurasia often used to crown their ritual poles with bird figures and place sacrificial offerings in their vicinity. The poles were regarded as a sort of conduit down which exalted spiritual beings could pass on their way to sample sacrifices. The Yuraks erect a pole behind the fireplace in their tent so that its tip protrudes through the smoke vent. This they call a *siimsi*. (The Vogul and Tungusian versions of this word are *sims-asla* and *shimka*, respectively.) The siimsi pole in the Yurak tent was clearly meant as a link between sacrifice and deity, for both Ränk and Lehtisalo mention that sacrificial bowls were placed near its foot. As the steam rose, the Yuraks addressed their supreme god as follows: "Eat, Old Num, watch over thy son."

If one compares the scene at Lascaux with the sacrifices made by circumpolar tribes during a shaman's spiritual journey, it does not seem illogical to regard the dying bison as a sacrificial beast, the bird on its perch as a link with an exalted spiritual being or deity, and the spread-eagled man as a shaman who has fallen into a cataleptic fit or trance during his soul's absence. If this is so, the departing rhinoceros either plays a subordinate role in the picture or has no connection with it at all.

If, as seems likely, the Lascaux drawing really does have shamanistic significance, some form of communication must have existed between the people of the Arctic Circle and the cave artists of France and northern Spain during the Upper Paleolithic period.

At Altamira in the Spanish province of Santander there are wall engravings of men in bird masks who seem to be dancing. Their arms are raised as though in conjuration and they are undoubtedly in a state of ecstasy. K. F. Karjalainen, Finnish ethnologist, says that when performing bear dances, the Ostyaks do no more than describe certain movements with their limbs, principally their hands, gestures whose meaning is unknown to the present generation of tribesmen. Shamans dance in a similar fashion, so it is not inconceivable that the bird-men of Altamira are also meant to be shamans.

Numerous wall engravings of masked figures have been discovered in the cave of Les Combarelles. It is hard to tell which are animals and which masked men, but it seems doubtful whether the figures belong to apes, as some authorities have suggested.

At Lourdes there is an engraving of a man wearing a tail, deer's antlers and a beard. Those who are familiar with the Tungus and other Siberian tribes will be tempted to assume that this picture, too, portrays a shaman, for the adoption of several animal characteristics is thought to increase a shaman's chances of sending his soul on its travels and establishing contact with the spirit world.

Drawings at Teyat, Abri Mège (Dordogne), include three strange figures resembling sea horses. They are obviously magicians and perhaps shamans, too. The upper part of their body is clothed in skins and they are wearing ibex masks and appear to be dancing.

One exceedingly interesting wall engraving is to be seen in the so-called Sanctuary in the cave of Trois-Frères. This is the celebrated sorcerer or *sorcier* which Abbé Breuil described as a god. The artist probably intended to depict a masked human being, not an animal, in order—as K. J. Narr puts it—to endow a unique magical or religious act with greater permanence by means of pictorial recapitulation. I regard this "magician," too, as a shaman because he has seen to it that his soul will receive a maximum of assistance from various animals while on its journey by assuming a deer's mask, owl's eyes, wolf's ears, a horse's tail and bear's paws. He, too, is dancing. Since the shamans of the Arctic cultures look upon deer's antlers and bear's feet as the most effective items in their magical equipment, and since the owl "who sees all" plays so important a role in the shamanism of the Arctic races, it can hardly be coincidental that we rediscover them in the sorcerer of the Trois-Frères cave. Having seen shamanism at first hand among the Tungus of northern Asia, I find it difficult to dismiss this wall engraving simply as a portrayal of a magician or a god. It betrays far too many shamanistic features for that.

The bison-headed man in the same cave is blowing a flute or playing some kind of stringed instrument, which may indicate that he is trying to put his audience into a state of ecstasy. Shamans among the circumpolar peoples of our own century also use musical instruments, though principally the drum, to intensify emotion, capture spirits and send their own souls ajourneying.

We have already mentioned the Paleolithic batons dating from the Middle Aurignacian and Magdalenian which have been found in western Europe, in Austria and Moravia, in the Ukraine and at Krasnoyarsk in Siberia. The term "wand" or "baton" was first used by Lartet, but may these objects not have been the drumsticks of fifteen, twenty or perhaps even thirty thousand years ago?

Let us compare them with the drumsticks used by shamans in the North Eurasian area. These are usually made of birch saplings and other wood, but are sometimes carved in reindeer's or deer's horn. They are flat, and their tips are covered with hare's or other animal's fur. At the upper or handle end is a hole equipped with a ring through which are passed the thongs or knotted cords that bind the stick to the shaman's wrist and prevent him from dropping it in the throes of his ecstasy. Among many arctic tribes this handle takes the shape of an animal's head. While I was with the Golds of Manchuria I saw a drumstick whose handle was carved with long, grotesque faces, and the Russian scholar Lopatkin appears to have seen sticks with similar ornamentation. S. V. Ivanov also recorded in 1954 that drumsticks (known in Russian as *kolotushki*) are adorned with carvings of human beings, spirits, animals, mythical creatures and plants. Among other motifs used to decorate these usually spatulate implements are water, mountains, paths, stars and celestial phenomena.

Horst Kirchner follows H. Obermaier in emphasizing that the batons of the Upper Paleolithic were more than just articles of everyday use. To the circumpolar tribes, drums and—to an even greater degree—drumsticks are regarded as sacred objects which must never be allowed to become "unclean." They are carefully stored in a special place and protected from damage while a tribe is on the march. The French scholars P. Girod and E. Massénat were the first to recognize a similarity between drumsticks made by the Lapps and used by their shamans and certain of the Paleolithic batons. These lengths of

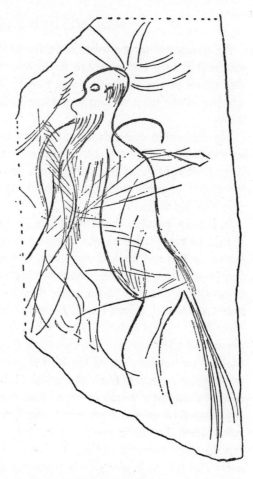

The so-called "magician of Lourdes" found by Nelli in the Grotte des Espeluges displays two features strangely reminiscent of the Tungusic shaman: an animal's tail and deer's antlers.

pierced reindeer's and deer's horn are, in fact, ideally suited for use as drumsticks, and only articles of considerable importance would have been as finely decorated. Certainly, no one would have taken as much trouble with a mere tent peg. Their inner edge is usually worn away as though by the persistent friction of leather thongs, while their handles also betray signs of what may be manual wear. There is little significance in the suggestion that some of these mysterious Paleolithic implements were made in pairs, for shamans only use one drumstick at a time. Moreover, the only site where paired sticks are thought to have been found is Petersfels.

All this points to the great antiquity of shamanism. The caves of southern France and northern Spain may well have echoed to the dull throb of the shaman's drum twenty or thirty thousand years ago just as the taiga of northern Manchuria did when I myself was there.

No Paleolithic shaman's drum has ever been found, but this is understandable because the rim of such a drum is very thin and would, if made of bent wood like the modern version, have completely disintegrated, together with the drumskin, during the immense span of time that has elapsed.

It is even possible that the female statuettes of the Aurignacian should be classified with the strange hybrids of cave art, the semi-human beings and masked magicians. Siberian tribes sometimes have female shamans, wise old sorceresses endowed with great skill and hypnotic powers. At Malta, some fifty miles northwest of Irkutsk near Lake Baikal, eleven female figures were found in company with some birds carved in bone. They probably represent duck and wild geese, and Kirchner remarks that these birds, "the artistic zenith of Malta," are reminiscent of the bird figures which modern Siberian tribes place on top of their sky poles. Holes had been bored in the tails of these little works of art so that they could be hung up like the small bird effigies with which the Tungusic shaman adorns his robe today. The same applies to the human figures which hang on the shamanic costume and serve as reception centers for wandering souls. Did the celebrated female statuettes, the earliest-known figurative representations in the world, act as "auxiliary dolls" in shamanistic rites? We do not know, but it is quite possible, for there seems to be a mysterious link between the shamans of northern Eurasia and the Paleolithic cave cultures with their magicians, wands and female statuettes.

We have some indications, therefore, that fifteen or twenty thousand years ago or even earlier there may have been shamans who practiced genuine magic, who were capable of finding and healing the souls of the sick and of themselves setting off in spirit on a journey into the world hereafter. Perhaps they were the doctors of the Stone Age.

Be that as it may, there is no doubt that the peculiar bird-headed figures, the masked magicians, the drumsticks and the Venus statuettes all belong to the hunter's world of ideas. Human figures with birds' heads, bears' feet and deer's antlers are so much at home in the world of Tungusic shamanism that the ancient cave pictures can hardly be evaluated on any other basis. Like the hunters of the taiga, the hunters of twenty thousand years ago were evidently familiar with the secret of the animal mask. They attempted to find a way to reach the transcendental world by releasing their souls from their bodies, seeing the bird as a symbol of untrammeled flight and deliverance from earthly bonds. By so doing, they hoped to reach their god and the lords of forest, mountain and sea, or, if this were impossible, at least to establish contact with disembodied souls.

The soul was created by God, and only God could have brought into being the faculty of abstract thought. But, before these divine creations—a soul and an ability to think independently of the body—were breathed into his mortal clay, man was probably very near the beast. Perhaps the artists of the Stone Age were trying to retrace this path. Perhaps they were trying, via the animal, to rediscover their primeval god or acquire a measure of divine power.

CHAPTER 28

ALFRED RUST'S GREAT DISCOVERY

*Since I assume it to be important and desirable that a better survey
be made as soon as possible, I respectfully request your permission
to dig. I shall not allow any discoloration of the earth by hut poles,
fireplaces, etc., to escape me.*

ALFRED RUST, in a letter to his
tutor Schwantes dated May 14, 1932

BETWEEN the years 1924 and 1928, Professor Gustav Schwantes, the eminent authority on prehistory and early history, gave a series of evening lectures at Hamburg University. Among the students who regularly attended his classes and took part in practical tests was one whose keenness, hard work and ability singled him out for special notice. He was an electrical engineer by the name of Alfred Rust.

One day, Rust informed his tutor that he was going to look for the original home of the so-called Ascalonian culture in southern Palestine, where J. Bayer had identified a prehistoric outdoor station at el Hulekat near Ascalon during the World War I. (Let it be said immediately that Rust himself later demonstrated the untenability of the Ascalonian theory in a paper published in 1936.)

When Schwantes asked Rust how he proposed to meet the cost of such an expedition, his undaunted pupil replied that all he needed were his traveling expenses and that, anyway, he owned a bicycle. Shortly afterward, on September 1, 1930, Rust set out. Striking south from Hamburg, he made his way through the Balkans to Istanbul. Here he met Bittel, the well-known authority on the Hittites, who warned him of the hazards of the rainy season and advised him to speed up his journey. Thirty days later, Rust had crossed "trackless" Anatolia and caught amoebic dysentery in the process, having lived almost exclusively on bread, sugar, tea and water, which in that area can harbor a wide variety of diseases. Almost penniless and without medical supplies, Rust reached Syria, often sleeping in caves on the way. At Hamar he met a fellow German who invited him to stay. It was a long time before the young archaeologist could eat a proper meal.

[104] Orochon tents pitched in the icy winter landscape of the taiga are heated by fires whose smoke escapes through vents in their roofs. At night, the Orochi sleep naked under furs, back to back in pairs to conserve warmth. The Orochon girl riding the white reindeer on the right is holding a *palma* or spear in her hand.

[105] The Orochi bury their dead in wooden coffins which they mount on tree stumps to prevent wolves from disturbing the bodies inside. They believe that a dead man should be laid to rest in an airy place where he can hear the rustle of the surrounding forest and from which his soul can float away unhindered.

[106] Tungusic raised coffin on the banks of the Lena, photographed by the Jochelson-Jesup North Pacific Expedition. The coffin consists of two hollowed-out balks of timber fitted together. One end has collapsed because the supports have rotted away.

[107] Raised coffin of a Yukaghir child.

[108] Coffin of a Tungusic shaman. The four posts are surmounted by figures of birds, apparently great northern divers. Their significance stems from the fact that human souls can assume the shape of birds and that bird figures are often used as aids in shamanism.

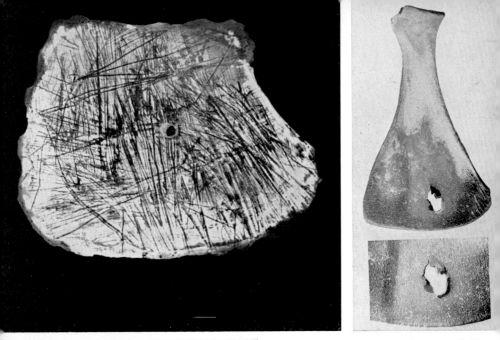

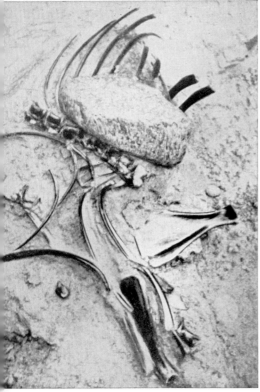

[109] This small amber disk was probably a hunting amulet. The numerous blackened grooves on either side were animal figures which the hunter of 18,000 years ago erased, as soon as they had fulfilled their magical purpose, to make room for fresh quarry. This interesting piece, on which a horse's head can be identified, was one of the finds made by Alfred Rust at Meiendorf.

[110] Made by hunters 18,000 years ago, these holes are marks left by weapons in reindeers' shoulder blades. In the case of the larger shoulder blade (*above*) the weapon remains unidentified, but the hole in the smaller shoulder blade was probably made by a harpoon launched from a throwing stick. Both pieces were unearthed by Alfred Rust in the Paleolithic reindeer hunters' camp at Meiendorf.

[111] Near the reindeer hunters' abode excavated by Alfred Rust at Meiendorf were found the remains of a reindeer on whose rib cage lay a large stone. The completeness of the skeleton and its position convinced Rust that the animal had been thrown into the water unskinned and that Upper Paleolithic man had made sacrifice there to a god of hunting—or just God—18,000 years before. Since the beast had immature antlers it must have been killed in May or June, and Rust suggests that it may have been sacrificed as a prelude to the summer hunting season.

[113] (*Right*) This so-called "dancing magician" of the Magdalenian period was discovered by Count Bégouen in the Trois-Frères cave in 1918. The man is naked but masked, wears stag's antlers, has a long beard, wolf's ears and a horse's tail. Note his striking resemblance to the Tungusic shaman from Siberia in the old engraving [112] above. Count Bégouen christened the deer-man a sorcerer, but it would probably be nearer the truth to describe both the twenty-thousand-year-old figure and the modern Tungusic shaman as genuine magicians.

[114] Did shamans exist during the Magdalenian period? This wall engraving (*left*) was discovered in the principal chamber or "sanctuary" of the Trois-Frères cave (Montesquieu-Avantès, Arièges). From the jumble of superimposed animals, Abbé Breuil extracted and interpreted the small group above [115]. On the right is a magician or god in animal garb. His body and legs are human, but not his arms. He has a tail and appears to be holding some kind of small musical instrument, perhaps a flute, to his lips. The reindeer on the extreme left is drawn true to life except for its forelegs, which end in semihuman hands. The animal in the center is half bison, half deer, but on its hump can be seen a brush of wiry hair (characteristic neither of bison nor reindeer) surmounted by a strange and unidentifiable object. The backward-facing head displays a mixture of bisonlike and deerlike traits. We are here confronted by a combination of four elements peculiar to Arctic shamanism: the magician with animal's head and antlers, the reindeer, and, finally, a dual being—half deer, half bison—which may represent a forest spirit. The Russian ethnologist A. F. Anisimov wrote in 1949 and 1950 of the Tungus' belief in a strange being which could appear either in human or animal guise.

[116] and [117] (*Above*) Early drawings from Monte Bego, Liguria. [118] (*Below*) The Chukchees of Siberia also believe in beings that are half human, half animal. Bogoras interprets them as evil spirits which dwell in the Siberian tundra and try to devour human beings.

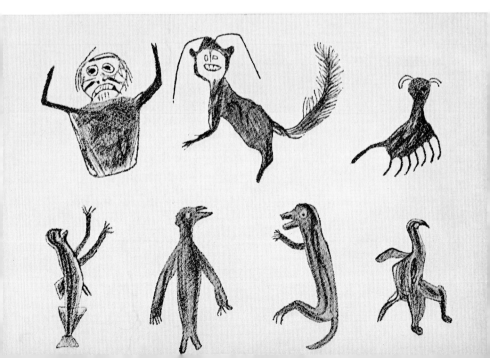

Leaving Hamar, Rust traveled via Homs to Nebek, where, to use his own words, the amoebae called a sudden halt. By now seriously ill, he managed to find one Arab among the three thousand inhabitants of the little township who spoke some English. When he mentioned that he was ill, the man told him that there was a Danish hospital in the village. Rust could hardly believe his ears, but it was true. Danish missionaries had established a hospital more than four thousand feet up in the desert highlands of Syria. Rust was taken in for treatment and learned on his recovery that only six miles away, some distance from the main road, lay the village of Jabrud, the erstwhile summer residence of Queen Zenobia of Palmyra. There, he was told, were some caves which might prove of archaeological interest.

Before long, Rust had unearthed flint tools in three rock shelters. He also found Lower Paleolithic settlements in the Nebek plain, hundreds of coups de poing, thousands of flake tools, scrapers, burins, saws, awls and blades, all relics of Stone-Age cultures collectively known to science as the Jabrudium.

Professor Schwantes admits that he did not at first take his pupil's audacious plan seriously, but adds: "He carried it out, for all that."

Having made a total of four trips to Syria, Rust returned home firmly resolved to discover bone tools belonging to glacial man in northern Germany. "Before a few months were past," writes Schwantes admiringly, "he had them!"

If this sounds easy, we should reflect that almost all students of prehistory had hitherto regarded northern Europe as uninhabitable during the Paleolithic gladiations and assumed that the cold was so intense that neither man nor beast could have endured the Arctic temperatures. It was thought that any signs of human life found in this area must date from the interglacial periods and, more especially, from the postglacial.

Rust, however, endorsed the view first expressed by his tutor in 1924 and later in a memorial lecture on the occasion of the fiftieth anniversary of Hamburg's Museum of Ethnology in 1928, which was that man existed in northern Europe during the Ice Age.

We have derived the bulk of our knowledge of the legacy left by Stone-Age man from the caves of central and southern Europe, where

289

his remains were not only sheltered externally but partially covered by clay and dust and thereby protected from complete decay. The glacial hunters of the North European plains, on the other hand, were forced to rely on man-made accommodation. Nothing has remained of their tents, for thousands of years of exposure to ice, rainstorms and wind have reduced them to dust. The only things that have withstood the passage of time are their implements and bones.

In 1932, Rust examined a freshly plowed field in a valley between Meiendorf and Ahrensburg in Germany and within a few hours found over a hundred tools dating from the Magdalenian. During the summer of 1933 and 1934, Rust and his colleague Karl Gripp carried out extensive digging. They unearthed a dwelling place and excavated what had once been a lake. In fact, Rust's discoveries of reindeer bones brought him so intimate a knowledge the life of the Paleolithic hunter that he was even able to identify some of the religious concepts which prevailed sixteen thousand years ago. Radiocarbon dating set the age of Layer I at Meiendorf at 13,800 B.C. Professor Schwantes says of this: "For me personally, the Meiendorf find signifies the ultimate and fullest realization, to an extent never envisaged in my wildest dreams, of decade-long attempts to shed light on the earliest period of human habitation in the North."

Alfred Rust may justifiably be called the Schliemann of northern Europe, for his unearthing of a sixteen-thousand-year-old culture is no less important than Heinrich Schliemann's discovery of Troy. The Homeric stratum of Troy dates from about 1200 B.C., the year of the city's destruction being 1185 B.C. And there is a great difference between excavating a three-thousand-year-old culture like that of Troy and using spade and shovel to unearth evidence of a life which became extinct sixteen thousand years ago. Although the incomparably greater age of such a civilization makes it much more difficult to excavate and interpret, what came to light at Meiendorf and Stellmoor surpassed everyone's boldest expectations.

CHAPTER 29

REINDEER SACRIFICE IN 16,000 B.C.

No one who first endeavors to understand the soul of the taiga reindeer herdsman and then visits the archaeological sites near Hamburg can fail to sense the presence of God.

HOW did men live sixteen thousand years ago in the lowlands of northern Germany? What impelled them to go there? Why did they migrate to the neighborhood of what is now the modern metropolis of Hamburg at the height of the last Ice Age? The earth boasted warmer zones sixteen thousand years ago, and there were no frontiers to prevent men from living farther to the south. Yet some of them preferred the cold and barren tundra of the north.

All is explained when we know that the people of the so-called Hamburgium were reindeer hunters. Reindeer have always fled the summer warmth with its plagues of gnats and flies. Eons ago they migrated to the Dordogne in southern France and even farther to the south in winter, but moved northward, and roamed through the valley that lies between Meiendorf and Ahrensburg in summer. This valley was once a drainage channel for melted snow, but when the glaciers' icy flanks withdrew, leaving it dry and full of debris, reindeer hunters found it a suitable district in which to pitch camp.

Nevertheless, the people who lived in northern Germany ten thousand years before the beginning of recorded history remain an unsolved enigma. We still do not know whether they entered this inhospitable region in pursuit of their main quarry, reindeer, or whether they made it their permanent home and hunting preserve, or whether they were tundra dwellers born and bred and had so thoroughly adapted to the cold climate of the North that they were literally compelled to live there.

Eskimos cannot be transplanted from north to south, and the people of the Hamburgium resembled Eskimos in their most important cultural attribute. They were reindeer *hunters*. Today only the Eskimos in the northernmost regions of the American continent still hunt the caribou. All other circumpolar races who depend upon the reindeer for their livelihood are reindeer owners and breeders. It is possible, therefore, that the Eskimos are the only people alive comparable to the tundra dwellers of the Upper Paleolithic. The hunters whose culture has been identified at Meiendorf and Stellmoor probably led a life much like that of the modern Eskimo, stubbornly defying the icy climate of the plains to hunt animals which would provide them with meat, fat and marrow to eat, bones and antlers from which to fashion tools, and skins to clothe themselves with or, perhaps, cover their tents.

People who owned weapons and manufactured tools of such diversity and fine workmanship were probably familiar with the tent as well. Acting on this assumption, Rust kept an eye open for traces of earth huts and fireplaces and for the rings of stones which usually mark the site of a tent. Not only did he fail to discover anything of this nature, but his efforts to find traces of tent poles or pit dwellings were equally unsuccessful. But at last Rust did succeed in identifying an Upper Paleolithic habitation in the Ahrensburg-Meiendorf valley. A large conglomeration of tools, principally siliceous, showed where the center of the dwelling place had once been.

Rust made still further discoveries. He traced the outline of a former lake and found that a Stone-Age settlement had been situated only about twenty-five yards from its shores.

So much ground water seeped into the pits while digging was going on that pumps had to be operated, but before the site had been drained Rust groped around in the water and brought out a fossilized length of antler. It was as well preserved "as if it had been thrown into the water a short while before." A strip eighteen inches long had been shaved from the antler's interior curve, and Rust immediately realized that it had been fashioned in a manner characteristic of the Magdalenian.

A reindeer's sacrum usually consists of four or sometimes five anchylosed vertebrae. Seventy-five of these composite bones were found on the site, all belonging to animals which had been killed in summer. This is a most interesting point, because it can be inferred that both reindeer and hunters left the area during the winter. Most of the bones and antlers were found around the shores of the former

lake. It is probable that hunting was done in a businesslike and un-
sentimental way, for young animals are in the majority. (Their age
can be deduced from the concrescence of their sacral vertebrae.)

Scratch marks on the vertebrae indicate that meat was pared off
with flint utensils. The hunters used to decapitate their quarry, cut
the carcass into several pieces and dismember it. Every skull was
found to have been smashed, as were the hollow bones containing
marrow. In all, diggers at Meiendorf unearthed 105 lengths of antler,
and it was possible, after expert scrutiny of coronal sutures and antler
formation, to determine the age and sex of individual animals.

Rust found no less than 2,426 flint tools in the hunters' abode and
another 272 specimens on the bottom of the former lake. Most of
these implements were flakes, unretouched stone blades, round-
bladed scrapers and angled burins—though this far from exhausts
the list of tools typical of the Hamburg culture.

During excavations in 1934 an amber disk came to light bearing
engraved representations of animals' bodies. Among them was a fine
horse's head and a pair of reindeer's legs. It was evident that once the
magic of the engraved animal figures had worked, they were obliterated. The only thing visible on another amber disk is an almost
frighteningly realistic horse's eye. One rounded piece of sandstone
was adorned with the head of a beast of prey, while on another,
somewhat larger piece can be seen the streaming mane of a terrified
horse which is trying to escape its pursuers. Yet another small sandstone slab is decorated with what may be a bird's head. Many stones
were merely adorned with a small cross, and one tool, presumably
a leather cutter, made of reindeer's antler bears two elongated crosses
which resemble written symbols and may have been the owner's
personal mark. Awls made of reindeer horn, arrowheads of the same
material, sewing needles and a harpoon all prove that the hunters
who lived here were well able to withstand the rigors of their natural
environment.

A length of young reindeer's antler had been worked in such a
way as to suggest that it might have been a wand. Two dorsal vertebrae and one cervical, all belonging to reindeer, show traces of fire,
and the scapulae of several beasts are pierced by almost circular

holes. Paleolithic spears, which were probably launched with a throwing stick, had remarkable powers of penetration. Smaller game were hunted with bow and arrow, as can be deduced from arrowheads and corresponding holes in the fossils of ptarmigans and cranes.

Perhaps the most interesting discovery was the carcass of a sacrificial beast which the tundra hunters had deliberately sunk in the lake. It was lying on its left side with an eighteen-pound lump of gneiss on its rib cage. That it was a sacrifice could be concluded from the fact that its marrowbones and the top of its skull were still intact. Even its antlers were untouched. Rust asserts that the skeleton's completeness and the position in which it was found are evidence that the animal was thrown into the water not only whole but probably unskinned.

Why? Certainly a glut of meat cannot be the answer. Rust points out that raw meat will keep fresh for weeks in an Arctic climate. And practical considerations such as softening the skin for leatherwork or feeding fish are dismissed by the ethnologist and religious historian Alois Closs in view of the special circumstances under which the animal was found.

It must be assumed that the hunters sank the reindeer's carcass for some more important reason, and it is impossible, taking into account the accompanying circumstances, to discount the likelihood of sacrificial intent. These men believed in divine power—perhaps in a single god.

The animal was a reindeer doe and had cuticular antlers, ample evidence that it must have been killed in May or June. This brings us to a still more interesting point. All the indications are that May or June was when the hunters took up their abode in the valley, and this suggests that they made sacrifice on arriving in their summer quarters, having completed the spring trek.

Rust also dug up remains of a second reindeer culture in a layer more than six thousand years younger than the first. In this layer, which dates from about 8000 B.C. and is known as the Ahrensburg level, was found a stake seven feet long and almost five inches thick. It had once stood in water and was crowned with the skull of a reindeer doe. From this skull the age of the beast was set at about sixteen, making it the oldest of all the reindeer (nearly a thousand of them) whose remains were identified on the site.

Cult pole and water sacrifice probably bore some kind of relationship to one another, Closs assumes, in both the earlier and later layers. Two submerged reindeer were found in the Hamburg level, and between twelve and eighteen in the later, Ahrensburg level. It seems obvious that only religious motives could have prompted men to renounce valuable game in this way. Then there is the wooden stake. A cult pole crowned with a skull is a sacrificial salutation which we have already met in the case of primitive Siberian races, notably the Tungus, whose custom of impaling reindeers' heads on stakes has been discussed in an earlier chapter. The German-Swedish ethnologist Henn Pohlhausen's suggestion that the submerged reindeer were not sacrifices at all but had been sunk in the icy lake for the purposes of preservation and storage seems implausible to someone who has learned in the taiga that reindeer or bear skulls are never exposed for practical reasons. Pohlhausen interprets the reindeer skull on the pole as a simple marker indicating the position of a submerged meat store, but people whose entire life is centered on hunting need no markers to help them find something, whether they have hidden it in the ground or thrown it into water. Rust, who was present throughout the excavations, had no doubt that these hunters of the Upper Paleolithic were complying with a religious tradition and that they believed in the existence of exalted beings, of gods or, even probably, of a single deity.

Like most Altaic peoples, the Tungus never throw anything unclean into water because it would offend the lord of that element. They also know that an animal sacrifice would soon putrefy under water, and would never offer their god an animal in this manner. Almost every lake in the taigi is regarded as sacred, so the Tungus avoid bringing unclean things into contact with the water. Men may have abandoned this early form of sacrifice by submersion when they ceased to hunt reindeer and started to domesticate it, when they grew to believe that there was a lord of the forests, a lord of the mountains and a lord of the water.

This glimpse into the religious ideas of men sixteen thousand years ago probably constitutes the most important result of the diggings carried out in the valley between Meiendorf and Ahrensburg. They afford evidence that long before the beginning of recorded history, eight or nine thousand years before the first signs of human activity made their mark on ancient river valleys like those of the Euphrates and Nile, Indus and Hwang Ho, a band of Upper Paleolithic hunters sought to pay homage to their god.

No one who first endeavors to understand the soul of the taiga reindeer herdsman and then visits the archaeological sites near Hamburg can fail to sense the presence of God or to realize that He was worshiped there with the same fervent and natural faith that later inspired the people far away in the forests at the other end of the Eurasian continent.

CHAPTER 30

MAN: THE UNSOLVED MYSTERY

*Where did modern man come from? Where did he first arise? ...
According to some authorities, Europe had some human inhabit-
ants who resembled modern men during the second interglacial
period (350,000 or more years ago), before the appearance of the
Neanderthalians.... The skull fragments found at Fontechevade in
France, at Swanscombe in England and at Steinheim and at
Ehringsdorf in Germany may have been rather* sapiens-*like, despite
their great age.*

THEODOSIUS DOBZHANSKY, *Evolution,*
Genetics, and Man, New York, 1955, p. 332

BELIEF in a supreme power is a prerequisite of sacrifice, and man
must already have entertained the idea of a god in Paleolithic times.
Certainly he would not have sacrificed to thin air, nor would he have
served many gods with one sacrifice, for a sacrifice is a personal
offering.

We can only guess at what took place at Ahrensburg some ten
thousand years ago. The reindeer hunters may have held full-scale
sacrificial festivals, dancing and singing around their fires. When we
consider that in even earlier times, about sixteen thousand years ago,
similar sacrificial ceremonies took place by the lake near Meiendorf
in Holstein, when we reflect that reindeer were ritually weighted
with stones and submerged as a form of sacrifice, it seems evident
that there, too, men were trying to approach the supreme being and
express their gratitude to him. Most prehistorians now acknowledge
that the finds made at Ahrensburg and Meiendorf denote religious
activity. Sacrifice is an inalienable symptom of divine faith, and
sacrifices belong not to magic but religion.

The Magdalenian bear cult of twenty thousand or so years ago,
the clay figure in the cave of Montespan and the rites that were for
so long associated with it—none of this was a game or a primitive
form of magic. It was, as we have deduced from comparisons with
the bear cults of the Gilyaks, Ainus and other Siberian peoples, an

earnest attempt to send an intercessor to the lord of the mountains and forests, i.e. to a supernatural being.

As we have seen, the Lower Paleolithic finds made in caves in the Swiss cantons of Saint Gallen and Appenzell have their parallel in the skull and marrowbone sacrifices of the primitive Arctic races, and the seventy-thousand-year-old relics of bear-skull sacrifices in the caves of Saint Gallen are eloquent testimony to man's quest for God in almost unimaginable distant times.

Even Pithecanthropus pekinensis of three hundred thousand years ago was capable of complex intellectual achievements. Not only did he manufacture tools and weapons and make use of fire, but the skulls which he left behind at Chou-k'ou-tien may have played their part in some sacrificial cult. Certainly he was a fully developed human being endowed with intellect. It is equally certain that he was monogamous and had social ties. It is also very probable that he was possessed of religious ideas and that, like the ethnologically ancient races, he believed in a supreme being.

If we probe still deeper into prehistory we find that the Australopithecines of six hundred thousand years ago used to assemble baboons' skulls and large quantities of mammals' bones. Was there a religious motive underlying this practice? Did the Australopithecines know how to use fire? It is impossible to tell, but few modern anthropologists care to dispute the intellectuality of this earliest-known form of man.

The world of the living is in a constant state of flux. The passage of time brings modifications in all living things, and it seems as though nature is forever forcing them from a lower to a higher estate, from fish to amphibians, amphibians to reptiles, reptiles to mammals, birds, primates and, finally, men. The whole process is one of progressive development. Nevertheless, the hypothesis of general evolution is beset by so many unsolved problems and interspersed with so many lacunae and obscurities that it should be treated with the utmost caution. Overhage wrote in 1959: "Thus the most interesting and important problem of all, the emergence of the grand design of the animal kingdom, remains unsolved. The family of vertebrates appeared unheralded and for the first time in the Silurian Age."

The phy[...] of the invertebrates are equally mysterious, no[...] how this multiform group attained the
heights of [...] which it exhibited in its basic design as early
as the Ca[...] The physicist Pascual Jordan puts it in this way:
"The dependence of life-processes on 'guiding' occurrences which
are not themselves subordinate to the causality of the over-all physical pattern fundamentally removes biological phenomena from the
realm of unbroken mechanical causality." It is even harder to prove
the continuous evolution of plant life in terms of the exact sciences.
As Jordan says, "The affirmation of derivation (descendancy) or
evolution thus remains, in its basic essentials, no more than an assumption or hypothesis designed to explain the gradated formal multiplicity and interrelationship which characterizes the whole realm
of organisms. It is founded not on direct observation but only on
indirect, circumstantial evidence."

We know of no instance where one form of life has gradually
changed into another. The ancestors of the horse were all horselike
ungulates. Paleontologists have dug up five-toed fossils the size of
foxes, and we know that very small horselike animals lived on earth
about sixty million years ago. We know the formal sequence or succession, "but there is something which this succession fails to teach
us. It tells us nothing about the relationship of the individual links
in this chain of sequence" (A. Portmann, *Probleme des Lebens*, 1955,
p. 87).

Beneath its cushions of blubber the whale possesses atrophied or
rudimentary limbs. Was the whale once a quadruped which lived
on land and later took to the water? Did its legs waste away as its
tail fin developed, or are its legs slowly developing so that it will one
day leave the water and live ashore? Paleontologists assume that the
whale was a land animal which returned to the water, but here again
exact science has to give way to supposition, for no one has yet found
a whale which lived on land. All the ancestors of the whale appear
to have been sea dwellers.

The famous Dresden naturalist and theologian Arthur Neuberg
has pointed out that a dog's embryo cell can never produce anything

but a dog, but children at school today are still being taught that long ago man was an amoeba, then a fish, then a reptile, and so on.

The red deer and the roe are closely related, but the red deer was never a roe nor the roe a red deer. Both are finished products, and if they did "evolve" it was by a phylogenic process entirely unknown to us. Paleontology, or the study of fossil animals and plants, provides us with no information about the origin of the species.

The distinguished German paleontologist Weissermel declared that one must either resign oneself to ignorance or assume, as he did, that the whole of evolution was underpinned by a spiritual force or Creator, while Emil Abderhalden, the world-famous Swiss doctor, zoologist and physiologist, stated that "to assume that every living thing originated from and by itself demands greater faith than to assume its creation by God."

The theory of organic evolution is even less well equipped to deal with man. O. Spülbeck says: "We do not know how man came into being, nor, biologically, can we pronounce upon the subject. When the time was ripe, when the conditions necessary for life were present, when his cue came, man suddenly appeared." [1] Man is a unique and extraordinary phenomenon; in Overhage's words "an event far transcending all organic evolutions." That is why we have no conclusive evidence of his physical derivation from animal forebears and why no theory that traces the development of the human form from the primates has been universally accepted. Views on this subject differ widely, and the number of suggested family trees is legion. If men really did evolve from animal rudiments, the earliest human remains ever found show that the process must already have been complete when their owners were alive. In any case, which are the earliest forms of human life?

There are certain facts which cast doubt on the whole theory of man's upward development and evolution by stages from the anthropoid via the Neanderthalian to the sapiens type. We owe our knowledge of these facts to American, British, French and German scholars, men like Leakey, Connolly, Oakley, Howell, Montagu, Remane and

[1] *Der Christ und das Weltbild der modernen Naturwissenschaft*, Berlin, 1957.

Overhage. Certainly man did not pass through anthropoid and Neanderthalian stages on his way to becoming Homo sapiens in the same way as a child reaches maturity via adolescence, because the sapiens types always coexisted and were contemporaneous with the earliest hominids ever identified.

Modern men are all of the sapiens type, the other groups having long since become extinct. We now know, however, that the sapiens type can be traced far back into the Ice Age. On March 29, 1932, in West Kanam on the southern shores of the Kavirondo Gulf of Lake Victoria Nyanza in Kenya, Dr. L. S. B. Leakey, director of the Nairobi Natural History Museum, discovered fragments, dating from the Lower Pleistocene, of a lower jaw with a well-developed chin. As he wrote, "Homo kamanensis must be regarded as standing much closer to Homo sapiens than do any known other human genera or species. In all probability Homo kamanensis is the direct ancestor of Homo sapiens" (Leakey, *The Stone Age Races of Kenya*, 1935, p. 23).

Unfortunately, the sapients-like shape of the lower jaw was obscured by a sarcoma or tumor which had distorted it in the region of the chin. Having for this reason conducted a fresh examination of the jaw, which reposes in the British Museum, Ashley Montagu declared in 1957: "It nevertheless remains highly probable that at one time it possessed a well-developed chin." Thus, Leakey's discovery preserves its validity. "The Kanam mandible shows such resemblances to Homo sapiens that it must be regarded as an ancestor and not a cousin." K. P. Oakley postulates that Homo kanamensis was a contemporary of Homo heidelbergensis, which would mean that men of the sapiens type existed in the very early glacial periods at the same time as members of the Anthropus group such as Pithecanthropus modjokertensis, which von Königswald dug up in Java.

A skull found in a gravel pit at Steinheim an der Murr (near Stuttgart, Germany) in 1933 hails from the middle of the Ice Age, more precisely, from the Mindel-Riss or Penultimate interglacial period. Le Gros Clark and other scholars place Steinheim man in the Homo sapiens group, and it is important to note that he existed before the appearance of Neanderthal man. "The antiquity of the skull must be very great," Le Gros Clark, professor of human anatomy at Oxford, wrote in 1958.

Clark states that the three skull bones found by A. T. Marston at Swanscombe in Kent represent "the oldest human fossils so far discovered on English soil," and goes on to say that "the bones are quite closely comparable with those of a modern skull." A. A. Abbie assented in 1952 that Swanscombe man was "indistinguishable from modern man."

Like Swanscombe man, the skull fragments found at Kanjera, northeast of Lake Victoria in East Africa, belong to the Middle Pleistocene and indicate that sapiens-type men were contemporary with the Anthropus types of Java, China and the coast of North Africa.

Discoveries made in 1947 in the cave of Fontéchevade proved that sapiens-like creatures had been living in France before the Neanderthalians. In 1954 the great French paleontologist Henri Victor Vallois classified the Swanscombe and Fontéchevade people as a presapiens family which ran parallel to the Neanderthalians from the second interglacial age onward. (Note that by "presapiens" Vallois means only a primitive form of sapiens.) The Fontéchevade finds are the earliest human fossils yet discovered in France.

For all these reasons, it seems probable that neither Peking nor Neanderthal man represents the outcome of a process of human evolution. The once popular theories of biological ascent and gradual succession are now regarded by many anthropologists with the utmost reserve, and if some of the oldest fossils exhibit sapiens-like characteristics, i.e. are similar to modern man, this suggests that we should speak less of evolution than of the human development which took place during the hundreds of thousands of years spanned by the various glacial periods.

"Sapiens characteristics are an age-old possession of mankind," stated Overhage in 1959. Today, many experts no longer regard the Neanderthalian group as our ancestors but look for them among the presapiens forms. The Freiburg paleoanthropologist J. Kälin considers the most noteworthy feature of this new phylogenic approach to be that, from the biological point of view, man is seen in an increasingly human light. The brute beast which the German biologist Ernst Haeckel envisaged in his *Natural History of Creation* (1866) has now given way to a creature endowed with reason from the very first.

Why do we cling so stubbornly to outmoded theories? Why do we prefer to look for our origins in the animal rather than in God? Why do we find it so hard to wean ourselves from a purely biological assessment of man?

For decades, people accepted an evolutionary sequence leading from Heidelberg and Peking man, via the Neanderthalians, to Homo sapiens, and that was why they automatically placed every sapiens type in the last and highest evolutionary stage. In that way, "scientific impartiality," i.e. the idea that to ascribe spirituality to men of the Lower Paleolithic was to yield to religious prejudice, became the greatest single obstacle to scientific progress. Completely obsessed by the thought that man's logical development could only be ascertained by biological means, scholars formed their opinion of early man without reference either to ethnology or cultural research.

It has at last been realized that the origins of man are not explicable by biological means alone. Attempts are at last being made to assess the intellectuality of early man and to disclose the essential humanity, the mind and soul, which once inhabited the crumbling relics so dispassionately examined by the "bone merchants" of former days. New excavations, far-reaching discoveries and, above all, more painstaking scientific research have combined to damage irreparably the old illusion of an evolutionary progression from ape-man to creative intellect.

Technical progress was so often confused with mental and physical development that the best scholars of our era found it immensely difficult to recognize the full humanity and intellectuality of the earliest human types known to us. Yet, as Leakey told the skeptics in 1938, sapiens forms existed on earth in the early glacial period.

What does all this add up to?

It means that the pretty drawings and diagrams which show a number of roots converging to form a tall tree at whose head the Homo sapiens of our time stands in lonely grandeur are largely without scientific foundation and must be relegated to the realm of crude simplifications.

Just as we are slowly learning that primitive men are not necessarily savages, so we must learn to realize that the early men of the Ice Age were neither brute beasts nor semi-apes nor cretins. Hence the ineffable stupidity of all attempts to reconstruct Neanderthal or even Peking man. Exaggeratedly hirsute plaster figures of bestial mien glower savagely at us in museums all over the world, their features usually chocolate-brown in color, their hair wild and unkempt, their jaws prognathous and their foreheads receding—and this despite the fact that we have absolutely no idea what color Paleolithic man's skin was or how his hair grew and virtually no idea of his physiognomy. The American authority T. D. Stewart rightly pointed out in 1948 the impossibility of reconstructing hair, eyes, nose, lips or facial expression. "The probabilities are that the expression of early man was not less benign than our own," he wrote.

When a museum displays models of Peking man, Neanderthal man and modern Homo sapiens side by side, it encourages a conception of physical and intellectual development which is not in accord with the views of contemporary science. Those who make such models tend to give their imagination free rein and stress the sensational and apelike traits of early man. Protruding mouth and receding forehead earn particular attention, although prognathism and a receding forehead are far from indicative of rudimentary or deficient intellectual powers. Both characteristics still occur today, often in extremely intelligent people. The exhibition of these half-human, half-animal figures is symptomatic of the moral arrogance of our era and latently inspired by a smug feeling of "look how far we've come!" It also illustrates the whole tragedy of the purely biological view of man, which devalues his intellectual side and insists, willy-nilly, that it must have evolved from the animal mind.

In point of fact, Homo sapiens has made his uninterrupted way down the millennia from the very beginning. There have been many varieties of the sapiens type, but the varieties and the forms of life which were distinct from the sapiens type from the first never merged with it and sometimes wandered off down the blind alleys which led to extinction.

"What I own" and "what I am" are the bases of two quite different criteria. It is difficult to believe that the natural disposition of men in the dawn of the earliest Ice Age was very different from that of modern Homo sapiens. What they possessed and what their intellect, imagination and inventive powers gave birth to in the material field may well have looked different, but the intellect that produced a stone knife was basically related to the intellect that succeeded in splitting the atom. Both achievements required creative energy and intellectual ability—and required them in an equal degree, for simple things are no easier to invent than complex systems which draw upon an established wealth of planning and experience. Men who have access to the painstakingly recorded results of other men's experimentation, research and designs naturally turn out products quite unlike those made by men who have acquired their craftsman's skill by word of mouth or mute demonstration alone.

Although the origins of man are more obscure than they ever were and the mysteries of life grow more unfathomable the farther we progress in the exact sciences, at least we confront the earliest tokens of human existence with more humility than our great-grandfathers did a hundred years ago. At least we perceive the unique and extraordinary nature of mankind more clearly than all the generations before us and recognize that the enigma of man's origin lies no less on the physical than on the spiritual plane. No longer shrinking from the assumption that there is a creative force or that behind all the secrets of existence stands a supreme being, we are daily drawing nearer to God.

CHAPTER 31

THE SECOND BEAM OF THE CROSS

All too often we tend to think of the world as being governed by natural laws which are independent of God. But perhaps the old Hebrew conception is nearer the truth, that the world is a sphere in which God can act directly at any time and in which he does act.

JOHN BRIGHT, *The Interpreter's Bible,*
New York, 1953, Vol. 2, p. 579

EVEN though it required a multiplicity of combined circumstances to make man's earthly existence possible, is it not conceivable that he exists on other planets as well, and that the creature Homo may not be unique in the cosmos? The numerous galactic systems contain innumerable suns, each surrounded by its own planets. Yet except for our own solar system, not one of these planets is visible to us, even through the finest optical telescopes in the world. We can only postulate their existence from, say, the periodic diminution of a sun's luminosity as its planets, invisible in themselves, pass between it and an observer on earth. The Russian astronomer Boris Vorontsov-Velyaminov believes that a proportion of the hundred million planets in the universe must carry highly organized forms of life.

We know that organic life, if only of the most rudimentary sort, is possible on three of the earth's neighboring planets—Mars, Venus, and Mercury. The prerequisites are a temperature which ranges between certain limits, an atmosphere which contains water, and a certain degree of atmospheric pressure. These conditions exist on Mars and probably Venus, but we also believe that higher forms of organic life could not exist on those planets.

Some doubt is justified in the case of Venus because astronomers are unable to penetrate the planet's swathing layers of cloud and it is thus impossible to ascertain the exact composition of its atmosphere. What is more, these layers of cloud must shield Venus from the sun's rays, so the temperature cannot be as high as that of Mercury. It is conceivable, therefore, that Venus supports organic life of the sort that existed on earth during the Tertiary period. Nevertheless, the possibility is an extremely distant one, and it is still further diminished by other factors too numerous to mention here.

The attempts now being made to pick up radio signals from outer space are prompted by the thought that some other planet may have been the scene of technical developments like our own and that rational creatures elsewhere in the universe may have arrived at exactly the same stage of technical development as we ourselves have done. Any such hypothesis founders on the fact that the cosmic "clock" governs the rate of growth and decay by temporal standards inconceivable on earth. Our galactic system is dominated by a continuous ebb and flow. Radiant new suns come into being while others pale and grow cold. New fixed stars are formed out of gaseous nebulae and clouds of cosmic dust only to die eventually. Meanwhile, the planets of these suns follow the same pattern of growth and decay. These occurrences take place over such immeasurably vast spans of time that the chances of two planets' reaching the same stage at the same time are slim indeed. In theory, planets may have existed whose careers matched that of our own, but logic tells us they probably existed eons ago and have since died. That the same thing should occur at the same point in time and that the technique and functions of living organisms should coincide exactly is contrary to all the laws of the universe, in whose illimitable history all events are no more than tiny specks swimming in a boundless ocean of time.

If man were not the result of a deliberate creative act, the million-fold conjunction of fortuitous circumstances which enable him to exist would be less easy to digest than the idea of divine intervention. However immense the number of planets in the universe, man remains such a miracle, his acquisition of intellect dependent on so many prior conditions and his existence governed by such an infinite chain of accidents that the theory of probabilities forbids one to assume a repetition of this highest form of life.

There are roughly a million animal species and three hundred thousand varieties of plant life on earth, but only one creature ever became man. This is a phenomenon at once so miraculous and so inimical to the theories of the traditional evolutionists that man must be regarded as unique.

But, even if the Russian Vorontsov-Valyaminov were right, I should like to point out that orthodox science is developing an entirely new approach to the universe: the idea of the interaction of mind and matter in space. The eminent British astronomer Sir James Jeans said that the universe more closely resembles a great thought than a great machine. Mind is no longer regarded as a chance intruder into the realm of matter. There is, in fact, a dawning presentiment that it should be regarded as the creator and controller of that realm. We are finding out that the universe betrays signs of a formative and guiding power which has something in common with the individual human mind.

Man is an extremely complicated machine, and his brain is unquestionably the highest and finest product of creation. No one has yet managed to explore the bodily machine in its entirety, and the design and capabilities of the brain may never be fully identified. Man's thoughts can range far beyond his material surroundings. He can capture his thoughts verbally and project them in any given direction. He knows what he is thinking and he can even ascertain why he is thinking it. He exploits his natural environment better than any other living creature. Indeed, he already possesses the ability to travel through space in an artificial abode.

The enormous domain spanned by the human intellect comprises some twenty-four distinct and complex sciences, each of them a world in itself, yet the scope of his intellectual processes extends far beyond them. Man is at once angel and devil, cruel and beneficent, greedy for new knowledge and daily beset by error, an eternal fantast and the most realistic and cold-blooded creature that ever walked the earth. Man is rapacious, all-devouring, all-consuming and all-destroying, yet he is capable of supreme self-sacrifice to the point of renouncing his body and dying a martyr's death.

Man has a past and is capable both of grasping that he is a historical being and of absorbing such of the past as is known to him. But man is not merely a creature endowed with reason. He is also a sentient being whose feelings belong and seem valid to him. He can re-create his own preferred conditions in the midst of alien surroundings and force nature to comply with his wishes. He is largely independent of his natural environment, and the world lies at his feet. He assimilates visible impressions and blends them with the invisible and intangible, with faith and powers of imagination.

All traces of man in the Ice Age indicate that they were left behind not by children of nature but by cultural beings. Man is so deeply rooted in the soil of intellect, religion and spirituality that no interpretation of his existence which is purely biological and fails to take cultural relationships into account can be regarded as scientifically valid or applicable either to the Paleolithic Age or to the present day. Man does not habitually look at the ground like other vertebrates. His gaze is directed at the horizon or even at the skies, and his upright stance is analogous with a mental orientation which transcends the corporeal and mundane and aspires to God. Man, in fact, possesses a soul, and Heraclitus knew five hundred years before the advent of Christ that the frontiers of the soul can never be traced "whatever road one travels."

Man is steeped in spirituality through and through and spends by far the greater part of his life in a conscious or unconscious quest for the supersensual. As we can read in Deuteronomy (viii, 3) and St. Matthew (iv, 4), man really does not live by bread alone. This is a truth which all the world's truly great men have grasped, and it is because religious founders, too, have realized this and have striven to assuage men's spiritual rather than their physical hunger that they occupy the foremost place in the annals of human memory. This is so and will remain so despite misrepresentation, prohibition, oppression or persecution of religions and their originators. No one has a claim to or expectation of posthumous respect who fails to realize the magnitude of man's essential spirituality and the momentum of his quest for God and, at the same time, for truth on the highest plane.

Man is ever restless, ever eager for new surroundings, ever on the move, still inhabited by the nomadic impulses of the Ice Age. He is always prepared to adopt innovations, mingle with other races, adapt himself to alien customs, exchange cultural assets. That he possessed all these attributes and impulses in the earliest stages of his history is demonstrated by the way in which he carried his stone implements from continent to continent during the Ice Age.

Man is at once creature and creator, shaper of his art and origina- tor of his culture; but art in particular and culture in general both stem from a single source, namely faith. Man is simultaneously the author of life's drama and its chief protagonist. Although he is part of nature, he molds it to his will. Yet the harnessing of natural forces has brought man no nearer to his most important goal, which is to control himself and render possible the coexistence of his own kind throughout the world. At the same time, man is the only creature who carries an awareness of the past about with him but lives more in the future than the present.

Man's future is not simply ordained for him by fate. History does not move in a perfect cycle, nor can we forecast the state of affairs which will prevail at a certain point in the future by consulting our knowledge of the past. The future is unfathomable because it de- pends on the decisions of each individual and of humanity at large.

The oldest primitive peoples never believed in the mechanical functioning of destiny or subscribed to the comfortless theory that each man's measure of weal and woe is inevitably determined or predestined at birth. The theory, borrowed from natural science, that races and cultures burgeon and wither like plants must necessarily lead to lethargy, heedless irresponsibility, fatalism and contempt for human life because it implies that all occurrences lie beyond the scope of man's will and endeavor. As soon as the doctrine that history is not shaped by the human will gains a hold it automatically para- lyzes that will, and whole nations subject themselves to a dictator or an overpowerful political system. Free will becomes atrophied, prayers are silenced, and the State takes the place of God.

Spengler regarded the course of history as a natural and immutable process which holds man in eternal bondage, and with his prophecies of decline there broke over the whole of central Europe a wave com- pounded of apathy and a passive and quite un-Western acceptance of suffering. Individual men renounced their right to independent thought, and free will found itself banned. "Time cannot be held in check," wrote Spengler in 1931. "There is no turning back, no shrewd retreat. Only dreamers believe in the possibility of evasion. Optimism is cowardice. We were born into this age and must resolutely tread the path that is allotted to us. There is no other. It is our duty to hold out, without hope, without escape. . . . This is greatness, this is what breeding means. This honorable end is the only thing of which man cannot be robbed." Shortly afterward, entire nations marched off to meet their allegedly inevitable end!

An inexorable and mechanical destiny precludes the possibility of God and renders every prayer superfluous and irrational. Fatalism is an approach to life which has long been popular in the Orient but which only achieved "popularity" in Europe when Spengler and Toynbee arrived on the scene. The ethnologically ancient races believed in a supreme being, and Paleolithic man's sacrifices prove that he regarded fate not only as accessible but also susceptible to influence. Humanity would never have survived three Ice Ages on a diet of blind fatalism. It may well be that man survived for over six hundred thousand years just because he lacked the trait which Spengler admired so extravagantly, the trait which goes hand in hand with a blind faith in predestination and lessens the prospect of a long life on earth. Courage is probably a very recent acquisition of our species.

The massive vulgarizations of the nineteenth century with its exaggerated respect for biological knowledge silenced the soul as it is always silenced by the cold scrutiny of pure knowledge. It is sadly paradoxical that in their attempts to enrich us and enhance our economic strength, scientists have only succeeded in making us poorer—and this despite the fact that the greatest scientists of all time, men like Copernicus, Kepler, Newton and Leibnitz, not to mention the leading physicists of our own day, have all clearly perceived the interaction of matter and creative force, a unity which probably represents the *ne plus ultra* of all science.

The physicist Pascual Jordan, whose works on quantum mechanics and the origin of the earth are of such fundamental importance, declares that "the results of modern physics are bringing about a complete change in the relationship between religion and science. The conception of the absolutely automatic natural occurrence has itself been refuted by physical experiment.... An unbiased examination of the conclusions which have stemmed from the cognitional-theoretic insights gained by science in recent decades makes it virtually impossible to maintain the scientist's traditionally anti-theological position. It is hardy an incautious prognosis to surmise that in course of time the inner logic of the thing will turn out to be stronger than emotionally colored and traditional inclinations." By "emotionally colored" Jordan means tinged with fanatical materialism.

The celebrated physicist Max Planck, author of the quantum theory and Nobel Prize winner, wrote: "Wheresoever and however far we look, we nowhere find a contradiction between religion and science but rather, and especially on vital points, complete agreement."

Erwin Schrödinger, whose research into wave mechanics, relativity and the quantum theory have won him world-wide recognition and the Nobel Prize for physics, regards the structural elements of life not as the clumsy work of man but as "the finest masterpiece that was ever constructed according to the guiding principles of God's quantum mechanics."

The secret of life and the secret of the world cannot be solved in a horizontal direction. We must take into account the second, the vertical beam of the Cross, like the circumpolar races who used to erect a tree of life.

Were the countless millions of men who died believing in God and a life hereafter no more than hecatombs offered in the name of mass delusion? Man realized, tens of thousands of years ago, that nothing can bar the gates of eternity to the soul. He let himself be interred beneath earth and slabs of stone because he knew that his faith was strong enough to burst the bonds of burial or imprisonment. It is our duty to execute the last will and testament of the Great Majority, men who could not take their bodies with them into eternity but to whom the spiritual aspect of human existence meant eternal life.

BIBLIOGRAPHY

1. *Spirituality Is Life*

BRIEFS, G. A.: The Crisis of Our Age, The Review of Politics, Vol. 4, No. 1, Notre Dame 1942, p. 319. — BRUNNER, A.: Die Religion, Freiburg 1956. — The Holy Bible, Romans 8, 6. — SCHEBESTA, R. P.: Congo, Brussels 1931, p. 9.

2. *The Problem of Our Time*

ALBRIGHT, W. F.: From the Stone Age to Christianity, Baltimore 1946, p. 310. — KUHN, H.: The Journal of Philosophy, 44, 1947, p. 491. — LIPS, J.: Einleitung in die vergleichende Völkerkunde. — OSGOOD, C.: Southwestern Journal of Anthropology, Vol. 7, 1951, pp. 202–214. — SCHMIDT, W.: Handbuch der Methode der kulturhistorischen Ethnologie, Münster i. W. 1937.

3. *Man 600,000 Years Ago*

BLACK, D.: Tertiary Man in Asia, Bull. Geol. Soc. China, Vol. 5, 1927, pp. 3–4. — BLANC, A. C.: Das Auftreten des Menschen, Handbuch der Weltgeschichte, Vol. 1, edited by A. Randa, Olten, and Freiburg i. Br. 1954, pp. 37–38. — BOULE, M.: Le Sinanthrope, L'Anthropologie, Vol. 39, 1929. Les Hommes Fossiles, Paris. — BREUIL, H.: Le feu et l'industrie de pierre et d'os dans le gisement du Sinanthropus à Chou Kou Tien, L'Anthropologie, Vol. 42, 1932, pp. 5, 6, 11. — BROOM, R. and ROBINSON, J. T.: Further Evidence of the Structure of the Sterkfontein Ape-Man Plesianthropus, Transvaal Museum Memoir, No. 4, Pretoria 1950, p. 82. Man contemporaneous with the Swartkrans Ape-Man, Am. J. Phys. Anthrop., Vol. 8, 1950, pp. 151–184. — DART, R. A.: The Predatory Implemental Technique of Australopithecus, Am. J. Phys. Anthr., New Series, Vol. 7, 1949. — DUBOIS, E.: Pithecanthropus erectus, eine menschenähnliche Übergangsform aus Java, Batavia 1894. — EHGARTNER, W.: Fossile Menschenaffen aus Südafrika, Mitt. Anthrop. Ges. Wien, Vol. 80, 1950, p. 207. Die stammesgeschichtliche Einstufung von Australopithecus Prometheus Dart, Mitt. Anthrop. Ges. Wien, Vol. 78–79, Vienna 1949, p. 2 et seq.—v. EICKSTEDT, E.: Der derzeitige Stand der Urmenschforschung, Arch. Jul. Klaus Institute, Vol. 24, 1949, p. 31. — FEHRINGER, O.: Die Welt der Säugetiere, Munich, 1953, p. 352. — GERVAIS, P.: Sur un singe fossile, d'espèce non encore décrite, qui a été decouvert au Monte Bamboli, C. R. Acad. Sci. 74, 1872. — HOLMES, A.: An Estimate of the Age of the Earth, Nature, Vol. 157, London 1946, pp. 680–684. The Age of the Earth, Endeavour, Vol. 6, London 1946, pp. 99–108. — HÜRZELER, J.: Oreopithecus bambolii Gervais, Basle 1958, p. 5. — KÄLIN, J.: Die ältesten Menschenreste und ihre stammesgeschichtliche Deutung, Historia Mundi, Vol. 1, Munich 1952, pp. 72, 75, 92–93.— v. KÖNIGSWALD, G. H. R.: Neue Pithecanthropusfunde 1936–1938, Wet. Meded. Dienst Mijnbouw Ned. Indie, Vol. 28, 1940. — KOPPERS, W.: Der historische Gedanke in Ethnologie und Prähistorie, Kultur und Sprache, Wiener Beitr. zur Kulturgeschichte und Linguistik, Vienna 1952, p. 34. — LE GROS CLARK, W. E.: New Palaeontological Evidence Bearing on the Evolution of the Hominoidea, Quart. J. Geol. Soc. London, Vol. 105, Part 2, 1950, pp. 225–264. — MILANKOVIĆ, M.:

BIBLIOGRAPHY

Astronomische Mittel zur Erforschung der erdgeschichtlichen Klimate, Handb. Geophys., Vol. 9, Berlin 1938. Kanon der Erdbestrahlung und seine Anwendung auf das Eiszeitenproblem, Ed. spec. Acad. R. Serbe, Belgrade 1941. – MOVIUS, H. L.: Early Man and Pleistocene Stratigraphy in Southern and Eastern Asia, Pap. Peabody Mus. Am. Arch. Ethnol., Harvard University, Vol. 19, 1944. – MUCKERMANN, H.: Der Mensch in der Weltwirtschaft, Berlin 1951. – OVERHAGE, P.: in: "Das stammesgeschichtliche Werden der Organismen und des Menschen," Basle-Freiburg-Vienna 1959, p. 238. – PEI WENZCHUNG: Notice of the Discovery of Quartz and Other Stone Artifacts in the Lower Pleistocene Hominid-Bearing Sediments of the Choukoutein Deposit, Bull. Geol. Soc. China, Vol. II, 1931/32. – REMANE, A.: in: Frankfurter Allgemeine Zeitung, 3.11.59, No. 255, p. 12, "Doch keine Frühmenschen." Ist Oreopithecus ein Hominide? Abh. Akad. Wiss. und Lit. Mainz, Nat.-Math. Kl. 12. – RÜTIMEYER, L.: Über Pliocen und Eisperiode auf beiden Seiten der Alpen, Basle 1876. – SALLER, K.: Art- und Rassenlehre des Menschen, Stuttgart 1949. Grundlagen der Anthropologie, Stuttgart 1949. – Schmidt, P. W.: Völkerkunde und Urgeschichte in gemeinsamer Arbeit an der Aufhellung ältester Menschheitsgeschichte, Report of the Natural History Society, Berne 1941. – TSCHUMI, O.: Urgeschichte der Schweiz, Vol. I, Frauenfeld 1949, p. 439. – VALLOIS, H. V.: Les preuves anatomiques de l'origine monophyletique de l'homme, L'Anthropologie, Vol. 39, 1929, pp. 77–101. – WEIDENREICH, F.: Die Sonderform des Menschenschädels als Anpassung an den aufrechten Gang, Z. Morph. Anthrop., Vol. 24, 1924. The Skull of Sinanthropus Pekinensis, Palaeontologica Sinica, n. s. D., No. 10, 1943. About the Morphological Character of the Australopithecinae Skull, Robert Broom, Commemor. Vol. Roy. Soc., South Africa 1948, pp. 153–158. – WEINERT, H.: Ursprung der Menschheit, Stuttgart 1932. – ZEUNER, F. E.: Dating the Past, London 1952, p. 307 et seq. Dating the Past, Third Edition, London 1952, p. 274.

4. No More Primitive Than Ourselves

ADRIAN, W.: Die Frage der norddeutschen Eolithen, Paderborn 1948. – ALIMEN, H.: Atlas de Préhistoire, Vol. I, Paris 1950. – BAYER, J.: Die ältere Steinzeit in den Sudetenländern, Sudeta, Vol. I, 1925. Das zeitliche und kulturelle Verhältnis zwischen den Kulturen des Schmalklingenkulturkreises während des Diluviums in Europa, Die Eiszeit, Vol. 5, 1928. – BLANC, A. C.: Sulla penetrazione e diffusione in Europa ed in Italia del Paleolitico superiore, Quartär, Vol. I, 1938. – BREUIL, H.: Les industries à éclats du paléolithique ancien, Préhistoire, Vol. I, 1932. – BREUIL, H. and KOSLOWSKI, L.: Études de stratigraphie paléolithique dans le nord de la France, la Belgique et l'Angleterre, L'Anthropologie, Vol. 42, Paris 1932, pp. 27–47. – BREUIL, H. and LANTIER, R.: Les Hommes de la Pierre Ancienne, Paris 1951. – BURKITT, M. C.: The Old Stone Age, Cambridge 1934. – GAHS, A.: Die kulturhistorischen Beziehungen der östlichen Paläosibirier zu den austrischen Völkern, insbesondere zu jenen Formosas, Report of the Anthropological Society, Year 1929–1930, Vienna 1930, p. 5. – LEAKEY, L. S. B.: Stone Age Africa, London 1936. – LEAKEY, L. S. B. and OAKLEY, K.: in: "The First Men." Recent Discovery in East Africa, by Ray Inskeep, Antiquity, Vol. 33, December 1959, pp. 285–289. – MENGHIN, O.: Weltgeschichte der Steinzeit,

BIBLIOGRAPHY

Vienna 1931. — MOIR, J. R.: The Darmsdenian Flint Implements, Proc. Prehist. Soc., Vol. I, London 1935. — MOVIUS, H. L.: Old-World Paleolithic Archeology, Bull. Geol. Soc. America, Vol. 60, 1949. Zur Archäologie des unteren Paläolithikums in Südasien und im Fernen Osten, Report of the Anthropological Society, Vol. 80, Vienna 1950. — NARR, K. J.: Zur Frage altpaläolithischer Kulturkreise, Anthropos, Vol. 48, 1953, pp. 773–794. Vorderasien, Nordafrika und Europa, Abriss der Vorgeschichte, Munich 1957, pp. 1–79. — OAKLEY, K. P.: Man the Tool-Maker, British Museum Natural History, London 1949. — OBERMAIER, H.: Der Mensch der Vorzeit, Berlin-Munich 1912. — PEYRONY, D.: Les industries "aurignaciennes" dans le bassin de la Vezère, Bull. Soc. Préhist. Franc., Vol. 33, 1936. Le Périgordien et l'Aurignacien (Nouvelles observations), Bull. Soc. Préhist. Franc., Vol. 33, 1936. — RUHLMANN, A.: Le paléolithique marocain, Publ. Serv. Antiqu. Maroc. Vol. 7, 1945. — RUST, A.: Betrachtungen über eurasiatisch-afrikanische Kulturzusammenhänge in der Steinzeit, Offa 8, Neumünster 1949. — SCHMIDT, P. W.: Die Urkulturen: Ältere Jagd- und Sammelstufe (Feuererzeugung), Historia Mundi, Vol. I, Munich 1952, pp. 424–427. — SCHULZ-WEIDNER, W.: Vorgeschichte Afrikas südlich der Sahara, Abriss der Vorgeschichte, Munich, 1957, pp. 85–111. — VAUFREY, R.: Le paléolithique italien, Arch. Inst. Paléont. Humaine, Mém. 3, 1928. — WARREN, H. S.: The Clacton Flint Industry: A New Interpretation, Proceed. Geologists Assoc., Vol. 62, 1951. — WEINERT, H.: Menschen der Vorzeit, Stuttgart 1947. Über die neuen Vor- und Frühmenschenfunde aus Afrika, Java, China und Frankreich, Zeitschr. Morph. Anthropol., Vol. 42, 1951. — WIELAND, W.: Schellings Lehre von der Zeit, Heidelberger Forschungen, No. 4, Heidelberg 1956. — ZOTZ, L. F.: Altsteinzeitkunde Mitteleuropas, Stuttgart 1951.

5. Early Man in America

ANTEVS, E.: The Age of "Minnesota Man," Carnegie Institution Yearbook, No. 36, Washington 1937, pp. 335–338. The Great Basin, with Emphasis on Glacial and Post-Glacial Times; Climatic Changes and Pre-White Man, University of Utah Bull., Vol. 33, No. 20, Salt Lake City 1948, pp. 168–191. — BRYAN, K. and RAY, L. L.: Geologic Antiquity of the Lindenmeier Site in Colorado, Smithsonian Misc. Col. Vol. 99, No. 2, Washington 1940. — CARTER, G. F.: Man in America: A Criticism of Scientific Thought, Scientific Monthly, Vol. LXXIII, No. 5, Washington 1951, pp. 297–307. — COTTER, J. L.: The Occurrence of Flints and Extinct Animals in Pluvial Deposits near Clovis, New Mexico, Proc. Phila. Acad. Nat. Sci., Vol. 89, 1937, pp. 2–16. The Occurrence of Flints and Extinct Animals in Pluvial Deposits near Clovis, New Mexico, Proc. Phila. Acad. Na. Sci., Vol. 90, 1938, pp. 113–117. — CRESSMAN, L. S.: Western Prehistory in the Light of Carbon 14 Dating, Southwestern Journal of Anthropology, Vol. 7, Albuquerque 1951, pp. 289–313. — DE TERRA, H., JAVIER, R. and STEWART, T. D.: Tepexpan Man, Viking Fund Publications in Anthropology, No. 11, New York 1949. — EISELEY, L. C.: The Paleo Indians: Their Survival and Diffusion, New Interpretations of Aboriginal American Culture History, Washington, D. C., 1955, 75th Anniversary Volume of the Anthropological Society of Washington. — FIGGINS, J. D.: A further Contribution to the Antiquity of Man in America,

BIBLIOGRAPHY

Proc. Colorado Museum of Nat. Hist., Denver 1933. The Antiquity of Man in America, Natural History, Vol. XXVII, No. 3, New York 1927, pp. 229–239. – GIDDINGS, J. L., JR.: Early Flint Horizons on the North Bering Sea Coast, Journal of the Washington Academy of Sciences, Vol. 39, 1949, pp. 85–90. – GROSS, H.: Mastodon, Mammoth, and Man in America, Bull. of the Texas Arch. and Paleontological Society, Lubbock 1951, pp. 217–224. – HANSEN, S.: Lagoa Santa Racen, E Museo Lundii, Vol. 1, Part V, Copenhagen. – HAURY, E. W.: A Mammoth Hunt in Arizona, Archaeology, 1955, pp. 51–55. – HIBBEN, F. C.: Evidences of Early Occupation of Sandia Cave, New Mexico, and Other Sites in the Sandia-Manzano Region, Smithsonian Misc. Coll., Vol. 99, No. 23, 1941. – IBARRA GRASSO, D. E.: Das Altpaläolithikum in Amerika, Zeitschrift für Ethnologie, Vol. 83, 1958, pp. 170–197. – Imbelloni, J.: La industria de la piedra en Monte Heroso, Anal. de la Fac. de Cienc. de Educación, Parana, II, 1928, pp. 147–168. – JENKS, A. E.: Pleistocene Man in Minnesota, Minneapolis 1936. – LIBBY, W. F., ANDERSON, E. C. and ARNOLD, J. R.: Age Determination by Radiocarbon Content: World-Wide Assay of Natural Radiocarbon, Science, 109, 1949, pp. 227–228. – LÜTKEN, C. F.: Indledende Bemaerkninger om Menneskelevninger i Brasiliens Huler og i de Lundske Samlinger, E Museo Lundii, Copenhagen, Vol. 1, Part IV. – MARINGER, J.: Contribution to the Prehistory of Mongolia, Reports from the Scientific Expedition to the North-Western Provinces of China under the Leadership of Dr. Sven Hedin, VII, Archaeology, Stockholm 1950. A Stone Industry of Patjitanian Tradition from Central Japan, Kokogaku Zasshi, XLII, No. 2, The Archaeological Society of Nippon, 1957. – MEGGERS, B. J.: The Coming of Age of American Archaeology, Washington, D. C.: 1955, 75th Anniversary Volume of the Anthropological Society of Washington. – MENGHIN, O. F. A.: Das Protolithikum in Amerika, Acta Praehistorica I, Buenos Aires 1957, pp. 5–40. – PERICOT, L.: South American Prehistory: A Review, Antiquity, 1955, pp. 89–94. – PÖCH, H.: Beitrag zur Kenntnis von den fossilen menschlichen Funden von Lagoa Santa (Brasilien) und Fontezuelas (Argentinien), Report of the Anthropological Society, Vienna 1938, pp. 311 et seq. – ROBERTS, F. H. H., JR.: The Folsom Problem in American Archaeology, Annual Report of the Board of Regents of the Smithsonian Institution, Washington 1939, pp. 531 et seq. – ROTH, S., SCHILLER, W., WITTE, L., KANTOR, M., TORRES, L. M. and AMEGHINO, C.: Nuevas investigaciones geológicas y antropológicas en el litoral maritimo sur de la provincia de Buenos Aires, Anal. del Museo Nac. 36, 1915, pp. 417–431. – SCHULTEN, A.: Tartessos, Hamburg 1950. – SOLECKI, R. S.: Archaeology and Ecology of the Arctic Slope of Alaska, Annual Report of the Board of Regents of the Smithsonian Institution, Washington 1951, pp. 469 et seq. New data on the Inland Eskimo of Northern Alaska, Journal of the Washington Academy of Sciences, Vol. 40, 1950, pp. 137–156. – WORMINGTON, H. M.: Ancient Man in North America, The Denver Museum of Natural History, Denver 1957. Origins, Program of the History of America, I, 1, Mexico, 1953. – YAWATA, ICHIRO: Anthropology, Contribution to the Prehistoric Archaeology of Northern Jehol, Report of the First Scientific Expedition to Manchukuo, 1940.

BIBLIOGRAPHY

6. Never a Time Without History

BARKER, SIR E.: Dr. Toynbee's Study of History, International Affairs, Vol. 31, 1955, pp. 5–16. – BERNHEIM, E.: Lehrbuch der historischen Methode, Leipzig 1908. – BREUIL, H.: Le Paléolithique ancien en Europe occidentale et sa chronologie, Bull. Soc. Préhist. Française, Vol. 29, 1932. – COLLINGWOOD, R. G.: The Idea of History, Oxford 1951. – COON, C. S.: The Races of Europe, New York 1939. – DAWSON, C.: Toynbee's Study of History, International Affairs, Vol. 31, London 1955, pp. 149–158. – GRAEBNER, F.: Methode der Ethnologie, Heidelberg 1911. – GURIAN, W.: Toynbee's Time Machine, The Review of Politics, Notre Dame, Ind., 1942, 4, pp. 508–514. – HEINE-GELDERN, R.: Herkunft und Ausbreitung der Hochkulturen, Almanach der Österr. Akad. d. Wiss., Year 105, Vienna 1956. L'origine des anciennes civilisations et les théories de Toynbee, Diogène, Janvier 1956, Paris. – KAERST, J.: Universalgeschichte, Stuttgart 1930. – KIRN, P.: Einführung in die Geschichtwissenschaft, Berlin 1952. – KOPPERS, W.: Das Problem der Universalgeschichte im Lichte von Ethnologie und Prähistorie, Anthropos, Vol. 52, 1957, pp. 369–389. Zusammenarbeit von Ethnologie und Prähistorie (Ein Beitrag zur Methode beider Wissenschaften), Zeitschrift für Ethnologie, Vol. 78, 1953, pp. 1–16. Der historische Gedanke in Ethnologie und Prähistorie, Kultur und Sprache, Vienna 1952, pp. 1–65. Der Urmensch und sein Weltbild, Vienna 1949. – KRAFT, G.: Der Urmensch als Schöpfer, Tübingen 1948. – KUHN, H.: Book Review: Toynbee, A Study of History, Journal of Philosophy, Vol. 44, 1947, pp. 477–485 and p. 491. – LÉVY-BRUHL, L.: Die geistige Welt der Primitiven, Munich 1927. Les carnets de Lucien Lévy-Bruhl, Paris 1949. – MENGHIN, O.: Weltgeschichte der Steinzeit, Vienna 1941. – PODACH, E. F.: Zum Abschluss von L. Lévy-Bruhls Theorie über die Mentalität der Primitiven, Zeitschrift für Ethnologie, Vol. 76, 1951, pp. 42–49. – SHIROKOGOROV, S. M.: Psychomental Complex of the Tungus, Shanghai-London 1935. – SCHMIDT, P. W.: Der Ursprung der Gottesidee, Münster i. W. 1955. – TOYNBEE, A. J.: A Study of History, London 1934–1954. – TYLOR, E. B.: Researches into the Early History of Mankind, 1865. Primitive Culture, 1871. Anthropology, 1881. – v. WINEL BEI BÜLACH, E. E. S.: Die philosophische und politische Kritik Oswald Spenglers, Zürich 1958.

7. The Origin of American Indians

BOAS, F.: Relationships Between North-West America and North-East Asia (1933); Race, Language and Culture, New York 1949. Classification of American Indian Languages; Race, Language and Culture (1929), New York 1949. Relationships between North-West America and North-East Asia, The American Aborigines, Their Origin and Antiquity, edited by Diamond Jenness, Toronto 1933. – BUSHNELL, G. McBURNEY, C.: New World Origins Seen from the Old World, Antiquity, Vol. 33, No. 130, 1959, pp. 93–101. – CHARD, C. S.: New World Origins: A Reappraisal, Antiquity, Vol. 33, No. 129, 1959, p. 44 et seq. An outline of the Prehistory of Siberia, Southwestern Journal of Anthropology, Vol. 14, 1958, pp. 1–33. – CRESSMAN, L. S.: Western Prehistory in the Light of Carbon 14 Dating, Southwestern Journal of Anthropology, Vol. 7, Albuquerque

BIBLIOGRAPHY

1951, pp. 289–313. — EISELEY, L. C.: The Paleo-Indians: Their Survival and Diffusion, New Interpretations of Aboriginal American Culture History, Washington, D. C., 1955, 75th Anniversary Volume of the Anthropological Society of Washington. — EKHOLM, G. F.: The New Orientation Toward Problems of Asiatic-American Relationships, Washington, D. C.: 1955, 75th Anniversary Volume of the Anthropological Society of Washington. — FREUND, GISELA: Die Blatspitzen des Paläolithikums in Europa, Bonn 1952. — GIDDINGS, J. L., JR.: Early Flint Horizons on the North Bering Sea Coast, Journal of the Washington Academy of Sciences, Vol. 39, 1949, pp. 85–90. — IBARRA GRASSO, D. E.: Das Altpaläolithikum in Amerika, Zeitschrift für Ethnologie, Vol. 83, 1958, pp. 170–197. — HANSEN, S.: Lagoa Santa Racen, E Museo Lundii, Vol. 1, Part V, Copenhagen. — HENTZE, K.: Bronzegerät, Kultbauten, Religion im ältesten China der Shang-Zeit, Antwerp 1951. — JENNESS, D.: The Indians of Canada, Ottawa 1932. — JENKS, A. E.: Pleistocene Man in Minnesota, Minneapolis 1936. — LÜTKEN, C. F. Indledende Bemaerkninger om Menneskelevninger i Brasiliens Huler og i de Lundske Samlinger, E Museo Lundii, Copenhagen, Vol. 1, Part IV. — MARINGER, J.: Contribution to the Prehistory of Mongolia, Reports from the Scientific Expedition to the North-Western Provinces of China under the Leadership of Dr. Sven Hedin, VII, Archaeology, Stockholm 1950. — MASON, J. A.: The Languages of South American Indians, Handbook of South American Indians, VI, 1950, 157–317. — MEGGERS, B. J.: The Coming of Age of American Archaeology, Washington, D. C., 1955, 75th Anniversary Volume of the Anthropological Society of Washington. — PERICOT, L.: South American Prehistory: A Review, Antiquity 1955, pp. 89–94. — PÖCH, H.: Beitrag zur Kenntnis von den fossilen menschlichen Funden von Lagoa Santa (Brasilien) und Fontezuelas (Argentinien), Report of the Anthropological Society, Vienna 1938, p. 311 et seq. — RIVET, P.: Les Origines de l'Homme Américain, Paris 1957. — ROBERTS, F. H. H., JR.: The Folsom Problem in American Archaeology, Annual Report of the Board of Regents of the Smithsonian Institution, Washington 1939, p. 531 et seq. — SCHAFER, R.: Athapaskan and Sino-Tibetan, International Journal of American Linguists, Vol. 18, Baltimore 1952, p. 12 et seq. — SOLECKI, R. S.: Archaeology and Ecology of the Arctic Slope of Alaska, Annual Report of the Board of Regents of the Smithsonian Institution, Washington 1951, p. 469 et seq. New data on the Inland Eskimo of Northern Alaska, Journal of the Washington Academy of Sciences, Vol. 40, 1950, pp. 137–156. — TSCHOPIK, H., JR.: Indians of North America, Man and Nature Publications, The American Museum of Natural History, New York 1958. — WISSLER, C.: The American Indian, Third Edition, New York 1938. — WORMINGTON, H. M.: Ancient Man in North America, The Denver Museum of Natural History, Denver 1957.

8. American Indians and The Supreme Being

BARETT, S. A.: A Composite Myth of the Pomo Indians, Journal of American Folklore, Vol. 19, 1906, pp. 37–51. Pomo Bears Doctors, University of California Publications of American Archaeology and Ethnology, Vol. 12, 1917, pp. 443–465. — BIRD, J. S.: Antiquity and Migrations of the Early Inhabitants of Patagonia, The Geographical Review, 28, 1938, pp. 250–275. Before Magellan, Natural

BIBLIOGRAPHY

History, XLI, 1938. New York. — BIRKET-SMITH, K.: A Geographic Study of the Early History of the Algonquin Indians, Internationales Archiv für Ethnographie, Vol. 24, 1918, pp. 174–222. — CHAMBERLAIN, A. F.: Nanibozhu Amongst the Otchipwe, Mississagas, and other Algonkian Tribes, Journal of American Folk-Lore, Vol. IV, 1891, pp. 193–213. — COOPER, J. M.: Analytical and Critical Bibliography of the Tribes of Tierra del Fuego and Adjacent Territory, Bureau of American Ethnology, Bulletins, LXIII, Washington 1917. Culture Diffusions and Culture Areas in Southern South America, Internationale Amerikanisten-Kongresse, Proceedings, Göteborg 1925. — DOBRIZHOFFER, M.: Geschichte der Abiponer, aus dem Lateinischen von A. Kreil, Vienna 1783–84. — FALKNER, THOMAS: A Description of Patagonia and the Adjoining Parts of South America, Hereford 1774. — GIFFORD, E. W.: Miwok Myths, University of California Publications of American Archaeology and Ethnology, Vol. 8, 1917, pp. 283–338. — GODDARD, P. E.: Kato Texts, University of California, Publications in American Archaeology and Ethnology, Berkeley 1909. — GUSINDE, M.: Die Feuerland Indianer, Mödling 1931. — HAEKEL, J.: The Concept of a Supreme Being Among the Northwest-Coast Tribes of North America, Wiener Völkerkundliche Mitteilungen, Year 2, Vienna 1954, pp. 171–183. — HARIOT, THOMAS: Narrative of the First English Plantation of Virginia, 1588 and London 1893. — HARRINGTON, M. R.: Indian Notes and Monographs, Religion and Ceremonies of the Lenape, New York 1921. — HECKEWELDER, J.: An Account of the History, Manners and Customs of the Indian Nations Who Once Inhabited Pennsylvania and the Neighboring States, Transactions of the American Philosophical Society, Vol. 1, Philadelphia 1819, p. 205. — HOFFMAN, W. J.: The Midewiwin or "Grand Medicine Society" of the Ojibwa, Seventh Annual Report of the Bureau of Ethnology, Washington 1891, p. 163. — JONES, W.: Ojibwa Tales From the North Shore of Lake Superior, Journal of American Folklore, Vol. 29, 1916, pp. 368–391. The Algonkin Manitou, Journal of American Folklore, Vol. 18, 1905, p. 183. — KOPPERS, W.: Die Erstbesiedlung Amerikas im Lichte der Feuerland-Forschungen (Ethnologie, Prähistorie, Anthropologie, Blutgruppenuntersuchungen), Bulletin der Schweizerischen Gesellschaft für Anthropologie und Ethnologie, Year 20, 1944, pp. 49–63. — KRICKEBERG, W.: Beiträge zur Frage der alten Kulturgeschichtlichen Beziehungen zwischen Nord- und Südamerika, Zeitschrift für Ethnologie, Year 66, 1935, pp. 287–373. — KROEBER, A. L.: Elements of Culture in Native California, University of California, Publications in Amer. Archaeol. and Ethnol., Berkeley 1922. Handbook of the Indians of California, Bureau of Amer. Ethnology, Reports, Washington 1925. Wishosk Myths, Journal of American Folk-Lore, Vol. 18, 1905, pp. 85–107. Wiyot Folk-Lore, Vol. 21, 1908, pp. 37–39, Vol. 6, p. 348, Vol. 7, pp. 117–119. — LANG, A.: Magic and Religion, London-New York-Bombay 1901. Myth, Ritual and Religion, New Impression, London-New York-Bombay 1901. — MARKHAM, C.: Early Spanish Voyages to the Strait of Magellan, London 1911. — MERRIAM, C. H.: The Dawn of the World, Myths and Weird Tales told by the Mewan Indians of California, Cleveland 1920. — MÉTRAUX, A.: Religion and Shamanism, Handbook of South American Indians, V, 1949, pp. 559–599. — MORENO, F. P.: Viaje a la Patagonia Austral, Buenos Aires 1879. — MUSTERS, G. C.: Unter den Patagoniern, aus dem Englischen von Martin, Jena 1873. — D'ORBIGNY, A.:

BIBLIOGRAPHY

Voyage dans l'Amerique Meridionale, Paris 1835-44. L'homme américain (de l'Amérique Meridionale) considéré sous ses rapports physiologiques et moraux, Paris 1839. – PENN, WILLIAM: A letter from William Penn, Proprietary and Governor of Pennsylvania in America to the Committee of the Free Society of Traders of that Province, Residing in London, London 1683, p. 6. – POWERS, ST.: Tribes of California, Overland Monthly, 1. Ser. Vol. 8-14. Tribes of California, Contributions to the North American Ethnology, Washington 1877.

9, 10, 11

The Death of the Yaghan
The Alacaluf: Earliest of All Americans
The Selknam and Their God Temaukl

BANKS, SIR J.: Journal of Sir Joseph Banks, edited by Sir J. D. Hooker, London 1896, pp. 43-61. – BARCLAY, W. S.: The Land of Magellanes, with Some Account of the Ona and Other Indians, The Geographical Journal 23, 1904, pp. 62-79. – BIRD, J. S.: The Alacaluf, Handbook of South American Indians, I, 1946, pp. 45-79. Antiquity and Migrations of the Early Inhabitants of Patagonia, The Geographical Review, 28, 1938, pp. 250-275. Before Magellan, Natural History, 41, 1938. New York. – BORGATELLO, M.: Notizie grammaticali e glossario della lingua degli indi Alakaluf, Turin 1928. – COOPER, J. M.: The Chono, Handbook of South American Indians, I, 1946, pp. 47-54. The Yaghan, Handbook of South American Indians, I, 1946, pp. 81-106. The Ona, Handbook of South American Indians, I, 1946, pp. 107-125. The Patagonian and Pampean Hunters, Handbook of South American Indians, I, 1946, pp. 127-168. Analytical and Critical Bibliography of the Tribes of Tierra del Fuego and Adjacent Territory, Bureau of American Ethnology, Bulletins, 63, Washington 1917. Culture Diffusion and Culture Areas in Southern South America, Internationale Amerikanisten-Kongresse, Proceedings, Göteborg 1925. – DARWIN, C.: Journal of Researches into Natural History and Geology of the Countries Visited During the Voyage of HMS Beagle Round the World, Under the Command of Capt. Fitz Roy, R.N., London 1845, Second Edition 1860. – EMPERAIRE, J.: Les Nomades de la Mer, Paris 1955. – FALKNER, THOMAS: A Description of Patagonia and the Adjoining Parts of South America, Hereford 1774. – GUSINDE, M.: Die Feuerland-Indianer, Mödling, 1, 1931, 2, 1937, 3, 1939 and Anthropologie, Urmensch im Feuerland, Berlin-Vienna-Leipzig 1946. – HILDEN, K.: Zwei Indianerschädel aus Feuerland, Helsinki 1930, Acta Geographica 3, No. 2. – KOPPERS, W.: Unter Feuerland-Indianern, Stuttgart 1924. Die Erstbesiedlung Amerikas im Lichte der Feuerland-Forschungen (Ethnologie, Prähistorie, Anthropologie, Blutgruppenuntersuchungen), Bulletin der Schweizerischen Gesellschaft für Anthropologie und Ethnologie, Year 20, 1944, pp. 49-63. – MARKHAM, C.: Early Spanish Voyages to the Strait of Magellan, London 1911. – MÉTRAUX, A.: Religion and Shamanism, Handbook of South American Indians, V, 1949, pp. 559-599. – MORENO, F. P.: Viaje á la Patagonia Austral, Buenos Aires, 1879. – MUSTERS, G. C.: Unter den Patagoniern, aus dem Englischen von Martin, Jena 1873. – NORDENSKJÖLD, O.: Das Feuerland und seine Bewohner, Geographische Zeitschrift, edited by A.

BIBLIOGRAPHY

Hettner, Leipzig 1896, pp. 662–674. Wissenschaftliche Ergebnisse der schwedischen Expedition nach den Magellansländern 1895–1897, Stockholm 1899–1907. – D'ORBIGNY, A.: Voyage dans l'Amérique Méridionale, Paris 1835–1844. L'homme américain (de l'Amérique Méridionale) considéré sous ses rapports physiologiques et moraux, Paris 1839. – RADIN, P.: Some Myths and Tales of the Ojibwa of Southeastern Ontario, Ottawa 1914. – SCHMIDT, P. W.: Der Ursprung der Gottesidee, Part II, Vol. II, Die Religionen der Urvölker Amerikas, Münster i. W. – SKINNER, A.: Plains Ojibwa Tales, Journal of American Folklore, Vol. 32, 1919, pp. 280–305. – SMITH, W.: General History of New England, 1606–1624. – STRACHEY, W.: Histoire of Travaile into Virginia Britannia, ed. Arber, Hakluyt Society, 1849. – TEIT, J.: Traditions of the Thompson River Indians of British Columbia, Boston-New York 1898. Memoirs of the American Folk-Lore Society, Vol. 6. – TYLOR, E. B.: Primitive Culture, Vol. 2, London 1871, p. 308. On the Limits of Savage Religion, Journal of the Anthropological Institute, Vol. 21, 1892, p. 284 et seq. – WAITZ, TH.: Anthropologie der Naturvölker, Part Three: Die Amerikaner, Leipzig 1862. – WINSLOW, E.: See under A. Young, Chronicles of the Pilgrim Fathers, Boston 1841, and Elliott, New England History, New York 1857. – ZEISBERGER, D.: History of the Northern American Indians, Ohio Archaeological and Historical Quarterly, Vol. XIX, Columbus 1910, p. 128.

12. Palaeo-Asiatics and Tungus

BOGORAS, W.: Chukchee, Handbook of American Indian Languages by F. Boas, Washington 2, 1922. – JAKOBSON, R.: Structure of the Gilyak, Journal of the American Oriental Society, The Paleosiberian Languages, American Anthropologist, Vol. 44, 1942, pp. 602–620. – JÖRGENSEN, J. B.: The Eskimo Skeleton, Meddelelser om Grönland, Vol. 146, No. 2, Copenhagen 1953, p. 114. – KORSAKOV, G.: Lingvisticheskiye materialy S. P. Krasheninnikova i ikh znacheniye dlya issledovaniya paleoaziatskikh yazykov, Sovetskiy Sever 2, 1939. Samouchitel' nymylanskogo yazyka, Moscow 1936. – LAUFER, B.: Einige linguistische Bemerkungen zu Grabowsky's Giljakischen Studien, International Archive of Ethnography 11, 1898. – RADLOFF, L.: Über die Sprache der Tschuktschen und ihr Verhältnis zu Korjakischen, Mémoires de l'Académie des Sciences, St. Petersburg, Series 6, Vol. 3, No. 10, 1861. – RAMSTEDT, G.: Über den Ursprung der sogenannten Jenissei-Ostjaken, Journal de la Société Finno-Ougrienne 34, 1907. – STEENSBY, H. P.: An Anthropogeographical Study of the Origin of the Eskimo Culture, Meddelelser om Grönland, Vol. 13, Copenhagen 1917, pp. 41–228. – STERNBERG, L.: Gilyaki, orochi gol'dy, negidal'tsy, Khabarovsk 1933. – Yazyki i pis'mennost' paleoaziatskikh narodov, Trudy po lingvistike Nauchno-issledovatel'skoy Assotsiatsii Instituta Narodov Severa, Leningrad 1934.

15. The Tungus: A Dying Race

ANISIMOV, A. F.: Rodovoye obshchestvo evenkov (tungusov), Leningrad 1936. – BENZING, J.: Einführung in das Studium der altaischen Philologie und der Turkologie, Wiesbaden 1953. – BOGARAS, V. G.: Ocherk material'nogo byta

BIBLIOGRAPHY

olennykh chukchey, SMAE I, St. Petersburg 1901. — Coxwell, G. F.: Siberian
and Other Folk-Tales, London 1925, p. 53 and p. 56. — Findeisen, H.: Aus
Ostsibirien, Drei Beiträge zur Religions- und Wirtschaftskunde der Tungusen,
Zeitschrift f. Ethnologie, Year 1953/1954. — Finnie, R.: Canada Moves North,
New York, 1942, p. 78. — Hančar, F.: Kulturelement Pferd, Saeculum, Vol. 7,
1956, pp. 442–453. — Jochelson, W.: The Yukaghir and the Yukaghirized Tungus,
The Jesup North Pacific Expedition, Vol. 9, Leiden-New York, 1926, pp. 361–
369. — Kolarz, W.: The Peoples of the Soviet Far East, London 1954, p. 72. —
Levin, M. G.: Antropologicheskiye issledovaniya na Amure i Sachaline, IEKS,
Vol. 5, 1949. — Minns, E. H.: The Art of the Northern Nomads, Proceedings
of the British Academy, London 1942, pp. 47–99. — Thiel, E.: Sowjet-Fernost,
Munich 1953. Die Mongolei, Land, Volk und Wirtschaft der mongolischen Volks-
republik, Munich 1958. — Shirokogorov, S. M.: New Contributions to the Problem of the Origin of Chinese Culture, Anthropos, Vol. 26, 1931. — Sirelius, U. T.:
Über die Art und Zeit der Zähmung des Rentiers, Journal de la Société Finno-
Ougrienne, Helsingfors 1916. — Vasilevich, G. M.: Materialy yazyka k probleme
etnogenesa tungusov, IEKS 2, 1946. Drevneyshiye etnonimy Azii i nazvaniya
evenkiskikh rodov, Sovetskaya Etnografiya, 1946. Evenkiskaya ekspeditsiya,
IEKS, 1949. Tungusskiy nagrudnik u narodov Sibiri, Sbornik muzeya antr. i
etnogr. Vol. 11, Moscow-Leningrad 1949. K voprosu o paleoaziatakh Sibiri,
IEKS 8, 1949. — Yakutski, N.: Der goldene Bach, Berlin 1951, pp. 295–296.

16. The Tungus' Original Home

Anisimov, A. F.: Predstavleniya evenkov o dushe i problema proiskhozhdeniya
animisma, Truly instituta etnografii, New Series, Vol. 14, Moscow 1951, pp. 109–
118. — Benzing, J.: Die tungusischen Sprachen, Akademie der Wissenschaften
und der Literatur, No. 2, Wiesbaden 1955. — Debek, G. F.: Antropologicheskiye
issledovaniya v kamtchatskoy oblasti, Trudy instituta etnografii, New Series,
Vol. 17, Moscow 1951. — Findeisen, H.: Aus Ostsibirien, Augsburg 1955. — Flor,
F.: Zur Frage des Rentiernomadismus, Mitteilungen der Anthropologischen
Gesellschaft in Wien, Vol. 60, Vienna 1930. — Graham, D. C.: Songs and stories
of the Ch'uan Miao, Washington 1954. — Harva, U.: Die religiösen Vorstel-
lungen der altaischen Völker, Helsinki 1938. — Hiekisch, C.: Die Tungusen, St.
Petersburg 1879. — Holmberg, U.: The Mythology of all Races, Vol. 4, p. 300. —
Jettmar, K.: Zur Herkunft der türkischen Völkerschaften, Archiv für Völker-
kunde 3, 1948, p. 9. Zum Problem der tungusischen "Urheimat," Kultur und
Sprache, Wiener Beiträge zur Kulturgeschichte und Linguistik, 1952, pp. 484–
511. — Koppers, W.: Tungusen und Miao, Mitteilungen der Anthropologischen
Gesellschaft, Vol. 60, Vienna 1930, p. 306. — Levin, M.G.: Antropologicheskiye
tipy Sibiri i Dal'nego Vostoka, Sovetskaya Etnografiya, Vol. 2, 1950. — v. Midden-
dorff, A.: Reise in den äussersten Norden und Osten Sibiriens während der
Jahre 1843 und 1844, St. Petersburg, 1875. — Mironov, N. D. and Shirokogorov,
S. M.: Sramana-Shaman Etymology of the Word "Shaman," The Journal of the
North China Branch of the Royal Asiatic Society, Vol. 55, 1924. — Okladnikov,
A. P.: Neoliticheskiye pamyatniki kak istochnik po etnogonii Sibiri i Dal'nego
Vostoka, KSIIMK 9, 1941. Istoriya Yakutii, Vol. 1, Jakutsk 1949. K izucheniyu

BIBLIOGRAPHY

nachal'nykh etapov formirovaniya narodov Sibiri, Sovetskaya Etnografiya, Vol. 2, 1950. – SAVINA: Histoire des Miao, Hongkong 1924. – SHIROKOGOROV, S. M.: Who are the Northern Chinese? Journal of the North-China Branch of the Royal Asiatic Society, Vol. 55, 1924, pp. 1–13. – v. SCHRENCK, L.: Reisen und Forschungen im Amur-Lande, Vol. 3, 1881, p. 11.

18. An Offering of Bears' Skulls

ALBERT, F.: Die Waldmenschen Udehe, Forschungsreisen im Amur–und Ussuri-gebeit, Darmstadt 1956. – ATKINSON, T. W.: Travels in the Regions of the Upper and Lower Amoor, New York 1860. – BÄCHLER, H.: Die Altersgliederung der Höhlenbärenreste im Wildkirchli, Wildenmannlisloch und Drachenloch, Quar-tär, Vol. A, 1957, pp. 131–146. – BILBY, J. W.: Among unknown Eskimos, London 1923. – BIRKET-SMITH, K.: Über die Herkunft der Eskimos und ihre Stellung in der zirkumpolaren Kulturentwicklung, Anthropos 25, 1930. – BRODAR, S.: Zur Frage der Höhlenbärenjagd und des Höhlenbärenkults in den paläolithischen Fundstellen Jugoslawiens, Quartär, Vol. 9, 1957, pp. 147–159. – BYHAN, A.: Die Polarvölker, Leipzig 1909. – CZAPLICKA, M. A.: Hastings' Encyclopaedia of Religion and Ethics, Vol. 12. Aboriginal Siberia, A Study in Social Anthropology, Oxford 1914. – DE DOBBELER: Eine Reise nach dem Tas-Busen, Globus, Vol. 49, 1886. Die Samojeden, Globus, Vol. 49, 1886. – DONNER, K.: Bei den Samojeden in Sibirien, Stuttgart 1926. – GAHS, A.: Kopf-, Schädel und Langknochenopfer bei Rentiervölkern, Vienna 1928, pp. 231–268. – GJESS-ING, G.: Circumpolar Stone Age, Copenhagen 1944. – HALLOWELL, A. J.: Bear Ceremonialism in the Northern Hemisphere, American Anthropologist, Vol. 28, 1926, pp. 1–175. – HARVA, U.: Die religiösen Vorstellungen der altaischen Völker, Helsinki 1938. – HATT, G.: Moccasins and Their Relation to Arctic Footwear, Mem. American Anthropologist, Vol. 3, 1916. – HAWKES, E. W.: The Dance Festivals of the Alaskan Eskimos, Philadelphia 1914. – HOESSLY, H.: Krano-logische Studien an einer Schädelserie aus Ostgrönland, Ergebnisse der Schwei-zerischen Grönlandexpedition 1912–13, Zürich 1916. – HOLMBERG, U.: Über die Jagdriten der nördlichen Völker Asiens und Europas, Société Finno-Ougrienne, Helsinki 1925. – JENNESS, D.: Report of the Canadian Arctic Expedition 1913–18, Vol. 12. The Life of the Copper Eskimos, Ottawa 1922, p. 189. – JOCHELSON, W.: The Korjak, The Jesup North Pacific Expedition, Memoir of the American Museum of Natural History, Vol. 6, Leyden-New York, 1908. The Yukaghir and the Yukaghirized Tungus, The Jesup North Pacific Expedition, Memoir of the American Museum of Natural History, Vol. 9, Leyden-New York, 1926. – LEHTISALO, T.: Entwurf einer Mythologie der Jurak-Samojeden, Société Finno-Ougrienne, Helsinki 1924. – LINDNER, K.: Die Jagd der Vorzeit, Berlin and Leipzig 1937. – LOT-FALCK, E.: Les Rites de Chasse chez les Peuples Sibériens, L'Espèce Humaine, Vol. 9, Bagneux 1953. – MADERNER, J.: Das Gemeinschafts-leben der Eskimo, Report of the Anthropological Society, Vienna 1939, pp. 273–348. – MALAURIE, J.: Les Derniers Rois de Thule, Paris 1955. – MATHESON, C.: Man and Bear in Europe, Antiquity, Vol. 16, 1942, pp. 151–159. – NORDENSKJÖLD, A. E.: The Voyage of the "Vega" Around Asia, 1881. Die Nordpolarreisen Adolf Erik Nordenskjölds 1858–1879, Leipzig 1880, p. 338 et seq. – PALLAS, P. S.:

BIBLIOGRAPHY

Merkwürdigkeiten der obischen Ostjaken, Samojeden, daurischen Tungusen, udinskischen Bergtataren usw., Frankfurt-Leipzig 1777. Reise durch verschiedene Provinzen des russischen Reiches, St. Petersburg 1776. – PAULSON, I.: Die Tierknochen im Jagdritual der nordeurasischen Völker, Zeitschrift für Ethnologie, Vol. 84, Part 2, Brunswick 1959, pp. 270–293. – RASMUSSEN, K.: Thulefahrt, Frankfurt 1921. Eskimo Folk-Tales, ed. by W. Worster, Copenhagen-Christiania, 1921. Report of the 5th Thule Expedition 1921–24, Vol. 9, Intellectual Culture of the Copper Eskimos, Copenhagen 1932, p. 120 and p. 124. Report of the 5th Thule Expedition, Vol. 7, No. 1, Intellectual Culture of the Iglulik Eskimo, Copenhagen 1929. – RUBTSOVA, E. S.: Materialy po yazyku i folkloru eskimosov, Moscow-Leningrad, 1954, Part 1. – SCHMIDT, P. W.: Der Ursprung der Gottesidee, Münster i. W., Vol. 3, 1931, p. 563 and Vol. 6, 1935. – STEFANSSON, V.: Das Geheimnis der Eskimos, Leipzig 1925, p. 240. – THALBITZER, W.: Knud Rasmussen in Memoriam, American Anthropologist, Vol. 36, 1934, pp. 585–594. Die kultischen Gottheiten der Eskimos, Archiv für Religionswissenschaft 26, 1928, pp. 364–430. – VASILEVICH, G. M.: Evenki in: Narody Sibiri, Moskow-Leningrad 1956. – ZÉLÉNINE, D.: Le culte des idoles en Sibérie, Paris 1952. – ZHITKOV: Poluostrov Yamal, Zapiski I. R., Geograf. Obshchestva po obshchey geografii, Vol. 49, St. Petersburg 1913.

19. God and Worship Seventy Thousand Years Ago

ABEL, O. and KYRLE, G.: Die Drachenhöhle bei Mixnitz, Speläologische Monographien, Vols. 7–9, Vienna 1931. – BÄCHLER, H.: Die Altersgliederung der Höhlenbärenreste im Wildkirchli, Wildenmannlisloch und Drachenloch, Quartär, Vol. 9, Bonn 1957, pp. 131–146. Wildkirchli, Drachenloch und Wildenmannlisloch in: Urgeschichte der Schweiz, Vol. 1, Frauenfeld 1949. – Bächler, E.: Das Drachenloch, St. Gallen 1921. Die prähistorische Kulturstätte in der Wildkirchli-Ebenalp-Höhle, St. Gallen 1906. Das Wildkirchli, die älteste prähistorische Kulturstation der Schweiz, Schriften des Vereins für Geschichte des Bodensees, Frauenfeld 1912. Das Wildkirchli, St. Gallen 1936. Das alpine Paläolithikum der Schweiz im Wildkirchli, Drachenloch und Wildenmannlisloch, Monographien zur Ur- und Frühgeschichte der Schweiz, Vol. 2, Basle 1940. – BACHOFEN, VON ECHT, A.: Der Bär, Monographien der Wildsäugetiere, Vol. 7, Leipzig 1939. – BEHN, F.: Vorgeschichte Europas, Berlin 1949. – BRODAR, S.: Zur Frage der Höhlenbärenjagd und des Höhlenbärenkults in den paläolithischen Fundstellen Jugoslawiens, Quartär, Vol. 9, 1957, pp. 147–159. – CHILDE, G.: What Happened in History, Edinburgh 1941. – EHRENBERG, K.: Die ontogenetische Entwicklung des Höhlenbären in: Abel und Kyrle: Die Drachenhöhle bei Mixnitz, Vienna 1931. 30 Jahre paläobiologischer Forschung in österreichischen Höhlen, Quartär, Vol. 5, 1951, pp. 93–108. Über Höhlenbären und Bärenhöhlen, Verhandlg. Zoolog.-Botanischer Gesellschaften in Wien, Vol. 95, 1955. – HÖRMANN, K.: Die Petershöhle bei Velden in Mittelfranken, Abhandlungen der Naturhistorischen Gesellschaft zu Nürnberg, Vol. 21, 1923, pp. 123–153. – KOBY, F. E.: Les soi-disant instruments osseux du paléolithique alpin et le charriage à sec des os d'ours des cavernes, Verhandlg. Naturf. Ges., Vol. 54, Basle 1943. Les paléolithiques ont-ils chassé l'ours des cavernes? Actes de la

BIBLIOGRAPHY

Société Jurassienne d'Emulation, 1953, Porrentruy 1954. – LANCZKOWSKI, G.: Forschungen zum Gottesglauben in der Religionsgeschichte, Saeculum, Vol. 8, 1957, pp. 392–403. – LARTET, E. and CHRISTY, H.: Comptes rendus de l'Académie des Sciences, 1865. – MARTIN, H.: Recherches sur l'Évolution du Moustérien dans le Gisement de La Quina, Vol. 2, Paris 1910. – NARR, K. J.: Die Steinwerkzeuge aus der Zeit des Neandertalers, Der Neandertaler und seine Umwelt, Bonn 1956. – NARR, K. J. and VON USLAR, R. J. C.: Fuhlrott und der Neandertaler, Der Neandertaler und seine Umwelt, Bonn 1956. – SCHLOSSER, M.: Die Bären-oder Tischoferhöhle im Kaisertal bei Kufstein, Munich 1909. – SCHMIDT, P. W.: Die Urkulturen: Ältere Jagd- und Sammelstufe, Historia Mundi, Vol. 1, Munich 1952, pp. 484–487. Der Ursprung der Gottesidee, Vol. 3, 1931, pp. 534–537. – SOERGEL, W.: Die Massenvorkommen des Höhlenbären, ihre biologische und stratigraphische Deutung, Jena 1940. – VAYSON DE PRAEDENNE, A.: La station paléolithique du Mont-Dol, L'Anthropologie, Vol. 39, Paris 1929, pp. 1–42. – VUKOVICH, S.: Petshina vindiya kao prethistorijtska stanitsa, Speleolog, Vol. I, Zagreb 1953, p. 18. – ZOTZ, L.: Die altsteinzeitliche Besiedlung der Alpen und deren geistige und wirtschaftliche Hintergründe, Sitzungsberichte der Physikalisch-Medizinischen Sozietät zu Erlangen, Vol. 78 (1955–57) 1958.

20. Cro-Magnon Man

ARAMBOURG, C., BOULE, M., VALLOIS, H., and VERNEAU, R.: Grottes paléolithiques de Beni Segoual, Arch. Inst. Paléont. Hum., Vol. 8, 1934. – BATAILLE, G.: Die vorgeschichtliche Malerei Lascaux, Geneva 1955, p. 18. – BEATTIE, J.: The Stone Age of Mount Carmel, Vol. 2, Oxford 1939. – BOULE, M.: Les Hommes Fossiles, Paris 1946. – BOULE, M. and VALLOIS, H.: L'homme fossile d'Asselar, Arch. Inst. Paléont. Hum., Mém 9, Paris 1932. – BULLETIN SOCIÉTÉ PRÉHISTORIQUE, Vol. 49, 50, p. 643. – COON, C. ST.: The Races of Europe, New York, 1939. – V. EICKSTEDT, E.: Rassenkunde und Rassengeschichte der Menschheit, Stuttgart, 1934. – GIESELER, W.: Die Fossilgeschichte des Menschen, Die Evolution der Organismen, Stuttgart 1957, p. 998. – HAUSER, O.: Der Mensch vor 100,000 Jahren, Leipzig, 1917. – McGOWN, T. D. and KEITH, A. The Stone Age of Mount Carmel, Vol. 2, Oxford 1939. – MOCHI, A.: La succession des industries paléolithiques et les changements de la fauna du Pléistocène en Italie, Florence 1912. – OBERMAIER, H.: Der Mensch der Vorzeit, Berlin 1912. Urgeschichte der Menschheit, Geschichte der führenden Völker, Vol. 1, Freiburg i. Br. 1931. – PEQUART, M., BOULE, M., and VALLOIS, H.: Teviec, station nécropole mésolithique du Morbihan, Arch. Inst. Paléont. Hum. Mém. 8, 1937. – RIETH, G. A.: Der Wildpferdfelsen bei Le Solutré, Antares, Vol. 1, Oct. 1952, pp. 97–99. – RUST, A.: Die Jüngere Altsteinzeit, Historia Mundi, Vol. 1, Munich 1952, p. 308. Die Höhlenfunde von Jabrud, Neumünster 1950. – DE SAINT-PÉRIER, R.: Les baguettes sculptées, dans l'art paléolithique, L'Anthropologie, Vol. 39, 1929, pp. 43–64. – SCHRADER, O.: Reallexikon der indogermanischen Altertumskunde, 2 Vols., 1911. – TSCHUMI, O.: Urgeschichte der Schweiz, Vol. 1, Frauenfeld 1949. – VALLOIS, H.: Recherches sur les ossements mésolithiques de Mugem., L'Anthropologie, Vol. 40, 1930. Nouvelles recherches sur le squelette de Chancelade, L'Anthropologie, Vol. 49, 1941–46. – VERNEAU, R. Les Grottes de Grimaldi, 3 Vols., Monaco 1906. –

BIBLIOGRAPHY

Weidenreich, F.: Apes, Giants, and Man, Chicago 1946. – Weinert, H.: Menschen der Vorzeit, Stuttgart 1947.

21. Handprints, Statuettes, Wands and Religious Art

Absolon, K.: Une nouvelle et importante station aurignacienne en Moravie, Revue Anthropologique, Paris 1927. Représentations idéo-plastiques anciennes et nouvelles de femmes du Paléolithique moravien, Congrès International d'Anthropologie et d'Archéologie Préhistorique, 15ᵉ Session, Paris 1931. Ergebnisse der neuesten paläolithischen Forschungen in Mähren, Mainzer Zeitschrift, Vol. 26, 1931. – Bandi, H. G.: Die Schweiz zur Rentierzeit, Frauenfeld 1947. – Bataille, G.: Lascaux, Geneva 1955. – Bégouën, H.: À propos de l'idée de Fécondité dans l'iconographie préhistorique, Bulletin de la Société Préhistorique Française, Vol. 26, 1929. – Dewdney, S.: The Quetico Pictographs, The Beaver, Winnipeg, Summer 1958, pp. 15–22. – Findeisen, H.: Karelische Hirtenzauberer und ihre Praktiken, Zeitschrift für Ethnologie, Vol. 78, 1953, pp. 103–110. – Furon, R.: Manuel de préhistoire Générale, Paris 1951. – Gaerte: Auf den Spuren des ostpreussischen Mammut- und Rentierjägers, Mannus, Vol. 18, 1926, pp. 253–257. – Gerasimov, M. M.: Raskopki paleoliticheskoy stoyanki v sele Malte, IGAIMK, Vol. 118, Leningrad, 1935. – Hančar, F.: Probleme und Ergebnisse der neuen russischen Urgeschichtsforschung, 33. Bericht der Römisch-Germanischen Kommission, 1943–1950, Berlin 1951, pp. 25–60. – Hoernes, M.: Urgeschichte der bildenden Kunst in Europa, Vienna 1925. – Kühn, H.: Menschendarstellungen im Paläolithikum, Zeitschrift für Rassenkunde, Vol. 4, Stuttgart, 1936. – Lemozi, A.: Fouilles dans l'abri sous la roche de Murat, commune de Rocamadour, Bulletin de la Société Préhistorique Française, 1924. La Grotte-temple du Pech-Merle, Un nouveau sanctuaire préhistorique, Paris 1929. – Lindner, K.: Die Jagd der Vorzeit, Berlin-Leipzig 1937. – Lips, J.: Fallensysteme der Naturvölker, Ethnologica, Vol. 3, Leipzig 1927. Paläolithische Fallenzeichnungen und das ethnologische Vergleichsmaterial, Tagungsberichte der Deutschen Anthropol. Ges., Leipzig 1928. Trap Systems among the Montagnais-Naskapi Indians of Labrador Peninsula, Stockholm 1936. – Louis, M.: Le Mont-Bego, haut lieu de l'âge du Bronze, Bulletin Société Préhistorique, Vol. 49, 1952, pp. 309–312. – Luquet, G. H.: Les Vénus paléolithiques, Journal de Psychologie, Paris 1934, pp. 429–460. – Meyer, E.: Geschichte des Altertums,Vol. 1, Sec. 1, 7th Edition, Stuttgart 1954, p. 245. – Petri, H.: Tanz und Schauspiel bei den Eingeborenen Nordwest-Australiens, Kosmos, 46th Year, Stuttgart 1950, p. 49. – Petri, H. and Schulz, A. S.: Felsgravierungen aus Nord-west-Australien, Zeitschrift für Ethnologie, 74th Year, 1942, Berlin 1944. – Peyrony, D.: L'industrie et l'art de la couche des pointes en os à base à biseau simple de Laugerie-Haute, L'Anthropologie, Vol. 39, 1930, pp. 361–371. – Pfizenmayer, E. W.: Mammutleichen und Urwaldmenschen in Nordost-Sibirien, Leipzig 1926. – Piette, E.: La station de Brassempouy et les statuettes humaines de la période glyptique, Anthropologie, Paris 1895. L'Art Pendant l'Âge du Renne, Paris 1907. – Riddell, W. H.: Cave-Paintings, Lascaux, Antiquity, Vol. 16, pp. 359–360. Palaeolithic Paintings-Magdalenian Period, Antiquity, Vol. 16, 1942, pp. 134–150. – Rust, A.: Die Jüngere Altsteinzeit Jungpaläolithikum, His-

BIBLIOGRAPHY

toria Mundi, Munich 1952. — SACCASYN-DELLA SANTA, E.: Les Figures Humaines du Paléolithique Supérieur Eurasiatique, Antwerp 1947. — DE SAINT-PÉRIER, R.: Les baguettes sculptées dans l'art paléolithique, L'Anthropologie,Vol. 39, 1929, pp. 44–64. — VERBRUGGE, R. P.: La main dans l'art préhistorique, L'Ethnographie, Vol. 51, Paris 1957, p. 13. — VERWORN, M.: Zur Psychologie der primitiven Kunst, Naturwissenschaftliche Wochenschrift, No. 46, Jena 1907. — ZAMYATNIN, S. N.: Raskopki u s. Tagarina, IGAIMK, Vol. 118, Moscow-Leningrad, 1935.

23. The Bear Festival

ADAM, L.: North-West American Indian Art and Its Early Chinese Parallels, Man, Vol. 36, 1936. — ANISIMOV, A. F.: Kult medvedya u evenkov i problema evolyutsii totemisticheskikh verovanii, Sb. Inst. istorii AN SSSR, Vopr. istorii i ateisma, Moscow 1950. — ATKINSON, T. W.: Travels in the Regions of the Upper and Lower Amoor, New York 1860. — BATCHELOR, J.: The Aino and Their Folklore, 1901. Ainu Life and Lore, 1927. — BIRD, I. L.: Unbeaten Tracks in Japan, 1880. — BOGORAS, W.: Ideas of Space and Time in the Conception of Primitive Religion, American Anthropologist, Vol. 27, 1925. — BUSCHAN, G.: Illustrierte Völkerkunde, Vol. 1, Stuttgart 1922, p. 60. — CESARESCO, E. M.: The Place of Animals in Human Thought, London 1909. — CHAMBERLAIN, B. H.: Aino Folk-Tales, 1888. — COLLINS, P. McD.: A Voyage Down the Amoor, New York 1860. — CZAPLICKA, M. A.: Aboriginal Siberia, Oxford 1914. — ERMAN, A.: Travels in Siberia, Vol. 2, London 1848. — FRAZER, J. G.: The Golden Bough, London 1912. — GJESSING, GJERTRUD and GUTORM: Lappedrakten, Instituttet for Sammenlignende Kulturforskning, Oslo 1940. — GONDATTI, N.: The Bear-Cult among the Aborigines of North-Western Siberia, Bull. of the Imperial Society of Friends of Natural Science, Anthropology and Ethnology, Moscow, 1888. — HALLOWELL, A. I.: Bear Ceremonialism in the Northern Hemisphere, American Anthropologist, New Series, Vol. 28, 1926, pp. 1–175. — HEINE-GELDERN, R.: Some Problems of Migration in the Pacific, Kultur und Sprache, Year 9, Vienna 1952. — HITCHCOCK, R.: The Ainos of Yezo, Reports, U. S. National Museum, Washington 1890. The Ainos of Japan, 1892. — INUKAI TETSUO: Ainu no kuma no atama no shochi ni tsuite, Tokyo-jinruigakkwai, Nippon-minzokugakkwai-rengo-daikwai dai-ni-kai-kiji, 1937. — KHARUZIN, N.: Ethnography, 1905, Vol. 4. — KINDAICHI, KYOKUKE: Kuma-matsuri no hanashi, Minzo-kugaku, Vol. 1, 1924. Aino, in Daihyakkwa-jiten, Vol. 7, 1935. Nihon-chiri-daikei, Vol. 10, 1930. — KROHN, K.: Bärenlieder der Finnen, Publication d'hommage offerte au P. W. Schmidt, Vienna 1928. Suomalaisten runojen uskonto, Helsinki 1915. — MAAK, R.: Reise an den Amur, St. Petersburg 1859, pp. 209–210. — MONTADON, G.: La Civilisation Ainoue, 1937. — MÜHLMANN, W.: Über den Anschluss der Polynesier an die Südasiatischen Hochkulturen, Baessler-Archiv, Vol. 18, Berlin 1935. — PILSUDSKI, B.: Niedzwiedzie Swieto u Ainów, Sphinx, Warsaw 1905. Das Bärenfest der Ainen auf Sachalin, Globus, Vol. 96, 1909. — PODACH, E. F.: Der angebliche Bart der Ainu-Frauen, Zeitschrift für Ethnologie, Vol. 75, 1950, p. 79. — v. SCHRENCK, L.: Reisen und Forschungen im Amurlande, Die Völker des Amurlandes, Vol. 3, St. Petersburg 1881. — SEELAND, N.: Die Ghiliaken, Russian Review, Year 11, St. Petersburg 1882, pp. 97–130 and 222–254. — SLAWIK,

BIBLIOGRAPHY

A.: Zum Problem des Bärenfestes bei den Ainu und Giljaken, Kultur und Sprache, Year 9, Vienna 1952. — STERNBERG, L.: Die Religion der Giljaken, Archiv für Religionswissenschaft, Leipzig 1905, pp. 244–274 and 1906, pp. 456–473. Kult orla u sibirskikh narodov, Leningrad 1925. The Ainu Problem, Anthropos, Vol. 24, 1929. — SUFFERN, C.: Review of "La Civilisation Ainou" by George Montadon, Man, Vol. 37, 1937, pp. 147–149. — TEICH, G. and RÜBEL, H.: Völker, Volksgruppen und Volksstämme auf dem ehemaligen Gebiet der UdSSR, Leipzig 1942. — VASILEV, B. A.: Medvezhiy prazdnik, Sovetskaya Ethnografiya, Vol. 4, 1948. — YONEMURA, YOSHIO: Kitami-Ainu, Abashiri 1937. — ZOLOTAREV, A. M.: The Bear Festival of the Olcha, American Anthropologist, Vol. 39, 1937, pp. 113 et seq.

24. Sorcery, Magic and Religious Cults

ABEL, O. and KOPPERS, W.: Eiszeitliche Bärendarstellungen und Bärenkulte in paläobiologischer und prähistorisch-ethnologischer Beleuchtung, Palaeobiologica, Vol. 5, 1933, pp. 7–64. — BATCHELOR, J.: The Ainu and Their Folk-Lore, London 1901. — BÉGOUËN, H.: La magie aux temps préhistoriques, Extr. des Mémoires de l'Académie des Sciences, Inscriptions et Belles-Lettres de Toulouse, Vol. 2, 12th Series, 1924. — BÉGOUËN, H. and BREUIL, H.: Les Ours déguisés de la caverne des Trois Frères (Ariège), Festschrift für P. W. Schmidt, Vienna 1928. — FROBENIUS, L.: Kulturgeschichte Afrikas, Frankfurt a. M. 1933. Erlebte Erdteile, Vol. 7, Frankfurt 1929, p. 31. Das unbekannte Afrika, Munich 1923, pp. 34–36. — HARVA, U.: Die religiösen Vorstellungen der altaischen Völker, Helsinki 1938, pp. 389–395. — JENSEN, A. E.: Mythos und Kult bei Naturvölkern, Studien zur Kulturkunde, Vol. 10, Wiesbaden 1951, pp. 143–155. — LANG, A.: The Making of Religion, London 1898. — NARR, K. J.: Interpretation altsteinzeitlicher Kunstwerke durch völkerkundliche Parallelen, Anthropos, Vol. 50, 1955, pp. 513–545. — OBERMAIER, H. and KÜHN, H.: Buschmannkunst, Felsmalereien aus Südwestafrika, Leipzig 1930. — SCHMIDT, P. W.: Der Ursprung der Gottesidee, Vol. 3, Münster 1931, p. 553. — WORMS, E. A.: Contemporary and Prehistoric Rock Paintings in Central and Northern North Kimberley, Anthropos, Vol. 50, 1955, pp. 546–566.

26. The Shaman's Secret

AGAPITOV, N. and KHANGALOV, M.: Materialy dlya izucheniya Shamanstva v Sibiri, Izv. VSORGO, Irkutsk 1883. — ANISIMOV, A. F.: Shamanskiye dukhi po vosreniyam evenkov i totemicheskiye istoki ideologii shamanstva, Sb. MAE, Vol. 13, Moscow-Leningrad 1951. — ANOKHIN, A. V.: Materialy po shamanstvu u altaytsev Sb. MAE, Vol. 4, Leningrad 1924. — ANUCHIN, V. I.: Ocherk shamanstva u yeniseyskikh ostyakov, Sb. MAE, Vol. 2, 1914. — AVRORIN, V. A. and KOSMINSKIY, I. I.: Predstavleniya orochey o wselennoy, a pereselenii dush i puteshetviyakh shamanov, izobrazhennye na "karte" Sb. MAE, Vol. 11, Moscow-Leningrad 1949. — BANSAROV: Chornaya vera ili shamanstvo u Mongolov, Uchomye zapiski Kazanskogo universiteta, Vol. 3, Kazan 1846. — BRUNNER, A.: Die Religion, Freiburg, i. Br. 1956, pp. 298–319. — DAMEYEV, D.: Legenda o

BIBLIOGRAPHY

proiskhozhdenii shamanstva i padenii volshebstva, Burjatowedchestk. sb., Vol. 3, 4, Irkutsk 1927. – DELATTE, A.: Les Conceptions l'Enthousiasme chez les Philosophes Présocratiques, Paris 1934. – DODDS, E. R.: The Greeks and the Irrational, Berkeley 1951. – DONNER, K.: Bei den Samojeden in Sibirien, Stuttgart 1926. – DYRENKOVA, N. P.: Materialy po shamanstvu u teleutov, Sb. MAE, Vol. 10, Moscow-Leningrad 1949. – ELIADE, M.: Le Chamanisme et les Techniques Archaïques de l'Extase, Paris 1951. – FINDEISEN, H.: Schamanentum, 1957. – FRAZER, J. G.: The Golden Bough, New York 1923. – FRIEDRICH, A.: Knochen und Skelett in der Vorstellungswelt Nordasiens, Wiener Beiträge zur Kulturgeschichte und Linguistik, Year 5, 1943, p. 189. – FRIEDRICH, A. and BUDDRESS, G.: Schamanengeschichten aus Sibirien, Munich 1955. – GRAEBNER, F.: Das Weltbild der Primitiven, Munich 1924. – GUNDERT, W.: Japanische Religionsgeschichte, Stuttgart, 1943. – HOLMBERG, U.: Der Baum des Lebens, Annales Academiae Scientiarum Fennicae, Vol. 16, Helsinki 1922–1923. – KATANOV: Shamanskiy buben i yevo znacheniye, Yenis. eparkh. vedom., No. 6, 1889. – KSENOFONTOV, G. V.: Legendy i rasskazy o shamanakh, Moscow, 1930. – LANG, A.: Magic and Religion, London 1901. – MIRONOV, N. D. and SHIROKOGOROV, S. M.: Sramana-Shaman Etymology of the Word "Shaman," Journal of the North China Branch of the Royal Asiatic Society, Vol. 55, 1924, pp. 105-130. – NACHTIGALL, H.: Die kulturhistorische Wurzel der Schamanenskelettierung, Zeitschrift für Ethnologie, Vol. 77, 1952, pp. 188-197. Die erhöhte Bestattung in Nord- und Hochasien, Anthropos, 1953. – NILSSON, M. P.: Geschichte der griechischen Religion, Handbuch der Altertumswissenschaft, Sec. 5, Part 2, Vol. 1, pp. 204, 205. – NIORADZE, G.: Der Schamanismus bei den sibirischen Völkern, Stuttgart 1925. – PFISTER, F.: "Ekstase," Reallexikon für Antike und Christentum, Stuttgart 1959, pp. 943-987. – POTAPOV, L. P.: Obryad ozhivleniya shamanskogo bubna u tyurko-yasychnykh plemen Altaya, Tr. Inst. etnograf, New Series, Vol. 1, Moscow-Leningrad 1947. – RÄNK, G.: Die heilige Hinterecke im Hauskult der Völker Nordosteuropas und Nordasiens, Helsinki 1949. – SHIROKOGOROV, S. M.: Versuch einer Erforschung der Grundlagen des Schamanentums bei den Tungusen, Baessler-Archiv, Vol. 18, 1935, pp. 41-96. – TOKAREV, S. A.: Sushchnost i proiskhozhdeniye magii, Trudy instituta etnografii, Vol. 51, Moscow 1959. – WEDEMEYER, A.: Das Verbergen der Sonnengottheit in der Felsenhöhle, Tokyo, 1935, p. 76. – WILBOIS, J.: Religion et Magie, Histoire des Religions, 1, 1953, pp. 30-34. – WOOLLEY, C. L.: Excavations at Ur of the Chaldees, 1923-1930, 7 Vols., 1923-1930.

27. Shamanism Twenty Thousand Years Ago

BÉGOUËN, H. and BREUIL, H.: Nouvelle gravure d'Homme masqué de la caverne des Trois-Frères associées à des animaux composites, C. R. Ac. Inscr., 1930. De quelques figures hybrides, mi-humaines, mi-animales de la caverne des Trois-Frères, Rev. Anthrop., 1934. – EPPEL, F.: Die Trois-Frères-Höhle und das Problem paläolithischer Kunst, Mitteilungen der Osterreichischen Gesellschaft für Anthropologie, Ethnologie und Prähistorie, Vols. 78-79, 1949, pp. 117-139. – FRIEDRICH, A.: Knochen und Skelett in der Vorstellungswelt Nordasiens, Wiener Beiträge zur Kulturgeschichte und Linguistik, Year 5, 1943, pp. 189-247. – GIROD,

BIBLIOGRAPHY

P. and MASSÉNAT, E.: Les Stations de l'Age du Renne, 1900. – GRAEBNER, F.: Das Weltbild der Primitiven, Munich 1924, pp. 95–104. – HARVA, U.: Die religiösen Vorstellungen der altaischen Völker, Helsinki 1938, pp. 449–561. – IVANOV, S. V.: Materialy po izobrazitel'nomu iskusstvu narodov Sibiri, 19. bis Anfang 20. Jahrhundert, Trudy instituta etnografii, New Series, Vol. 22, Moscow-Leningrad 1954, pp. 182, 183, 319, 376, 385, 739. – KARJALAINEN, K. F.: Jugralaisten uskonto, Por. – KIRCHNER, H.: Ein archäologischer Beitrag zur Urgeschichte des Schamanismus, Anthropos, Vol. 47, 1952, pp. 244–286. – LEHTISALO, T.: Entwurf einer Mythologie der Jurak-Samojeden, Helsinki 1924. – LOPATIN, I. A.: Goldy Amurskiye, Ussuriskiye i Sungariskiye, Vladivostok 1922. – MANKER, E.: Die lappische Zaubertrommel, 1938. – MARINGER, J.: De Godsdienst der Praehistorie, 1952. – NARR, K. J.: Interpretation altsteinzeitlicher Kunstwerke durch völkerkundliche Parallelen, Anthropos, Vol. 50, 1955, pp. 513–545. – PETERS, E.: Die altsteinzeitliche Kulturstätte Petersfels, 1930. – RÄNK, G.: Die heilige Hinterscke, Helsinki 1949, pp. 107, 113–114. – SEROSHEVSKIY, V. L.: Yakuty, St. Petersburg 1896. – WINDELS, F.: The Lascaux Cave Paintings, London 1949, p. 49 et seq.

28 and 29.

Alfred Rust's Great Discovery
Reindeer Sacrifice in 16,000 B.C.

CLOSS, A.: Das Versenkungsopfer, Wiener Beiträge zur Kulturgeschichte und Linguistik, Vol. 9, Vienna 1952, pp. 66–107. – GROSS, H.: Die geologische Gliederung und Chronologie des Jungpleistozäns in Mitteleuropa und den Angrenzenden Gebieten, Quartär, Vol. 9, Bonn 1957, p. 28. – LAUFER: The Reindeer and Its Domestication, Mem. Amer. Anthrop. Ass., Lancaster 1917. Reindeer Once More, American Anthropologist, Vol. 22, 1920. – LEHTISALO, T.: Beiträge zur Kenntnis der Rentierzucht bei den Juraksamojeden, Oslo 1932. – POHLHAUSEN, H.: Nachweisbare Ansätze zum Wanderhirtentum in der niederdeutschen Mittelsteinzeit, Zeitschrift für Ethnologie, Vol. 78, 1953, pp. 64–82. Das Wanderhirtentum und seine Vorstufen, Brunswick 1954. – RUST, A.: Die Höhlenfunde von Jabrud, Neumünster 1950. Die alt- und mittelsteinzeitlichen Funde von Stellmoor, Neumünster 1943. Das altsteinzeitliche Renntierjägerlager Meiendorf, Neumünster 1937. Die Funde vom Pinnberg, Neumünster 1958. Die jung-paläolithischen Zeltanlagen von Ahrensburg, Neumünster, 1958. – SCHMIDT, W.: Zu den Anfängen der Tierzucht, Zeitschrift für Ethnologie, Vol. 76, 1951, pp. 201–204. Zu den Anfängen der Herdentierzucht, Zeitschrift für Ethnologie, Vol. 76, 1951, pp. 1–41. – SCHWANTES, G.: Nordisches Paläolithikum und Mesolithikum, Festschrift des Museums für Völkerkunde, Hamburg 1928. Die Bedeutung der ältesten Siedlungsfunde Schleswig-Holsteins für die Weltgeschichte der Steinzeit, Festgabe für Anton Schifferer, Breslau 1931. Eine neue jungpaläolithische Zivilisation in Holstein, Nachrichtenblatt f. Deutsche Vorzeit, Year 8, No. 2, 1932. – SKALON and KHOROSHIKH: Ob olennykh pisanitsakh Severnoy Azii, 1951. – SOLOTAREV and LEVIN: K voprosu o drevnosti i proiskhozhdenii olenevodstva, Problemy proiskhozhdeniya, evolyutsii i porodoobrazovaniya

domashnikh zhivotnykh, Vol. 1, Moscow-Leningrad 1940. — VASILEVICH and
LEVIN: Tipy olenevodstva i yikh proiskhozhdeniye, Sovetskaya Etnografiya,
Vol. 1, 1951.

30 and 31.

Man: The Unsolved Mystery
The Second Beam of the Cross

ABBIE, A. A.: A New Approach to the Problem of Human Evolution, Trans-
actions of the Royal Society of South Australia, Vol. 75, Adelaide 1952, p. 79. —
BREITINGER, EMIL: Das Schädelfragment von Swanscombe und das "Praesapiens-
problem," Mitteilungen Anthrop. Ges. Wien, Vols. 84–85, 1955, p. 1 et seq.
Zur Phyletischen Evolution von Homo Sapiens, Anthropologischer Anzeiger,
Year 21, Stuttgart, 1957, pp. 62–83. — BRIGHT, J.: The Interpreter's Bible, New
York 1953, Vol. II, p. 579. — CONOLLY, C. J.: Brain Morphology and Taxonomy,
in Anthrop. Quarterly 26, 1953. External Morphology of the Primate Brain,
Springfield 1950. — DENNERT, E.: Die Natur—das Wunder im Lichte der modernen
Forschung, 5th Edition, Bonn 1950. — DOBZHANSKY, T.: Evolution, Genetics,
and Man, New York 1955, p. 332. — ENGELS, H.: Die grössten Geister über die
höchsten Fragen, Constance. — FALKENBURGER, F.: Kritische Bemerkungen zur
Entwicklung des Sapienstypus, Actes du IVème Congrès International des
Sciences Anthropologiques et Ethnologiques, Vol. 1, Vienna 1954, pp. 105, 106.
— HAAS, A.: Naturphilosophische Erwägungen zum Menschenbild des Schöp-
fungsberichtes und der modernen Abstammungstheorie, Scholastik, Year 23,
1958, p. 369. — HOOTON, E. A.: Up from the Ape, London 1931. — HOWELL, F. Cl.:
Place of Neanderthal Man, Amer. J. Phys. Anthrop. 9, 1951. The Evolutionary
Significance of Variation and Varieties of Neanderthal Man, Quart. Review
Biol. 32, 1957. — JEANS, J. H.: The Growth of Physical Science. The Universe
Around Us, London. — JORDAN, P.: Zeitgeist im Spiegel der Naturwissenschaft,
Hochland, Munich, Dec. 1951, pp. 138–139, Die Physik und das Geheimnis des
organischen Lebens, Brunswick 1948, 6th Edition, pp. 155–56. — KÄLIN, J.: Die
ältesten Menschenreste und ihre stammegeschichtliche Deutung, Historia Mundi
I, Munich 1952, p. 96. — KOPPERS, W.: Der Urmensch und sein Weltbild, Vienna
1949. — KROEBER, A. L.: Anthropology Today, Chicago, Illinois, 1957. — LEAKEY,
L. S. B.: Adam's Ancestors, London 1953. The Stone Age Races of Kenya,
London and New York 1935, p. 23. — LE GROS CLARK, W. E.: The Antiquity
of Homo Sapiens in Particular and the Hominidae in General, Scientific Progress 42, 1954, No. 167. The Fossil Evidence for Human Evolution, Chicago 1955.
— MONTAGU, M. F. A.: The Chin of the Kanam Mandible, American Anthropologist, Vol. 59, 1957, pp. 355–383. — MUSCHALEK, H.: Gottbekenntnisse moderner
Naturforscher, Berlin 1954. — NEUBERG, A.: Das naturwissenschaftliche Weltbild
der Gegenwart, Göttingen 1944. — OAKLEY, K. P.: Dating Fossil Human Remains, Anthropology Today, Chicago 1957, p. 43 et seq. — OVERHAGE, P.: Das
stammesgeschichtliche Werden der Organismen und des Menschen, Basle, Freiburg, Vienna 1959, pp. 166–370. Um das Erscheinungsbild der ersten Menschen,
Basle, Freiburg, Vienna 1959. — PLANCK, M.: Kausalgesetz und Willensfreiheit
in: Wege zur physikalischen Erkenntnis, Reden und Vorträge, Leipzig 1944. —

BIBLIOGRAPHY

PORTMANN, A.: Biologie und Geist, Zürich, 1956. Das Tier als soziales Wesen, Zürich 1953. Probleme des Lebens, Basle 1955. Die Biologie und das neue Menschenbild, Berne 1942. Biologische Fragmente zu einer Lehre vom Menschen, Basle 1951. – REMANE, A.: Methodische Probleme der Hominidenphylogenie III. Die Phylogenie der Lebensweise und die Entstehung des aufrechten Ganges, Zeitschr. f. Morph. u. Anthrop. 48, 1957. Paläontologie und Evolution der Primaten, Primatologia, Vol. 1, ed. by H. Hofer, A. H. Schultz, D. Starck, Basle-New York 1956. – SALLER, K.: Aufstand des Geistes, Düsseldorf 1953. – SCHRÖDINGER, E.: Was ist das Leben? Berne 1951, 2nd Edition, p. 151. – SPENGLER, O.: Der Mensch und die Technik, Munich 1931, p. 62. – SPÜLBECK, O.: Der Christ und das Weltbild der modernen Naturwissenschaft, Berlin 1957, pp. 180, 188, 189, 225. – STEWART, T. D.: American Journal of Physical Anthropology, Vol. 6, 1948, p. 321 et seq. – VALLOIS, H. V.: Neandertals and Praesapiens, Journ. Roy. Anthrop. Inst. 84, 1954, pp. 111–130.

SOURCES OF ILLUSTRATIONS

Between pages 32 and 33

1 Skull of Peking man (Pithecanthropus pekinensis). Photo: Musée de l'Homme, Paris
2 Tools of Peking man. Photo: Musée de l'Homme, Paris
3 Skulls of Australopithecus africanus. Photo: Musée de l'Homme, Paris
4 Lower jaw of Homo heidelbergensis. Photo: Musée de l'Homme, Paris
5 Fossil skull of a Plesianthropus. Photo: Musée de l'Homme, Paris
6 Coups de poing from Saint-Acheul (Somme). Photo: Musée de l'Homme, Paris
7 Hand-fashioned coup de poing from the Abbevillian. Photo: Musée de l'Homme, Paris
8 Grooved stone used for polishing bone tools. Photo: Musée de l'Homme, Paris
9/10 Yaghan man and girl. Photo: Martin Gusinde
11/12 Selknam (Ona) man and woman. Photo: Martin Gusinde
13/14 Alacaluf man and girl. Photo: Martin Gusinde
15 Old Copper Eskimo. Photo: R. M. Anderson
16 The vast taiga. Photo: Hans von Schiller
17 Forest in the Amur Bend. Photo: Hans von Schiller

Between pages 64 and 65

18 The Lena. Photo: Hans von Schiller
19 Tunguska. Photo: Hans von Schiller
20 Swamp taiga (*totschki*). Photo: Hans von Schiller
21 Taiga marshes. Photo: Hans von Schiller
22 An Orochon. Photo: Völkerkundemuseum, Berlin
23 Old Orochon and his wife. Photo: Völkerkundemuseum, Berlin
24 Orochon children. Photo: Völkerkundemuseum, Berlin
25 Construction of an Orochon tent. Photo: Völkerkundemuseum, Berlin
26 River spanned by wickerwork weir baskets. Photo: W. Jochelson, *The Jukaghir, The Jesup North Pacific Expedition*
27 Manego. Photo: Völkerkundemuseum, Berlin
28 Orochon women smoking. Photo: Völkerkundemuseum, Berlin

Between pages 96 and 97

29 Garments of the Orochon. Photo: Völkerkundemuseum, Berlin
30 Golds of Khabarovsk and of Manchuria. Photo: Musée de l'Homme, Paris
31 Orochon girl. Photo: Völkerkundemuseum, Berlin
32/33 Koryak girls. Photo: W. Jochelson, *The Koryak, The Jesup North Pacific Expedition*
34 Koryak reindeer-drawn sledges. Photo: W. Jochelson, *The Koryak, The Jesup North Pacific Expedition*
35 Sunken hut of the Sea Koryaks. Photo: W. Jochelson, *The Koryak, The Jesup North Pacific Expedition*
36 Tent of the Reindeer Koryaks. Photo: W. Jochelson, *The Koryak, The Jesup North Pacific Expedition*

SOURCES OF ILLUSTRATIONS

37-40 Three Yukaghirs. Photo: W. Jochelson, *The Jukaghir, The Jesup North Pacific Expedition*

41 Children of the Tundra Yukaghirs. Photo: W. Jochelson, *The Jukaghir, The Jesup North Pacific Expedition*

42 Funeral of a Yukaghir girl. Photo: W. Jochelson, *The Jukaghir, The Jesup North Pacific Expedition*

43 Old Yukaghir woman. Photo: W. Jochelson, *The Jukaghir, The Jesup North Pacific Expedition*

44 Love letter of a Yukaghir girl. Photo: W. Jochelson, *The Jukaghir, The Jesup North Pacific Expedition*

45 Old Yukaghir woman. Photo: W. Jochelson, *The Jukaghir, The Jesup North Pacific Expedition*

Between pages 128 and 129

46 Drachenloch cave. Photo: from Bächler, *Das Drachenloch*

47 Ascent to the Drachenloch. Photo: from Bächler, *Das Drachenloch*

48 Limestone missile. Photo: Musée de l'Homme, Paris

49 The celebrated Neanderthal skull. Photo: Musée de l'Homme, Paris

50 Neanderthal male skull. Photo: Musée de l'Homme, Paris

51 Hip-joint sockets of cave bears. Heimatmuseum Saint Gallen. Photo: from Bächler, *Das Drachenloch*

52 Bone tools from the Drachenloch. Heimatmuseum Saint Gallen. Photo: from Bächler, *Das Drachenloch*

53 Bisected skulls of a brown and a cave bear. Heimatmuseum Saint Gallen. Photo: from Bächler, *Das Drachenloch*

54 Cave bears' claw marks. Photo: Musée de l'Homme, Paris

55 Cave bear's jaw. Heimatmuseum Saint Gallen. Photo: Rietmann-Haak

56 Fragments of iron pyrites and limestone, charcoal, charred bone, and a tapir jaw. Heimatmuseum Saint Gallen. Photo: Rietmann-Haak

57 Fragments of cave bear's marrowbone. Heimatmuseum Saint Gallen

58 Skeleton of cave bear from the Wildkirchli (Ursus spelaeus Blum). Heimatmuseum Saint Gallen

59 Dart, Broom, Breuil and van Riet Lowe. Photo: Musée de l'Homme, Paris

60 P. Wilhelm Schmidt

61 H. V. Vallois. Photo: Musée de l'Homme, Paris

62 Pierre Marcellin Boule. Photo: Musée de l'Homme, Paris

63 The so-called "marriage of death." Photo: Musée de l'Homme, Paris

Between pages 192 and 193

64 Skull of an old man (Cro-Magnon). Photo: Musée de l'Homme, Paris

65 Skull of the Chancelade people. Photo: Musée de l'Homme, Paris

66 Cro-Magnon skull with shells. Photo: Musée de l'Homme, Paris

67 The "pseudo-Venus" from the Wildenmannlisloch cave. Heimatmuseum Saint Gallen. Photo: Rietmann-Haak

68 The famous *tête à la capuce* of Brassempouy. Photo: Musée de l'Homme, Paris

69 Statuettes from Gagarino. Photo: Musée de l'Homme, Paris

70/71 Venus of Lespugue. Photo: Musée de l'Homme, Paris

334

SOURCES OF ILLUSTRATIONS

72 Stone-Age lamp. Photo: Musée de l'Homme, Paris
73 Two white owls. Magdalenian drawing. Photo: Musée de l'Homme, Paris
74 *Tol-nir* (bird-shaped tool). Gilyaks. Naturhistorische Gesellschaft Nürnberg. Photo: Rauchwetter
75 *Lankh-chonsh-charsh* (club). Gilyaks. Naturhistorische Gesselschaft Nürnberg. Photo: Rauchwetter

Between pages 224 and 225

76 Gilyak cradle. Naturhistorische Gesselschaft Nürnberg. Photo: Rauchwetter
77 Toy seals. Gilyaks. Naturhistorische Gesellschaft Nürnberg. Photo: Rauchwetter
78 Tall birch-bark box. Gilyaks. Naturhistorische Gesellschaft Nürnberg. Photo: Rauchwetter
79 Gilyak fish tureen. Naturhistorische Gesellschaft Nürnberg. Photo: Rauchwetter
80 Wooden bowl and soup spoon. Gilyaks. Naturhistorische Gesellschaft Nürnberg. Photo: Rauchwetter
81 Gilyak dipper. Naturhistorische Gesellschaft Nürnberg. Photo: Rauchwetter
82 Ainu girl.
83 The last surviving Ainus (map).
84 Slaying of a bear (Magdalenian period).
85 Roped bear being shot with arrows.
86 Headless clay figure of a bear. Photo: Musée de l'Homme, Paris
87 Bear ceremony of the Gilyaks. Photo: Musée de l'Homme, Paris
88 Gilyak bear amulet. Naturhistorische Gesellschaft Nürnberg. Photo: Rauchwetter
89 Kichikagi (spirit aid of the Gilyak shaman). Naturhistorische Gesellschaft Nürnberg. Photo: Rauchwetter
90 At-Kegn, the tiger-man. Gilyaks. Naturhistorische Gesellschaft Nürnberg. Photo: Rauchwetter

Between pages 256 and 257

91 Spirit (protector of the household). Gilyaks. Naturhistorische Gesselschaft Nürnberg. Photo: Rauchwetter
92 Nyokhul-Chsai (spirit which cures breast pains). Gilyaks. Naturhistorische Gesellschaft Nürnberg. Photo: Rauchwetter
93 Pansh-Omugu. Gilyaks. Naturhistorische Gesellschaft Nürnberg. Photo: Rauchwetter
94 Bearskin used as dancing mask. Naturhistorische Gesellschaft Nürnberg. Photo: Rauchwetter
95 Bear skull with hooks and spear blade. Gilyaks. Naturhistorische Gesellschaft Nürnberg. Photo: Rauchwetter
96 *Takhai* (root fragment). Gilyaks. Naturhistorische Gesellschaft Nürnberg. Photo: Rauchwetter
97 Gilyak carved meat ladle. Naturhistorische Gesellschaft Nürnberg. Photo: Rauchwetter
98 Gilyak fishskin smock (front). Naturhistorische Gesellschaft Nürnberg. Photo: Rauchwetter

335

SOURCES OF ILLUSTRATIONS

99 Gilyak fishskin smock (back). Naturhistorische Gesellschaft Nürnberg. Photo: Rauchwetter
100 Orochon shaman. Photo: Völkerkundemuseum, Berlin
101 Yakut shaman. Photo: W. Jochelson, *The Jukaghir, The Jesup North Pacific Expedition*
102 Tungusic shaman's drum.

Between pages 288 and 289

103 White reindeer of the Tungus. Photo: Völkerkundemuseum, Berlin
104 Orochon girl with *palma* (spear). Photo: Völkerkundemuseum, Berlin
105 Wooden coffin on tree stumps.
106 Tungusic raised coffin. Photo: W. Jochelson, *The Jesup North Pacific Expedition*
107 Raised coffin of a child. Photo: W. Jochelson, *The Jukaghir, The Jesup North Pacific Expedition*
108 Coffin of a Tungusic shaman. Photo: W. Jochelson, *The Jukaghir, The Jesup North Pacific Expedition*
109 Amber disk hunting amulet. Photo: Alfred Rust, *Das altsteinzeitliche Rentierjägerlager Meiendorf*
110 Reindeer shoulder blades pierced by weapons. Photo: Alfred Rust, *Das altsteinzeitliche Rentierjägerlager Meiendorf*
111 Rib cage of reindeer on large stone. Photo: Alfred Rust, *Das altsteinzeitliche Rentierjägerlager Meiendorf*
112 Siberian magician (old engraving).
113 Dancing deer-man from the Trois-Frères cave. Photo: Musée de l'Homme, Paris
114 Wall engraving (Trois-Frères cave). Photo: Musée de l'Homme, Paris
115 Detail of the wall engraving. Photo: Musée de l'Homme, Paris
116/117 Early drawings from Monte Bego. Photo: Musée de l'Homme, Paris
118 Spirit beings of the Siberian Chukchees. Photo: Musée de l'Homme, Paris

INDEX

INDEX

338

INDEX

INDEX

INDEX

INDEX

INDEX